A volume in the

DOUGLASS SERIES IN EDUCATION,
edited by HARL R. DOUGLASS, Ph.D.,
DIRECTOR OF THE COLLEGE OF EDUCATION,
UNIVERSITY OF COLORADO

VOLUMES IN

DOUGLASS SERIES IN EDUCATION

Principles and Practices of
SECONDARY
EDUCATION

By

VERNON E. ANDERSON
DIRECTOR OF THE CURRICULUM CENTER
UNIVERSITY OF CONNECTICUT

PAUL R. GRIM
DIRECTOR OF LABORATORY EXPERIENCES
UNIVERSITY OF MINNESOTA

WILLIAM T. GRUHN
DIRECTOR OF PRE-SERVICE TEACHER EDUCATION
UNIVERSITY OF CONNECTICUT

THE RONALD PRESS COMPANY ⟡ NEW YORK

Library of Congress Catalog Card Number: 51-10239
PRINTED IN THE UNITED STATES OF AMERICA

To the many able secondary school teachers and administrators who are devoting their lives to giving youth a fruitful educational experience, whose work has been an inspiration and a source of information for the illustrations of forwarding-looking practices in this book.

PREFACE

This book is an examination of secondary education in mid-twentieth century America—of the society and the pupils whom it serves, of its purposes and its practices. It seeks to appraise the organization, administration, curriculum, and guidance services of the secondary school, and the education of the secondary school teacher, in terms of stated desirable principles.

Written especially for the student in pre-service education courses and for the beginning teacher, this book is designed for use in the newer integrated education courses as a basis for evaluating secondary school practices in terms of democratic principles, physiological principles, and youth needs. It is equally useful for separate courses in principles of secondary education, especially where the instructor wishes to relate the work to other courses in education. In either case, the book is intended to be used where various types of laboratory experiences are considered desirable. Principals, supervisors, and college teachers of education should also find it useful for the in-service education of beginning teachers and for experienced teachers who wish to evaluate critically the experiences provided for youth in the secondary schools.

The first three chapters are devoted to a discussion of general principles and information by which the program of the modern secondary school can be judged. In each subsequent chapter except two, a distinct pattern is followed: (1) A discussion of the principles which apply specifically to that chapter; (2) the description and evaluation of some typical practices; (3) descriptions of some better practices which illustrate the principles; and (4) recommendations for first steps that can be taken to improve the situation. Particular attention is given to helping the future teacher and the beginning teacher to understand his duties, responsibilities, and opportunities.

Several distinct features have been incorporated. First, using the principles as a yardstick, both poor and good practices are described, thus enabling the undergraduate student to picture different types of school situations in which he may find himself when actually teaching. Second, general statements are illustrated by descriptions of actual practices. In presenting these, the experience background of the pre-service student is taken into consideration. Third, the book is written from a particular point of view; the authors have no desire

v

to be eclectic but wish to present the direction in which they believe
the secondary school should move. They are interested in developing teachers who use the experience, or problem-solving, approach,
both in their teaching procedures and in their professional and civic
life. Students are urged, however, to read from other sources with
differing philosophies so that they may establish principles of their
own—principles based upon facts from psychology, sociology, education, and other areas that deal with human beings and their relationships.

As an essential part of the teacher's education, the authors stress
the use of direct experiences and varied sources of information in
approaching a problem or reaching a conclusion: individuals of di-
verse backgrounds, schools, communities, audio-visual aids, and many
written sources. As a guide to additional material, a list of annotated
references will be found at the end of each of the chapters.

In reading the text, it is important to understand how the terms
"some typical practices" and "practices in the better secondary
schools" are used. In those sections describing "some typical practices," the intention is to present examples of practices that future
teachers may encounter in the schools where they will teach—many
of which fail to satisfy when measured in terms of the principles
advocated. These practices have been taken from actual situations
that are typical of *some* schools and *some* teachers. Unless so stated,
they are not practices found in the majority of the high schools of
the country, nor are they presented as statistical averages. The
"practices in the better secondary schools" were selected from schools
recommended by state departments of education as having developed
certain outstanding practices, or from schools with whose work the
authors were familiar. Neither the authors nor the schools described
would claim that these schools are "better" in all respects, or that
these are the best practices in the country. They are, however, practices that effectively illustrate the principles outlined in this book.
Measured in these terms, and *in the specific phases of school life described,* the schools are generally better than the schools discussed
under the sections "some typical practices." The authors invite information concerning other outstanding practices which might be
used in a future revision of this book.

The writing of the book was a cooperative venture; the coordination and the editing of the work were the responsibility of the senior
author, who developed the plan for the book as a whole and for each
chapter. The fundamental principles were agreed upon at the beginning. Each author then read and criticized the chapters written by

the other two authors. Thus, while utilizing the experiences of the three authors for certain chapters, the book is an integrated work. The section on general principles, the first six chapters on the curriculum, the chapter on pre-service education, and the chapter on challenging needs of secondary education were the particular responsibility of Vernon E. Anderson; the section on organization and administration, the chapter on the secondary school and the community, and the chapter on evaluation and reporting were the particular responsibility of Paul R. Grim; and the section on guidance, the two chapters on the beginning teacher's in-service education and responsibilities, and the chapter on extraclass experiences were the special responsibility of William T. Gruhn.

Storrs, Connecticut   VERNON E. ANDERSON
Minneapolis, Minnesota   PAUL R. GRIM
Storrs, Connecticut   WILLIAM T. GRUHN
January, 1951

ACKNOWLEDGMENTS

The authors wish to express their indebtedness to many secondary school principals and teachers for providing illustrative materials about their schools, for the permission to use these illustrations, and for reading the illustrations to check on their accuracy. We are also appreciative of the helpful guidance and criticism given by Harl R. Douglass, University of Colorado, throughout the writing of the manuscript. Valuable contributions resulted from the criticisms of the following persons, who read portions of the manuscript: Arthur Adkins, University of Minnesota; Jean H. Alexander, University of Minnesota; G. Lester Anderson, New York City Colleges; William H. Burton, Harvard University; J. Louis Cooper, University of Connecticut; Mary Lombard Eukers, University of Connecticut; C. Irene Hayner, University of Minnesota; Urbane Hennen, University of Connecticut; Kenneth Hovet, New York University; W. Howard Martin, University of Connecticut; Warren G. Meyer, University of Minnesota; Paul R. Pinckney, Oakland High School; P. T. Pritzkau, University of Connecticut; and I. N. Thut, University of Connecticut.

We wish to express our appreciation to the authors and publishers of copyrighted materials who have generously given us permission to quote from their publications.

For valuable assistance in typing the manuscript, we are indebted to Alice P. Anderson, Anne Marie Berggren, and Myrtis Gruhn.

CONTENTS

PART I

General Principles of Secondary Education

PART II

Curriculum and Instruction of the Secondary School

PART III

Guidance Activities of the Secondary School

ix

PART IV

Organization and Administration of the Secondary School

PART V

The Secondary School Teacher

PART VI

A Look Ahead for Secondary Education

PART I

GENERAL PRINCIPLES OF
SECONDARY EDUCATION

GENERAL PRINCIPLES OF SECONDARY EDUCATION

In Chapters 1 through 3, the stage is set for the rest of the book. They contain what the authors believe are the basic principles of secondary education. They attempt to answer the questions:

What is the job of the secondary school? What do we mean when we say that the secondary school should meet the needs of youth? How can we judge whether a secondary school is good?

Even more important, they present questions and data that should stimulate students of education to think seriously about secondary education and formulate principles of their own, based on facts and information. It has been the authors' specific intention in these chapters to present a point of view; consequently, statements and questions are phrased to that end. It is, however, their belief that the student should read widely and come to his own independent conclusions. Each of the other chapters in the book is discussed within the basic setting provided by Part I; the principles in the chapters of Part II through V are derived from the general principles outlined here.

Chapter 1

GUIDES FOR JUDGING A PROGRAM
OF SECONDARY EDUCATION

We often hear people say, "This is a good high school"; "Their English department is one of the best I have seen"; or "I think it is a splendid idea; I'm going to use it in my classes." On what bases did these people make their judgments? How can one know what constitutes a good high school? Good in what ways? How does a teacher decide whether to use an idea?

There are several bases on which we may make our decisions as to what a school should be like; a great deal will depend upon which of the following influence our attitude.

1. Tradition
2. Whim
3. Personal interest
4. The idea that it is "the thing to do"
5. Democratic values
6. Scientific knowledge about human growth and development
7. Information about the needs of particular adolescents
8. Information about how people learn
9. Information about our society

Some teachers shop around for gadgets. At teachers' conventions they look for the latest tricks by which the teaching of spelling can be sugar-coated, or for ideas which will make pupils accept the study of Rome more agreeably. A few accept without question the segregation of boys and girls in high school because it has always been done in their particular school. Others teach *Macbeth* in the twelfth grade because it is accepted by all English teachers in that region as the thing to do. Still others spend most of the time on aerodynamics in an aeronautics class because it is their particular "hobby."

Where do we stand? Which of the nine criteria listed above do we accept as valid? Much more important, however, is how we will be making our choices some years from now as experienced teachers. It is of momentous consequence to the future of education whether or not teachers have *valid* bases for making choices. Every teacher

3

has to make innumerable decisions every day. We cannot expect to run to a book or to the principal for information on what to do in regard to each disciplinary case as it arises, for each case will be different as long as young people differ. Nor can we continue practices that have been carried on in secondary schools simply for the reason that they have always been done that way. It is imperative that we have some guides to judging why we teach certain content or use particular methods. But first of all, we need to get into the habit of asking, "Why?"

This chapter proposes to set up principles that will serve to help the teacher in making better judgments. They are principles based on research and on information that we have gradually accumulated. If decisions are made by school people using principles such as these for criteria, youth in secondary schools will find a greatly enriched program of living in their schools.

The practices in secondary schools discussed in the rest of this book will be judged in the light of these principles. Students in teacher education classes are urged to examine these and other practices in the same manner. It is not intended that anyone should accept these principles as his point of view without questioning them. In fact, it is hoped that all who read this book will examine them critically on the basis of the most recent inquiry and research in the areas included. But practices should be submitted to a critical eye— practices in curriculum, guidance, administration, teacher education, and other aspects of secondary education.

1. Principles Based on How People Learn

Mechanistic Explanation of Learning Found Wanting.—The idea that learning proceeds through establishing simple neural connections has proved inadequate as an explanation of what goes on in the process. The S-R bond theory of learning, the theory that learning takes place through establishing in the neural system a bond or connection between a specific stimulus and its response, falls far short of explaining the complexity of the learning situation; it is too atomistic and does not adequately account for interrelationships and meanings in the learning process. Students of learning have expanded research into areas much broader than the stimulus-response concept can describe. The organismic theory has contributed much to understanding the learning process in school situations. It stresses that the nervous system functions as a whole in a total, unified situation. The whole organism reacts to stimuli in its environment. To the educator, this theory makes sense, for he is aware that the child is constantly developing attitudes, that emotions enter significantly into the learning situation when the child is studying arithmetic, history, or typing.

Whether the stress on drill and the learning of facts has resulted from the application of the stimulus-response bond theory, or from a misinterpretation of the theory, as some psychologists claim, makes little difference. The important point is that this theory of learning has not helped to produce in schools learning practices that take into consideration the balanced development of the child. Many practices in schools today testify to its influence that has permeated secondary education.

The influence of the organismic theory and recent research in learning is evident in a number of secondary schools. Examples of good practices described in this book indicate that teachers and administrators are applying a more functional concept of learning. The application of principles based on modern developments in the psychology of learning is found most frequently among teachers and schools imbued with the child development philosophy and among those genuinely interested in keeping up with new developments in this field and their implications for the teaching-learning situation.

Learning Results in Changed Behavior.—What is involved in learning? This is a deliberately simplified explanation of a complex process. Learning is a form of adaptation in which man adjusts to his environment; it is a change of behavior. It is only through interaction with our environment that we learn. To know if learning is going on, we must look for changes in the behavior of an individual, for learning products are forms of changed behavior. Throughout the text, "change of behavior" refers to changes in the emotional sphere and in implicit mental activity, as well as in motor skills and overt, physical action. Changes in a pupil's conduct, his attitudes, his ways of meeting a situation or solving a problem, are examples of important changes that take place. These changes occur when a person is striving to attain his goals and is blocked in some way because his responses are inadequate to meet the new problem. Thus, the learning situation is essentially a problem-solving one.

Adolescents may be, for example, striving for independence, seeking security, or desiring the approval of classmates and friends. It is important to realize that learning is goal-seeking behavior and is the result of the individual's working to achieve those goals. In the process he meets obstacles that cause him to try out new methods and find new ways of arriving at his goals. He discovers that certain types of behavior are successful in reaching his goals. These behaviors are what is learned.

Although it is a fearsome thought, we may be teaching pupils how to cheat effectively, or how to lie, even though we are not conscious of that learning. If tasks become too difficult for the pupil to achieve in legitimate ways, he tries other means. If our examinations are too difficult for a pupil to pass, he may resort to devious means to arrive at his goals, for we have made it important for him to pass. The whole process of learning is a complicated one, never as simple as learning a formula, arithmetic tables, or names and dates. There are all types of other learnings involved in acquiring skills or facts—many of which may not be regarded as desirable.

Principles Regulate Practices.—The implications of research in the psychology of learning must be carefully examined if we are to expect that applications will be made. The principles listed here are selected in terms of the value that they have for appraising secondary school practices. They are stated in such form that they may be readily applicable to teaching-learning practices, whether they be pupil-teacher, teacher-administrator, or school-community relationships. The following section is not intended to be a theoretical explanation of learning, but rather a statement of principles that can be used throughout the book as a basis for examining the secondary school in American society. A number of questions intended to stimulate the student's thinking in regard to practices are raised under each principle. In order to arrive at a further understanding of how people learn and what can be done to promote learning, the student in education courses should examine the references listed for this chapter; they are selected in terms of how well the authors interpret learning as it applies to the school. It is important to understand that these principles are applied to a particular kind of social situation.

The significant and lasting products of learning for living in a democratic society are attitudes, appreciations, skills, and understandings, not facts and information for their own sake.

Facts are not useful unless they are the basis for thinking through a plan, idea, or problem. By themselves they become as meaningless as nonsense syllables to the adult, or as words to the young child who has no experience background for understanding them. Used to clarify ideas or to stubstantiate a point, these bits of information become important factors in contributing to understandings.

What do we find, however, in many classrooms in secondary schools? Pupils recite facts about history because it is important to know history. The classifications of the animal kingdom are glibly listed to show that the biology lesson has been "learned." What has been learned? Is it of any value? Is it probable that the learning that actually remained with the pupils was an attitude of disgust for scientific studies, or the idea that the science of living things has no relationship to or value for understanding the pupil's own surroundings?

As teachers, we need to be concerned with "learnings" which, because they are understood and used, affect the behavior of young people. These are the attitudes that are built up toward people, things, or ideas; the appreciations or enjoyments of life; the understanding of life and man's attempt to control his environment and improve living conditions; the skills by which we communicate, or earn a living, or use any kind of tools. These are the only real learnings of value. What has been found when adults are tested on information supposedly "learned" in school; for example, on the facts of American history? It would be worth while to ponder the reasons for the findings. The principles discussed here are concerned with the most lasting types of learning, not the nonsense-syllable variety which has no permanance or social significance.

In any learning situation, the individual should accept the goals as worthy ones for him.

The purposes must be real to the learner, not just someone else's purposes. He must accept them as *his* goals. Just because the teacher has certain goals in mind does not mean that they are also the pupil's goals. What does this signify for school experiences of youth, for teacher education, for teachers' meetings? Is a teachers' meeting most successful if the principal decides upon how the group is to devote its time? In high school classes, should the teacher alone make all the decisions as to how the group will proceed?

The adolescents' goals of gaining prestige, being liked by others, having friends among the group, satisfying their curiosity about themselves and the world, pleasing their parents, improving their personalities, or earning a living, are real to them. School experiences must be related to these goals if they are to make sense to the pupil. Why do pupils sometimes question the value of a subject? Have these pupils accepted what is being done in the class as progress toward worthy purposes for them?

When, by sugar-coating an assignment, we use incentives for

pupils to do something that we want them to do, we are using so-called "extrinsic" motivation, which technically is not motivation. Motivation refers to the needs, drives, wants, and interests of the individual. Untold amounts of time and effort are spent in trying to get pupils to do things for which they see no reason. The school may force them to do the work in order to get good marks or to graduate, both of which may be very important to attaining the pupils' own goals. How much more satisfactory it would be, and how much less time would be spent, if school tasks were really centered around youth's interests and needs! The interests and needs already existing and those that may be developed must be discovered and stimulated by the teacher. Such a procedure involves knowing more about adolescents—a challenge to both pre-service and in-service teacher education.

If the goals are not accepted by the pupils, the learning will probably be incomplete and transitory, since people do not use skills or information for which they see no need. Research shows us that such learning disappears as rapidly as items "crammed" for a final examination. What would happen in secondary education if goal-setting became a cooperative process among teacher and pupils in every course? Would we be able to recognize courses as they are often taught today?

The learner should participate actively in the learning situation.

The laity show rather keen discernment of how learning takes place most effectively when they say, "Experience is the best teacher." John Dewey stated this concept in another way when he said at length that we *learn by doing*. There must be interaction between the person and his environment: people, written words, objects, living things, and ideas. Kilpatrick has stated that we learn what we do, "we learn our responses, only our responses, and all our responses." [1] There must be interaction with our environment in order for us to learn.

These experiences that we have do not need to be overt activity. If one is thinking, he is reacting to his environment. However, in judging a lecture-test or read-recite-test procedure as a learning experience, we need to determine how actively the individual is entering into the situation. In such circumstances in school classes the pupil usually copies verbatim, sees no purpose except to pass a test, listens half-heartedly, or engages in some other activity that interests him

[1] William Heard Kilpatrick, *Modern Education: Its Proper Work,* New York: Hinds, Hayden & Eldredge, Inc., 1949, p. 15.

more at the moment. Consider, also, the teacher's own experience. The give and take of a good faculty meeting is fruitful for clarification of ideas and for exploring the possibilities of any plan. How much more is learned in such a situation compared with one in which people only listen to an outside speaker who knows none of the local problems?

It is rather uncommon to find high school classes that are not working as one large group at all times, except when supervised study is carried on in the classroom. Would learning be facilitated if small groups could be formed to work within the class? We ought to ask ourselves such questions as: Do we give many pupils the opportunity to participate in class? Are we giving pupils every opportunity to perform tasks or take charge of activities in the school day? Who profits most when the teacher always answers questions, reads notices, takes charge of room responsibilities, and makes decisions—the teacher or the pupils? What do we do for pupils that they could better do for themselves? Are we using the rich resources about us in the community that would provide for pupil participation?

Learning experiences should be unified for the individual around some real problems of which he is clearly aware.

In a demonstration class in a summer workshop, the pupils had two classes immediately following each other in the same room; one class was English and the other, social studies, taught by different teachers. It was strikingly brought home to the observers that the pupils were often confused by the period or time barriers separating the two classes, since at times they did not recall which rules they had agreed upon for the particular class. The work was purposeful and related to their living. The time divisions that represented a change of classes were artificial to them. If they had decided in the English class that they were to work on improving their speech, it was obviously ridiculous to forget about such purposes when they were working on social studies problems.

Yet, for the most part, the barriers set up between classes are even more rigid and difficult to cross. Pupils may be told that "this is history; we are not concerned with literature." In taking principles of secondary education one hour and methods of teaching the next, is there unity for learning for the college student? Are problems in these two courses closely interrelated? Could an effective undergraduate education program be based upon a series of problems, real to the students?

The unit organization of class experiences was devised to provide for unity in learning. Nevertheless, we often find a teacher who talks about "unit teaching" when there is really no unity for the learner. There may be unity of content, but none whatsoever in the experiences that pupils have. Unity cannot be achieved without a concept of a clear, specific goal for some real problem. In cases where there is real unity, there is no question of fear of treading on another department's or course's "territory." The problems for study have been planned with pupils as ones that need to be studied to achieve certain goals.

The individual has a desire for and an interest in learning.

The normal adolescent—in the sense of one who is able to profit by formal education—is certainly not without interest in anything, as some teachers claim. The chief trouble is that those teachers have not discovered the interests nor stimulated the learning of new interests. If they were to live with a youngster for a day on a camping trip, his joys, sorrows, and concerns would probably stand out in bold relief. Every parent knows that young children have an insatiable curiosity and a desire to learn. Is this interest lost in the process of growing up?

Of course, pupils are not interested in school work that has little meaning and less relation to their past or present experiences. The problem for teachers is to find the kinds of experiences in which pupils will want to participate because they see a need for them. Is it not the teacher's job to guide pupils to select experiences that will broaden and expand interests? Is it true that, in the case of some young people, school experiences have so maladjusted them that they cannot enjoy activities in which the normal adolescent participates? What light is thrown on this question by the facts of mental hygiene?

The learning products are many, since the complex learning process involves the whole individual: physically, socially, mentally, and emotionally.

Learning has no neatly classified pigeonholes, such as mathematics or science or civics. The feelings are brought along to the mathematics class, and, even though the teacher may not be aware that attitudes are being formed, they are most certainly being learned. It is no secret to parents that a crabby, sarcastic teacher may contribute to their child's unhappiness more than to his understanding. The whole child learns, not just part of him. Learning is not the simple process of forming a connection between stimulus and response as was once propounded and is still widely accepted. Emotional blocks are severe handicaps to learning skills. How well do any of us do in an examination when we have seemingly insurmountable worries?

Do high school teachers generally take into consideration the physical growth of the adolescent? Do they consciously work for improvement in ability of pupils to get along with each other, to make decisions, or to be acceptable socially to others? Why not? Are these goals of less importance than knowing how to communicate or to understand historical development and scientific phenomena?

Individuals differ markedly in their ability to learn.

It is well known among teachers that some individuals learn much more readily than others. Tests of intelligence and achievement have long indicated that individuals differ in rate and retention of learning. Not so common, however—if we are to judge by practices—is the knowledge that individuals differ in kinds of abilities other than the verbal. They vary considerably in how readily they learn to function in a social situation: getting along with others, meeting others halfway, being able to see themselves, making friends, and the like. Some may be able to acquire a high degree of skill in creativeness by use of brush, drawing pencil, or other art media. The ability of others can be highly developed along mechanical lines.

Do secondary schools generally recognize the importance of these various types of abilities? Why do we have such an excessive premium placed on verbal learning? Do "slow-learners" also acquire new attitudes slowly? What kinds of teaching materials should a class of thirty different pupils have? These questions confront any beginning teacher. We may puzzle over the setting up of standards that all pupils are expected to meet, when it is a known fact that good instruction develops even greater differences among individuals. Standards should be individual standards, requiring a higher level of achievement from the most capable students. The approach of having everyone meet just minimum standards, the same for all students, is a means of fostering mediocrity. We may not see as readily the inconsistency of some practices in regard to ability grouping. But we run up against a serious conflict in trying to resolve practices with known facts when we find schools that divide pupils according to ability and then continue to give each group the same types of experiences, the same books, and the same examinations. As puzzling to the uninitiated is the practice of having all thirty pupils in the same class use the same book, read the same stories, do the same exercises or problems. Do any known standardized tests of skills or understandings substantiate such practices?

Experiences are fruitful only when they have meaning for the learner.

Foreign languages are not really learned unless they become a part of the individual's means of communication. Being able to recite vocabulary meanings for a test and forgetting them the next week or the next year is not the kind of learning with which schools ought to be concerned. An experience in apparently meaningless diagraming of sentences or the memorization of a grammatical rule may be confusing and irritating to a pupil who does not understand what he is doing nor see any reason for doing it.

This is a rather obvious principle; yet, we find pupils doing many tasks that to them do not make sense. They may prepare reports on the Industrial Revolution from encyclopedias or reference books too difficult for them to understand. As a result, most of the material is copied from the reference. What is the learning in such a case? Are these experiences fruitful in developing attitudes and understandings needed in our society? Are advanced mathematical problems which are not really understood by pupils learned when they are laboriously solved with the assistance of others, or memorized, as in the case of geometry theorems? Has the college student learned anything useful to him if he can merely give a definition of a unit or of the core curriculum?

Individuals can reasonably be expected to learn effectively only when, by reason of physical, mental, and social development and previous experiences, they are mature enough to profit by the new experiences.

We know that young children who are forced to learn to read before they are ready for that new experience develop maladjustments that are often serious handicaps in later school life, as well as in developing reading skills at the time. Experiential background must be built up before formal reading begins. The same thing is true with older individuals. Consider the skills required for self-control. Are they acquired by giving a new freedom to pupils who have never had any experience in self-direction? Can cooperation be practiced by a secondary school group that has had no opportunity to use this skill in previous years? Maturation of the individual has a great deal to do with readiness to learn not only physical skills such as walking but also skills and understandings in other areas.

Forcing learning produces abnormal behavior, frustration, and tensions instead of producing early learning or any acceleration of the process. In other words, the learning products will be entirely different from those desired. What does this mean when the inauguration of a plan of student government is being considered for the school? Does it have anything to do with the failure of a home room program as it is sometimes initiated by the administrator? What does it mean as to the grade level at which certain concepts and skills should be taught? Does a seventh grade child's maturity enable him to profit more by the study of American history or by the study of his own problems of social adaptation?

The learning situation should provide for continuity of experience.

This principle is closely related to the forgoing, for only if by previous experience a pupil is prepared for a new experience can there be any continuity *for him*. School systems often spend considerable effort, as a part of curriculum revision, to eliminate the overlapping of content or to establish a sequential program of subject matter from grade level to grade level. Does such a revision actually guarantee continuity? Is it reasonable to expect each of thirty or more different students to come out with the same level of understanding at the end of the year? Are college courses built on an assumption that they will? Do systematized courses of study built for the "average" pupil promote sequential growth from year to year for all pupils?

The principle that we should begin teaching a person where he is, rather than according to where we think he should be, is sound. In other words, at any stage, continuity can be provided for a person only if we build our work on what he has already learned, not on what he has "covered," for there is a tremendous difference between the two. One can hear high school teachers blaming elementary teachers for pupils' lack of preparation, or college teachers putting the responsibility on high school teachers. When such remarks are made, do the teachers assume their responsibility for assisting the student? What does it show about their belief in how continuity can be obtained?

Learning is more effective under the type of teaching that guides and arouses interest rather than awes and dominates.

Teacher-dominated classrooms are perhaps one of the greatest hindrances to effective learning of important goals in American secondary schools. They can be found everywhere. Observe these classes to see whether the teacher ever allows the pupils to take over the control of the class. Occasionally, when this has been allowed, a teacher will apologize for not "teaching" a class when the supervisor comes into the room. They are sincere persons, but their principles are built upon outmoded or misunderstood concepts of learning. Supervisors and college instructors have often helped to perpetuate these concepts.

Some feel that they must know all the answers. Administrators, as leaders of teachers, may be in this category. They do not realize that a good learning situation is creative, one in which the teacher as well as the pupil learns. Of course, this statement does not mean that a teacher does not need to know the subject which he is teaching. But if he does not learn something new about pupils, if he is not constantly stimulated to probe into new ideas or facts about the subject, how dreary and monotonous teaching can become! A good teacher is a guide who assists students in finding the answers; he does not give them. What happens when a teacher is reluctant to allow pupils to make mistakes? Will they learn as effectively if they are always told how, instead of being allowed to make errors and profit by their mistakes?

2. Principles Based on the Nature and Growth of the Adolescent

There are two important means of studying the adolescent to find out more about his nature, needs, growth, and development: (1) through the investigation of research findings in the areas of child development, adolescent psychology, and mental hygiene, and (2) through observation and study of individual youngsters and groups of adolescents. Fortunate indeed is the student of education who, at the time he is taking courses in education and psychology, has ready access to elementary and high schools where pupils can be observed and studied at first hand.

It is assumed in this book that time will be spent on this important phase of teacher preparation and that other references will be studied to achieve a more complete understanding of the adolescent. The authors have not attempted to include in the principles listed here all the facts about the adolescent's nature and development, but rather have selected principles, based on research, that they believe will serve to guide the teacher in his judgments about how to assist young people with their adjustment problems and in his selection of desirable experiences for them. Other aspects of youth are discussed in Chapter 3.

No one of these principles may appear as significant by itself as when seen in relationship to the others. But when we look at all nine together, far-reaching implications for the secondary school program become evident. For example, if we possessed a thorough understanding of adolescent actions and thinking, would we continue to use the same content that most schools do now, or would general education aim more directly toward helping young people solve their conflicts and assisting them with their developmental tasks?

We can examine almost any of the practices discussed in this book in the light of these principles of adolescent nature and development. The curriculum, activities, evaluation of progress, guidance services, organization of the school, scheduling of the school day—all are involved directly or indirectly. Let us ask ourselves sincerely: What would these phases of school life be like if we applied these principles to the best of our ability?

School experiences should recognize the adolescent's striving to achieve independence and adult status as a normal phase of growing up.

A normal part of growing up is the desire to gain independence from the family in matters of dating, money, bedtime, and other life activities. The adolescent wants to make decisions for himself. Often this desire may result in rebellion against interference with his plans or revolt against authority. For him it is a period of conflict in more than one way, since he is torn between loyalties to his friends and to his parents. Although this is a fortunate aspect of natural development, some parents fail to recognize it as such. Witness the unhappy individuals who are still "tied to mother's apron strings" after reaching adulthood and suffer serious emotional conflicts in their efforts to disentangle themselves.

If a pupil is misunderstood both at home and at school—if his parents or teachers regard these manifestations of growth as deviltry or "cussedness"—his chances of attaining desirable growth in attitudes and emotions will be considerably lessened. Should the adolescent-parent relationship happen to be particularly strained or unnatural at this period, the pupil will need all the more sympathetic understanding at school. Can the teacher help the pupil toward a more responsible use of newly gained freedom? Of what value are pupil activities in providing the needed experience that gives youth a feeling of being adult? Or should the teacher apply repression and punishment for the critical attitude that usually accompanies this period of growing independence? The way these questions are answered will make a considerable difference in the kinds of experiences pupils have in class and extraclass activities.

School experiences should assist the adolescent in working out a desirable orientation to his age mates of both sexes.

Approval and acceptance by one's own age group are powerful determiners of behavior of adolescents. At this age, status with peers is more important than adult approval. Young people will imitate each other in dress, speech, and mannerisms in order to be accepted by the group. They may feel more secure if accepted by the gang that counts, or by a select group. An example of this manifestation can be seen in the development of high school fraternities and sororities in spite of school opposition to them. Again, cheating and lying may be adjustments to a normal growth process, for the group feeling may be so strong that these actions become a way of protecting one's friends. Can school situations be planned to minimize opportunities for such behavior? What may the usual type of report cards do to the relationships between pupils?

Social recognition, and consequently the development of social skills, becomes important to school experiences. The teacher in his classes and activities can make use of this group spirit and desire for acceptance. Yet, in how many high school classes do we find small-group work being used? Some teachers will tell you that pupils are too unruly; group work cannot be carried on. Does this attitude square with the facts, or is it a cover-up for their own inadequacies? Could the teacher help in preventing the formation of antisocial groups of adolescents which defy acceptance by the group as a whole? What responsibility does the secondary school have for providing social activities that appeal to young people?

The desire for status with the opposite sex and the groping for ways of solving these new relationships should be of concern to the school. Is showing off regarded as undesirable behavior? It may be just a desire for gaining the attention of the opposite sex. The beginning teacher may be particularly disturbed by the keen interest of adolescents in obscene jokes and vulgar language, although this may be simply another manifestation of seeking prestige with their classmates. Does the school have a rich program of activities suited to every pupil to help make these social adjustments? How well trained are teachers to guide pupils in making wholesome adjustments to these problems?

The school program should help the adolescent make adjustments to his changing body.

The adolescent is likely to have abnormal fears and worries about the rapid changes in his body that occur at this time. Uneven growth or failure to develop may cause him to worry about whether he is normal. These factors call for a straightforward discussion of sex and well-trained teachers who can help pupils over the rough spots by giving friendly advice. What does this principle mean as to the type of health service that should be provided by the schools? The need for development of physical coordination and skills that assist youth in gaining social recognition furnishes an important guide in the planning of physical education experiences. Does the school really make use of these deep-seated interests and important needs for assistance in development? Can the school afford to slight these phases in favor of the typical college preparation, mistakenly believed to be the best preparation for future study? What relation does a healthy body and a wholesome attitude toward the body have to college success?

Educational experiences should give the adolescent a sense of security and satisfaction with his own development as a person.

It is important for the pupil to succeed in something and to feel that he is accepted in at least a few groups important to him. He should feel that there are some things which he can do better than others can. Constant failure is a terrible load for any personality to carry. The results often are unfortunate or tragic. The development of the adolescent must include opportunities for satisfaction in accomplishments. As teachers, we need to ask ourselves if the curriculum we provide in a course, or to a group, includes many opportunities for every boy and girl to succeed. What does ability grouping and the division of the high school program of studies into college-preparatory and other curricula or "courses" do to the individual's security and confidence in himself? Can we get away from grouping that places a premium on only one kind of ability, the academic or verbal?

Security is closely related to the need for affection and for belonging to certain groups, such as a club, a social "set," or a group of young people who do things together. How secure does a child feel if he sees no evidence that anyone cares what happens to him? As teachers, who are the hub of the school's guidance program, what will be our responsibility in this respect? What implications do these facts have for our marking system? What responsibility have we for helping pupils become active in extraclass activities?

A part of the business of growing up involves the building of a personal philosophy, a basic evaluation of self as a physical and social being, as a person. Satisfaction with one's own development and one's relations to others helps to build the right kinds of attitudes toward life. How much responsibility should the beginning teacher feel for helping to build such a philosophy? Perhaps it may be one of the most important tasks before him.

The successful teacher understands that normal adolescent behavior is not necessarily desirable nor pleasing from the point of view of the teacher or the adult.

The high school teacher is often inclined to look upon shoving or shouting in the halls, throwing spitballs, or aggressive behavior of various types as something out of the way or "abnormal" for boys. In fact, it may be the most normal type of adjustment for a boy in his desire to be admired or noticed for his "independence." If he is not given proper opportunities in class to be somebody in the eyes of his classmates, he may engage in activities that are neither constructive nor wholesome.

Adolescents may develop codes of behavior to demonstrate their defiance of adults, such as being noisy to disturb the teacher. Particularly is this true in cases where the class is dominated by the teacher and the pupils have no say in establishing codes to regulate their own behavior in class, study halls, or halls. How many teachers accept, as normal-growth phenomena, stubborn or "tough guy" behavior, hiding real feelings by acting in the opposite way, or using the classroom as a place for social experimentation? Do you agree with this statement: "Behavior is desirable if it is a natural and necessary part of the growth process"? What are the implications for evaluation of growth?

Teachers should face realistically the fact that an adolescent in his relations with the school and the outside world lives in a confusion of double standards.

We know that the moral code of the police department in a large city is not often the same as the standards set by the church. Young people are confused by what they hear professed at church and what they see adults doing. Political "deals" are very different from the idealism set for behavior in the school. Parents' standards of conduct may differ from those taught at school.

What is the young person going to do? If the school is totally blind to these confusions in culture, what will he do? Should mature young people actually delve into the facts and get at the basic issues? If pupils are not given an opportunity to make choices based on facts, how well will they be able to face these confusions as they grow up? There is certainly a crying need for an understanding of the terrific impacts that such confused standards make on an adolescent, especially when they concern him directly.

Every adolescent behavior problem has a cause or causes that the school may be helping to alleviate or which it may be helping to aggravate.

Behavior problems of pupils have a relationship to every phase of school life: experiences in class, extraclass activities, guidance, the use of community resources. Whether or not some of these areas of school living are directed successfully depends to a large extent upon the understandings which teachers and administrators have of pupil behavior.

The whole concept of discipline has changed to one based upon the understanding of behavior. Each case is a problem in itself into which the teacher must probe to find the causes. Defiance, bullying, truancy, and showing off are not meanness, but are ways by which pupils attempt to adjust. What are the real causes behind truancy? Is it home conditions? What are the pupil's relations with his brothers and sisters? Does he really feel secure?

Teaching that permits shy, quiet youngsters to isolate themselves from the rest of the group does irreparable harm to those individuals, for they are the real problem cases. What should a teacher do to assist such a pupil? How does one get at the causes of the problem? The whole area of mental hygiene is one that has such a direct bearing on progress in learning that every undergraduate student ought to have a good understanding of this field before he goes out to teach.

Growing up is a total, unified process for the adolescent.

In more recent years, teachers in elementary schools have been interested in the concept of the "whole child." Particularly in the primary grades, a definite attempt has been made to plan experiences for children to develop their total personalities. Good teachers everywhere know that the process of growing up has unity. Mental, social, emotional, and physical development must all be considered if we are to view an individual's growth process. A teacher familiar with the principles of child and adolescent development is concerned about cases in which maladjustment results from the failure of an individual to develop in a normal fashion in all these phases.

The significant studies of Willard C. Olson at the Child Development Laboratory of the University of Michigan[2] have supported the idea of unified growth. These studies have been made with younger children over a period of years. Different types of development have been traced, such as dental, mental, height, and weight development, and ossification of the bones. When growth in these areas is translated into age equivalents and charted, the different growth lines follow about the same pattern in a well-adjusted child.

In the face of such growing evidence, we need to examine certain instructional and administrative practices that are based on a consideration of the growth of only one phase of the child's life. Should we continue to use honor rolls, graduation awards, and credit systems that do not reflect the total growth of the pupil? Can a parent really understand what is happening to a child if he receives reports only on progress in academic skills and understandings? What does this growth concept mean for guidance; what does it mean for the kinds of activities in which pupils engage?

Adolescents vary in the rate at which they grow and their level of growth.

Adolescents of the same age and grade may be found to differ by as much as six to seven years in their progress as measured by different standardized tests. They vary as to their stage of maturation, physically and psychologically. Teachers are familiar with the fact that pupils are not alike, that what will help one pupil learn will not necessarily help another. Yet, we still have mass production methods used to an overwhelming degree in secondary school instruction.

Studies show that everyone is unique in his manner of growth. He grows at his own rate; consequently, forcing or attempting to speed up the process beyond a certain point results only in frustration and maladjustment. The teacher with the growth point of view understands that it takes much more time for some pupils to develop

---

2 Willard C. Olson and Byron O. Hughes, "Concepts of Growth—Their Significance," in *About Children, How They Learn, Feel and Grow*, Washington, D.C.: Association for Childhood Education, 1945, pp. 5-15; Willard C. Olson, *Child Development*, Boston: D. C. Heath & Co., 1949, 417 pp.

to a certain degree than others. Moreover, some probably can never reach the degree of development possible for others.

Uniform assignments, single textbooks, rigid schedules, and minimum essentials for all, are thus called into question. Should the fast-growing pupil, with rich potentialities for creativity and leadership, be held to a low standard of minimum essentials with the rest of his group? The slow learner, whom research shows us cannot be forced to speed his process of growth, suffers equally in this attempt to set a minimum for a total group. We ought to examine critically what is happening to adolescents who spend the same time during the day on the same type of materials because they constitute what is known as English I, American history, or algebra.

3. Principles Based on the Democratic Way of Life

Astonishing as it may seem, many of the traditional practices in secondary schools fail to measure up to the principles of a democratic society. Most practical school people concede that schools in a democracy must aim to perpetuate the ideals of that type of society. Differences in interpreting the meaning of a democracy have contributed to the confusion in implementing democracy in the schools. Lack of clear thinking about what democratic principles mean in practice has resulted in the apparent contradictions between theory and practice.

Concepts of school administration derived from business management have pervaded staff organization, courses in administration, school surveys, and various administrative practices for the past three or four decades. Only in the more recent years has the idea of democratic leadership gained a foothold. More schools are using teacher committees to share in the determination of policy. Interest in the group process and the function of leadership in the group is gaining momentum. Genuine democratic leadership will be apparent in many of the school situations to be described in this book.

The authoritarian teacher has thrived in the former type of environment. It is difficult for democratic teacher-pupil relations to develop in an atmosphere of autocratic administrator-teacher relationships. However, there is an increasing number of teachers who live up to the full meaning of democratic principles in their work with pupils. Yet, beginning teachers will be sadly disillusioned if they expect to go into almost any school on their first job and carry out democratic practices in the classroom without receiving some severe jolts from the attitudes of fellow teachers.

The principles of the democratic way of life discussed here attempt to define what democracy actually means. It is not only a form of government, as some persons think. It is not a way of living that never changes. It is, instead, a set of principles guiding the relationships of the individual to the group in a society, large or small. These principles, or this manner of living, apply to the classroom as well as to the school, the community, the nation, or a group of nations.

Every person is regarded as worthy of optimum development of his potentialities, and his importance and contributions to the group are recognized.

When we make an application of this principle to the school situation, we wonder what is happening to the thousands of pupils who drop out of school every year because of a lack of interest in school, failure, or a desire to go to work as soon as possible. Have these young people been considered by their teachers as worthy of the fullest development of their potentialities? If so, would they have been considered failures in a subject because they did not measure up to standards of academic achievement set for the "average" pupil?

We have but to look at the barren offerings in the curriculum of some secondary schools to see that the possibilities for a number of pupils to develop their potentialities are extremely slight. For example, in a curriculum without art, music, shop work, or opportunities for creativity in English or other classes, what chance has a pupil to develop potential creative talents?

We need to examine school programs to see if democracy of race, religion, nationality, and social class exists. Only if the individual is accepted as a person, if everyone is considered as important, is such equality present. Many barriers to equality of opportunity will be found. They are not all based on discrepancies in the amounts of money spent for schools in different localities. Segregation, unsuitable instructional materials, and college preparatory curricula of the traditional type with their high prestige value, all are as effective in producing inequalities. A few other practices that need to come under a critical scrutiny are academic barriers to entering interscholastic activities, election to membership in pupil organizations, and the usual concept of failure. To help pupils develop maximum potentialities, far more attention needs to be paid to adequate health services, including psychiatric, dental, and medical services.

Differences in opinions, abilities, and interests among individuals are valued.

How often have we heard a teacher say, "If only I could get all my pupils up to this standard"? That teacher does not understand that growth of individuals comes through encouraging differences, that these differences are most essential to a democracy. Specialized interests and abilities are fundamental to the innumerable types of pursuits with which people occupy their time in our society; they are fundamental to invention and progress. What little progress we would make in thinking if everyone thought alike! Yet, that is the very practice encouraged by teachers who test for the answers in the book.

Can we teach effectively if all pupils in a class do the same things at the same time? Should there not be a choice of experiences for different groups of pupils within any class? Do we value differences if we give a teacher one set of books to be used by all pupils? If we really value differences, we will not be afraid to trust pupils to think for themselves, to criticize, and to help evaluate what the teacher and pupils are doing in the class.

A democratic society is characterized by an ever widening concern and responsibility for the welfare of others and for the social consequences of one's acts.

This principle is concerned with the development of a realization that privileges entail corresponding responsibilities. Studies of secondary school pupils' opinions about democracy seem to indicate that they are far more concerned about their privileges than about their responsibilities. Living in a school community demands subjecting individual wishes to the good of the group, just as in a larger community. However, school people sometimes act as though they believed that the self-control necessary to such a way of living can all be learned after youth have left school.

Self-control is acquired in an atmosphere in which ample opportunity is given to exercise it. Pupils must realize that they are actually responsible for others' welfare in study halls, halls, lunch rooms, and other areas of school living, through being delegated full responsibility for control and management. Too often student government is a mere sham in this respect. Are competitive marking systems and competition through contests consistent with this principle? Is an autocratic form of teacher discipline conducive to developing a realization of the social consequences of what individual pupils do?

This principle also refers to the extension of common concerns to other groups. If young people are sent to exclusive schools, will they be concerned about the social classes who live across the tracks? Can we do more about extending interests into the community through use of field trips and the study of real social problems in our own community? This principle has implications for a clear understanding of peoples of other countries, through giving such study an important place in the curriculum.

Then, too, an interest in the welfare of others means an interest in change and in progress. Teachers do not stop growing in a school that lives up to this principle.

In a democracy, the control comes from inside the group concerned, not from the outside.

Group participation in making policies and rules that affect individuals in the group is basic to our democratic freedoms. Our country was formed out of rebellion against autocratic measures. Fundamental to the liberty of any people is a right to participate in making rules for their own living.

It is not difficult to find out if this principle is violated in different phases of the life of a secondary school. Examine the relations between administrator and teachers. Do they as a group determine policies regarding wages, contracts, and other aspects of teacher welfare? Do they share in setting administrative regulations, the framework within which instruction takes place? Examine the classroom. Are pupils and teachers planning together, setting up their purposes together? Do you find the teacher among the pupils or in front of the room? Note the arrangement of pupils' desks and the teacher's desk in relation to each other. Do pupils take charge of responsibilities for the welfare of the group? Do they participate in making rules for classroom conduct? We should also investigate how much pupils have to say in the management of the school, in the formation of policies for social functions, school activities, hall traffic, and other matters of living in their school community. It is extremely doubtful if democracy functions unless practices measure up to this yardstick of democratic living.

The democratic method necessitates determining all the facts and arriving at intelligent decisions cooperatively.

If a democracy is to function, people must have the attitude of inquiring critically into questions and problems of civic life. All sides of the question are examined and the decision is based on facts. Is this method of scientific thinking stressed in secondary school classes in social studies or science? Do we find a great deal of independent and group investigation of problems by students, a critical attitude in class discussions, and a readiness to defer judgments until all the facts are discovered? Do colleges encourage the development of this skill through the form of admission requirements used?

The method of intelligence applied to problems is imperative in a secondary school program if it is to perform its function of developing competent citizens. Yet, what is happening in some schools regarding controversial issues? Can high school classes study about Russia without critisism from some sources? Do pressure groups frighten teachers away from a frank and open consideration of communism? Do social studies classes investigate what is happening in American life today because of fear and intimidation? Do they study school issues and local problems?

As future teachers, we need to be militant about freedom to express one's beliefs and to make inquiries without fear or reprisal. The democratic method will work successfully only in such an atmosphere. We need to be concerned about cooperation through group work, the use of committees in our classes, and sharing experiences. Moreover, as an important objective, we should see that discussion among students often results in social action for the good of a small group, the school, or the community.

SUMMARY

It would be unfortunate, indeed, if the principles listed in this chapter were regarded as points to be learned for a course in which this text is used. The principles are not the final word; they represent some guideposts for thinking through the problems and practices in secondary educations, and are derived from information on how people learn, on adolescent growth and development, and on the democratic way of life. In fact, they ought to be applied as a yardstick to college classes as well as to the secondary schools. It is hoped that students will develop other principles throughout their study and investigation of the secondary school in this country, of its purposes, its nature, and its effectiveness in American life.

The authors use these principles as a means of evaluation of practices to be discussed. Each chapter dealing with practices, in turn, lists further specific principles that apply particularly to the subject discussed. The most important outcome of the study of this book, and others which may differ in point of view, should be the formation of a set of values or principles which students of education accept and will use as their own when they serve as teachers in secondary schools.

SELECTED REFERENCES

ASSOCIATION FOR SUPERVISION AND CURRICULUM DEVELOPMENT. *Fostering Mental Health in the Schools* (1950 Yearbook). Washington, D.C.: National Education Association, chaps. 1, 6, 7.—These readable chapters on conditions of good mental health and the developmental tasks and their implications for the school are especially pertinent.

BURTON, WILLIAM H. *The Guidance of Learning Activities.* New York: Appleton-Century-Crofts, Inc., 1944, Part I.—An excellent reference on the application of principles of learning to the classroom, modern in its point of view and practical in its application. The author uses many illustrations from everyday life and school activities.

CASWELL, HOLLIS L. (ed.). *The American High School* (Eighth Yearbook of the John Dewey Society). New York: Harper & Bros., 1946, chap. 5.—Another good chapter on the developmental tasks of youth.

COREY, STEPHEN M., and OTHERS. *General Education in the American High School.* Chicago: Scott, Foresman & Co., 1942, chaps. 4, 5.—These excellent chapters on "Scientific Study of Developing Boys and Girls Has Set Up Guideposts" and "For Vital Learning, Students Must Have Materials Related to Their Goals," discuss the developmental tasks of adolescents and principles of learning.

EDUCATIONAL POLICIES COMMISSION. *Policies for Education in American Democracy.* Washington, D.C.: National Education Association, 1946.—Books I and II, published previously as separate bulletins, are most helpful references on the nature of the democratic way of life and its application to our society. These two parts are "The Unique Function of Education in American Democracy" and "The Education of Free Men in American Democracy."

NATIONAL SOCIETY FOR THE STUDY OF EDUCATION. *Learning and Instruction* (Part I, Forty-Ninth Yearbook). Chicago: University of Chicago Press, 1950, 352 pp. —One of the most recent and complete summaries of information on how children learn and on the application of these principles to instruction.

OLSON, WILLARD C. *Child Development.* Boston: D. C. Heath & Co., 1949, 417 pp.—One of the best references to use with undergraduate students. It is written from the organismic and developmental point of view of growth, and deals with both children and adolescents. Stresses implications for the school situation.

PETERS, CHARLES C. *The Curriculum of Democratic Education.* New York: McGraw-Hill Book Co., Inc., 1942, chap. 8.—Discusses the meaning of democracy and its relation to progress.

Chapter 2

THE TASK OF THE AMERICAN SECONDARY SCHOOL

A good program of secondary education moves with the times. It is not static, sluggish, or lagging behind the conditions and needs of the society in which it exists, trying to preserve the status of things as they are. Evidence of a growing, alive society has always been the presence of a keen desire to improve conditions, to move ahead, and to plan for the future, using the past to provide guidance and wisdom. A static society, on the other hand, has a backward look. The orientation is in the past; it worships the old, is reluctant to change, and follows tradition because past generations are thought to have had a higher intelligence or a better sense of values than the present.

The secondary school is an important key in determining what kind of a society we shall have in years to come. Will the American way of life mean life as it is today, or will it develop and grow in harmony with scientific advances, human needs, and the changed relationships of peoples throughout the world?

1. The Secondary School In a Democracy

The Secondary School, an Essential of Democracy.—The early statesmen of America realized that the public school is essential to a continuing democracy, that people must keep alive to changing conditions and the new issues that arise. Although Jefferson and Washington were not confronted with problems of extending medical services, controlling atomic development, or feeding the needy peoples of the world, they knew that men could participate intelligently in governing themselves to the extent that they made themselves intelligent about public affairs, or as Washington expressed it, "In proportion as the structure of government gives force to public opinion, it is essential that public opinion be enlightened." There were no pat answers to the social issues and problems of their times, certainly none that could readily be applied to the uncertain years that lay ahead.

The history of the public high school in this country shows that, once established, its development was considered fundamental to the interests of democratic government. The free public high school movement was opposed to the theory of educating only the elite, which some favored. It opened opportunities for the individual to become self-sufficient and independent. Stress was placed on the need for the citizen to be informed on political and economic matters in order to participate in a democratic form of government. During the early "battle" for free public education, the idea that the secondary school should be made available to all became firmly entrenched in American ideals.

An Understanding of Democracy Needed.—Although the student of education may be firmly convinced that the secondary school is a bulwark of democracy, his zeal will be of no value in promoting democratic institutions unless he understands the full significance of what the democratic way of life means. He will be confused by rabble-rousers who shout "A hundred per cent American!" He will find many persons who put out the flag on holidays, obey the laws, and pay homage to early American leaders, yet at the same time work for ends that deprive other sincere Americans of the rights and privileges that are guaranteed them by the Constitution. The student who is preparing to be a teacher in the United States needs to be a student of democracy. He must realize that it is not an irrevocably crystalized pattern of government, not an unchanging economy, and not a social order that guarantees rights for special groups. As the five principles in Section 3 of Chapter 1 indicate, it is much deeper than that.

Democracy stresses, first of all, human welfare—the welfare of all individuals as individuals, and as individuals-in-the-group. It is a faith, an ideal, a way of life that seeks to extend human rights and privileges through an exercise of responsibility and a concern for others. In a democracy, the individual is considered important and his potentialities are believed worthy of being developed to the fullest degree. Considered in this light, restrictions placed on minority groups operate only as cancers on a healthy, growing community of peoples. Democratic ideals call for all individuals to participate in deciding questions that are of concern to them. Any drastic means of keeping individuals from voting on issues or selecting their representatives can be truly evaluated by this standard as inimical to democratic living.

In other words, the effectiveness of a democracy can be evaluated only by measuring practices against the principles that constitute the ideals of a democratic way of life. It cannot be accepted on the faith of someone's flowery oratory nor appraised solely in terms of past practices. Only as teachers study democracy and understand its real meaning will they recognize the most important tasks confronting the secondary school.

Secondary Education Designed for Democracy.—In a totalitarian state, secondary education is definitely designed to perpetuate the concepts of that type of society. The kind of education that was provided for youth in Nazi Germany sought to forward the idea of the master race. The aims of such an education are as out of place in a democratic society as is flogging in a modern school. The secondary school that seeks to develop citizens who will live by and seek to improve the democratic way of life has unique goals of its own. Cooperation, responsibility for the welfare of others, and intelligent action are a far cry from subservience, thought control, and blind obedience. Out of the ideals of democracy grow definite aims determining what the secondary school should do for individuals. A certain type of behavior is demanded of the individual in order that he might be a healthy, happy, well-integrated person who contributes to the social good.

Moreover, each democratic society and each age has problems of its own. The knotty problems of Paul Revere's day have either faded, changed, or multiplied a hundredfold by invention and the increased complexity of society. The Philippines certainly do not face exactly the same problems that our own country does today. Making democracy work in India presents still different problems. Thus, the secondary school has a specific setting and specific ideals to inculcate in a certain culture with characteristic traditions and problems of its own.

Study of the Social Scene Demanded.—Those who are responsible for carrying out the aims of secondary education, therefore, also have a responsibility for continuous study of the social setting in which the school exists. What are the current social trends and issues? What are the blocks to improvement of human welfare, the forces working against progress? First to be considered in this chapter are the goals of the secondary school in a democratic society, evaluated in terms of human behavior. Then, the serious difficulties that stand in the way of promoting democratic ideals and institutions—in furthering the welfare of human beings—are presented as questions for study and deliberation. The student of education needs to be a student of his own world.

2. The Goals Of The Secondary School In A Democratic Society

The conscientious study of what democracy means should lead to the questions : How does an individual behave if he lives according to these principles and is best able to cope with the problems of his society? What kinds of behavior lay the basis for a growing, healthy, democratic life? In other words, what is the product for which the secondary school in a democracy should strive?

Importance of Knowing the Kinds of Outcomes Wanted.— Every teacher must know for himself what kind of individuals a democracy demands if he is to know the *direction* in which boys and girls in his charge need to develop. A teacher who works without distinct goals in mind is not fulfilling the trust placed in him by society. Anyone who sets out to teach so much subject matter or to cover a book has no intelligent aim as to what he wants to accomplish for individual youngsters. As a successful teacher, he should be able to answer, first of all, what he hopes to do for his pupils—what should be the real outcomes of their study together.

The aims that the teacher formulates should be the result of co-operative study and group thinking of the school faculty. They must be thought out together and clearly analyzed, for mere verbalisms in the form of a well-sounding statement of objectives on paper do not give direction to teaching. More important than well-turned phrases is the teacher's acceptance of the goals as his own.

Goals Reflect Social Policy.—Since the social policy of the United States is democracy, the purposes of the secondary school should be vitally concerned to advance that policy. Schools in a democracy can best be judged by the manner in which they contribute to the principles of democratic living, how they equip individuals to act intelligently on social problems of the day in order that the society may move forward. Emphasis on the purposes of the secondary school must therefore be placed on social goals.

If social policy is to be used as one of the main criteria for determining the goals of the secondary school, what weight should be given to statements such as these, often given as reasons for including certain subject matter in the secondary school curriculum?

1. All well-educated and cultured persons have studied it.
2. The colleges require it for admission.
3. It trains the mind.
4. It is the usual required subject matter.

An analysis of social principles, problems, and needs would show up these reasons as superficial and shallow, the result of lazy thinking that does not gather all the facts. Experiences that pupils have in high school should be the result of a keen-sighted concept of social goals rather than of a justification for what is being done or a sham to avoid intelligently directed change.

Such goals as the following, stated in the eighth yearbook of the John Dewey Society,[1] a professional organization committed to the ideals of the great educational philosopher, are examples of social goals that help to determine what subject matter and experiences the secondary school should include in its program:

1. Secondary education should give primary attention to developing citizens competent and willing to make every needed sacrifice to make democracy work for all men.
2. A concomitant of this primary responsibility is the task of developing a consuming desire for that kind of public behavior toward other nations which produces peaceful international relationships.
3. Secondary education should be committed to teaching youth that we have adequate resources to meet the economic and social needs of all our people and that these resources must be used for this purpose.
4. The high school should direct the attention of youth to the fact that successful living depends upon adequate personal and public health and to physical fitness for employment, social and family life.
5. The high school should teach youth that America is committed to an economic system of private enterprise and that this system must be healthy, but government regulation is required to insure its serving the public good.
6. Youth need to learn that all men must work to produce for individual and group welfare and that opportunities for work must always be available.
7. The high school should see that each young person has the knowledge he needs to improve his social and economic status to the limit of his capacities. He should know that each occupational level carries its own rewards and affords each individual an opportunity to enrich his life. He should not strive to rise to levels where he cannot succeed.

If these goals were regarded as really important jobs of the secondary school, what would the curriculum be like? Would countless young people go through high school with only two years of social studies, or four years of a perfunctory study of history, a dreary recitation of facts without meaning or significance?

---

[1] Hollis L. Caswell (ed.), *The American High School* (Eighth Yearbook of the John Dewey Society). By permission of Harper & Bros., copyright 1946, pp. 67-69. (Explanatory discussions of each point, found in the original, are not reproduced here.)

Adolescent Needs Related to Goals.—The needs of the adolescent certainly must be considered in the setting up of goals for the secondary school. His nature, his developmental tasks, and his biological and psychological needs are guideposts showing what the school should do for him to help him become a well-integrated individual in our society. But these needs are not at variance with social needs, for in a democracy each individual is considered important, worthy of the highest development of his potentialities. The social welfare of all individuals stands foremost. In such an atmosphere are found the best possibilities for developing well-integrated personalities. Adolescent growth phenomena become guides in assisting the individual to develop into a citizen whose personal and social adjustment will enable him to contribute to the democratic way of life.

Goals Stated by National Committees.—An historical study of aims of the secondary school would reveal a number of statements by educators who have attempted to put into words what the school should accomplish. Most of them have been broad, and in a sense vague and indefinite since they are subject to various interpretations. The best known of these statements, which has undoubtedly had significant influence on American secondary education, is the *Cardinal Principles of Secondary Education,* published in 1918 by the Commission on the Reorganization of Secondary Education, a committee appointed by the National Education Association.[2] The seven objectives of education listed were these:

1. Health
2. Command of fundamental processes
3. Vocation
4. Worthy home membership
5. Citizenship
6. Worthy use of leisure
7. Ethical character

The Commission listed several principles to carry out these objectives, many of which sound as though they might have been written today instead of more than thirty years ago. While the Commission made some attempt at interpreting these statements, it did not go very deeply into translating them into individual behavior. Moreover, education courses have used them more often as a list to be recited rather than to be understood and analyzed in terms of their meaning for high school practices. Few have thought to ask: "How

---

[2] *Cardinal Principles of Secondary Education,* U.S. Bureau of Education, Bulletin 35, 1918, Washington, D.C.: Government Printing Office, 1919, 32 pp.

does a pupil act if he is a worthy home member?" "Are my pupils making any progress toward this way of behaving?" Many recount these objectives glibly, but secondary schools have not adequately carried out these goals for all their pupils.

The Educational Policies Commission of the National Education Association has written a useful, easily understood statement of the purposes of education in American democracy. This is a commission of well-known educators, a deliberative body appointed by the N.E.A. to consider general policies in American education. *The Purposes of Education in American Democracy,* published in 1938, was one one of its three statements on education's function in our society, all now available in one volume.[3] The entire report should be read by future teachers.

The statement dealing with purposes of education first discusses the meaning of the democratic process. It then points out that advancement of the democratic way of life is the inclusive purpose of American education, and describes the educated individual as a person, as a member of the family and community group, as a producer or consumer, and as a citizen. The objectives of education are grouped under four headings, those of self-realization, human relationships, economic efficiency, and civic responsibility.

The usefulness of this statement lies in the fact that each of these objectives is defined in terms of what the educated person who lives up to these goals is like. The following lists the Commission's description of the educated individual:[4]

THE OBJECTIVES OF SELF-REALIZATION

THE INQUIRING MIND. The educated person has an appetite for learning.

SPEECH. The educated person can speak the mother tongue clearly.

READING. The educated person reads the mother tongue efficiently.

WRITING. The educated person writes the mother tongue effectively.

NUMBER. The educated person solves problems of counting and calculating.

SIGHT AND HEARING. The educated person is skilled in listening and observing.

HEALTH KNOWLEDGE. The educated person understands the basic facts concerning health and disease.

HEALTH HABITS. The educated person protects his own health and that of his dependents.

PUBLIC HEALTH. The educated person works to improve the health of the community.

---

[3] Educational Policies Commission, *Policies for Education in American Democracy,* Washington, D.C.: National Education Association, 1946, 277 pp.

[4] *Ibid.,* pp. 192, 212, 226, 240.

RECREATION. The educated person is participant and spectator in many sports and other pastimes.

INTELLECTUAL INTERESTS. The educated person has mental resources for the use of leisure.

AESTHETIC INTERESTS. The educated person appreciates beauty.

CHARACTER. The educated person gives responsible direction to his own life.

THE OBJECTIVES OF HUMAN RELATIONSHIPS

RESPECT FOR HUMANITY. The educated person puts human relationships first.

FRIENDSHIPS. The educated person enjoys a rich, sincere, and varied social life.

COOPERATION. The educated person can work and play with others.

COURTESY. The educated person observes the amenities of social behavior.

APPRECIATION OF THE HOME. The educated person appreciates the family as a social institution.

CONSERVATION OF THE HOME. The educated person conserves family ideals.

HOMEMAKING. The educated person is skilled in homemaking.

DEMOCRACY IN THE HOME. The educated person maintains democratic family relations.

THE OBJECTIVES OF ECONOMIC EFFICIENCY

WORK. The educated producer knows the satisfaction of good workmanship.

OCCUPATIONAL INFORMATION. The educated producer understands the requirements and opportunities for various jobs.

OCCUPATIONAL CHOICE. The educated producer has selected his occupation.

OCCUPATIONAL EFFICIENCY. The educated producer succeeds in his chosen vocation.

OCCUPATIONAL ADJUSTMENT. The educated producer maintains and improves his efficiency.

OCCUPATIONAL APPRECIATION. The educated producer appreciates the social value of his work.

PERSONAL ECONOMICS. The educated consumer plans the economics of his own life.

CONSUMER JUDGMENT. The educated consumer develops standards for guiding his expenditures.

EFFICIENCY IN BUYING. The educated consumer is an informed and skillful buyer.

CONSUMER PROTECTION. The educated consumer takes appropriate measures to safeguard his interests.

THE OBJECTIVES OF CIVIC RESPONSIBILITY

SOCIAL JUSTICE. The educated citizen is sensitive to the disparities of human circumstance.

SOCIAL ACTIVITY. The educated citizen acts to correct unsatisfactory conditions.

SOCIAL UNDERSTANDING. The educated citizen seeks to understand social structures and social processes.

CRITICAL JUDGMENT. The educated citizen has defenses against propaganda.

TOLERANCE. The educated citizen respects honest differences of opinion.

CONSERVATION. The educated citizen has a regard for the nation's resources.

SOCIAL APPLICATION OF SCIENCE. The educated citizen measures scientific advance by its contribution to the general welfare.

WORLD CITIZENSHIP. The educated citizen is a cooperating member of the world community.

LAW OBSERVANCE. The educated citizen respects the law.

ECONOMIC LITERACY. The educated citizen is economically literate.

POLITICAL CITIZENSHIP. The educated citizen accepts his civic duties.

DEVOTION TO DEMOCRACY. The educated citizen acts upon an unswerving loyalty to democratic ideals.

Although these objectives are written for education in general, they should be studied with the part of the secondary school in mind. Each teacher, no matter what subject area he teaches, should ask himself: "How can I further objectives from each of these four areas in my classes?" "Which of them should be my particular concern?"

Kinds of Behavior Basic to Effective Functioning of Democracy.—These objectives serve as a scale of values for what the school should accomplish. But what do they mean in terms of specific pupil behavior? How does a pupil act if he is a cooperating member of a world community? What does he do if he puts human relationships first? These are goals that must be observed in the pupil's behavior here and now in the school. In other words, goals for the teacher must be specific enough so that they can be observed or evaluated in some manner. Moreover, they must apply to an individual's growth and development and to the individual-in-the-group. The Educational Policies Commission points out this fact: "The general end of education in America at the present time is the fullest possible development of the individual within the framework of our present industrialized democratic society. The attainment of this end is to be observed in individual behavior or conduct." [5]

Such an approach is vastly different from one that begins with a textbook or a section of subject matter and sets out to cover the material. Subject matter and experiences, as will be elaborated on later in this book, instead should be selected in terms of their con-

---

[5] *Ibid.,* p. 186.

tribution to the behavior set up as the outcomes which the secondary school seeks to attain.

What are these behaviors? They can best be stated in terms of understandings, attitudes, appreciations, and skills, the real outcomes of learning. Unless they are thought of as applying to pupils, they may become high-sounding terms useful for tests and teachers' conventions but with little application to youngsters in a classroom. In the following pages, a number of specific objectives are listed to indicate the kinds of behavior the teacher in a secondary school in a democratic society should strive to develop. They are not all inclusive. If we take the Educational Policies Commission's list as a basis and state our goals in specific pupil behavior terms (such as those that follow), we will have a more concrete guide in determining our responsibilities as a teacher.

The goals are not intended merely for the social studies teacher but for the mathematics teacher, the science teacher, the homemaking teacher, and all others who are responsible for the growth of boys and girls in the secondary school. Each teacher would certainly need to add other skills, understandings, or appreciations that apply specifically to his area of teaching responsibility. Some teachers are more responsible for homemaking skills, for language skills, or for mathematics skills in our present secondary school organization. But the point is that *all* teachers should be responsible for the pupil's growth toward a more balanced, integrated, and informed person who can serve to further the aims of democracy. To the extent that any teacher is contributing to development of such specific behaviors as these, he is contributing to the democratic goals of the secondary school. This is but a partial list, one that applies to several of the broad objectives.

SPECIFIC OUTCOMES FOR THE SECONDARY SCHOOL
(Listed in terms of pupil behavior)

Attitudes

1. The pupil accepts responsibility for his contributions to group welfare.
2. He respects the rights of others and treats them with the same respect he demands for himself.
3. He accepts the consequences of his own actions.
4. He adjusts his own behavior to the decisions of the group.
5. He is open-minded to new ideas.
6. He welcomes honest differences of opinion and respects others' points of view.

7. He feels free to express his own beliefs without fear of reprisal.
8. He bases judgment on reliable information.
9. He withholds judgment on important issues until he has all the facts.
10. He considers the effect of his actions on other members of the group.
11. He respects duly constituted authority.
12. He works for the solution of problems in his own school community and for the advancement of the welfare of others.
13. He enters freely into service activities of his community.
14. He judges an individual on his own merits as a person rather than on the basis of nationality, creed, race, or economic level.

Appreciations

1. The pupil appreciates the values to the individual of democratic participation in school affairs.
2. He enjoys reading about the social scene and desires to understand the problems that confront society.
3. He appreciates the American heritage of freedom.
4. He admires the achievements of all cultural groups and appreciates their contributions to American life.
5. He shows sympathy and sensitiveness to human misery and want.
6. He has a wide interest in art, music, science, history, and literature.
7. He enjoys reading good books and periodicals.
8. He has a desire to learn and explore.
9. He appreciates beauty in his surroundings.
10. He enjoys expressing himself creatively in some form.
11. He finds pleasure in participating with others in recreation.
12. He is interested in enlarging his vocabulary.

Understandings

1. The pupil realizes the need for limitation of individual and group freedom in order that greater liberties may be enjoyed by all.
2. He realizes that democracy is in a constant process of adjustment and that democracy in this country has not been fully achieved.
3. He understands that the individual who places the interests of his racial, cultural, religious, economic, or social group above the good of society as a whole endangers his own freedom.
4. He understands that democratic living includes full opportunity for political, economic, social, and religious rights.

5. He recognizes the necessity of law in establishing and maintaining an orderly society.
6. He realizes the value of group effort in arriving at decisions.
7. He understands that controversial issues are best solved through open discussion and objective study.
8. He understands that minority rights must be protected within majority rule.
9. He understands that citizenship in a democracy demands a responsible, actively participating people.
10. He realizes that intelligent effort is essential to success.
11. He understands that harmonious participation in the home and family life are basic to healthy and desirable social relationships.
12. He understands that nations must forego national sovereignty to achieve world cooperation and peace.

Skills

1. The pupil is able to analyze data, observe relationships, and note causes and effects in arriving at a solution.
2. He selects reading materials with increasing discrimination.
3. He is able to locate and use sources of information.
4. He is able to organize information effectively.
5. He can draw logical and reasonable conclusions from his investigations.
6. He is able to distinguish between fact and opinion.
7. He has the ability to make intelligent choices for himself.
8. He can work independently.
9. He is able to work cooperatively with others.
10. He is able to express ideas effectively in written or oral form.
11. He can discriminate reasonably between socially desirable and undesirable behavior.

These are goals to be approximated, reached in degrees according to the individual's needs and capacities. They are a direction in which to move in the same way that principles of democracy are ideals. Some pupils are slower in attainment than others and can achieve only so much in a certain number of years. Some can never go beyond a certain point. But there are no grade standards for achievement in objectives of this kind. There are, on the other hand, the maturity and nature of the individual youngster to be considered. Only as specific behaviors of this kind are evident in the growth of pupils in the secondary school will that school achieve its purposes of serving a democratic society.

3. Problems Of Making Democracy Work In The United States

Since American society has democracy as its goal, the examination of how effectively democracy is put into action and the invention of better forms of living for achieving democratic ends become major goals for the secondary school. Thus, if the American secondary school is to be suited to the society in which it exists, it must be concerned about the difficulties that democracy faces in the modern world. Headway will be made in improving human welfare only as problems that stand in the way are tackled squarely. The problems of making democracy work are many and will change in seriousness and import from time to time. A selected list of questions that beset mid-twentieth century America are presented here. It is hoped that the prospective teacher, through his reading and courses in the social sciences, will develop others for consideration by himself and his classes in pre-service education, and that he will read widely in search of the facts essential to reach intelligent conclusions concerning these problems.

Problems of Earning a Living.—In a democracy, an individual theoretically has a freedom of choice of his vocation, subject to the limitations of his own abilities, capacities, and interests. He should be able to secure training necessary for the occupation for which he is best suited—an occupation that will enable him to provide a comfortable living for his family. Those who lived through the 1930's as laborers, farmers, businessmen, or in the professions, many forced to subsist on relief or on WPA, had good cause to wonder what had happened to the economic system of their society. Although the problems of earning a living are not now as dramatically highlighted, there are grave issues awaiting solution by a world shaken and confused by tremendous conflict and the consequent economic readjustments. The secondary school of mid-twentieth century America exists in an environment where problems such as these demand an adequate solution:

1. *Settling differences between labor and management.* What basic causes underlie the frictions between labor and management? What is the responsibility of management for establishing satisfactory relationships with labor? What is the responsibility of labor? What can the government do to maintain satisfactory labor-management relationships?

2. *Developing fair employment practices for all races and ethnic groups.* Does the idea of restricting some occupations to certain groups of people square with democratic ideals? How can we eliminate discrimination against various racial and ethnic groups in these occupations? How can the gains made toward a solution of this problem in many communities and states be extended? What part should education play?

3. *Maintaining adequate production to provide full employment.* How can industry and labor best provide for full employment? What is the responsibility of each and what has each been doing to encourage full employment? To hinder full employment? How may the government contribute to full employment? What is the responsibility of the government for those industries closely related to the public welfare?

4. *Providing employment for the beginning and older wage earner.* Will youth find it increasingly difficult to secure employment in business, industry, and the professions? Why do unions and professional organizations restrict the number of youth who can enter some occupations? What effect does the rising age for beginning employment have on the lives of young people? How does the increased specialization of jobs relate to the type and length of secondary education? Will the wage earners past forty experience greater difficulty in finding employment? What relation do retirement or pension systems have to this problem?

These and other problems connected with making a living must be considered in determining what are desirable outcomes of the secondary school.

Problems of Providing Adequate Living Standards.—The opportunity to work under favorable conditions should result in an income sufficient to provide for the necessities and comforts of life. The fact that there are, in a country of the highest standards of living, children and adults who are living in crowded conditions in substandard homes, improperly nourished, and suffering from disease and ill-health that medical science now has the power to alleviate, indicates a need for further improvement in our economy. Science has placed at our disposal means by which those standards can be raised for all. Some of the chief problems in our country today relating to the living standards of its people are these:

1. *Solving the increasing cost of living.* Are government controls necessary to stop or prevent inflation? Can the matter be han-

dled adequately through private action? What effect will controls have on initiative and expansion in business and industry? Is control of wages a necessary corrollary to price control? What are the effects of the diminishing dollar value upon savings represented by government and other pensions, bonds, and life insurance?

2. *Furnishing adequate housing.* What responsibility does the state or federal government have for providing decent living quarters? What are the difficulties in establishing low-cost public housing projects? What needs to be done to enable low-income families to build or purchase homes of their own?

3. *Providing needed medical attention.* Will voluntary free medical services, private health insurance plans, or compulsory health insurance furnish the medical attention needed by low-income families? Can the family of below average income provide for the health of its members without assistance? Are there sufficient doctors in this country to take care of the needs of the total population?

4. *Eliminating restrictive covenants and "ghetto districts."* How can we eliminate restrictive practices in housing which result in certain minority groups living in less desirable districts? What are the basic causes of these practices? What has been the effect of the recent Supreme Court decision on such practices?

Obviously, democratic principles would be opposed to special interest groups securing their own advantages at the expense of the health and welfare of others. These are issues that deal with the important principle of concern for the common welfare. No secondary school can afford to sidestep such vital issues to humanity.

Problems of Securing the Finer Things of Life for More People.—While these problems are not as severe, they are, nevertheless, of real concern to education. Countless homes have little music, are drab in appearance, and contain no books or magazines except of the comic book variety. It is a challenge to secondary education to develop in our society a people who will be interested in things of cultural value; who will broaden their interests; who will find creative things to do with their hands; and who will, as a result, lead richer and fuller lives. In an industrial age of shorter working days and weeks, the general morale of the people will depend upon how constructively they use their leisure time.

1. *Using profitably the increased amount of leisure time.* Do crime and delinquency have any relationship to use of leisure hours?

Will beer taverns and "joints" continue to draw a larger number of the American public? Whose responsibility is it to assist people to develop a heightened appreciation of music, art, drama, literature? Does the way leisure time is spent have any bearing on the effectiveness of democratic life and institutions?

2. *Selecting desirable reading materials.* How has the rapidly multiplying amount of reading material created a greater problem for the schools? From an observation of the newsstands, what picture do we get of the moral level, cultural interests, and sociocivic interests of the American people? Is this condition an indication of the outcomes of secondary education?

3. *Choosing radio and television programs and movies.* What relation does public demand bear to the kind of radio, television, and movie programs available? Can more discriminating tastes be developed for these newer cultural and educational media? What is the secondary school's responsibility?

4. *Developing skills for hobbies and recreation.* Is proficiency in such skills associated with the mental health of a people? What should the local community do about public recreation? How can we become more of a nation of participators in recreational activities rather than one of spectators? Is developing these skills an important purpose of the secondary school?

5. *Beautifying one's living surroundings.* How can communities improve the appearance of the village, city, or community neighborhood? How can we provide more artistic arrangements, color harmony, attractive landscaping, and simple beauty in our small homes? Is it entirely a matter of finances? Should the advancement of this phase of living be a part of the general education of all secondary school pupils?

Some may take issue with the points listed here under the finer things of life. For millions of people, however, living a richer, fuller life is a matter of broadening interests in nature, people, places, sports, music, books, and different forms of everyday artistic expression or appreciation of beauty. A firsthand study of the life of the coal miner, farmer, trucker, mill worker, sharecropper, or those in the many other occupations in American life will give a realistic picture of the task of education.

Problems of Preserving Freedom and Securing Equal Rights. —One of the most serious problems that faces our country is the constraints limiting certain minority groups. Negroes, Mexicans, Japanese, Indians, and other ethnic, religious, and racial groups are often treated in a manner befitting criminals excluded from society. Bigotry is certainly not limited to any one section of the United States. It is an unhealthy and repulsive blot on American life wherever it is found. Conditions vary in different sections of the country. While substantial progress has been made in many places, these groups are still too frequently relegated to a lot in life in which they are able to earn only enough money to keep alive; dependent upon others, they are deprived of many of their liberties and rights as American citizens. If the United States is to maintain and extend its place of leadership among democratic nations, it must improve the implementation of our democratic ideals at home. The successful efforts toward alleviating these conditions are encouraging, and school people need to be leaders in continuing and supporting these achievements.

Then, too, there is the need for maintaining freedom of thought and expression, vital to a healthy democracy. Any form of thought control is a serious threat to all Americans. We have recently witnessed a first step in this direction when demagogic politicians attacked liberal and patriotic citizens, labeling them "communist."

Listed for consideration by all concerned with a better nation and world are these phases of the problem:

1. *Maintaining civil liberties.* What should the federal government do to assure the civil liberties guaranteed by the Constitution? What is the responsibility of the states? What controls should be exercised over organizations that oppose our democratic way of life? How can these controls be exercised effectively without interfering with the liberties of others? How can we protect the interests and freedom of minority groups as guaranteed by the Constitution? What is the responsibility of individual citizens in this matter?

2. *Preserving freedom of communication.* How do various subversive organizations endanger freedom of communication? How can these organizations be restrained without limiting the freedom of expression of all citizens? How can citizens obtain complete factual information as a basis for decisions on public issues? What factors today may hinder the dissemination of factual information?

3. *Emphasizing freedom of thought in education.* Should there be any limitation on the freedom of teachers and pupils to discuss controversial issues in the schools? If such discussions are carried on, what are the responsibilities of the teacher? The responsibilities of the pupils? Should newspapers and periodicals

expressing the views of all groups be provided in the schools? What are the dangers if, in certain communities, publications expressing one view or another are excluded from the schools?

4. *Exercising the right to participate in government.* What is the danger if only a small percentage of voters exercise the right of suffrage? Should the voting age be lowered from twenty-one years to twenty or eighteen? How can we protect the right of all minority groups to vote? What is the responsibility of the individual citizen in encouraging everyone to exercise the right to vote?

5. *Combating communist and fascist ideologies and aggression.* How can the concept of freedom and democracy be extended into areas of the world under communist control? What means are available to communicate with people in those areas? What is the potential danger from organized communist and fascist groups in this country? How important in combating the spread of communism and fascism are such factors as education, maintaining a high standard of living for all peoples, and an open and calm discussion of the issues involved?

6. *Securing equality of educational opportunity.* Will some school districts and states be able to achieve equality of educational opportunity for children in that area without state and federal aid? Do segregated schools provide equal opportunity for children? To what extent should society provide scholarships for worthy youth to attend college?

A real understanding of the facts and issues involved in the situation is needed. Investigation of different points of view, freedom of choice, and a concept of changing civilization are attitudes and understandings of the kind that will help to preserve freedom for our people in the years to come.

Problems of Establishing Effective World Government and Peace.—The question that will test present and future statesmanship is whether or not we will be able to set up an effective world government before events lead us into another world conflict. Peace is desired by people all over the world. A universal popular poll would undoubtedly show that the overwhelming majority would like to avoid war. To most educated people, war seems a barbaric, inhuman means of settling differences. We have been told repeatedly since World War II that another war, with its newly developed instruments of destruction, could wipe out civilization. Yet, we seem to have advanced no closer to effective methods of settling international differences. The aftermath of war and the continued preparation for possible future conflicts create situations that require the best of intelligent thought.

1. *Mitigating hatreds built up by the war.* Should we solicit the cooperation of former enemy countries to preserve world peace? How can we relieve the international distrust built up during World War II? What is the school's responsibility for changing attitudes of dislike of people in other countries, developed through war experiences?

2. *Shifting emphasis from national sovereignty to world govern-ment.* Can a world government, strong enough to prevent war, be built up while strong feelings of nationalism prevail? How can the United Nations become an increasingly effective force? Will direct national or regional action promote world harmony and peace? Should the United Nations have a military force to resist aggressions? Should economic action be brought against aggres-sors?

3. *Coping with the effects of increased mechanization of warfare and scientific advance in potential instruments of destruction.* How can international control of atomic energy be established in the face of sharp differences among the great powers? What should be the direction of research in atomic energy? What effect will the increased cost of war equipment, materials, and manpower have on our economy if constant preparedness must be main-tained?

4. *Achieving a mutual understanding between peoples of different nations and settling differences between nations.* What is the re-sponsibility of the schools for helping pupils understand better the cultures of other peoples? Should the schools provide study of peoples whose ideologies are opposed to ours? How can our citi-zens become fully informed concerning other nations and cultures? How can the United States establish effective relationships for international peace with other nations?

These questions are of such far-reaching significance for future civilization that consideration of them as immediate problems must be given a recognized part in the program of the secondary school.

Problems of Conserving Human and Natural Resources.—With advances in transportation and mechanization of our way of living have come such a phenomenal increase of accidents on the highway and on city streets that they head the list of causes of accidental death.

Although medicine has made great strides in conquering many ailments, heart disease, poliomyelitis, rheumatic fever, and cancer still are among the areas where a great deal of medical research is needed. Conservation of human life remains a foremost problem of society. Sickness, pestilence, accident, and disease, while less dramatic than war, are the concern of every individual in whatever social or economic position.

In spite of the many excellent efforts to educate the people to use natural resources wisely, a great deal of carelessness, exploitation, ignorance, and greed still continues to destroy forests, deplete soil, kill wildlife, and ruin natural beauty. Since man is dependent upon his environment for his livelihood, means must be found to prevent such abuses.

1. *Using wisely soil, forests, mineral deposits, wildlife, and other natural resources.* To what extent should the public control waterpower, mineral deposits, and forests to avoid their exploitation for personal gain rather than their use for the social good? Will a program of education suffice to secure the wise use of resources?

2. *Preventing loss of life through accidents.* What means are warranted for preventing the great loss of life through automobile accidents? Should drivers' licenses be as carefully controlled as pilots' licenses? Are uniform traffic codes needed?

3. *Reducing death from disease and illness.* What prevents more money being spent on medical research and preventive medicine? Should research foundations or public taxation bear the cost of such research? How can quack patent medicines and fake practitioners be dealt with effectively?

Education for preservation of life and limb and for wise use of natural resources has gained momentum in secondary schools. It is as legitimate a function as education for home life. Undoubtedly, educators and the public will need to decide whether it is important enough as a goal on which to spend more time, money, and effort. The study of this area will call for increased use of the community as a laboratory and for instructional materials other than textbooks.

Problems of Strengthening Spiritual and Moral Qualities of the People.—Should secondary education be concerned with matters of a spiritual and moral nature? Is this a question related to the teaching of desirable attitudes? In seeking the essential purposes of the secondary school in the modern age, these are questions that need consideration. The problem in the public schools is one of keeping free from the sectarian differences that may deter any real progress toward consideration of moral values.

1. *Reducing crime and delinquency.* Why does one fifth of all arrests occur among youth under twenty-one? What does this fact indicate for the responsibilities of the church, the home, and the school? Are present methods of punishment and rehabilitation in line with psychological findings? What basic sources of crime does our society need to attack?

2. *Strengthening family life.* What can be done to provide more activities for the family as a unit? Is modern life necessarily conducive to weakening family social and spiritual life? What can replace the opportunities for work experience in the home? How do the emphasis on sex in movies, magazines, and books, and the tension of modern living, affect marriage relations?

3. *Reinvigorating spiritual life and moral strength.* Are the congestion and indifference of urban living contributing to lowered moral standards? Who is responsible for the moral guidance of children and youth if the family fails in its duties? Have the spiritual qualities of the people served to improve democracy in recent times? What stand should churches take regarding the treatment received by minority groups?

4. *Strengthening the church as a social institution.* How vital a part does the church play in American life? Why are there millions of nonmembers or indifferent church members? Should the church assume a militant social purpose for human welfare?

5. *Expressing spiritual values in behavioral terms.* Are human brotherhood, love for one's neighbor, and helping the needy merely verbalisms to many who profess these principles? How can they become functioning parts of the lives of people? How does one behave if he practices brotherly love? Can the school express spiritual values in terms of behavior?

Church, school, and home are a responsible team of social institutions that should serve to strengthen the moral fiber of a people. Inhuman warfare, the inability of countries to get along with each other, the bigoted treatment of fellow American citizens, and self-righteous attitudes pose the question of how their teamwork can be improved. Although we may be better morally as a people than in the past, it staggers one's imagination to consider what a militant, cooperating body of churches and schools might accomplish through working toward improved attitudes and behavior as a major common goal.

Other Problems of an Increasingly Complex Social, Economic, and Political Life.—This section has discussed some of the most significant problems of the society which the American secondary school serves. They warrant analysis, study, and discussion by all concerned with education of youth. A few others are cited here to indicate the urgent need for developing greater social intelligence and social interest among the general population in an increasingly complex society.

1. An expanding role of government with a greater degree of regulation of local communities, private enterprises, and individuals.
2. The diminishing of direct contacts with policy-making in government.
3. The diminishing of direct contacts among individuals and groups that are a part of a total social organization.
4. An increasing mobility of population with continuously new adjustments demanded.
5. An increasing difficulty in getting facts because of propaganda, advertising methods, and biased news.
6. An increasing interdependency in economic life.
7. A seeming inability to adjust production and consumption to human needs for food, clothing, and shelter.
8. The possibility of the replacement of independent small business and industry by modern mass production and by national and international business organizations.

SUMMARY

Secondary education plays a vital part in producing an intelligent citizenry in a democracy. In order to accomplish this aim, the secondary school in our society must have goals that are fashioned to serve democratic ends. Constant study of democracy and of the current social setting is necessary to keep the secondary school suited to the times. The most important goals for the Latin Grammar school are not the foremost ones for the mid-twentieth century American high school.

The school and the teacher should know what those goals are. Moreover, they need to be translated into specific behavior of pupils in order that there may be some basis for evaluations to determine whether or not the goals are being achieved. Only as teachers thus interpret goals in school and classroom will the secondary school become most effective as an agency for promoting democratic ends. Each major subject area taught in secondary schools has a potential contribution to make to social goals if appropriate content is employed and appropriate objectives are emphasized.

Furthermore, problems that beset our American life need to be studied and discussed in order to strengthen democracy in this country. Solutions will no doubt be tentative, but as human relations are improved, many of these problems will fade into the background. In order to forward democratic aims, the difficulties in making democracy work must be understood. Here the teacher has a very definite obligation. These are questions which the secondary school must face squarely.

Material on socioeconomic trends and on social problems is available in abundance in technical and popular books and journals. It is the intention of this chapter to stimulate the student of education to inquire into these issues critically in order that he might be a responsible leader of youth, not a demagogue or a blind, uninformed follower, and that he might more clearly understand what should be the purpose of the secondary school of this day and age.

Selected References

Bossing, Nelson L. *Principles of Secondary Education.* New York: Prentice-Hall, Inc., 1949, chaps. 4-11.—Contains a good summary of how the secondary school has developed historically and statements of its present purposes by different professional groups in American education.

Caswell, Hollis L. (ed.). *The American High School* (Eighth Yearbook of the John Dewey Society). New York: Harper & Bros., 1946, chap. 4.—Raises some critical issues regarding the social policies of this country and discusses the need for planning at the local and national level.

Douglass, Harl R. (ed.). *Education for Life Adjustment.* New York: The Ronald Press Co., 1950, chaps. 1, 2, 3.—Gives the history of the development of the Life Adjustment Education movement, discusses changes in American life, and presents the objectives of Life Adjustment Education, good objectives for a secondary school program that meets life needs.

Douglass, Harl R. *Secondary Education for Youth in Modern America.* Washington, D.C.: American Council on Education, 1937, chaps. 2, 4.—The author presents a concise statement of trends in American life and the objectives of secondary education.

Douglass, Harl R. (ed.). *The High School Curriculum.* New York: The Ronald Press Co., 1947, chaps. 4, 5.—Further information on technological, industrial, and social changes in American society will be found in this reference.

Educational Policies Commission. *Policies for Education in American Democracy.* Washington, D.C.: National Education Association, 1946.—Book III of this publication, also printed separately, is a significant report of the Commission dealing with "The Purposes of Education in American Democracy." Although it applies to the whole school, it is especially pertinent for the secondary school.

Kilpatrick, William Heard. *Modern Education: Its Proper Work.* New York: Hinds, Hayden, & Eldredge, Inc., 1949, 26 pp.—A contrast of the aims of modern education and the older outlook, which stressed knowledge, is well presented. Personal characteristics demanded in a democracy are indicated.

LEONARD, J. PAUL. *Developing the Secondary School Curriculum*. New York: Rinehart & Co., Inc., 1946, chaps. 3, 4, 8.—Presents contrasting points of view in educational theory and what they mean for the school program.

PETERS, CHARLES C. *The Curriculum of Democratic Education*. New York: McGraw-Hill Book Co., Inc., 1942.—Part III presents a long list of specific behaviors demanded of an individual in a democracy, the "components of effective living in a democratic society."

QUILLEN, I. JAMES, and HANNA, LAVONE A. *Education for Social Competence*. Chicago: Scott, Foresman & Co., 1948, chap. 3.—This chapter on "Social Competence and Human Behavior" contains one of the clearest explanations of the need for stating objectives in behavioral terms.

Chapter 3

MEETING THE NEEDS OF YOUTH THROUGH THE SECONDARY SCHOOL

The secondary school has been criticized rather severely in recent years by a number of educators for its failure to meet the needs of youth in a modern world. They claim that it is an "academic aristocracy" where youth with academic ability are privileged over those with other types of abilities. They are concerned about the fact that comparatively little attention is paid to youth's own life problems. They feel that the school eliminates earliest those young people who are least able to cope with civic and vocational problems. In the main, they are bothered by the slowness of secondary schools to adjust to the changing times.

To determine for ourselves the accuracy of these statements, we need to look into such facts or questions as these:

> How much has the nature of the pupil population changed?
> Who is eliminated and who remains to graduate?
> Why do pupils drop out of high school?
> Do all youth have an equal opportunity to attend high school?
> Does the high school show equal concern for youth of all types of ability?
> Are youth concerns and problems an important part of the curriculum?
> Are special services of the school organized to deal effectively with youth problems?
> Do secondary school teachers understand the problems of youth in growing up?
> Do youth who have completed or left high school show competency in facing the problems of living?

In this chapter will be presented information about the youth who are enrolled in secondary schools. Students of education may want to investigate further the original studies on elimination data, follow-up, and the like. Research is plentiful in these areas. The chapter does not recount all the data found in these studies since they have been made easily accessible through a number of publications on

the secondary schools. Some of the real life problems and needs
of youth are outlined briefly here. A number of the chapters throughout the book indicate, through descriptions of current practices, how
well these needs are being met. The student should keep them
constantly in mind in judging present practices for himself.

1. THE YOUTH IN SECONDARY SCHOOLS

*Approximately 75 per cent of youth are enrolled in secondary
schools.* The six to seven million youth enrolled in secondary schools
of the United States include approximately 70 to 80 per cent of all
youth 14 through 17 years of age. The rise in birth rate following
1941 undoubtedly will substantially increase high school enrollments
from 1955 to 1960 or 1962. In 1890, only 7 per cent of young people
of these ages were attending high school. In fact, the pupil population in secondary schools practically doubled every decade from 1880
to 1940.[1] This fact is of tremendous significance for curriculum,
guidance services, and other aspects of the secondary school program.
An extremely selective group formerly composed the student body,
even up to 1920, when only three of ten youth of high school age
were in school. In just twenty years, the proportion skyrocketed
to seven of ten youth. Many persons fail to consider this change
in the pupil population when they advocate the same type of program
of studies that prevailed in 1920.

The figures for the proportion of high school youth enrolled
in school vary for different sections of the country and for urban
and rural areas. Some states of the Far West, Middle West, and
East have the highest proportion enrolled. In some states in the
South, where educational support is not as favorable, the lowest
proportion is found. Density of population and the different types
of life led by the people are factors of importance affecting these
figures. Rural areas where school facilities are less easily accessible
have a smaller percentage of youth going to high school. World War
II caused a temporary decline in secondary school enrollments. Other
factors will be discussed in the following pages.

There is a wide variety of abilities and interests. In the days
when only 7 to 15 per cent of youth attended high school, the

---

[1] See the latest biennial survey report of the Office of Education. The most
recent at the time of publication was "Statistical Summary of Education, 1945-46,"
chap. 1 in *Biennial Survey of Education in the United States, 1944-46,* Washington,
D. C.: Federal Security Agency, Office of Education, Government Printing Office,
1949, pp. 9-11.

great majority was interested in educating themselves to enter the professions. A much larger percentage of high school graduates went on to college than the proportion continuing their education today. The highly verbalistic curriculum was within the grasp of a group that represented the higher levels of intelligence; in fact, only those persisted in high school who found such a curriculum "learnable."

As the secondary school has become more and more a place where "all the children of all the people" attend, the heterogeneity of the group has increased remarkably. We find vast differences in reading ability ranging from fifth grade to fifteenth grade; intelligence quotients varying from the 60's to the highest levels. The influx of pupils who have no great interest in cultural things, nor ability to master abstract formulas and concepts, has baffled a number of secondary school teachers who have been used to failing those who could not meet their 1920 school population standards. Those teachers have not understood how to cope with youngsters whose ability lies in areas other than the academic—in art, music, social relations, and mechanical pursuits.

The youth come from home backgrounds of all types. A high school education for their children has become the ambition of parents of all economic classes. The rapid democratization of secondary school education in this country is in striking contrast to the selective character of European secondary education. Here the people of semiskilled and unskilled occupational groups have found free public education a boon which provides greater opportunities for their children.

The increasing enrollment in public schools has brought together pupils from all walks of life, from various economic and social classes, from different religious and racial groups. This development in itself has been of utmost importance in giving the pupil a significant part of his secondary school education, that of learning to live together with all types of people. In most sections of the country, different racial groups attend classes together and form lasting friendships there. Pupils from the home of the plumber, the mechanic, the itinerant worker, the doctor, and the business executive go to the same high school. They come from broken homes as well as from homes where family harmony and solidarity give an added advantage. Their home may be an eighteen-room mansion overlooking the beach, or a shack by the river.

Some teachers and principals who still look back with longing at the days when the secondary school could readily force out the "misfits" are bewildered by pupils who come from slum environ-

ments and broken, unhappy homes, bringing their many maladjustment problems with them to school. Teachers who go on blindly
making homework assignments to all pupils, as though all still came
from homes where there were both a place and encouragement to
study, fail to realize that the pupils of today's secondary schools are
different from those of the 1920's because they represent all groups
in the American population. In such sociological studies as "Elmtown," a study of the impact of social classes upon adolescents, there
is some evidence to show that teachers discriminate against pupils
whose families come from the "lower classes." [2]

*Only a small percentage of high school pupils will continue their
education in college.* Although approximately one third of the high
school graduates continue their education in college, only about 15
per cent of the pupils who enter high school continue their education
past the twelfth grade.[3] The latter is a more accurate measure since
the high school curriculum must be planned in terms of all its pupils,
not just those who graduate. These proportions are considerably
smaller than those of twenty years ago, when many of the rather
highly selected group of secondary school graduates went on to college. In other words, today the student body of the secondary school
is composed mainly of youth who will terminate their education when
they leave high school. Even in junior colleges, three fourths of the
students terminate their education before or by the end of the
fourteenth year. Has the secondary school program kept pace with
this significant change in the nature of pupil population?

2. THE EXTENT OF DEMOCRATIZATION OF OPPORTUNITY FOR ALL YOUTH

Although the facts indicate that the American secondary school
has gone a long way toward becoming a universal school, we need to
examine additional data to determine whether it is genuinely democratic in providing an equal opportunity for all youth. To what
extent does the economic group into which a child is born determine
his chances of receiving a high school education? Is the American
secondary school geared to all its youth except those who, because of
severe mental or physical handicaps, cannot support themselves or
take the responsibility for their own lives? Whose children does the
secondary school serve? How well does it serve different groups?

---

[2] A. B. Hollingshead, *Elmtown's Youth,* New York: John Wiley & Sons, Inc.,
1949, chaps. 8, 13.

[3] "Statistical Summary of Education, 1945-46," *op cit.,* p. 31.

Slightly more than one half of the young people who enter the ninth grade graduate from high school. The actual figures show that, in 1947-48, 61.6 per cent of those who entered high school in 1944-45 graduated.[4] There is a gradually diminishing number remaining from year to year as the group progresses through high school. The number dropping out is significant. Evidently high school is not meeting the needs of these youth, or other circumstances in their environment prevent them from continuing.

Youth of higher intelligence levels have a better chance of survival through high school. Our first finding as we look into the question of why so many youth fail to complete high school is that those from the lower brackets of intelligence are more likely to drop out. It should be emphasized that this is academic intelligence as measured by the verbal type of test. Studies show that the average I.Q. of seniors is usually greater than that of freshmen, but they do not indicate the differences in other types of abilities: mechanical, artistic, or social. Evidently there is somewhat of an "intellectual aristocracy" in the upper years of high school. We can assume that the secondary school is not geared as well to youth of the lower levels of academic ability. If it really served youth of all types of abilities equally, it is doubtful if we would find selectivity on this basis.

Youth from homes of low socioeconomic status drop out in greater numbers than those more fortunately situated. A number of studies have shown that the father's occupation is an extremely important factor in determining how long a boy or girl will attend high school. Whether a child is born into the home of a proprietor, a store manager, a doctor, a coal miner, a waiter, or a factory worker determines to a large extent his chances of being in the line on commencement day, and consequently of attending college or securing certain types of employment. These studies show convincingly that the youth from the lower economic brackets do not have equal opportunity in attending high school. For example, such evidence as the following has been presented from time to time in the last fifteen years:

1. A young person from a home in the highest economic level is five times as likely to complete high school as one from the lowest income group.

---

[4] Data from "Statistical Summary of Education, 1947-48," supplied by David **T.** Blose, Office of Education, November 30, 1950.

2. One of ten youth from underprivileged homes continues school after high school graduation as contrasted with eight of ten from the top of the economic scale.

3. One of the chief reasons given for dropping out of school is the need to work or the lack of money to stay in school. This was particularly true in the findings of the youth studies conducted during the latter part of the 1930's.

4. Two of every three youth who drop out of school below the ninth grade are from homes in poor economic circumstances.[5]

In the homes of the lower income group, the family members are usually many and the dollars few. Older children are needed at home on the farm or must begin earning money early to supplement the family income. There may be less encouragement for them to continue high school. Certainly, the father and mother often see little chance of their being able to send the children to college. The total family culture, including its mores and accepted pattern of living, is a powerful factor in determining how long a child will continue in school. For example, the Elmtown study indicated that the great majority of the withdrawees from school were from families of the two lowest of five social classes in the community.[6]

Is this a democratic situation as far as equality of opportunity is concerned? What does it mean for the effectiveness of democratic institutions? We might also ask ourselves what can be done about it. During the depression days of the 1930's, the National Youth Administration, created by Congress, performed yeoman service in aiding many young people to earn money enough to stay in school.

The cash cost of attending high school is an important factor in determining whether youth will continue in school. The findings of research that has been done on the cost to pupils for textbooks, student tickets, dances, laboratory fees, gym uniforms, class rings, and the like have raised the question whether the public high school

---

[5] The student may wish to investigate these studies further. Some of them are: R. E. Eckert and T. O. Marshall, *When Youth Leave School*, New York: McGraw-Hill Book Co., Inc., 1938, 360 pp.; George S. Counts, *The Selective Character of American Secondary Education*, Chicago: University of Chicago Press, 1922, 162 pp.; Newton Edwards, *Equal Educational Opportunity for Youth*, Washington, D.C.: American Council on Education, 1939, 189 pp.; Howard M. Bell, *Youth Tell Their Story*, Washington, D.C.: American Council on Education, 1938, 273 pp.; William Lloyd Warner, *Who Shall Be Educated?* New York: Harper & Bros., 1944, 190 pp.; A. B. Hollingshead, *Elmtown's Youth*, New York: John Wiley & Sons, 1949, 480 pp.; *Encyclopedia of Educational Research*, Walter S. Monroe (ed.), New York: The Macmillan Co., 1950, pp. 1157-59 (summarizes studies made).

[6] Hollingshead, *op. cit.*, chap. 13.

is "free." The average cash cost per year has varied, usually amounting from $80 to $100 or more. As these figures represent costs of about ten years ago, the expense undoubtedly is greater today because of the diminished value of the dollar. One notable fact in these studies is that children from the lower economic groups spend less than one half the amount spent by children of homes in the upper bracket. These figures, in themselves, tell the story of the difficulty and sacrifices of parents from low income homes in order to send their children to high school. They do not tell of the heartaches and disappointments of many youth who are not able to be like other pupils in the school because of the lack of money to spend on clothes, dances, games, or "cokes" at the corner drug store.

Harold Hand of the University of Illinois has been a leader in conducting these studies, the most recent of which is the Hidden Tuition Costs Study in the state of Illinois.[7] This study breaks down various types of costs instead of presenting them as a total figure. Some representative findings from this preliminary report are these: the total annual cost to a pupil for taking an English course ranged from nothing to $24; class rings cost from $11 to $24 in three fourths of the schools studied; activity books for athletic contests ranged from $1.75 to $10.

These studies throw further light on the reason why pupils from certain homes drop out of high school before graduation. They indicate that the American public high school is not "free" in the complete sense.

Many youth drop out of high school because the curriculum is not suited to their abilities and interests. Ranking with economic factors as an important reason for leaving high school is the lack of interest in school. In studies of dropouts, made on a large scale and in individual high schools, many youth have indicated their reasons for leaving school as "didn't get along," "tired of school," "subjects too hard," or "didn't interest me." A recent study of those who leave school confirms the findings of earlier investigations: that the majority dropping out of school do so for economic reasons, because of a lack of interest in school, or because of a desire to work.[8]

---

[7] Harold C. Hand, "For Whom Are High Schools Designed?" *Educational Leadership,* 6 (March, 1949), pp. 359-65; see also his chapter "America Must Have Genuinely Democratic High Schools," in *General Education in the American High School,* Chicago: Scott, Foresman & Co., 1942, pp. 17-20. Also, see Paul B. Jacobson, "The Cost of Attending High School," *Bulletin of the National Association of Secondary School Principals,* 28 (January, 1944), pp. 3-28.

[8] Harold S. Dillon, *Early School Leavers.* New York: National Child Labor Committee, 1949, p. 50.

Pupils in college preparatory curricula drop out in fewer numbers than those in vocational and general curricula. In other words, the secondary school has been better suited to youth of academic ability, granting that the economic status of the family is a factor that operates here. To many of those who have interests other than books, high school has not proved satisfying. In no sense of the word can a secondary school be said to offer equal opportunity to all youth if it does not offer an equal chance of success to pupils of all types of abilities and interests. The days of the high school teacher who could cover his own inadequacies by flunking out pupils who did not meet his standards are numbered. Secondary school leaders and communities in general realize the need for serving all youth, even though the ways are not always clear to them.

Young people from certain racial and ethnic groups frequently do not have equality of opportunity in attending high school. The inferiority of schools for Negroes, in sections of the country where segregated schools exist, is well known. In many cases, teachers' salaries are lower than those of teachers in schools for white children, the pupil-teacher ratio is much higher, poorer physical facilities exist, and less money is spent for instructional materials. Statistics in the United States Census also indicate that smaller proportions of all Negro children are in attendance during the high school years. In the Southwest, children of Mexican parentage are found to attend high school in fewer numbers than children of the rest of the population. More children of native white parentage reach the twelfth grade than those of foreign-born parentage, according to census figures. To these people, equality of opportunity for a secondary education is still a dream.

Youth from the upper economic and intellectual groups participate more frequently in extraclass activities. Another study of the Illinois Secondary School Curriculum Program, investigating participation in extraclass activities, has found that the socioeconomic status of the youth's family has a relationship to his participation in school activities. Pupils from homes of the upper socioeconomic level participated in greater proportion.[9] Other research and informal studies made by individual high schools have found the same conditions to be true. The "Elmtown" youth who came from the two lower social classes had by far the largest proportion of non-

---

[9] Harold C. Hand, "For Whom Are High Schools Designed?" *Educational Leadership.* 6 (March. 1949), pp. 359-65.

participators.[10] Here again we find a segment of the youth population deprived of some of the worth-while experiences in secondary
school. Although cost of participation is a factor, the culture pattern
of high schools makes it impossible for pupils with failing marks in
school subjects to participate in extraclass activities. This is another
instance of the curriculum being geared to the pupil of academic
ability. The reason given for the practice—that it will stimulate better work in classes—does not erase the fact that many youth are being
deprived of experiences more suited to their abilities and interests
than classwork.

*Relatively few secondary schools are equipped to give service to
youth past the twelfth grade or to out-of-school youth.* If all youth
are to be served equally, those who plan to enter semiskilled or
skilled occupations should find opportunity for public education
beyond high school. The largest proportion of youth will enter
occupations other than the professions or executive and managerial
positions. Yet, few states or communities make provision for these
youth to extend their education beyond the twelfth grade.

Junior colleges offering education of a general and vocational
nature for community living are available to relatively few youth.
Some of these programs, as well as those of the extended secondary
school and evening high school, offer splendid part-time and evening
school opportunities to young people in the community. A few
make guidance services available to out-of-school youth. Most secondary schools lose interest in youth when they drop out of school.
Equal opportunity to all youth would mean that educational facilities
such as post-high school courses, placement services, guidance services, and evening or part-time school facilities would be available to
youth of the community.

3. RECOGNITION OF YOUTH NEEDS AND PROBLEMS

The modern secondary school should meet the needs of youth
through the experiences and services that it provides. Whether or
not it is fulfilling this obligation can be decided by the student of
education when he has read about the practices described in this
book and investigated further for himself what the American secondary school is doing. This section presents some important needs
and problems facing youth as a natural part of their development in a
twentieth-century American culture.

---

[10] Hollingshead, *op. cit.,* chap. 8.

Needs are discussed by various authors in terms of biological needs, psychological needs, current interests, lacks in society, or skills and understandings that adults feel youth should acquire in order to live successfully in a particular type of society. The definition given by Quillen and Hanna is accepted here. They define needs as "individual wants and desires plus lacks and inadequacies which are expressed in the interaction of the individual with the social environment of which he is a part."[11]

Understanding Adolescents' Nature and Problems.—In order to help youth with their daily problems of adjustment to their environment, teachers of the secondary school must know youth. They must be familiar with the nature of adolescents' whims, fancies, worries, fears, and hopes. The competent teachers of our secondary schools look on much of the behavior in a classroom as social experimentation on the part of boys and girls in establishing themselves as "grownup." These teachers spend much of their time in observing individual behavior and in trying to find ways to help pupils make the transition from childhood to adulthood. To them the characteristics of the adolescent boy and girl are displayed through their interests in conversation, reading, hobbies, radio, movies, and other daily activities.

They know that adolescents differ a great deal in their stages of physical, social, and psychological development. In other words, the teachers do not expect the same type of reaction or intensity of problems from young people of the same age. For instance, one boy may reach the stage of wanting to assert his independence much earlier than another of like chronological age. The way in which the teacher helps him make this adjustment is a considerable factor in determining how rapidly and well it will be made.

Teaching for Behavior Changes.—The secondary school that has change of behavior rather than learning subject matter as the chief aim of its teaching is realistically helping youth with their problems and needs. In such a setting, the focus is on boys and girls and how they can be helped to develop in desirable ways. Secondary schools in which this point of view predominates among faculty members are concerned about assisting young people—in classes, in activities, and in counseling—with their real life problems. The kinds of desirable behavior changes toward which the secondary school should aim were outlined in Chapter 2.

---

[11] I. James Quillen and Lavone A. Hanna, *Education for Social Competence*, Chicago: Scott, Foresman & Co., 1940, p. 30.

These behavior changes, which are the teacher's aims, are related in school living to the pupil's own desires and needs. For example, the teacher provides for activities that will give pupils an opportunity to be successful in the eyes of their peers and, at the same time, to make progress toward the attitude of respect for others as individuals or toward the ability to express ideas effectively. In the modern secondary school, it is more important to help the adolescent find friendship and prestige than to see that he reads *Julius Caesar* or memorizes the date of the Louisiana Purchase. It is also extremely important, however, to guide him to gain information as a basis for solving or thinking through social problems and to learn to like increasingly the reading of better literature. The learning of these skills and appreciations goes hand in hand with gaining social approval and success.

Recognizing Basic Psychological Needs.—Psychologically, the individual has certain needs that are just as vital to his welfare as need for rest, food, and other physical needs, even though deprivation will not bring on as drastic and immediate results. If we deprive a person of such fundamental needs as the need for affection, belonging, security, social approval, success, or recognition, his mental health will certainly be twisted and warped.

In secondary schools, pupils are often given tasks which are far beyond their attainment. The slow student finds himself a misfit in an academic environment of symbols, formulas, and abstractions. He cannot "be somebody" in the eyes of his fellows through succeeding in assigned lessons; the school deprives him of accepted ways of receiving social recognition; and so he takes recourse in means frowned upon by adults—boisterousness, rudeness, loudness, lying, or other ways of gaining recognition that are within his grasp. The way in which these fundamental needs are satisfied will help to determine what kinds of attitudes youth will develop.

In his actions and attitudes, the young ninth grader may belie his real feelings in order to avoid revealing his insecurity. He may be cocksure and defiant. Another pupil may resort to flights of fancy instead of facing the realities of the classrooms that are too much for him. In secondary schools where teachers understand these basic needs, pupils are given important jobs so that they may demonstrate their ability—jobs in which they can succeed.

In the modern secondary school, opportunities for experiences in art, shop work, music, dramatics, and social activities are a part of the curriculum. Pupils can find areas other than the academic in which they can gain recognition and find security. Moreover, these phases of school life are given high prestige value as important learnings for pupils. We seldom find these pupils saying, "Why, I'd be branded if I took home economics!" for these schools have made it their business to arrange the program of studies so that such outrages against youth do not occur.

Stating Predicated Needs of Youth as Goals.—Statements of what adults feel that youth need in order to fit into the society in which they live are actually the goals of education. One important statement of such predicated needs has been made by the Educational Policies Commission and has been widely discussed. These are termed the "ten imperative needs of youth." [12]

1. All youth need to develop salable skills and those understandings and attitudes that make the worker an intelligent and productive participant in economic life. To this end, most youth need supervised work experience as well as education in the skills and knowledge of their occupations.

2. All youth need to develop and maintain good health and physical fitness.

3. All youth need to understand the rights and duties of the citizen of a democratic society, and to be diligent and competent in the performance of their obligations as members of the community and citizens of the state and nation.

4. All youth need to understand the significance of the family for the individual and society and the conditions conducive to successful family life.

5. All youth need to know how to purchase and use goods and services intelligently, understanding both the values received by the consumer and the economic consequences of their acts.

6. All youth need to understand the methods of science, the influence of science on human life, and the main scientific facts concerning the nature of the world and of man.

7. All youth need opportunities to develop their capacities to appreciate beauty in literature, art, music, and nature.

8. All youth need to be able to use their leisure time well and to budget it wisely, balancing activities that yield satisfactions to the individual with those that are socially useful.

9. All youth need to develop respect for other persons, to grow in their insight into ethical values and principles, and to be able to live and work cooperatively with others.

10. All youth need to grow in their ability to think rationally, to express their thoughts clearly, and to read and listen with understanding.

Identifying Real Problems of Living and Growing Up.—The adolescent's life is as full of thrills, sorrows, joys, and adventure as

---

[12] Educational Policies Commission, *Education for All American Youth*, Washington, D.C.: National Education Association, 1944, pp. 225-26. See also "The Imperative Needs of Youth," *Bulletin of the National Association of Secondary School Principals,* Vol. 31, No. 145 (March, 1947), 164 pp.

that of the adult. He must make adjustments to people and to established institutions and customs as does the adult. Moreover, he has the added burden of making a transition from childhood to adulthood, where accepted values and mores are different from those he has been used to. The problem of growing up is in itself a difficult one. Yet, a study of the curriculum of some secondary school classes would convince one that the adolescent has no unique problems, that his life resembles that of adults.

When we speak of real life problems in the curriculum, we refer to the recognition given to the everyday living affairs of youth. A list of family problems,[13] checked by youth in a large number of high schools, is illustrative of what youth consider as their specific problems:

Getting to use the car
Quarreling in the family
My folks understanding me
Get along with brothers and sisters
Dad understanding my problems
Getting along with my parents
Mom understanding my problems
Having a happy home life
Understanding my folks
Sickness in the family
Treated like a child at home
Father or mother dead
Too much teasing at home
Drifting away from the family
Parents are always quarreling
Folks ridicule my ideas

Relatives in the home
Parents separated or divorced
Being from a broken home
Being allowed out oftener
Want to leave home
Breaking home ties
Don't want to leave home
Parents don't like my friends
Have to work at home
Parents spend no time with me
Afraid home is being broken up
No one has an interest in home
Being neglected by parents
Ashamed of my parents
Parents don't like me

Does the curriculum recognize these problems? It may be that the literature selected for study in an English class is chosen for the purpose of helping youth understand and meet adolescent-family conflicts, or perhaps units on home and family living are included in social studies classes. Perhaps such youth concerns are given no recognition whatsoever, or at best considered as the "territory" of the home economics teacher.

Significant problems that youth face in their everyday living are outlined briefly here. They serve as a type of check list for the curriculum, services, and organization of the secondary school. A curriculum that neglects to assist young people in solving their problems is as unrealistic as a guidance program that is concerned exclusively with vocational and educational guidance. If youth work at these problems, they will see the need for developing communication skills,

[13] L. S. Elias, *High School Youth Look At Their Problems,* Pullman, Washington: State College of Washington, 1949, p. 35.

social skills, tool skills, and other "fundamentals" considered important by society.

Problem of making friends and group contacts. Young people want to widen their contacts and have friends among their school group. Many have a real problem of making any friends at all because of their shyness, physical characteristics, or social maladjustments. Do the planned experiences of the classroom and activity program assist them in getting acquainted with new people? Do these experiences help youth to analyze themselves? What help is extended to the youngster who has just moved into the community, or the awkward and the shy?

Problem of being accepted by and gaining the approval of one's peers. This is a potent factor in determining behavior, for being accepted by fellow pupils is far more important to youth than is social convention or the authority of a teacher who little understands what youth think or feel. There is a real fear of not being liked by others or of not being popular. Witness the many fads that high school pupils follow. Does the school put this knowledge of youth to work, or does it try to quell fads as "foolish"? How do teachers try to help youth gain status within the group?

Problem of making adjustments to the family. Problems in this area may be minor, or they may be enormous and tragic in their consequences. They will vary from the ordinary adjustments to sisters and brothers to jarring emotional adaptations some adolescents are expected to make to broken and unhappy homes. Who helps these youth in school with the more difficult type of adjustments? Is there any flexibility in the program to meet their specific needs? Does adjustment to the family come up for discussion in classes?

Problem of planning for marriage and family responsibilities. The secondary school authorities used to frown upon the girl who married while in high school. In most cases, she was politely asked to leave school. What recognition does the school of today give to the fact that many youth in the upper high school grades, extended secondary schools, or junior colleges are planning to be married in the near future? Do such questions as choosing a mate, marriage adjustments, and the like come into the curriculum? What are guidance services doing about them?

Problem of establishing relations with the opposite sex. Questions of dating, going steady, having boy friends or girl friends, and being attractive to the other sex are uppermost in adolescents' minds before serious thoughts of marriage arise. Some authors have said that youth spend most of their time working at the problem. Radio programs and young people's magazines deal with these questions. How prominent a place do they have in curriculum content in the secondary school?

Problem of sexual maturation. Although it is actually a phase of the preceding problem, this is a normal part of adolescent life that brings fears and misunderstandings of its own. Youth may worry about "abnormal" developments, either underdevelopment or over-development of sex characteristics. They want to understand their own bodies and need help in doing so. Not the least of the adjustments to be made is conformity to social convention and moral codes in a society in which the marriage age is being constantly advanced for many youth. Is this matter of physical and mental health regarded as "controversial" in the community, or does the secondary school forthrightly and frankly tackle it as an important problem in youth's life?

Problem of differences in physical development among adolescents. Research has demonstrated vividly the differences in the age of onset of puberty. There are rapid spurts of growth among youth of both junior high school and senior high school age. In the more extreme variations, feelings of abnormality are frequent. Are these dissimilarities merely topics for ridicule by students in the hallways, or are they matters of concern to the teachers?

Problem of physical and mental health. Youth are concerned about such unsatisfactory health conditions as overweight, skin blemishes, frequent illness, tiring easily, and constant worries. It is a pertinent question to ask whether the study of health in secondary schools is concerned with these problems—the health of the boy or girl in the class—or with classifying and memorizing diseases and bodily functions from a book.

Problem of gaining independence from the family and attaining adult status. This problem in itself causes many family misunder-standings; it is often a difficult adjustment for young people to make. They want to make decisions for themselves, choose their own friends, go to work—in other words, "live my own life." Over-protective parents make the adjustment more difficult by trying to shield their children from hardships and mistakes. During this transition, youth are expected to fit into the pattern and mores of adult society. Yet, how youngsters are frowned upon for smoking, drinking, wearing cosmetics, driving fast, or telling "dirty" stories!

Do high school teachers recognize this developmental task and provide understanding and sympathetic direction to youth?

Problem of formulating values acceptable to one's own group, to parents, and to the culture mores. Youth may find that the moral standards of adults and those of their own group vary considerably. They may be torn between receiving the approval of the "crowd" and following the accepted mores of the type of culture in which they live. As has been shown in recent research, these standards differ a good deal among groups of different economic levels. The question of necking and petting may be ridiculous to old-maid school teachers of both sexes, but it is real to youth. Do experiences that youth have in school help them to formulate an adequate philosophy of life and adopt acceptable moral values?

Problem of solving questions and doubts concerning religion and spiritual life. Youth are concerned about life and death. Many have serious doubts at times concerning the teachings of the Bible and their own faith. Some become intensely religious; others lose faith in religion. As previously mentioned, conflicts between religion and the life in which youth find themselves, or between religious teachings and adult actions, are puzzling to many. Is this an area of responsibility only for the church and the home, or is it also one for the school?

Problem of securing money for spending and buying personal necessities. The great majority of youth have difficulty in getting spending money enough to keep up with "the rest of the kids," to buy sodas, take trips with the team, bowl, go to the movies, or pay for the innumerable items included in the cost of attending high school, as discussed previously in this chapter. This problem is tied up with popularity and friendships. Some young people are faced with humiliating experiences because they are ashamed of their clothes, their home, their neighborhood, or their parents. Some have to contribute to the support of the family.

Problem of maintaining a sense of personal achievement. A good deal has already been said about this obvious problem. Every youth wants to "be somebody," to develop himself, and to find himself. It is a serious question how much the secondary school, with its stress on academic achievement and on marks, report cards, prize contests, awards, and competition, assists youth in this problem. Is there sufficient consideration on the part of secondary schools to help the so-called "lower 20 per cent" attain this goal?

Problem of establishing relations with teachers and adjusting to school and its demands. The adjustment that a seventh grade youngster must make in going from a self-contained classroom to an entirely departmentalized situation is often a real hurdle. Any high school youth works hard at making adjustments to four or five different teacher personalities and spends a good deal of energy in trying to figure out how to get good marks from each one. Pupils have difficulty in learning how to study, in getting into the courses they want, in getting into clubs, in meeting homework demands which are sometimes unnecessarily heavy, and in adjusting to a new school situation. Does the seventh or ninth grade social studies course help pupils with these *real social* problems of their own lives, or is it concerned only with problems of other generations?

Problem of choosing and buying clothes and other goods and services. In the life of youth, the selection of one's own clothing becomes a jealously guarded privilege. Adolescents also want to buy other personal items by themselves. They are now becoming consumers in a new sense. Secondary schools have begun to recognize the need for knowing how to buy wisely. As yet, relatively few pupils in the typical high school study how to become good consumers.

Problem of finding something to do with leisure time and places to go with other youth. For the boy or girl in the small town, this is often a serious matter. They may wander the streets, drive to the next town, or perhaps travel fifty miles to a dance when they find nothing provided by church, school, or community for their evening's amusement. Churches may frown on dancing, an appealing form of recreation to youth. What obligation does the school have to provide desirable forms of recreation for young people?

Problem of being accepted by the community. Where adults jealously hang on to political positions, community responsibilities, and the right to decide what is good for the community, young people indeed have a difficult time learning how to take an active part in community affairs. For all youth, there is a period when they are still considered by older people of the community as "kids" without the good judgment or ability to participate in community affairs. Is this a problem for social studies classes to tackle? Should social study end in social action?

Problem of understanding and doing something about world conditions. A high school teacher of social studies knows—if he has given pupils a chance—that youth are interested in current affairs. The teacher who has always taught history from the chronological sequence in the textbook without reference to current happenings has a pleasant surprise when he shifts to a consideration of history in terms of today's events. As young people mature this interest grows and deepens, and idealistic youth will champion "causes" for human betterment. To what extent is this interest being carefully guided and stimulated? Is the experience of reading one book and giving factual answers for a mark conducive to helping youth solve their questions about current issues?

Problem of getting along with people. Not as broad in scope, but fully as important for effective democratic participation in community life, is the ability to meet people, to get along with fellow classmates, fellow workers, and others with whom youth are in daily contact. Young people are concerned about this matter. They are concerned about quarreling with friends, hurting others' feelings, helping others, and making a good impression.

Problem of choosing a vocation and getting a job. This choice faces every high school pupil. He wants advice. Parents may insist on one type of occupation in which he is not interested. A girl may need to make the choice between marriage and a career. Some want to leave school to begin work. Many have unrealistic ambitions. All need help in knowing how to get a job and in finding one that is suitable and to which they are adapted. Do guidance services give the help needed? Is a ninth grade course or unit in vocations sufficient to help solve the problem of choosing an occupation? How can other courses and activities contribute?

Problem of planning what to do with regard to further education. The choice between work and further schooling is involved here. Youth often want to go to college when they have little chance of succeeding. Others find the financial barriers too great. Pupils in high school seek and rightfully expect advice on further educational opportunities from which to choose. Does the secondary school, through its practices, encourage an interest in continued education? Does it help them to make wise choices in this area?

Examining the Findings of Follow-Up Studies and Youth Surveys.—A good many studies have been made of youth who have completed high school or dropped out of school. The follow-up studies conducted in specific school systems (usually reported in educational periodicals) furnish considerable insight into how youth value their school experiences as meeting their needs, and tell something about their vocational and educational activities following their leaving school. A few of them report information on other phases of living.

There are also a number of comprehensive studies of larger regions, many statewide in nature, that have been made to find out what youth do after leaving school in order to evaluate the effectiveness of the school program. Many good studies were made in the 1930's when the American Youth Commission, created by the American Council on Education in 1935 to study the problems of youth, stimulated the consideration of the plight of youth during the depression. The Regents' Inquiry in New York State which resulted in several published volumes, the Occupational Adjustment Study of the Secondary School Principals Association, and the Maryland Survey reported by Howard M. Bell are some of the best known of these.[14]

A summary of some of the important findings of the youth studies in the accompanying list of references is presented here, since these facts are important in revealing how well the secondary school has met youth needs. Although employment conditions have changed since these studies were conducted, many of the conditions doubtless still apply to out-of-school youth today, or may again apply at some future time. It should be pointed out that the youth studied were usually between the ages of sixteen and twenty-four; a number

---

[14] The student can find a good deal of information on youth in the following studies. The general summary in this section of the chapter comes from these and from the author's study indicated below:

American Youth Commission, *Youth and the Future,* Washington, D.C.: American Council on Education, 1942, 296 pp.; Vernon E. Anderson, *Evaluation of Proposals for Reorganization of Terminal Education at the Junior College Level,* Unpublished Doctor's thesis, Boulder, Colorado: University of Colorado, 1942, 504 pp.; Howard M. Bell, *Youth Tell Their Story,* American Youth Commission Study, Washington, D.C.: American Council on Education, 1939, 273 pp.; Ruth E. Eckert and Thomas O. Marshall, *When Youth Leave School,* The Regents' Inquiry, New York: McGraw-Hill Book Co., Inc., 1939, 360 pp.; Raymond G. Fuller, *A Study of Youth Needs and Services in Muncie, Indiana,* American Youth Commission Study, Washington, D.C.: American Council on Education, 1938, 199 pp.; Edward Landy, "Occupational Adjustment and the School," *Bulletin of the National Association of Secondary School Principals,* Volume 24, 154 pp. (November, 1940); Gordon W. Lovejoy, *Paths to Maturity,* Cooperative Personnel Study, Chapel Hill: University of North Carolina, 1940, 310 pp. (North Carolina youth study.); Nettie P. McGill and Ellen M. Mathews, *The Youth of New York City,* New York: The Macmillan Co., 1940, 420 pp.; Stanley L. Payne, *Thirty Thousand Urban Workers,* Social Problems Series No. 6, Works Progress Administration, Washington, D.C.: Government Printing Office, 1940, 35 pp. (Interviews with 30,000 youth.); Homer P. Rainey, *How Fare American Youth?,* New York: Appleton-Century-Crofts, Inc., 1937, 186 pp.; Francis T. Spaulding, *High School and Life,* The Regents' Inquiry, New York: McGraw-Hill Book Co., Inc., 1939, 377 pp.; Claudia Williams, Drayton S. Bryant, and Aaron E. Jones, *Youth—California's Future,* Sacramento, California: Department of Education and State Relief Administration, 1940, 72 pp.

had not finished high school. The facts, presented under various phases of the life of youth, should give ample reason for a serious re-evaluation of the secondary school in terms of serving *all* youth adequately.

Civic life

1. Few youth were engaged in any organized activity of a civic nature, belonged to community organizations, or participated actively in community betterment.
2. The majority had no interest in current affairs and were not even awake to local problems.
3. They recognized their rights and privileges much more readily than their responsibilities.

Vocation

4. A large number had not decided what to do upon leaving school.
5. Few had received adequate guidance or had received any help from the school in being placed on the job.
6. The majority had taken the first job that came along and most of them were dissatisfied with their jobs.
7. Many lacked knowledge of how to advance on the job.
8. There was little relation between scholastic achievement and later ability to adjust to the job.

Home and family life

9. Because of financial conditions and schooling, many youth had been forced to delay marriage.
10. Very few had received any sex education at school.
11. A number of youth were helping to support families with total incomes often below subsistence level.

Recreational, cultural, and social life

12. Most out-of-school youth engaged in passive recreation such as reading, listening to the radio, going to the movies, or attending games.
13. A large proportion read no books or mainly books of fiction of inferior quality.
14. The majority had no type of social activity except seeing friends and going with friends to the movies.
15. Many took no part in church activities of any type.
16. An alarming number reported no leisure-time activities other than loafing and "hanging around."

Health

17. A considerable number had never had a physical or dental examination.
18. Many suffered from disease and malnutrition.

Education

19. Many had no funds with which to complete their education.
20. Most revealing of all, few ever returned to school for counsel or had ever been invited to do so.

SUMMARY

The public secondary school in the United States has been committed to a policy of providing an education for all youth, the sons and daughters of rich and poor alike. An examination of the facts reveals that many drop out before they graduate. Among the most potent factors for determining survival in high school are the economic ones. Youth from the Negro district, from across the tracks, or from the foreign-born section have the poorest chances of surviving until they have amassed the needed sixteen units. Those who are fortunate enough to be able to handle with ease abstract concepts and "book larnin' " find the high school program much more palatable than those young people who have talents along the artistic, mechanical, or social lines.

A number of youth's real problems of living have been presented in this chapter as a guide to future teachers in deciding what they can do to make high school more interesting and worth while for young people of all kinds, circumstances, and abilities. These problems are not the concerns of the intellectually gifted—they are the problems of *all* youth. These concerns, and the facts about young people in our high schools, should offer the student who uses this book a further yardstick for evaluation of secondary school practices.

SELECTED REFERENCES

ALBERTY, HAROLD. *Reorganizing the High-School Curriculum.* New York: The Macmillan Co., 1947, chaps. 1, 2, 3.—Discusses the purposes of secondary education, the present status of progress in secondary education, and the study of the adolescent. The section on trends in adolescent development is especially good in pointing out the concerns and needs of youth.

ASSOCIATION FOR SUPERVISION AND CURRICULUM DEVELOPMENT. *Fostering Mental Health in Our Schools* (1950 Yearbook). Washington, D.C.: National Education Association, chaps. 6, 7.—Has a convenient list of developmental tasks and discusses their implications for the school program. This is an excellent reference to use in connection with the observation of children.

CASWELL, HOLLIS L. (ed.). *The American High School* (Eighth Yearbook of the John Dewey Society). New York: Harper & Bros., 1946, chaps. 2, 3, 4.—Discusses youth problems and basic social trends and issues. The chapter on the "Assets and Liabilities of the High School" could well be read when purposes of the secondary school are being discussed.

COOK, LLOYD ALLEN, and COOK, ELAINE FORSYTH. *A Sociological Approach to Education.* New York: McGraw-Hill Book Co., Inc., 1950, Part III.—This section on "Community, Child, and School" supplements the information in this chapter on the social class of youth and its relation to his school and future life in society. A case based on *Elmtown's Youth* is included.

COREY, STEPHEN M., and OTHERS. *General Education in the American High School.* Chicago: Scott, Foresman & Co., 1942, chaps. 2, 3.—These chapters deal with the historical development of change of purposes and the present purposes and new conceptions of secondary education.

DOANE, DONALD C. *The Needs of Youth.* New York: Bureau of Publications, Teachers College, Columbia University, 1942, 142 pp.—Reviews the literature on youth needs and problems, and has additional information on youth problems. It is especially helpful in clarifying what is meant by youth needs.

HOLLINGSHEAD, A. B. *Elmtown's Youth.* New York: John Wiley & Sons, Inc., 1949, 480 pp.—Presents a thought-provoking sociological study of adolescents, both in school and out, in a mid-western community, written in readable style, in such a manner that it will be enjoyed by students of education and laymen alike. It is a fare very different from most educational books or reports of research.

JERSILD, ARTHUR T., and TASCH, RUTH J. *Children's Interests.* New York: Bureau of Publications, Teachers College, Columbia University, 1949, 173 pp.—Discusses the likes, dislikes, wishes, and interests of children in Grades 1-12 as discovered through research by teachers in public schools. It is important for the searching questions raised concerning the school program.

JONES, HAROLD E. *Development in Adolescence.* New York: Appleton-Century-Crofts, Inc., 1943, 166 pp.—Contains a record of the study of an adolescent over a period of several years, valuable for understanding both youth in a specific culture and all the forces that impinge on his life. Written in an informal style.

"The Imperative Needs of Youth of Secondary School Age." *Bulletin of the National Association of Secondary School Principals,* Volume 31, No. 145 (March, 1947), 164 pp.—A committee of the National Association of Secondary School Principals presents illustrations of what secondary schools are doing to meet the ten imperative needs of youth.

PART II

CURRICULUM AND INSTRUCTION
OF THE SECONDARY SCHOOL

CURRICULUM AND INSTRUCTION OF THE SECONDARY SCHOOL

Part II is the longest section of the book because the curriculum is the heart of the school program. Since the curriculum is defined in terms of pupils' experiences, the principles and the illustrations in the nine chapters in this section indicate the kinds of experiences youth should have and do have in the secondary school. The organization or framework of the curriculum and the teacher's part in planning the curriculum are indicated as having a definite bearing on those experiences. From this point of view, class work, extraclass activities, the school's relation with the community, and the manner in which evaluation and reporting is done are all important in determining those experiences. Throughout the section, the differences between an experience-centered curriculum and a subject-centered curriculum are pointed out.

Chapter 4

NEWER CURRICULUM CONCEPTS

To the beginning teacher, the job of developing values and meeting youth needs may be extremely challenging, but may be puzzling as well. His own experience as a secondary school pupil might have been one of learning what was in the book, remembering facts for tests, and being told what to do. He may ask: What possible connection did these school experiences have with *youth problems* or *social action* or *democratic values?* On the other hand, he may see how many of his experiences in high school did apply directly to these concepts as they were discussed in the preceding three chapters.

The student preparing to teach needs to understand that some school practices represent a point of view about education different from the philosophy expressed in the previous section of this book. It is the purpose of this chapter to show the different ways of thinking about curriculum and how teachers who hold these differing points of view plan a curriculum for their pupils. In order that the terms used in this book may be clearly understood, a portion of this chapter is devoted to definitions. As we shall see, it makes a considerable difference just how we interpret the meaning of the word "curriculum." If we follow the concept of curriculum given in this book, our attention is bound to turn a good deal more to what happens to pupils than to what books we use or what outline of content is studied.

1. THE MEANING OF TERMS

The *curriculum* consists of the experiences that pupils have under the direction of the school. It is the school's job to plan worthwhile experiences that will help develop the type of behavior outlined in its objectives. Definitely the curriculum *is not* the inert material in the pages of a course of study. It is the things children do, plan, write, read, construct, talk about, react to, and think about. It includes their field trips, their extraclass experiences, their student council activities, the study of the community that they make, their farm projects in connection with their agriculture courses, their work experience under school supervision. All these are significant learning experiences planned by the school to further the growth of pupils.

The *course of study* is a more limited term than curriculum, since it refers to the outline, bulletin, or written plan that serves as a guide to the experiences that the teacher will plan for, and with, the pupils. It is not difficult to visualize how unlike the experiences might be for two groups of pupils under different teachers, different in temperament and background but following the same course of study.

A *curriculum improvement program* refers to the plan of action adopted by a school, a state, or a group of teachers in order to consider ways of providing better experiences for pupils. A school usually selects some phase of the curriculum for study by the faculty for the year, or over a period of years. "Curriculum revision," "curriculum building," "curriculum development program" are other terms used. In the past, some subject in the curriculum was invariably selected for study. In recent years, when school people have begun to think of the curriculum in terms of experiences provided for pupils, schools are more frequently attacking any significant problems that deal with the improvement of instruction. Generally, such study has yielded better results in actually *improving* the kinds of experiences that children and adolescents have. Examples of these types of problems studied in secondary schools are as follows:

1. Youth needs and adolescent development
2. Case studies of pupils
3. Recording and reporting pupil progress
4. Cooperation with the home and community agencies
5. Follow-up of high school dropouts and graduates
6. The occupational opportunities in the community
7. Use of the community for pupil experiences
8. Adapting materials used in class to pupil needs, interests, and abilities.

The *common learnings* refer to those types of experiences in the high school curriculum that all pupils should have. They are the learning experiences considered essential for all people in order to become competent citizens, competent members of a family, and well-adjusted individuals. For example, in a democracy it is considered essential that people know how to make decisions based on facts and how to carry on discussions and social action as members of a local, state, national, or international group. Experiences planned to promote these ends are a part of the common learnings. Another way of expressing it would be to say that the common learnings refer to the general education needed by all pupils. Some authors have used the term as synonymous with "core curriculum." However, for clarity in thinking, a clear-cut distinction is made in this book.

The *core curriculum* is a specific form of organization of the curriculum that cuts across subject fields and includes a greater block of time in the school day than the usual period. It refers to a way in which a number of the important common learnings are organized within the total high school curriculum. The core consists of a number of problems important to youth that are studied together by the group, which selects subject matter from various areas to solve these problems. Usually English and the social studies are fused in the core, and the guidance function is always a part of the core. However, it consists of basic behavior patterns common to all and is based upon problem situations. It is *not*, therefore, a mere fusing of subject matter. It is explained in greater detail in Chapter 6.

Other terms sometimes used in educational literature as synonymous with core curriculum are "unified studies," "general education," "integrated curriculum." The term as it is used here does not refer to the required subjects of the high school curriculum, such as physical education, English, and social studies.

These are some of the basic terms that will be used in a discussion of the curriculum. The student is referred to the *Dictionary of Education* for definitions of other terms that he does not understand.[1]

2. Basic Approaches to Curriculum Development

The student of education will find in his reading reference to "the activity curriculum," "the child-centered curriculum," "the community-centered curriculum," "the integrated curriculum," and the like. No attempt will be made here to discuss what is meant by these various types, for often several of these terms are used to mean approximately the same thing, and such a classification is more apt to confuse the future teacher than to assist him in understanding how he should function in developing the curriculum for his pupils.

Instead, this chapter will concentrate on the two fundamental approaches to curriculum development which represent opposing points of view of how the teacher should function, how content should be selected, what types of evaluation of progress should be made, and how books and other materials should be selected for the classroom. One is the subject-centered (or subject) approach to

---

[1] *Dictionary of Education*, Carter V. Good (ed.), New York: McGraw-Hill Book Co., Inc., 1945, 495 pp.

curriculum development, undoubtedly used by the majority of secondary school teachers. The other is the experience-centered (or experience) approach, used by a growing number of secondary school teachers who understand the principles of child and adolescent development and are familiar with recent information concerning how effective learning takes place. The latter is the approach used in the core curriculum.

Both approaches represent definite points of view. A teacher who holds the one position acts differently in the classroom from one who holds the other position. It will be the purpose of this discussion to indicate how the teacher behaves if he uses either approach. It should be understood, however, that this is not an either-or proposition. A person can be *moving toward* the experience approach, accepting a number of the things that he feels that he can carry out.

This book takes the position that if any *fundamental* improvement in the secondary school curriculum is to be effected, an experience-centered approach must replace the traditional subject-centered approach. The experience approach is in line with the principles outlined in Chapter 1, as guides to a good secondary school.

The subject approach results in a subject-centered curriculum in which learning the subject is considered most important; the experience approach, in an experience-centered curriculum in which the focus is on the kinds of experiences pupils have in order to develop specific kinds of behavior. The inexperienced teacher needs to be warned constantly, however, that the issue here is not subject matter versus experience, for the teacher using the experience approach uses as much subject matter as, or more subject matter than, the teacher using the subject approach, and, moreover, this subject matter is used with a real purpose.

The Subject-Centered Approach.—The student in education courses will be familiar with the subject-centered approach to curriculum development, for it is predominant in high school courses and even more so in college courses. He experiences it every time he sits through a lecture that has no significance or interest for him; he experiences it when his entire course is structured by the textbook as the material to be learned. The predominant characteristics can be singled out as indicated in the following discussion. To the extent that a teacher does not follow these principles, he is moving away from the subject approach toward the experience approach. The characteristics listed here describe more of the extreme position. Most teachers will be found somewhere on the scale between a subject approach and an experience approach.

Subject matter represents what is to be learned. It is assigned chapter by chapter, recited back in the form of factual questions, objective tests, and semester examinations. Measurement of progress in learning is by the amount of subject matter acquired. Pupils pass or fail on the basis of the amount of subject matter learned. Distinct lines are kept between subject departments in the school. Drill for college entrance examinations, makeup work, review drill, and the short "recitation" period are all evidences of teaching subject matter rather than teaching the child.

Even though the teacher may be sincerely interested in developing the character of young people, attitudes can receive only scant attention in an atmosphere of the stress and strain of covering so much subject matter. Skills are often mishandled in the rush to cover the book or the course. The habit of thoroughness takes a back seat.

The subject matter to be covered and the kinds of experiences pupils will have are determined before the course begins. These decisions are made without any knowledge of what the pupils will be like except that they will be in a specific grade, of a general age level, and probably of a certain "ability grouping." The books are selected first, and the teacher plans his work around the text. There may be an outline of what is to be covered in the course, with specific time limits for different sections, or the textbook serves as the outline. If a course of study is provided, it prescribes definitely what is to be taught.

The same predetermined subject matter is intended for all pupils, and the teacher is supposed to bring every pupil up to a stipulated "minimum essentials" level. Consequently, the teacher finds that he has to spend a good deal of time coaching slow pupils to attempt to bring them up to a standard often unattainable and unrealistic, and consequently has little time for the outstanding student.

The subject matter studied often has little or no bearing on youth problems and present-day social issues. The content of such courses as ancient history, Latin, and algebra may be considered desirable to be studied by all pupils because it is needed for college entrance, because it trains the mind, or for some reason other than meeting pupil needs in the world of today. Even such science courses as physics and chemistry, which offer wonderful opportunities to relate activities to the lives of the pupils, often remain sterile when so approached.

In American history or world history, the major portion of the time may be spent on the history up to World War I, or up to the twentieth century, with little thought given to the pressing contemporary problems that call for the best informed intelligence of the citizenry. Asia is often a relatively unexplored continent because there is too much material to cover.

The problems of youth in their relations to their peers, their family, and their future occupation are not considered as content with sufficient "status" to be studied in regular classes. The significance of the subject lies in the subject matter itself, not in what it can do to help youth become better adjusted or change their behavior.

The teacher acts as the external authority who exercises control over the learning situation. Because so much subject matter must be learned in a certain period of time, the teacher acts as the authority on what is to be learned, how much time is to be spent on it, and what is to be done by the class. There is no time for planning together what is to be done because it takes too much time away from what must be done.

As a consequence, the teacher finds himself spending a good deal of the study periods "policing" the group, seeing that they behave and are busy. Pupils for whom the subject matter has little interest, is too difficult, or is so easy that it is boring, often become troublemakers. Discipline occupies a good deal of the teacher's energies, for the control all comes from him as an authority, not from the group itself.

The subject-centered approach is described further in the following section in contrast with the experience-centered approach.

The Experience-Centered Approach.—In speaking of the experience-centered approach to curriculum development, we are referring to the use of a series of significant and worth-while experiences to develop young people in desirable ways. These experiences will be with subject matter, with the community, with school activities, with vital issues and problems. The essential difference from the subject approach is that the pupil's development—how his behavior should be changed—is considered *first;* then, the experiences to develop those behaviors are planned and subject matter is used as a means of bringing about these desirable behavior changes.

The experience approach, while not so common, is used by an increasing number of teachers. Students of education often make the mistake of asking where they can find a progressive school so that they might see new ideas in action. Instead of looking around for schools with neatly tagged labels—especially such meaningless labels as "progressive"—the future teacher would do well to search out good teachers who do many of or all the things described here as characteristic of the experience approach. They can be found in many schools. The following pages discuss the distinguishing characteristics of this approach.

The development of the child or adolescent, his mind, body, emotions, and social nature, all are considered equally important. As opposed to the stress on learning subject matter, the child's development is of first and foremost importance. His balanced growth is the goal of the teacher. Adjustment problems become as important as English skills. The teacher is conscious of physical defects and health problems. As contrasted with learning subject matter to be stored for future use, the situation calls for learning social skills for present-day life, developing attitudes toward fellow pupils, and becoming a well-adjusted individual. It is recognized that the pupil's emotional state often makes it impossible for him to learn, and as much assistance is given him in achieving mental health as in learning how to write effective sentences.

Subject matter is used as a means to an end, to lead to desirable outcomes in behavior changes. The teacher who follows the experience approach uses subject matter to achieve the goals set for the group. For example, subject matter from history is selected to achieve an understanding that the struggle for freedom involves continuous conflict with reactionary forces bent on keeping special privileges for their own group. Or subject matter is selected that may best lend itself to the skill of distinguishing between propaganda and reliable information. In the same way, subject matter is used to develop desired attitudes and appreciations.

Starting with desirable behavior changes as goals is as different from starting with a book to be studied or a certain portion of subject matter to be covered (as is done in the subject-centered approach) as night from day. The objective of the latter is to learn the material covered. Understandings grow out of such a procedure if the material is not too difficult for the learner, but attitudes and appreciations are neglected. Attitudes do develop, however, often undesirable ones, since there is no conscious attempt to strive for those that are worth while. Dislike rather than appreciation of good literature frequently is the result of beginning with the selection of a piece of literature to study instead of selecting literature in terms of pupils' maturity and interests in order to achieve appreciation. In the experience-centered approach, the skills of finding sources of material, contrasting different points of view, or choosing more reliable data are developed through using many sources, reading from different books, and checking for accuracy in facts. In other words, the experience is selected in terms of the objectives to be attained. A part of that experience is the use of subject matter that lends itself to achieving the desired aims.

The content is a series of purposeful, well-planned experiences growing out of the pupils' background, needs, interests, and daily living, and out of the social and physical environment. Pupils and their nature and background become the point of orientation for selection of activities. The present social scene—particularly in the secondary school—is a main source of problems and issues studied. The subject-centered approach would, on the other hand, begin with the chronological starting point and go forward to present issues and concerns, under the assumption that the background gained would sometime help to solve current problems. The experience approach uses historical information directly to solve these present-day problems.

The content grows out of pupils' daily living. It includes, in addition to issues of the day of worldwide significance, the immediate concerns of the pupil. The student council and problems with which it deals become important content. Rules and regulations of school and classroom are studied. Such problems as orientation to high school life, improvement of the lunchroom situation, the seating arrangement in the room, an understanding of school organizations, and good citizenship in a school are considered. Adolescents' concerns about their own personality, their home, their relations with others, receive attention. Writing or speaking activities grow out of ongoing life activities in and out of school. There is a purpose for writing, rather than a theme assigned simply for the sake of practice in writing it. The teacher is always on the lookout for ways of relating classroom activities to the school, home, and community life of his pupils.

The experiences are selected cooperatively by teachers and pupils, based on a study and knowledge of those pupils and their previous experience. In the experience approach, the subject matter is selected during the learning situation to meet the needs. It will differ from year to year because pupils differ and the persistent life and social problems differ. This procedure contrasts with that of the subject approach in which those who select the subject matter may be far removed from the teacher. In the subject approach, the selection may come entirely from such sources as the state department of education, the central administration of the school, the supervisor, a central committee, the textbook writer, or some other source that specifies the subject matter to be taught.

A mistake often made by the uninformed is that the experience approach means a lack of planning and a selection of class activities based on the whims of the pupils at the moment. Nothing could be further from the truth. More careful planning is required by teachers cooperatively, by teachers and parents, by teachers and supervisors, and by individual teachers themselves before the learning situation takes place. The difference is in the type of planning. It is not a simple planning that merely sets down subject matter to be covered; it concentrates instead on pupil growth toward aims to be achieved, types of materials to achieve that growth, kinds of experiences to be used, and means of evaluating progress toward the goals.

Cooperative planning in the classroom is a planning of pupils *and* teacher. The teacher is the guide who, by virtue of his greater experience and knowledge, helps pupils to select genuinely important problems. It is not a haphazard process of asking "What are we going to do today?" Instead, skilful planning may take a number of days, and continues after a unit is under way. The group sets up the goals that it wants to achieve and then checks often on how well it is accomplishing those goals. It knows specifically what it hopes to accomplish and how it is proceeding, something that cannot be said for the usual material-to-be-covered situation.

It should be obvious that in the experience approach the teacher needs to be better trained and needs to have a better understanding of adolescents and life outside the classroom than in the subject approach. Moreover, he must have a broader knowledge of subject matter. He must make a constant study of the behavior of his pupils to observe their growth; he must study their abilities, interests, and their previous school background. Also, he must be more expert in handling pupils in a cooperative classroom situation in which there must be a greater degree of self-control than in the class where the teacher decides what experiences pupils will have. Rules for the classroom are set by the group as a desirable type of experience in learning self-control and democratic procedures. The "home work" of the teacher using the experience approach will be of a different kind; it is apt to require much more time and definitely more clear, creative, imaginative thinking.

The teacher is concerned with the growth and development of each individual pupil rather than with preconceived ideas of what the mythical "average pupil" should know at a certain grade level.

Each individual pupil is taken where he is and helped to grow from that point. The myth that all pupils can learn effectively by doing the same things and using the same materials belongs only to the subject-centered curriculum. Research demonstrates that such uniformity of achievement is indeed a fantasy—moreover, a serious mistake, for effective learning produces greater differences. In the experience-centered curriculum, minimum standards for the gifted pupil are not the same as for those who learn more slowly. Appropriate activities, materials, and content are planned for individuals. There is no uniform material or books to be covered by all. Social Studies I includes skills and appreciations appropriate to the pupils in a specific class and may differ considerably in content from class to class or school to school. The objectives set up may in general be similar, but different expectancies will be evident for different groups and individuals, depending upon their previous background and maturity.

SUMMARY

The authors have defined curriculum in terms of experiences that pupils have. Succeeding chapters describe the curriculum of secondary schools in these terms, for it is our conviction that a mere discussion of courses offered in a high school program of studies tells very little about what is happening to boys and girls in the school. It would not describe the total curriculum, but merely the externals, or the structure within which the curriculum operates.

In this chapter, a contrast of the subject-centered approach and the experienced-centered approach to curriculum development has been made, indicating how a teacher operates in planning a curriculum and the kinds of experiences he provides for pupils in each approach. The two approaches represent fundamentally different points of view, for the one begins with the subject matter to be learned, the other with the desired development of the pupil: the skills, appreciations, attitudes, and understandings to be learned.

It is up to the student of education to decide which approach he wishes to use. Evidence from the field of learning, child and adolescent psychology, and the principles of a democratic society point toward the experience-centered curriculum. However, a teacher must *accept* the approach before he can use it effectively. The important thing is that beginning teachers should *move toward* the experience approach and attempt to use each year more practices that consider the pupil as a whole, that meet his particular needs and interests, and that conform with the best of knowledge about how adolescents grow and develop. They do not need to be discouraged because many of their colleagues will use a subject-centered approach. Good teachers in all sections of the country are finding a real satisfaction in teaching by working as partners with their pupils in this business of learning. Even though they may work in traditional situations, they find it possible to use the newer approach to curriculum development.

In this book, an attempt is made to illustrate what teachers and administrators who believe in this approach are doing as contrasted with those who follow the traditional approach. In the description of school practices in the following pages, it will be made clearer that it is not an issue of subject matter versus experience, but it is a question of *how* subject matter is used and *what kind* of subject matter is dealt with.

It should be also pointed out that the experience approach can be used most effectively in the area of the common learnings. The core curriculum is a type of curriculum organization that has been set up to facilitate its use. In some areas of specialized learnings, it is more difficult to apply an experience approach. However, that does not give a teacher a handy excuse for failing to apply many of the principles; rather, it should be a challenge to study how they can be applied.

Selected References

Alberty, Harold. *Reorganizing the High-School Curriculum.* New York: The Macmillan Co., 1947, chaps. 4, 5.—Includes a good discussion of the two approaches, illustrated by examples from school programs. The discussion of the improvement of the subject-centered curriculum in chapter 4 points out how more of the experience approach can be used in academic subjects.

Burton, William H. *The Guidance of Learning Activities.* New York: Appleton-Century-Crofts, Inc., 1944, Part II.—In a discussion of subject matter units and experience units, a contrast between the two types of approaches is illustrated.

Douglass, Harl R. (ed.). *The High School Curriculum.* New York: The Ronald Press Co., 1947, chap. 2.—Explains the nature and the function of the curriculum. Further curriculum definitions are given.

Hildreth, Gertrude. *Child Growth Through Education.* New York: The Ronald Press Co., 1948, chaps. 2, 5, 6.—Concrete examples are given that will help the student understand the concepts involved in the experience approach to curriculum development. It will be helpful reading even though it is pitched toward the elementary level.

Hopkins, L. Thomas. *Interaction: The Democratic Process.* Boston: D. C. Heath & Co., 1941, chap. 1.—Although not easy reading, this is one of the best single references on this topic. Students who become interested in Hopkin's book are urged to read on for further clarification of the two approaches.

"The Experience Curriculum in Action." *Educational Leadership,* 6 (January, 1949), pp. 194-244.—The entire issue is devoted to articles illustrating the experience-centered curriculum in public schools and teacher-education programs, and to articles clarifying the nature of the experience-centered curriculum. Olson's and Parker's articles are best for the latter purpose.

THUT, I. N., and GERBERICH, J. RAYMOND. *Foundations of Method for Secondary Schools.* New York: McGraw-Hill Book Co., Inc., 1949, chaps. 6, 7, 9, 10, 12, 13.—These authors contrast the daily assignment method, the subject-matter unit method, and the experience unit method and describe each of these methods in action. Essentially, the first two are the subject approach and the third, the experience approach. This book is written for undergraduate classes.

Chapter 5

THE TEACHER AND THE SECONDARY SCHOOL CURRICULUM

There are many adults who have some influence on the curriculum, including the teacher, the principal, the superintendent, the supervisor, the textbook writer, members of the state legislature, the curriculum committee, the public, and the consultant. The teacher's part in building the curriculum is considered in this chapter. The discussion centers around the importance of the teacher's place in the process called "curriculum making," and what he does to make the secondary school curriculum either a vital one or a lifeless package of books for youth in school.

1. THE PRINCIPLES

The teacher is the one who largely determines the curriculum of the pupils with whom he works.

Whether the teacher follows a single textbook or uses experiences as the basis for the curriculum, he is the one who determines what the experiences of pupils will be. Others influence many of those decisions through administrative decrees, legislative acts, or other means, but in the final analysis the teacher is by far the most influential of the curriculum makers.

The day by day and year by year planning for and with pupils determines the content for the class. Whether pupils will spend a great deal of time memorizing facts and unrelated information or search for information to solve significant problems will depend upon the teacher's approach. He creates the type of learning situation that will determine the attitudes, understandings, skills, and appreciations that boys and girls develop. He has it within his control to give pupils experiences either in democratic participation in the classroom or in sitting and listening to orders handed out by someone else. In the same way, he sets the stage for what is going to happen in the club or the student council for which he is adviser, although traditionally pupils have more freedom in these activities.

The teacher also determines what the curriculum will be like through the selection of materials to be used by the class. He may participate in selecting books and learning aids to be purchased. At least, he can determine how to use those books, the school library, and other sources of information. The very attitude that he displays toward other persons and toward life, his mental health, will have considerable influence on what kinds of experiences pupils will have. A well-adjusted teacher who likes people and enjoys living also makes school living a joy for his pupils.

The teacher's point of view concerning education and the functions of the secondary school is of utmost significance, since it serves as a basis for decisions concerning the kinds of experiences he will provide for pupils.

In the first chapter, certain principles were stressed as being fundamental for judging a good secondary school program. In the second chapter, we indicated that school people who have not clarified for themselves the purposes of the secondary school are floundering around with no beacons to guide them. Such principles and purposes should be a part of every teacher's equipment. There are many decisions that a teacher must make each day. Only a philosophy developed through critical thinking about young people, about the society in which they will live, and about the application of facts of learning to the school situation, can assure consistent and wise choices.

In addition to holding some point of view, the teacher should clearly recognize its implications. It is here contended that a person should be open-minded to new ideas and ready to change his philosophy if he is convinced by the facts and by results as he finds them. The teacher who looks for tricks of the trade and tries them all merely because they worked for someone else, without contemplating what the results may be, is indeed a dead weight on progress of secondary education. An orientation, a point of view, is one of the important outcomes that can be developed by students in preservice education courses. The study of methods and techniques means little unless an inexperienced teacher at the same time develops a philosophy to guide his procedures.

The philosophy that he holds, whether or not coherently developed, guides the manner in which the teacher works with pupils. It guides the choices he will make in planning the experiences that pupils will have in his classes. Consider the kinds of experiences pupils would have in the classes of two teachers who hold these different points of view:

1. Teacher A believes that all pupils should be brought up to relatively fixed standards of achievement during a year's time. In his classroom, pupils will be likely to do all the exercises in the book. Everyone will do the same exercises, no matter what his background or ability. As a student teacher remarked, "I get the feeling that these kids know all this material that we're working on in the grammar text." He had not given any pretest to find out what different pupils knew before he began teaching, but he had been told by the supervising teacher to assign certain chapters in the text. In teacher A's class, certain books will be read by all. Objective tests will determine how much of the fixed standards of achievement the pupils have attained. If some are at the bottom of such tests, they will fail *no matter how much progress they have made.*

2. Teacher B believes that each pupil should be considered as an individual and that standards are relative, depending upon the pupil's capacity. His pupils are more likely to study different short stories in literature, or read different books in social studies. He will probably be the type of teacher who develops drill materials himself to use with his pupils, and has them work in groups based on their own needs. Pupils of outstanding ability will be able to go ahead at their own pace rather than going through the motions with everyone else in the class.

In the modern secondary school, curriculum building involves a knowledge of pupils, community, social trends in the modern world, and principles of learning, as well as subject matter.

The student of education may have an instructor in a college course who says, "I am interested in education, but not in the art of teaching." Such a person, whether he teaches in high school or college, shows a profound ignorance of what good teaching involves. Enough is known about human behavior to indicate that a continuous study of how learning takes place, of adolescent nature, and of individual pupils is essential to developing a curriculum that will facilitate proper growth. A knowledge of the subject alone can no longer lead—or for that matter never has led—to a dynamic secondary school curriculum. Knowledge of subject matter itself must take on a broader concept, for a background drawn from sociology, economics, political science, anthropology, psychology, and other fields is necessary to fruitful participation in building the secondary school curriculum by the teacher.

The secondary school teacher's many responsibilities in connection with planning a curriculum demand that he know:

1. How to study boys and girls
2. What adolescents are like
3. Under what conditions effective learning takes place
4. What are the significant trends and problems in society
5. What a democratic society demands
6. How to work with others
7. What the community in which he works is like
8. What subject matter is suitable for different maturity levels and interests
9. How to evaluate progress toward goals

This is a far cry from knowing well only the subject matter to be taught to a certain class. Only as the teacher is a student of these problems and conditions will he be able to plan worth-while experiences that lead to significant goals. Such understanding calls for continuous study and planning in summer schools, with the staff throughout the year, and individually.

Democratic participation demands that the teacher have an important part in making decisions concerning curriculum policies and practices.

Teacher-pupil planning of experiences together on a democratic basis will be nurtured best in an environment of sharing and cooperation among principal, other administrators and supervisors, and teachers. Many decisions that are made in schools affect the curriculum. Included are decisions about these aspects of the school program:

1. The content to be taught at specified grade levels
2. The basis or framework, sometimes known as design, for the arrangement and plan of the curriculum
3. The marking and reporting system
4. Testing programs
5. The teacher's part in guidance
6. Books to be purchased; the plan for use of books
7. The flexibility of the course of study
8. The part parents and pupils will play in curriculum planning
9. The extent to which teachers will be encouraged to experiment and to use democratic participation
10. The degree of responsibility that pupils will have in managing school activities
11. The policy in regard to community excursions
12. The plan for use of audio-visual aids

13. The budget for purchase of instructional materials; and policies in regard to their distribution
14. The selection of teachers and principals who will carry out curriculum policies

The greater the extent of participation of teachers in these functions, the better the chance will be for developing teacher leadership and guidance of pupil activities that will lead to the desired goals of secondary education in a democracy. If secondary schools are going to live up to democratic principles, they will need seriously to consider giving teachers greater opportunity to take part in these important aspects of policy-making that affect the curriculum.

The teacher should have freedom to experiment and plan the curriculum with pupils and colleagues, unhampered by inflexible courses of study or administrative fiat.

Progress in curriculum development will result from teachers' experimentation with new content, procedures, and materials, with the interested assistance of the principal. Some teachers will be ready only for certain types of experimentation with ideas new to them; others will be further along. Curriculum improvement occurs as individual teachers feel secure in trying out new procedures; whereas, insistence on uniform use of new practices by all staff members would probably result in much unhappiness and frustration, and eventually in failure for the entire plan. There have been cases of such failure in secondary schools that have tried to put the core curriculum into practice as a schoolwide experiment without giving time for the necessary teacher in-service growth.

Much planning together is necessary in each school, with parents, pupils, and other teachers taking an active part. Rigid courses of study to be followed by all scarcely permit planning for individual needs. Such use of courses of study assumes that all schools, pupils, and teachers are alike. We have but to visit two secondary schools in a single city or rural consolidated school district to realize the fallacy of this assumption. We know that pupils differ, but we would also see how communities differ: the reflection of different types of homes in the pupils, the differences in morale in the school, and the differences in the character of the school staff.

Courses of study and resource units should be used as guides and sources from which to gather ideas for the selection of activities and experiences, materials, and means of evaluation. They should be helpful to the teacher in furnishing leads to units, indicating how to study pupils, and how to plan the curriculum with pupils. If the teacher wants to find materials available on a topic, he should be able to go to the course of study as a source of information. Although the staff in a school agrees on large areas of experience for pupils in a certain grade or class, such an agreement does not necessarily limit the teacher's freedom to develop units that grow out of classroom activities. If the course of study is considered as something to be adapted to local needs, to be studied as professional resource materials, it will not restrict the teacher.

2. Some Typical Practices

Since this chapter is concerned with the teacher's relation to the curriculum, in this section will be described practices to indicate how much freedom the teacher has in the development of the curriculum and how great an opportunity he has to participate in setting curriculum policy in the typical secondary school.

Restrictions Under Which the Teacher Works.—It must be recognized from the outset that the restrictions discussed here may or may not be desirable. They may serve the purpose of protecting children against the whims of incompetent school administrators or teachers. They may be distinct aids to the teacher in his first year of teaching. They may also form the basis for the kind of uniformity that is advantageous to schools in the same community. On the other hand, when these restrictions limit the good teacher's possibilities for planning a curriculum suited to his pupils, they are a hindrance to progress in secondary education. Some of them, such as legal requirements determining what should be taught in the schools, are built on the assumption that school people are not competent to develop the curriculum needed for the secondary schools of the state.

Among the restrictions that circumscribe the curriculum in the typical secondary school today, in addition to the education, experience, and vision of school personnel, are the following:

State laws and requirements by state departments of education and
    other accrediting agencies
Local school policy
Courses of study
Attitudes of the teaching staff
Attitudes of the community
College entrance requirements

1. State Laws and Requirements by State Departments of Education and Other Accrediting Agencies.

State Departments. State departments of education are established to carry out the laws of the state relating to education and to set general policies and regulations necessary for the good of the schools. The best state departments are planning legislation and necessary regulations with school people and working with them in a leadership capacity, rather than exercising mainly an inspectorial function.

Traditionally, state departments have exerted greater influence on the secondary school curriculum than on the elementary school curriculum. To a considerable extent, this action has been due to the pressure of college entrance requirements. Although, fortunately, the trend is away from this practice, most high schools still have their graduation requirements—in terms of total number of credits or subjects to be completed—determined by the state department of education or regional accrediting agency.

State Legislation. More common is the regulation of the curriculum through state legislation. The subjects most frequently required by law are these:

American history and the Constitution
Health and physical education
State history and government
Civics and citizenship
Driver training and education

Some laws specify definite areas of health education, such as teaching the effects of alcohol. Others prohibit certain practices, such as teaching organic evolution, giving religious instruction, and using any subversive form of instruction. High schools that wish to receive federal aid under the Smith-Hughes Act, George-Deen Act, or other acts of Congress, must include such subjects as agriculture, home economics, or distributive education, since this aid is provided specifically for such vocational subjects. State departments of vocational education exercise considerable control of the curriculum in these courses since they prescribe what the course should be.

State Examinations. In the State of New York, the Regent's Examinations, a statewide system of examinations given to high school pupils in the different subjects, limit considerably the curriculum. Teachers naturally try to include all subject matter on which pupils may be tested, since their teaching success is often judged by the proportion of pupils passing these tests. Statewide tests of this type are a definite hindrance to progress in secondary education and retard the development of an up-to-date curriculum.

State Courses of Study. Fortunately, state departments generally no longer publish state courses of study that must be rigidly followed by the schools. Instead, published courses and curriculum bulletins of other types are intended as a service feature of the state department's work with the schools and are furnished to give assistance and guidance to those teachers who want and need it. A few states have a list of state-adopted textbooks, usually selected by a state commission on textbooks, from which schools must select books for their use. These regulations in most instances do not apply to large city school systems. In effect, this plan of selection of books is as restrictive on the curriculum as state courses of study that must be followed.

Accrediting Agencies. Regional accrediting agencies are working to a greater extent through state departments of education and exert leadership through promoting secondary school evaluations and publishing pertinent information on standards. These agencies receive reports from schools as a check on standards for accreditation. They compile lists of accredited schools for use by colleges and universities for admission purposes.

A means of supervising and evaluating secondary schools, used to a considerable extent in many states, is the "Evaluative Criteria" published by the Cooperative Study of Secondary School Standards. The Cooperative Study of Secondary School Standards originated early in the 1930's through the efforts of the United States Commissioner of Education and the six regional associations for accrediting secondary schools, an example of which is the North Central Association that accredits high schools in the Midwest. The purpose of the study was to find better ways of evaluating a secondary school. Criteria for evaluating the curriculum, administration, library services, building, and other phases of the secondary school program, were developed to be used by the evaluators. Schools are first appraised by their own faculty and then by a visiting committee from the state department, universities and colleges, and public schools. The committee usually spends from two to three days in each school.

Norms have been developed for schools of different sizes, and reports of the evaluation are received by each school in the form of graphs known as "educational thermometers." The most important characteristics of these cooperative secondary school evaluations are (1) that the appraisal is made in terms of the school's objectives, and (2) that the school's own staff evaluates itself first. Usually these evaluations are under the direction of the state department of education. Although the evaluation of the curriculum still deals more with externals than with actual pupil experiences, these surveys have had considerable influence in improving the curriculum in secondary schools. Recent revisions have been made in the criteria.[1]

2. LOCAL SCHOOL POLICY. The degree to which the teacher has freedom in planning the curriculum for his pupils will depend to a considerable extent on the policies established by the board of education, the superintendent, and any supervisors which the school may employ. In a small and decreasing number of secondary schools, the textbooks are selected by the superintendent or supervisor without teacher participation. Selection by a department head or a small committee, which sometimes takes place, may be equally limiting if the materials do not suit the pupils in a particular class. Especially is this true if there is little choice among books on an adopted list. As the school system becomes larger, it is more difficult for a central administration to select books to fit different school situations.

School policy relative to required courses, schoolwide achievement tests, and the purchase of instructional materials influences the teacher's opportunity to develop a functional curriculum for his pupils. Most secondary schools require certain courses or specific units to be taught in courses taken by all pupils. An example of the latter is a unit in driver education added to some existing course. It is a rather common practice for larger school systems to give achievement tests to all pupils in specific subjects. The value of this practice depends upon the emphasis given to the use of the tests. Too often they are used for survey purposes without consideration of other outcomes of teaching, rather than for instructional purposes. This practice may result in an undesirable uniformity and undue emphasis on learning the facts asked for in the test.

The type of supervision found in some schools that is properly termed "snoopervision" has long been a drag on progress in secondary education. Its main purpose is to see that teachers are following the prescribed course or doing what the supervisor thinks is right; it does not build on an individual teacher's strengths nor give opportunity for democratic participation in determining policy. The

---

[1] Cooperative Study of Secondary School Standards, *Evaluative Criteria, 1950 Edition,* Washington, D.C.: American Council on Education, 1950, 305 pp.

prevalent practice of using subject supervisors in larger systems has in itself tended to perpetuate the emphasis on subject matter.

A practice that has more powerful influence on the curriculum than is generally conceded is the competitive marking system found in most secondary schools. The principles behind the system are not consistent with the principles of an experience-centered curriculum. As long as teachers have to mark pupils in the traditional manner on the basis of subject matter learned, the experience approach will have a difficult time in making headway.

3. COURSES OF STUDY. The type of course of study used in secondary schools has changed considerably in the last two decades. The change is from an outline of content to be covered toward the resource type of bulletin with suggested objectives, activities, means of evaluation, and materials. There are many schools that use rather brief outlines agreed upon by the teachers in order that all should cover similar content. Others do not use a course at all, but follow rather closely the textbooks selected by the school. In these cases the textbook becomes the course of study.

Most important, however, is the *use* made of the course of study. Some high schools use it as a means of keeping all classes together doing the same thing and covering the same material. Such use is hardly consistent with principles of a good learning situation. The individual differences of pupils—and teachers as well—tend to be lost in a forced uniformity that may result in pupils developing undesirable behaviors.

4. ATTITUDES OF THE TEACHING STAFF. A new teacher in a school will find that he can or cannot do certain things in his classes depending upon the attitudes of the teachers in the school. In certain schools, he will find that teachers frown on "new-fangled" ideas and do all they can to discourage new teachers from using them. They realize that it requires more work to carry on the newer practices, or they may feel insecure in the face of new developments which they lack confidence in being able to carry out successfully. In other situations, beginning teachers may find that they are left to themselves without anyone knowing or caring what they are doing or extending a helping hand to them. The school in which the staff works together with the principal in determining policy and procedure will generally have a high morale situation in which undesirable staff relations do not have a chance to develop.

5. ATTITUDES OF THE COMMUNITY. The beginning teacher will find that the mores of the community have a good deal to do with

what he can teach in the classroom. If the dominant group is one with an eye on the social calendar, there will be pressure exerted to include what traditionally has had prestige value for college preparation. Many a secondary school principal or teacher knows what it means to have ambitious parents insist on the academic program for a child, even though he has more talent for carpentry than for college.

Community attitudes toward sex education, toward liberal ideas, toward religion—toward manifold other topics—help to determine what the secondary schools in this country are teaching. If the community is not favorable to labor, and often if the majority of the more influential leaders in the community is not, labor's position may not be fairly presented in the school, or labor-employer problems and relationships may not be studied at all. Sometimes the teacher is cautioned that he must go easy on the topic.

The community should play a vital part in determining what is to be taught in the school. The tragic part is that, in such communities as the above, teachers and parents rarely have had the opportunity to get together professionally to understand what the school is trying to do or should do. Instead, timid administrators may try to please everyone and to stir up as little comment as possible, or virtually to keep the school isolated from the community in particular and the world in general.

Pressure groups are found in every community. The difference is that some schools work with them and bring leaders from such groups together to work out the best solutions and achieve a better understanding of the school's purposes; others try to ward them off as much as possible. Today, more than ever, it is unfortunate that freedom of thought and investigation is being encroached upon by supposed defenders of democracy who have but a twisted and warped idea of what democracy actually means. There are groups in some communities that have effectively prevented teaching about Russia or teaching youth the essential differences between democracy and communism, because that would be teaching "about communism." Others have been successful in keeping out of the schools some more liberal publications, such as the *Nation*.

6. COLLEGE ENTRANCE REQUIREMENTS. Colleges, of course, exert an influence on the high school curriculum by requiring certain subjects for college entrance, even though countless research studies have indicated that the pattern of high school subjects has no relation to subsequent college success. The colleges' influence on the content that teachers include in courses, although more indirect, is perhaps even more powerful. Literary selections for study in English are

sometimes made with the thought in mind that college teachers expect all high school students to have read *Macbeth, Hamlet, Ivanhoe,* or the *Lady of the Lake.* Formal grammar is often emphasized in English classes because it is considered good preparation for college. Chemistry classes of the college preparatory variety are much more formal and academic than the noncollege classes, which more often are centered around chemistry in life activities.

It is the College Entrance Examination Board, however, that is most effective in controlling the curriculum in some secondary schools. In the eastern section of the United States, where most of the well-known nonpublic institutions of higher learning use these examinations for admission purposes, some teachers plan their courses to fit the examinations, hold coaching classes in the afternoon, and strive to cover all the "essential" content which the examination may include. There is little chance for cooperative planning to develop under this pressure, and many vital experiences that grow out of the present-day life of youngsters go unnoticed in the strain to finish everything needed to prepare students for the examination. In Chapter 17 there is a more complete discussion of college admission requirements.

Teacher Participation in the Total School Curriculum Development.—The principles in this chapter indicate that the teacher is the most important curriculum maker, that under his direction experiences of one type or another are made possible. As we have seen, many influences are brought to bear upon the teacher in his direction of those experiences as he daily develops them with his pupils. Those curriculum activities which are broader in scope than the work of the teacher and the pupils in individual classes are (1) the planning of courses of study, course content, activities, and curriculum policy; (2) the selection of materials for use in classes; and (3) cooperative study of curriculum problems by the whole staff or a group of teachers. In this section will be discussed the extent to which teachers take part in these aspects of curriculum development in the secondary school.

In the development and use of courses of study. The new teacher is more likely to find courses of study to guide him if his first position is in a large city. Most school systems of cities with a population of 100,000 or more either (1) have some type of organization for continuous curriculum study, or (2) have produced courses of study spasmodically whenever a demand was felt. In the former, the emphasis is on the professional growth of the teacher in order to plan more effectively experiences for pupils; in the latter, on providing outlines for the content to be taught in the classroom. Either plan may produce courses of study or curriculum bulletins. In the high schools of medium size, there is more likely to be a mimeographed outline, usually briefer than the course of study published by large city systems or state departments of education. However, the majority of high schools, including practically all the smaller ones, either depend upon the use of the state courses of study or have none at all. Sometimes sketchy outlines of the books to be used and the required content are provided.

In the large cities, many teachers do participate in course of study development to a considerable extent, usually as representatives on committees of their departments. The number who serve on committees represents but a small proportion of all the teachers. In smaller school systems with only one high school, there is more opportunity for all teachers to take part in such work. In most instances, it is a departmental job where, for example, science teachers have little to do with developing the course for the social studies.

Most courses of study give suggestions for objectives, activities, content, and materials. Some are nothing more than a supplement to the textbook. The extremely long courses containing a detailed outline of subject matter content fortunately are declining in popularity. More and more suggestions relating to types of classroom activities and to materials of all types are being included.

The use made of a course of study is most important. Too often it is expected to be followed as an outline of content, uniform in nature for all classes. Classes may be grouped homogeneously, but one course of study, geared to the academic mind, is presumably supposed to fit all equally well. Voluminous courses, in the making of which teachers have had no part, gather dust on the shelves while good ideas for teaching go unheeded. Much more rarely than should be the case, the course of study is regarded as a source and a help, to be studied together by the staff and adapted to the local situation.

In the selection and use of textbooks. Since the great majority of the secondary schools in the nation are small, textbooks are most frequently chosen by the superintendent or the teacher, or the two in conference. In some of these schools, where there is a considerable turnover of teachers each year, the superintendent may find it more expedient to select the books himself every four or five years. He may believe that his knowledge of the school or acquaintanceship with book representatives will enable him to make a better selection than the teacher. More frequently, individual teachers choose texts themselves and recommend them for purchase. In the smaller high schools,

there is less likely to be cooperative study of what the school is trying to do, how materials should be used, and what is needed in a
text before it is selected. Insufficient consideration of the entire field
of books available may result in a hasty choice of "something that
looks good" at first glance.

In larger secondary schools, teachers usually have more to say
about which books are to be purchased, although there is ordinarily
little study together to determine what policy is most desirable for a
good learning situation: a single textbook for the whole class,
smaller sets of books for different levels of ability within the class,
a text and supplementary books, or classroom libraries of single
copies.

The student of education may ask if the use of books in the
secondary school has kept up with current knowledge of how to
promote effective learning. It is a well-established fact that a pupil
cannot profit by reading materials that are too difficult for him.
Research also shows that pupils in any one grade differ widely in
their ability to read. Yet, there are countless pupils in secondary
schools who fail in mathematics because they cannot understand the
mathematical vocabulary, or who cannot master the books provided
in social studies, or for whom the classics are as bewildering as a new
language to a freshman on his first day in class. There is a universal
lag in the secondary school between research and practice in selecting
books that are suitable for the different levels of reading ability.

In the study of curriculum improvement and problems. The
teacher for the most part must discuss informally with colleagues or
with the principal the experiences which he is providing for pupils.
The number of secondary schools that carry on a continuous study
and evaluation of the curriculum, in the broader sense, is relatively
small. Such study requires a mutual understanding of purposes of the
school—what it is trying to do for young people—of the real pupil
needs in that school, and of the nature of the community. To reach
that understanding would require meetings more often than once a
month and a longer tenure of staff members than one year or two
years.

The situation that the beginning teacher would be likely to find in
a secondary school is represented by one or more of the practices
discussed below:

1. Faculty meetings are held once a month with the main consideration given to administrative matters, school functions, school regulations, or pupil conduct.

2. In larger high schools, departmental meetings by subject areas are held more frequently than general meetings of the entire staff or meetings of small groups representing a cross-section of subject interests.

3. There are few meetings in which elementary and secondary school teachers work together on problems of common interest.

4. Curriculum study is more often interpreted to mean only the consideration of content of courses, selection of texts, course requirements in the program of studies, and course of study construction, than to include also problems dealing with adolescent development, recording behavior, adjustment problems, use of community resources, and pupil experiences in classes and activities.

5. The activities carried on by clubs, dramatic productions, and speech activities are less likely to be discussed by a group of teachers.

6. The teacher who is alert and interested professionally often volunteers or is usually called upon time and again for committee work; the teacher whose professional growth has come to a halt is but an infrequent participant in cooperative study.

7. Teacher participation in local or university workshops is confined to the minority who are taking graduate degrees or who are particularly interested in improving their work.

3. PRACTICES IN THE BETTER SECONDARY SCHOOLS

Although in many secondary schools the teacher is hemmed in by regulations, straight-laced courses of study, and tradition, there is an increasing number of forward-looking schools whose principal considers it his responsibility to release, if not really to stimulate and develop, creativity in his teachers. He assists them in many ways to make it easier for them to experiment and to build the kind of curriculum that will make a difference in the lives of youth. Such a principal is a leader of people, not a slave of custom. In secondary schools, too, are found teachers who can work with others, who have not forgotten how to try out new ideas, who can give leadership in curriculum improvement, and who use effectively the freedom they have by exercising imagination and resourcefulness in planning for pupil experiences.

Teacher Experimentation in Building an Improved Curriculum.—Where teachers are encouraged to have ideas and to explore them, there is considerable experimentation with content, activities, materials, and means of evaluation. The Metropolitan School Study

Council, composed of schools in the vicinity of New York City, has a committee that collects and publishes information concerning informal experimentation by teachers.[2] Educational periodicals include numerous articles concerning what teachers are trying out in class and extraclass activities.

Experimentation of the informal type and exploration by secondary school teachers take several forms:

1. Exploration by individual teachers of the use of the core curriculum by combining English and social studies in a two-hour class period. Gradually, provision is made for pupil planning and for the inclusion of guidance activities and new content closely related to the pupils' lives.

2. The use of democratic practices, particularly pupils setting up their own goals, taking charge of many class functions, practicing leadership, and assisting in evaluating their own progress.

3. More utilization of community resources and organizations, films, people, and instructional aids other than books.

4. A change from a single textbook for all pupils to classroom libraries containing books for different levels of reading ability, pamphlets, magazines, and newspapers.

5. Introduction of the use of the anecdotal record for recording progress of pupils, as well as other newer methods of evaluation.

6. The use of a different type of orientation or center of interest for courses, such as centering a chemistry course around industrial processes or life applications.

7. Gradual introduction of the use of experience units.

8. Developing a new organization of a course, such as starting all units in modern history from current places and events in the news and building the consideration of historical events around present problems.

9. Using school activities and school life as a source of experiences for courses.

It should be understood that these may not be new practices in education, but they are new to the teachers trying them out. For them, this experimentation and exploration represent progress toward procedures more consistent with sound educational principles.

The Horace Mann-Lincoln Institute of School Experimentation of Teachers College, Columbia University, is an organization that en-

---

[2] Bulletins available from Metropolitan School Study Council, Teachers College, Columbia University, New York.

courages local school experimentation. Consultants' services are furnished to schools working with the Institute in a program of experimentation of the "action research" type, a type of research that is done in schools on school problems with consultants from the Institute and local school people cooperating in the study.

Resource Units Used as Aids.—In the secondary schools where teachers are given freedom to try out new ideas, resource units, written units that contain many suggestions for content, activities, and materials, are used as a source of information for the teacher. Some schools develop a file of resource units of their own, some that have been written by the teachers of the school and others that may be secured from schools, state departments of education, and organizations concerned with education.[3] These units are most appropriately named since they contain a rich fund of suggestions for goals, activities, problems, materials, and evaluation. Schools often prefer to use these units, which can be filed away and used as needed, in place of voluminous courses of study.

An example of a resource unit developed by a teacher is a unit entitled *Free and Equal? The Japanese-Americans in Oregon,* prepared in a workshop in intercultural education in 1945 in the Portland Public Schools, Portland, Oregon. The unit was prepared at a time when the Japanese-Americans were going through a difficult time on the West Coast. Teachers recognized their responsibility for giving the facts about Japanese-Americans and building good human relations. Since there was very little collected information on this topic, many facts were gathered from magazine articles, newspaper articles, personal interviews, and other original sources. A skeleton outline of this unit [4] is given below:

    I. Introduction
   II. Objectives
  III. Possible Methods of Approach
  IV. Outline of Subject Matter
       A. Japanese-Americans at War
       B. Characteristics of Japanese-Americans
       C. Problems of Integration into American Life

---

[3] Examples of good units are those published by South Bend, Indiana, Public Schools; Portland, Oregon, Public Schools; Denver, Colorado, Public Schools; Center for the Study of Intergroup Relations, University of Chicago; The Problems in American Life units, by the National Association of Secondary School Principals and National Council for Social Studies; and units of the Consumer Education Study, National Association of Secondary School Principals.

[4] From Beatrice Stevens, *Free and Equal? The Japanese-Americans in Oregon,* (mimeographed), Portland, Oregon: Portland Public Schools, 1945, 42 pp.

Modern Courses of Study Serve as Guides.—The most useful courses of study are resource pamphlets in form and purpose. As previously mentioned, the trend in published courses, either mimeographed or printed, is toward including suggestions as to methods and activities, helpful, well-annotated bibliographies of books and other teaching aids, and techniques on how to study pupils and evaluate their growth. The following suggested outline for a course of study, from the Kalamazoo, Michigan, public schools,[5] is an example:

Suggestive Course of Study

Subject or Subject Area	Grade	Date
Characteristics of Pupils Involved		
Curriculum Implications		
Possible Objectives		
Suggested Points of Emphasis, Units, Activities		
Suggested Materials		
Suggested Methods of Teaching		

Other courses that students of education may wish to examine to see what the modern type is like are those published by cities such as Shorewood, Wisconsin; Seattle, Washington; Minneapolis, Minnesota; Santa Barbara, California; and Salem, Oregon.

There is also a definite trend toward developing curriculum bulletins that deal with specific instructional problems. These bulletins may either supplement or supplant the traditional course of study. In

---

[5] Condensed from mimeographed pages published by Department of Curriculum, Kalamazoo Public Schools, Kalamazoo, Michigan.

the schools developing such bulletins, it is rightfully assumed that uniformity is achieved, not through printed courses, but through discussions and thinking through purposes and procedures as a group. These curriculum bulletins on specific problems are used as a study guide for staff meetings and in-service classes and groups.[6]

Policies concerning the use of courses of study are more important than those concerning their form. Good schools are realizing that teachers do better work when they do not have to follow courses of study rigidly. Such is the policy, for example, of the Battle Creek, Michigan, public schools:

We believe that the individual classroom is the basic unit for curriculum development. It is the individual teacher planning with her children who, in the final analysis, determines which experiences and needs will be selected for study. This planning is done, with such help as desired or possible from the principal and supervisor, within the broad framework of educational goals agreed upon by the building faculty and the entire school system.

There are available for suggestion and help to the teacher the guides listed below. . . .

It is to be emphasized that these are guides and not outlines of work necessarily to be covered. Teachers are encouraged to depart from these guides if in so doing they are more adequately meeting the needs of their pupils.[7]

Teacher Participation in the Selection of Instructional Materials.—In good secondary schools throughout the country, teachers are responsible for choosing teaching aids, including books, maps, films and slides, library materials, and other types of materials that enrich the possibilities for varied and fruitful experiences of pupils. The selection does not come about through a hit-or-miss procedure, but rather is the result of careful analysis and study. Better results are obtained in the schools that select books as an outgrowth of a study of the curriculum, not as a separate function.

One plan followed by a larger school system involves careful selection of books. First, a committee of teachers and principals studies

---

[6] Examples of such bulletins are the following: *A Guidebook in Literature, Grades 7 and 8,* Chicago, Illinois: Chicago Public Schools, 1948, 216 pp.; *Effective Learning for Use in Junior High School,* Denver, Colorado: Denver Public Schools, 1949, 72 pp.; Grace Weston and Others, *Democratic Citizenship and Development of Children,* Detroit, Michigan: Citizenship Education Study, 1949, 43 pp.; *Improving Communication,* Bulletin No. 672, Baton Rouge, Louisiana: State Department of Education, 1949, 109 pp.; Ohio State University School, *How Children Develop,* Columbus, Ohio: Ohio State University, 1946, 79 pp.; *Planning and Working Together: A Guide to Curriculum Development in Michigan Secondary Schools,* Bulletin No. 37, Lansing, Michigan: State Department of Public Instruction, 1945, 191 pp.; *The Good School, The Home of Good Teaching,* Augusta, Maine: Division of Curriculum and Instruction, State Department of Education, 1948, 101 pp.

[7] *Aims and Policies of the Instructional Program* (mimeographed), Battle Creek, Michigan: Division of Instruction, Battle Creek Public Schools, 1947, p. 5.

the recent trends in the field in which books are to be chosen. Second, the committee sets up criteria for the selection of the books on the basis of the purpose of the course. This includes such policy decisions as whether one or more books will be used, whether there should be a selection of books of different levels of reading ability, and the like. These decisions are based on study and discussion with many teachers throughout the schools. Third, the committee develops an evaluation sheet, studies the books available, and rates them on the sheet. Book representatives usually meet with the committee if city-wide adoptions of texts are being considered. Policies are determined to govern the relations between publishers' representatives and the committee in order to avoid any unfair advantages being given to certain publishers or undesirable types of solicitation. The final decision of the committee is submitted to the administration for adoption by the board of education. Pupils have a part through the exploratory use of books in the classrooms of committee members and other teachers who secure evaluations by pupils.

In Portland, Oregon, such committees spend a year's analysis and study on the selection of textbooks, maps and globes, and classroom library materials. In the choosing of classroom library books for the junior high school level and for eleventh grade literary selections, the following standards were set up for evaluation of books:[8]

Some of the definite reading interests to remember are:
1. Biography
2. Personal adventure
3. Information books
4. Stories of vocations, adventure, mystery, school, and animals.

Books of biography should:
1. Be about heroes of action and achievement
2. Deal with outward events and struggles rather than with character analysis
3. Be presented sympathetically
4. Be idealistic without being didactic.

Books of personal adventure should be:
1. Vividly written but without undue exaggeration
2. Of wholesome exploits worth reading about.

Informational books should have:
1. The same characteristics of accuracy, good organization and presentation as in younger children's books
2. In addition, splendid indexes and bibliographies where the subject calls for them.

---

[8] This example was taken from mimeographed materials used in the Portland Public Schools, Portland, Oregon, in the selection of books, 1945.

Fiction in general should have:
1. An authentic background
2. Characters which are not types
3. Genuine character development
4. A plausible plot
5. Wholesome and normal relationships
6. Problems of interest to adolescents, the solutions of which may be helpful in their own lives.

The resulting list of books then serves as a list from which teachers may select purchases for their own classrooms.

Teachers also participate in choosing audio-visual aids to be purchased by the school. They preview films and slides and recommend those aids that fit in with needs of their classes. Some schools have standing committees for this purpose; others receive recommendations from individual teachers. Teachers are called upon to recommend new library acquisitions each year, especially where the library is more of an integral part of class work and is used extensively as a resource center.[9]

Teacher Participation in Developing Curriculum Policies and Plans.—The group activities of teachers constitute an important means by which the individual teacher participates in curriculum-building. Through these avenues, teachers have a part in determining policy concerning the curriculum and administrative matters that affect the curriculum. They take part in several ways:

1. Participation through staff meetings and local school policy-making
2. Participation through system-wide committees to study specific phases of the curriculum and through coordinating or curriculum councils for the school district
3. Participation through planning by small groups
4. Participation through in-service classes
5. Participation through workshops.

An illustration of how teachers take part in the policy-making of a larger high school is the cooperative planning in Oakland High School, Oakland, California. The staff participates in different groups:

1. *The administrative staff,* composed of the principal, the two vice-principals, and three teachers elected by the faculty. This staff

---

[9] See also mimeographed textbook adoption procedures of the Oakland Public Schools, Oakland, California.

meets weekly to discuss and recommend administrative practices in the school.

2. *An instructional council* composed of the principal, vice-principals, curriculum assistant, and department heads. This council directs the over-all instructional problems of the school. The problems of different departments are brought to the attention of this group and, in turn, the department heads discuss with teachers in the department the curriculum problems for the entire school. Teachers meet once a week with their department heads.

3. *Interdepartmental meetings* of groups of teachers. The faculty is divided into six groups; membership in each group is determined by the time when the teacher has a conference period scheduled. These meetings are for the purpose of clarification of administrative, guidance, and curriculum practices. These groups also discuss reports on talks presented at faculty meetings of the total staff. Teachers bring up any problem upon which there is need for better understanding.

4. *Teacher committees* selected to study and recommend to the faculty changes in the curriculum as well as other changes. Examples of these are:

    Committee on Home Rooms
    Committee on Evaluation and Grading
    Committee on Improvement of Family Life

5. *Monthly faculty meetings* to consider reports, hear talks by a teacher, the principal, or an outside consultant.

There is also a guidance council in the school. The participation is such that it breaks down departmental barriers at the same time as it permits teachers to participate in policy-making.

4. First Steps

Achieving more extensive teacher participation in developing curriculum policy, selecting teaching aids, studying curriculum problems, choosing experiences with pupils, and producing curriculum bulletins should be the goal of the modern secondary school. Restrictions that hamper creative work should be considered in their real light as inimical to the best interests of youth. Some of the first steps that schools and teachers may take in making the changeover are indicated:

1. If teachers have had little to say about policy, the election of an advisory group for the building or the school system is a good

place to begin. That teachers will welcome such an opportunity is evidenced by the constantly expanding movement among them to organize to secure better salaries and working conditions.

2. Such a group might well begin by investigating what teachers desire in the way of changes in the curriculum, ferreting out and publicizing the significant things teachers are doing, and starting some plan for study and recommendation on certain problems. It would be a serious mistake if the group went about its job on the basic assumption that it was a reform group.

3. In trying to arrive at some common philosophy among teachers of the school, it would be far better to have them work on real problems of significance than to set out to develop a statement of philosophy for the system. Philosophy grows out of thinking and analysis of such problems. Teachers will tire of the study of philosophy that seems to get nowhere.

4. The emphasis should be placed on cooperative planning within the individual building. In large secondary schools it will mean some division into groups. Problems dealing with the reasons for dropouts, with home conditions, the use of field trips, and the like will lend themselves to group study that cuts across subject fields. In small high schools, staff meetings are a more simple procedure.

5. Meetings of principal and teachers should begin—and continue —on a friendly and informal basis that considers teachers' problems. Administrative matters can be conveniently handled through a small principal's council or through bulletin form. If teachers are given a chance to talk about what concerns them, there will be little difficulty in getting teacher participation.

6. In schools where textbooks are adopted on a citywide basis, these books can be supplemented with classroom libraries to suit the demands of individual teachers. Purchases may be small at first, but the library can always be called on to furnish classrooms with short-time loans of books.

7. In experimenting with new content and procedures, the change should begin with teachers who want to participate. The attempted all-school changeover is often doomed to failure. In the former method, there will be several leaders who will work for the change rather than the probable one or a few.

8. A plan can be developed whereby teachers who wish to experiment are encouraged to do so and will receive cooperation from the administration. As the school becomes committed to a policy of progress and freedom for the classroom teacher to develop

suitable experiences with pupils, the formal procedure of securing permission to experiment by trying out new ideas will no
longer be necessary.

9. Teachers in schools where courses of study are supposed to be
followed closely may usually obtain permission to experiment
with new content if they outline their plans carefully.

10. Schools can make the first step away from more rigid concepts
of a course of study by considering in faculty meetings how adaptations can be made.

11. Teacher-centered curriculum improvement programs in large
cities can be achieved if the school unit rather than the central
office is regarded as the hub of curriculum activity. The latter
should be for coordinating and leadership purposes. This policy
would permit individual secondary schools desiring to go ahead
by themselves to explore new procedures and content.

SELECTED REFERENCES

DEPARTMENT OF SUPERVISION AND CURRICULUM DEVELOPMENT. *Group Planning in
Education* (1945 Yearbook). Washington, D.C.: National Education Association, chaps. 13, 14, 15, 16, 18.—Describes how teachers and administrators
have planned together in workshops, councils, and group conferences.

DOUGLASS, HARL R. (ed.). *The High School Curriculum.* New York: The Ronald
Press Co., 1947, chaps. 15, 16.—Chapter 15 deals with characteristics and construction of courses of study, giving further examples of modern courses. In
chapter 16 the teacher's part in curriculum construction, in choosing textbooks,
and in building and using courses of study is discussed.

GILES, H. H., McCUTCHEN, S. P., and ZECHIEL, A. N. *Exploring the Curriculum.*
New York: Harper & Bros., 1942, chaps. 6, 7.—One of five volumes that describe the Eight-Year Study of the Progressive Education Association. It contains accounts of how the twenty-nine schools organized the staff for curriculum
study, illustrations of the problems teachers studied together, and examples of
policy-making by staffs, coordinating councils, and faculty meetings.

HOPKINS, L. THOMAS. *Interaction: the Democratic Process.* Boston: D. C. Heath
& Co., 1941, chap. 5.—This chapter on "How Does Philosophy Affect the Cur-
riculum?" shows how the teacher's values determine experiences pupils will have.
It is a good reference for more mature students.

KRUG, EDWARD A. *Curriculum Planning.* New York: Harper & Bros., 1950, chaps.
1, 2, 4, 5, 7.—Indicates the role of teachers and others in curriculum planning,
how a school faculty works together effectively, the use of curriculum guides and
units, and means of system-wide curriculum study. The teacher's part is stressed
throughout, and the book contains good, concrete examples.

LEE, J. MURRAY, and LEE, DORIS MAY. *The Child and His Curriculum.* New York:
Appleton-Century-Crofts, Inc., 1950, chap. 6.—Contrasts the traditional and the
modern point of view of the teacher regarding the curriculum. Although written
for the elementary level, it also applies to secondary schools.

PIERCE, PAUL R. *Developing a High-School Curriculum.* New York: American
Book Co., 1942, chaps. 2, 4.—These two chapters, especially, tell how a principal

and his teachers worked together to improve the curriculum of Wells High School, Chicago, in a fascinating book that reads like a story.

SPEARS, HAROLD. *The Emerging High-School Curriculum.* New York: American Book Co., 1948, chaps. 2, 16.—Points out the weaknesses of curriculum study in secondary schools, such as lack of teacher participation, and describes certain city and state curriculum development programs.

Chapter 6

THE FRAMEWORK FOR THE CURRICULUM

Previous chapters have dealt with the approach that the teacher uses in selecting curriculum experiences and the teacher's part in curriculum planning. Material in this chapter will cover the way in which experiences and subject matter are organized for learning, both in the day's schedule and in the total program of studies. Since subject matter is important in any approach to curriculum development, we need to be concerned about how it is arranged and used for most effective growth of pupils. The chapter includes a description of attempts of secondary schools to achieve an organization in which the relationships of different subject fields are made evident, and in which the experiences of pupils in school may form a more unified pattern within the school day and school year. The course offerings of the school, the blocking of time for courses, and the organization of content within courses are all a part of this topic. The sequence of the content of the curriculum is not discussed here; the student is referred to books dealing with the curriculum, listed at the end of this chapter, for that information.

1. THE PRINCIPLES

The more effectively the organization of the curriculum provides for the student's seeing relationships among different experiences during the school day, the more efficient will be the learning.

There is little that is consistent with good learning principles in a policy of extreme departmentalization of subjects, with different teachers for each course that the pupils take during the day, and few, if any, attempts made to coordinate the work done in various courses. The college student is well aware how limited is the coordination among his courses, how few are the attempts of instructors to help students integrate in their own minds information received from various courses. Stress on learning the facts in each course without guiding students to use subject matter from all courses in solving questions and clarifying issues serves to block such integration. Relationships between learning experiences are not encouraged in any situation where material is to be learned in order to be recited back in class or in examinations. Subject matter must serve some more useful purpose, or learning will continue to be far less efficient than is possible.

Attempts of teachers to correlate English and history courses, that is, teaching related subject matter at the same time, and to fuse or combine geography and history into a single course in social studies illustrate how schools are trying to help the pupils see relationships in subject matter. A better learning situation is one in which information from various subjects is drawn as needed to solve problems of significance. It is most commonly found in the primary grades, where the teacher has the pupils in the room for the entire school day and time is taken to work on specialized phases of the curriculum, such as arithmetic or spelling, as needed. The core curriculum in the secondary school is designed to provide for an organization of the curriculum that permits more integrated experiences in the school day.

The phases of the curriculum of the secondary school common to all pupils should be organized around problems significant to their present-day lives and the culture in which they live, rather than around the logical arrangement of subject fields.

This is a principle that we realize will probably not be universally accepted in the secondary school for some time to come. However, we find that many good secondary schools are following it in providing for the common learnings through the core curriculum, as described in the section of this chapter dealing with outstanding practices. Departmentalization of subjects is rather firmly entrenched, however, in the secondary schools. This is because it is easier to teach a well-organized subject, where the teacher, principal, and pupils have less to do in planning the organization. It means fewer hours of cooperative planning by the teachers as a group, less time spent on making plans for organization of experiences and content for the class, and less extensive knowledge of the subject fields involved. However, even within a subject such as modern history or senior science, it is possible to organize the experiences around problems to a certain extent.

Using this principle means an entirely new organization of subject matter around problems vital to youth and live issues of the day. Materials will be drawn from different fields to solve these problems; desired skills will be developed in the study, investigation, and reporting involved. For example, a trip to the United Nations would involve investigating what it is, facts about what it has done and its purposes, information concerning travel possibilities and costs, making reservations for accommodations, setting up rules for the group, reporting on information, discussion, interviewing, and other activities. Practice of good speech habits, opportunities for writing, and discussion of socioeconomic questions would all be a part of the class work.

This principle does not preclude the study of specific subjects in a logical fashion. It applies to the phases of general education that are common to all pupils—the types of common learnings needed by everyone as a citizen of democracy. Pupils in secondary schools need to have an opportunity to specialize in areas of interest or special ability.

The unit organization of the curriculum in the classroom facilitates the learning of desirable attitudes, appreciations, skills, and understandings for a democratic society.

The unit organization of the curriculum is considered here as referring to the organization of activities, experiences, and subject matter around a central problem or purpose of a group of pupils. It is not correctly defined as merely a block of subject matter. The daily assignment-recitation type of teaching involves a certain type of organization of experiences in the classroom, including the teacher's planning of assignments by himself, discussion around assignments as decided by the teacher, and tests on material covered. These activities scarcely promote democratic skills. On the other hand, the unit organization has several definite advantages in facilitating desirable learnings:

1. Learning is more effective if the learning experiences are integrated rather than divided into minute segments or small areas.
2. The pupils have a chance to participate in setting their own goals, which should have meaning and purpose to them.
3. The pupils plan together their experiences to meet their goals; they practice the skills in cooperative planning and living essential to democracy.
4. Several areas of subject matter are drawn upon to solve the problems involved.
5. There is an opportunity for varied experiences, with different pupils doing the things most suited to their abilities and interest and using materials of varied difficulty.

6. The unit provides for constant group evaluation of progress and a knowledge of the progress being made.
7. The investigation, weighing of information, interviewing people, evaluating sources, and reporting information are important skills that are a part of unit teaching.

The program of studies in a secondary school should provide both common learnings for all pupils as a part of their general education for living and varied experiences to develop diversified and special interests and activities.

There are certain experiences to develop skills, understandings, and attitudes that all citizens of a democracy need, known as common learning experiences. They are not merely a compilation of required subject matter. These experiences should be common to all pupils, those who go on to college and those who do not. When the history of the mid-twentieth century high school is finally written, one of its indictments will undoubtedly be that some schools, in an atomic age, went blindly on monopolizing the attention of future citizens with foreign languages, higher mathematics, and other "college-preparatory" subjects without adequate consideration of the social issues of the day. These common experiences should be suited to the maturity and abilities of the pupils; they should not be uniform books, assignments, or tests for all. Secondary schools are beginning to realize that there needs to be some body of experiences, some goals, that should be a part of everyone's high school life. The core curriculum is a result of efforts to achieve this: to bring together within a longer portion of the school day, in one course, some of the common learnings for all pupils.

In addition to the common learnings, the secondary school must provide for the diversity that builds a strong democratic society, for the many interests, the variation in ability, the special abilities, and the needs of those who are handicapped. The citizens of the community are often surprised to learn what certain students with special talents have been able to do in school, for example, in music, in art, in creative writing, or in scientific experimentation. It is a function of the modern high school to furnish experiences that will help youth to discover and develop special talents of any kind.

The common elements of the program of studies should embody a well-balanced general education that includes the civic, social, cultural, health, adjustment, and family-life needs of every citizen no matter what his occupation will be.

Achieving a balance in the general education of the citizen for community and family living is no easy task, but it is an important goal of the secondary school. Civic responsibilities and intelligent voting on issues are fast becoming more complicated in a world constantly brought closer to each individual through scientific inventions in transportation and communication, and made ever more perilous through new and terrible instruments of destruction. Even so, the cultural and aesthetic phases of living cannot be neglected in a good general education.

How does the typical four-year high school program of a pupil preparing to go on to college stack up against this principle? How well-rounded an education for living fully in today's world would a boy or girl have after completing these courses in high school?

1 year of ancient history
1 year of American history
2 or 3 years of mathematics
3 or 4 years of foreign languages
2 or 3 years of advanced science courses
4 years of English
2 years, of two periods a week, of physical education.

There are countless numbers who go through grades nine to twelve and receive just such limited contact with the areas of experience advocated in *The Cardinal Principles of Secondary Education* [1] some thirty years ago.

Every pupil—whether he intends to go to college, to business school, or to get a job after finishing high school—should have some experiences in the areas of arts and crafts, science, literature, music, and family living. He needs to give considerable thought to happenings in his world and to social, economic, and political questions. He must develop skills of communication. A balanced education would not be complete unless he had a chance to consider personal problems of his own living, health, and adjustments to his age mates.

The common learning experiences should include more than subject content. They should provide practice in democratic skills, experience in living in an atmosphere where mental health is valued and fostered, skills in investigation and weighing of information, and attitudes and appreciations that go to make up a full and rich life—rich in friends, beauty, interests, and satisfaction.

---

[1] See p. 32.

The curriculum should be organized so as to give each pupil abundant experiences in democratic living.

At this point, it would be well to review what democratic living involves. Among other things, we recall that it gives each individual a share in deciding policy that affects his own welfare, it provides an atmosphere in which each individual is regarded as important and respected for what he is as a person, and it places a great deal of value on concern for others and their welfare. Segregation of pupils on a basis that places less value on any one group of young people than on others is inimical to these democratic principles. The student of education should ask himself: How were pupils in general or commercial curricula regarded in my school? Did these divisions, based on future plans, help pupils with less academic ability to achieve self-respect and security? Certainly, grouping for instructional purposes, where pupils with particular learning difficulties are separated from others for remedial instruction, has proved helpful to these pupils. But we ought to be greatly concerned about what the constant, year-in-and-year-out segregation does to the people in the group regarded as "lower" or "dumb." [2]

Parents who place their children in costly private high schools to give them an exclusive environment are actually robbing them of the rich experience of learning to know and live with all kinds of people, so essential to a functioning democracy. Impoverishment of social skills will be a serious deficiency that cannot be counterbalanced by enrichment of the social graces. The importance of development of desirable attitudes for democratic living is overlooked.

The organization of the curriculum around pertinent problems which draw upon information from several subject areas for their solution assures a greater probability of cooperation by the group in the work of the classroom, of learning the skills of planning and small group procedures, and of experiences in democratic leadership. According to this principle, the core curriculum represents progress in the right direction.

2. Some Typical Practices

In the typical American secondary school, the logical subject organization is the basis for organization of curriculum experiences. There has been little change in this respect during the history of secondary education in this country. The changes have been in new

---

[2] Read A. B. Hollingshead, *Elmtown's Youth,* New York: John Wiley & Sons, Inc., 1949, especially chap. 8.

content added or substituted for the old, in line with new developments in American life. Just as Latin or Greek was taught quite separately from history or rhetoric in the early public high school, English in most schools is a distinct subject with a clear-cut subject content separate from home and family living, world history, or social-economic-political problems.

Logical Organization of Subject Matter.—The logical organization of subject matter in secondary school classes is by far the predominant type. Geometry is a typical example of a subject that has changed little over the years. In the great majority of high schools, American history is still taught as a chronological arrangement of events. Physics and chemistry are organized much in the same fashion that they have been for several decades, with, of course, new content added in keeping with scientific advances. Foreign languages generally begin with the simple vocabulary and grammatical structure, going on to stress reading in the advanced classes, a traditional procedure.

It is in the newer subjects, such as home economics, agriculture, business education, industrial arts, problems of democracy, social living, art, and music that the organization of experiences tends to be centered around problems, or larger units of work. Home economics classes generally organize experiences around such units as different aspects of foods, child care, good grooming, the personal budget, and care of clothing. In agriculture, the projects on the boys' farms, along with different regional aspects of farming, form a basis for organization of the work. Art and music also are more likely to acquire characteristics of the experience-centered curriculum than the traditional academic subjects. In these newer courses, problems closely related to the lives of the pupils, and projects, are used more often as the basis for organization of subject matter and experiences. It must be recognized, however, that many pupils have little contact with these courses since they have traditionally, but erroneously, not been considered as the basis for good preparation for college.

In the academic classes, such as English, science, and history, which constitute a large portion of the high school pupil's program, the unit organization of experiences has gained little headway. It should be pointed out that the division of a textbook into units does not in itself assure unit teaching. Such units are merely divisions of subject matter, or a new name for chapters, not unified experiences in the true sense. In more specific skills subjects, such as mathematics, typewriting, and shorthand, which are sequential in nature, the unit organization is not as applicable.

Departmentalization of Subjects.—The net result of the emphasis on a subject-centered curriculum in the secondary school has been a continuation, and even an intensification, of barriers that separate subject field from subject field and class from class. Subjects have been kept in their respective compartments, rather than used in such a manner as to achieve correlation and integration. Departmentalization is not as common in the junior high school, in which a teacher often teaches a group of pupils in a home room for a half a day. In some eastern sections of the country, unfortunately, junior high schools are almost completely departmentalized.

These are some of the practices and trends that reflect this point of view in secondary education:

1. Teachers believe that their prerogative and responsibility is to teach only their own subjects and, consequently, hesitate to infringe on others' subject areas. Hence, the possible interrelationships are not developed.

2. The departmental organization with one teacher as a department head, commonly found in large senior high schools, promotes teacher planning mainly by departments. Jealousies have arisen over subject requirements and "intrusions" of some subjects in the list of required courses at the expense of others. Each group has fought to keep its hold on the curriculum.

3. City school supervisors have generally been subject supervisors. Only in recent years has general supervision made appreciable gains.

4. Subjects in a single field are assigned to teachers. As the high school size increases, the teaching assignment is likely to consist of duplicate sections in English I or in American history, for example. The emphasis is more on the subject matter than on pupil needs.

5. The certification of teachers by many state departments of education is for the teaching of a specific subject or subjects.

6. Teacher education is patterned after a compartmentalization of subject matter, teachers often being able to major only in narrow fields, such as physics or history, whereas they need to be well grounded in broader areas of related subject matter.

7. The high school schedule of classes shifts pupils from one teacher to another after each of the five or six class periods.

The beginning teacher may expect to experience difficulty in trying to use community resources effectively, for many teachers will resent any intrusion on the time scheduled for their classes which would reduce the time available for covering the subject matter planned for the year. He will soon become conscious of the sharp divisions that actually exist between subjects, the many teachers who know little about what is happening in other departments, and the subtle rivalry between subject matter groups.

Increase in Number of Courses Offered.—The list of courses offered by secondary schools has continued to multiply since the days of the Latin grammar school. For example, Van Dyke found in a study of course offerings in thirty-five schools that the total number of different courses had increased from 828 in 1908-11 to 1,683 in 1929-30, doubling in about a twenty-year period.[3] The last twenty years have seen another substantial increase. Most frequent offerings are English, mathematics, science, social studies, and physical education.

The expansion to include new courses follows the idea of curriculum enrichment through adding courses rather than through improving experiences in those already offered. Undoubtedly, these additions have given high school youth an improved program. Often they contain the significant life experiences that have had a difficult time to infiltrate the established academic courses. However, it represents a faith that addition of new courses will meet youth needs without the necessity of changing the orientation and experiences offered in existing courses. It also implies the assumption that differentiation cannot be provided within courses. The actual condition is that many students are not affected by these new courses since they usually are found in the elective rather than the required category.

The Organization of Subjects into Different Curricula.—The list of subjects offered in the high school, available to students in each grade, is known as the program of studies. Two general arrangements of courses within the program of studies are found in secondary schools of the country. There are variations of these patterns, but they represent the typical situation in secondary schools. The first organizes subjects into "curricula" or "courses"; the second just lists the required and elective courses for all students.

One of the common ways of organizing the program of studies in secondary schools is the grouping of subjects into different combinations (called "curricula" or "courses") around future vocational or educational objectives. This plan, known as the multiple curriculum type of organization, was popular with the early academy and high

[3] G. E. Van Dyke, "Trends in the Development of the High School Offering. II," *School Review*, 39 (December, 1931), 737-47.

school. It was intended to meet varying needs of pupils, for both the college preparatory and noncollege groups. In the late nineteenth and early twentieth centuries, this method of differentiation in the curriculum grew to ridiculous heights, ten or twelve curricula being offered by many schools. The number of curricula offered has decreased in the past twenty-five years.

The practice is still prevalent, especially in the larger high schools. It is more typical in eastern areas than in the Midwest, West, or South. Those most commonly found are college preparatory or academic, general, commercial or business, technical or industrial, and home economics curricula. Further breakdowns of the academic into classical and scientific curricula are sometimes made, emphasizing different groupings of subjects for the college preparatory students. Required and elective subjects are listed for each curriculum. An example of a program of studies of this type is presented here.

PROGRAM OF STUDIES I

College Preparatory

Ninth Grade	Tenth Grade	Eleventh Grade	Twelfth Grade
English I	English II	English III	English IV
Algebra I	Algebra II	Plane Geometry	History IV
History I	Biology	Foreign Lan-	Algebra III
Physical Educa-	Elective—1	guage I	(½ yr.)
tion		Chemistry or	Foreign Lan-
Elective—1		Physics	guage II
			Solid Geometry
			(½ yr.)

General

English I	English II	English III	English IV
General Mathe-	General Mathe-	Junior Business	Salesmanship
matics I	matics II	Training	Electives—2
History I	Biology	Industrial Arts II	
Physical Educa-	Industrial Arts I	or Home Eco-	
tion	or Home Eco-	nomics II	
Elective—1	nomics I	Elective—1	

Commercial

English I	English II	English III	English IV
General Mathe-	Biology	Bookkeeping I	Office Practice
matics I	Commercial	Stenography I	(½ yr.)
History I	Arithmetic	Elective—1	Commercial Law
Typing I	Typing II		(½ yr.)
Physical Educa-			Stenography II
tion			Elective—1

Electives

General Science	History II	History III	Trigonometry
Latin I	Latin II	Music	Music
Music	Music	Chemistry	Physics

In critically examining this program of studies, the student should appraise it in terms of principles outlined in this chapter. Such questions as these should be considered:

Would a pupil who completed the college preparatory curriculum probably receive a balanced education for life as a citizen?

Do the various curricula indicate that the school is providing any common elements of general education to all pupils, regardless of vocational objectives?

What phases of good general education for living in a modern world do not seem to be included?

What special interests and abilities are evidently provided for in the electives?

Obviously a list of courses cannot furnish specific answers as to the types of experiences provided in them, but they are the framework within which those experiences can be planned.

This type of organization, which has many advocates among secondary school people, served as a means of introducing new emphases into the program of studies of large numbers of pupils whose high school education was terminal. It may have been the most effective plan of guiding pupils in taking the needed courses for their vocational or educational objective at a time when guidance was in the infant stage, but it can be seriously questioned as fitting the needs of the modern secondary school on several counts:

1. Often about one half of the high school pupils enroll in the college preparatory curriculum since it has prestige value with parents, teachers, and pupils. In effect, this defeats the purpose of the plan, since a number of pupils are obviously misfits in that they are not college bound.

2. In many schools, strict adherence to a pattern of courses within one of these curricula is a barrier to a student who wishes to take some subject, such as art or typewriting, to fit his special needs and interests. The rigidity and inflexibility that often result do not serve the guidance function.

3. One result of this differentiation is an unfortunate social distinction. Pupils of academic ability are guided into the college preparatory curriculum, and others into the general, commercial, agriculture, or industrial arts curriculum. The consequence is to divide pupils into two groups, the college preparatory and the vocational. Pupils in the latter group often become identified as the "dumbbells," or other harsh terms are used by high school

pupils. The school helps to accentuate social class distinctions that already exist.

4. In effect, the result is a form of ability grouping that continues throughout high school and does not provide for different groupings for different purposes and skills. The criticism is not directed against grouping for instructional purposes but against inflexible grouping.

Program of Studies Organized into a Single List of Subjects or "Curriculum" for All Pupils.—The second typical kind of organization of the program of studies is a listing of prescribed courses and electives for each of the four years without regard for vocational or educational objectives, known as the constants-with-electives type. This organization is generally found in the smaller secondary schools, where in many cases programs of offerings have been too limited to permit much differentiation. In a number of larger high schools, it has gained considerable favor in recent years. Some have adopted its use generally, and others have confined it to the first two or three years of a four-year high school. In junior high schools, this type of "curriculum" is the one most frequently found.

In this plan, the program of studies includes certain required courses, considered as essential for the general education of all pupils. As yet, these required courses do not ordinarily include as balanced a program as is desirable. The schools depend upon the guidance program to help pupils make wise choices of courses each year. Often specific courses listed for certain grades are not open to pupils in other high school grades. A sample program of studies from a junior high school, shown on page 124, illustrates this type of organization.

This type of organization is better than the multiple type, especially if accompanied by adequate educational guidance. It permits greater freedom of choice of certain courses to fit special needs and interests; tends to give more pupils who plan to go to college an opportunity to elect subjects such as music, art, vocational subjects, and industrial arts; creates less of a distinction between academic and nonacademic subjects; and does not label specifically the "noncollege" and "college" groups.

An examination of programs of studies from secondary schools throughout the country will reveal that they are increasingly including music, art, shop, homemaking, vocational, and other special courses. Only in the small high schools does the scope of the program remain rather barren.

PROGRAM OF STUDIES II

Seventh Grade		Eighth Grade	
Subject	Periods Per Week	Subject	Periods Per Week
English	5	English	5
Mathematics	4	Mathematics	4
U.S. History to 1866	4	U.S. History, 1866-1949	4
General Science	4	General Science	4
Geography	4	Practical Arts	3
Practical Arts	3	Guidance	1
Music	1	Auditorium	1
Guidance	1	Art	1
Auditorium	1	Club	1
Club	1	Music or Study	2
Study	1		
Total periods	30	Periods required	26

Elect one of the following:

Geography	4
Additional Practical Arts	4
Latin	4
French	4
Total periods	30

Ninth Grade

Subjects Required	Periods Per Week	Units Credit
English	5	1
General Mathematics or Algebra	5	1
Guidance	1	¼
Auditorium	1	¼
Music or Study	1	0
Club	1	0
Periods required	14	Units required 2½

Elect two of the following:

Latin	5	1
French	5	1
Ancient and Medieval History	5	1
Civics	5	1
Business Training	5	1
Art	5	1
Agriculture	10	1
Mechanical Drawing and Pattern Making (½ yr. of each for boys)	8	1
Textiles and Clothing (girls)	6	1
Periods elective	10, 11, 13, or 15	
Periods for study	6, 5, 3, or 1	
Total periods	30	Units elective 2

Restricted General Education of Youth.—Education aimed at developing behavior desirable for the individual's life activities other than his vocational pursuits is considered as his general education. It includes the common learnings needed by all citizens. The principle that a program of studies should provide for a well-balanced general education is quite generally accepted by secondary school people. Essentials for a full, happy, and worth-while life in modern society demand civic participation, understanding of a modern, scientific, and complicated world, cultural and leisure-time interests, good physical and mental health, a well-adjusted family life, skills in communication, and other skills. The type of education that is common to all high school youth of today does not measure up very well against this standard.

Two sources of data will indicate what the majority of young people going through high school are experiencing as to a balanced general education: (1) a study of courses that have been pursued by high school graduates, and (2) the existing graduation requirements. A study of courses pursued by dropouts will generally reveal that these pupils have had less of a balanced education than graduates have.

The typical program of studies pursued by a pupil in one of the numerous small high schools of the country includes: English, four years; mathematics, two years; science, two years; social studies, two years; foreign language, two years; and other courses in business, industrial arts, physical education, agriculture, and home economics or—more likely—additional units in the academic subjects, four to six units. Since the small high school of a hundred pupils is limited in the number of subjects it can offer, the pattern is largely college preparatory or academic in nature. Studies of credits earned by high school graduates indicate that about three fourths of the subjects taken were of the academic type. In the junior high school, the pupil is more likely to get a broader program; art, music, industrial arts, or home economics are frequently a part of the common learnings of all pupils. The practice there is to offer some of these subjects one, two, or three times a week.

Sixteen units, or full-year courses, are generally required for graduation from a four-year high school, or twelve for graduation from a senior high school. There has been a notable tendency in recent years to extend this number in order to make it possible to include a broader general education. Credits in physical education and "extracurricular" activities have often been added to the basic sixteen. Many schools schedule ninth grade pupils in five or six classes a day, rather than use an ineffective study hall period. This practice is in line with those of the other junior high school grades. Except in junior high schools, important phases of general education, such as art, music, and homemaking, are still found largely in the columns of elective subjects.

3. Practices in the Better Secondary Schools

Attempts to improve the organization of the curriculum in secondary schools have centered around two general purposes: (1) providing for the common learnings that should be a part of the experiences of all pupils, no matter what their vocational objectives; and (2) achieving a situation for improved learning experiences through better integration of subject content from the various fields. There are secondary schools in all states that are experimenting with a better organization of experiences that constitute the general education of pupils. Although recent emphasis has been on seeking how to provide the common elements, these schools recognize that provision must also be made for specialization to take care of individual differences in abilities, interests, and needs.

The different aspects of the organization of the curriculum will be discussed in this order: first, organization of experiences into units; second, organization of subject content into courses that are broader in nature than many typical courses; third, improved coordination among courses; fourth, provision for common learnings and special interests in the total program of studies; and fifth, the core curriculum as a means of providing for significant common learnings. Each of the first four may illustrate the improvement of either standard practices or the core curriculum. The core is given special attention since it is doubtful whether we shall get marked improvement in the secondary school curriculum until concepts underlying the idea of the core curriculum are accepted. In situations where the core is not permitted, progress can be made toward a more integrated program, as pointed out in the "first steps" at the end of this chapter.

The Unit Organized Around Significant Life Problems.—The unit organization of experiences in the classroom is used by good teachers in growing numbers, especially in the general education areas where it is more applicable than in special fields. The kind of unit considered here is not merely a major subdivision of a course of study into larger blocks of work. It is, instead, an organization of activities and experiences around a central problem or purpose of importance to the group, developed cooperatively by teachers and pupils, exemplifying the experience approach.

In this type of unit, pupils draw on many areas of subject matter to find information to the solution of a problem. For example, a group may plan to study the problem of what forces operate in the disagreement between the United States and Russia. Information would need to be drawn from history, government, and economics to understand what are the basic differences and the causes for them. The study of propaganda and human relations would be involved. Science and its influence on the modern world would not be neglected. At the same time, pupils would be speaking, writing, and using tool skills in gathering information.

Examples of units that draw from various subject fields for information to solve problems are the following, included in the seventh grade social studies program at Wilson Junior High School, Wilson, Arkansas:

> Improved Community Health
> Housing Affects Our Community
> Room Beautification
> Educational Opportunities Offered by the Secondary Schools

At the Floodwood High School, Floodwood, Minnesota, these units were included in the tenth grade general education (core) course in 1948-49:

> Unit on Credit
> Early Minnesota History
> Reading for Pleasure
> Geography of the States
> School Handbook (the development of a handbook)
> School Store (run by a committee)

Broadening the Base of Experiences in Courses.—In working to improve the learning situation, courses with a broader base of subject content are replacing narrower courses. In junior high schools, this trend is particularly noticeable. Seldom are geography and history found as separate subjects in forward-looking junior high schools. Science includes a broad area in the course, general science. The course in problems of democracy, usually offered in the twelfth grade, is another example. Several schools, instead of giving the entirely inadequate course in ancient history, have changed to community civics or a broader course in social studies for the ninth grade. In the latter, for example, subject matter may be selected from the areas of community government, economics, history, sociology, problems of the school society, and other personal problems of the pupils. In junior colleges, or extended secondary schools, survey courses in literature, science, and social studies are sometimes offered.

Newer courses that have been added to the high school curriculum to meet the needs of youth in the modern world often center around current problems or developments in society and around life problems that face youth. When a course deals with problems of such nature, it necessarily draws from a wider area of subject matter, cutting across the traditional fields. Examples of such courses are these, taken from the programs of studies of selected high schools:

Consumer buying	Art in home and clothing
Home nursing	Personal development
Personal living	American life
International relations	Applied science

Moving Away from Compartmentalization.—In secondary schools where teachers and principals see the education of youth as a total process, attempts are being made to break down the departmental barriers between subjects. Teachers work consciously to help pupils see relationships between different subjects. Different ways are used:

1. The correlation of subjects taught by different teachers: for example, art and social studies.
2. One teacher teaching the same pupils in two classes and correlating or integrating much of the work: as history and English. This plan is most common in the junior high school.
3. Weekly planning, during periods scheduled for that purpose, by teachers who teach a common group of pupils.
4. Discussing all-school curriculum problems in department and department head meetings.
5. Part-time cooperative education programs, in which pupils work half a day and relate a good deal of their program to the job during the other half day.
6. The core curriculum in which the secondary school employs the same principles as the elementary school in its self-contained classroom and in which there is a complete breakdown of walls between related subject fields.

Emphasis on a Well-Balanced Program of Common Learnings in the Junior High School.—Since each of the major subject areas has been divided into specific courses, the question that confronts the secondary school staff is how to assure each pupil a balanced program of general education and still leave him time for specialization. In order to take care of this need, new units are often included in existing required courses to take care of the general education needs, or additional "units" beyond the usual sixteen may be required for graduation. The core curriculum, however, has been one of the outstanding contributions of the twentieth-century school to the solution of the matter of providing common learnings.

In junior high schools, a major portion of the program is generally included as required subjects, especially in the seventh and eighth grades. The trend is to require a larger block of the common learnings in the ninth grade as well, with provision for individual differences within the courses. The junior high schools of Amarillo, Texas, for example, have set up the entire seventh grade program as common learnings as follows:

	Periods Per Week
Language Arts	5
Arithmetic	5
Social Studies	5
Art	(2 or 3)
Music	(2 or 3)
Physical Education & Health	(2 or 3)
Science	(2 or 3)
Industrial Arts or Homemaking	5

In the eighth grade, both music and art are required for a full semester, five periods per week.

The program of studies for the seventh and eighth grades in the University Demonstration High School, Morgantown, West Virginia, is basically all common learnings, with a few choices:

	Units Required in Each Grade (7 and 8)
Integrative or Core Activity	2
General Mathematics	1
Physical Education	¼
General Shop or Crafts and Arts	½
Vocal Music or Instrumental Music	½
General Science (Boys)	½
Home Economics	½

It will be noted that pupils are scheduled for the full day, or practically the full day, in classes rather than in study halls for a part of the day. Also illustrated is a well-balanced program of general education, attained through offering certain courses, such as music and art, for less than five periods a week and through the core activity, supplemented by other important common learnings.

Provision for Common Learnings in the Senior or Four-Year High School.—

1. Revised graduation requirements.

Some secondary schools have broadened their requirements for graduation from high school to include more of the commonly accepted areas of general education. Music and art, although accepted by many educators as important for all pupils, are very seldom included as a constant, or required, subject in the program of studies. In some states, the schools are no longer restricted by graduation requirements set by the state department of education. There is a trend toward requiring more units for graduation. Many schools have added to the usual twelve units required in the senior high school, or sixteen in a four-year high school, some requiring as many as twenty or more.[4] In a number of cases, these units represent credit for extraclass activities. The trend is also to include only the three senior high school years as graduation requirements.

The following examples of graduation requirements illustrate some of these different trends:

New Trier Township High School, Winnetka, Illinois
(A Four-Year High School)

	Years Required
English	3
Social Science	2
Science	1
Physical Education	4
Art Appreciation	½
Physiology, Music Appreciation,	
Vocational Guidance (6 weeks each)	½

Other courses elected to meet the graduation requirements of 85 "credits," which, according to the definition of a credit by this school, are about the equivalent of 17 units. (Requirements are listed in terms of years for purposes of clarity.)

East High School, Denver, Colorado
(A Senior High School)

	Units
General Education	1
Reading	½
Composition English	½
American History	1
Physical Education (4 semesters)	1
Health Education	½
Electives	10½
Total	15 units (in three years)

---

[4] A "unit" is defined as a course taken one hour daily, five days a week for a full year (two semesters). The term "credit" is used in connection with secondary schools to refer to a course taken five days a week one hour a day for a semester. Thus, sixteen units equal thirty-two credits. A confusing factor about this terminology is the practice of assigning only partial "credit" (½, ¼, etc.) to such subjects as physical education or music taken the same length of time.

Sequoia Union High School, Redwood City, California
(A Four-Year High School)

	Semester Periods [5]
Orientation	10
English	40
Social Studies	20
Mathematics	10
Science	20
Homemaking (Girls)	10
Physical Education	40
Electives	50 to 90
Total	200 to 240

2. Provision for common learnings in the program of studies.

There is a tendency in secondary schools to increase the proportion of constants to insure well-rounded preparation for life, e.g., more units of social studies, art, crafts, music, home and family living, and the like. Both the preceding and the following examples of programs of studies illustrate this trend in various degrees.

When we examine the curricula in schools whose program of studies is arranged according to the multiple curriculum plan, we often find a richer program of general education offered to noncollege than to college preparatory groups. For example, the cooperative home economics curriculum of Springfield High School, Springfield, Vermont, includes attention to the homemaking area for both boys and girls, a practice that is rather unusual among secondary schools. The whole program includes a larger number of important areas than usual among the common learnings:

COOPERATIVE HOME ECONOMICS CURRICULUM
Springfield High School, Springfield, Vermont

Ninth Grade

Required:
    English
    General Science
    Elementary Social Studies
    Physical Education

Electives: (elect 2)
    Home Economics I (for girls)
    Arts and Crafts
    Art
    General Business Training

Tenth Grade

Required:
    English
    World History
    Physical Education
    Home Economics I (Boys)

Electives:
    Home Economics II (for girls who
      have had Home Ec. I)
    Arts and Crafts
    Art
    General Business Training

[5] Ten semester periods are the equivalent of one year unit. Two hundred semester periods are required for graduation. In other words, in this school pupils would take the equivalent of five daily courses and may take six.

Eleventh Grade

Required:
Cooperative Home Economics (cafeteria) *
English
U.S. History
Physical Education

Twelfth Grade

Required:
Cooperative Home Economics (on-the-job experience) *
English
Social Studies
Physical Education

* In the junior year, the pupils receive twenty periods of training in the cafeteria; in the senior year, they spend twenty to twenty-five hours a week in job experience in commercial institutions. Two units are given for each of these courses.

In the general curriculum of Avenal High School, Avenal, California, such aspects of general education as shop work, child care, psychology, and homemaking are given prominent places among the required subjects. The electives, including music, art, and many others, are not listed here:

GENERAL CURRICULUM

Avenal High School, Avenal, California

Ninth Grade	*Tenth Grade*
English IB	English IIB
Physical Education	Physical Education
Orientation	Mechanical Drawing
General Mathematics	Biology or General Science
General Shop or Home Economics	Metal Shop II
1 Elective	Home Nursing and Child Care
	1 Elective

Eleventh Grade	*Twelfth Grade*
English IIIB	English IVB
Physical Education	Physical Education
U.S. History	Senior Psychology
Interior Decoration and Household	Advanced Shop or Auto Mechanics II
Management	Advanced Food and Clothing
2 Electives	2 Electives

A bulletin [6] of Highland Park High School, Highland Park, Illinois, written to assist pupils in selecting courses, stresses the desirability of a balanced education:

In the four years here your program should reveal some recognition of a a well-rounded life. Since education is a matter of learning to live better, our courses reflect the specific aspects of living that make up a person's life. Once you have planned a four-year program, test it by seeing if in the 32 or more

[6] *Highland Park High School Curriculum Bulletin* (mimeographed), 1947-48, pp. 1-2.

semester courses you have selected that there is provision for education for *all* the areas of living listed below—the areas that play a part in a well-rounded life.

(1) Training in living with others, cooperation, assuming responsibilities in the group life, respecting the other fellow, developing civic pride and civic consciousness, etc.

(2) Better understanding a person's relationship to his natural and physical environment.

(3) Development in physical, mental, and emotional health.

(4) Experience in the arts, in expressing one's self with the hands or through music, esthetic development, better appreciating the beauty of life, developing one's taste and appreciations of the good things of life, etc.

(5) Self-advancement, self-realization, improvement of one's self in all desirable lines as one looks ahead to maximum efficiency in the occupation, the home, and the community.

It should be noted that in this school, in a single "curriculum" plan, the pupil is advised to choose electives to round out a well-balanced general education in addition to the required subjects, the

Program of Studies

Highland Park High School
Highland Park, Illinois
1947-48

Ninth Grade

Required:

English 1, 2
 or
Core Curriculum 1, 2
Mathematics 1, 2 (Alg.)
 or
Consumer Math. 1, 2
Gym. 1 and Health
Science here or in any
 other year

Elective Courses:

Art 1, 2
Exploratory Art 1, 2
SS 3, 4 (English Hist.)
Freshman Civics, SS 1-2
General Science 1, 2
Introduction to Business
 1, 2
Home Economics 1, 2
 (Foods & Clothing)
Industrial Arts 1, 2

French 1, 2
German 1, 2
Italian 1, 2
Latin 1, 2
Spanish 1, 2
Band
Chorus
Orchestra
Training Band
Music History and Ap-
 preciation

Tenth Grade

English 3, 4
 or
CC (English 3-4-Biology
 1, 2) or
CC (English 3, 4-SS 7, 8,
 Modern European His-
 tory)
Gym. 2 (see bulletin for
 choices)

Art 3, 4
Auto Mechanics 3, 4
Biology 1, 2
College Typing 1, 2
Commercial Arith. 1, 2
Crafts 1, 2
Global Geography
Harmony
Home Ec. 6, 7 (Interior
 Decoration)
Mathematics 3, 4 (Geom-
 etry)

SS 7, 8 (Mod. European
 History)
Mechanical Drawing 3, 4,
 7
SS 5, 6 (World History)
Machine Shop 3, 4
Typing 1, 2
French 3, 4
German 3, 4
Italian 3, 4
Latin 3, 4
Spanish 3, 4
Wood Shop 3, 4

Eleventh Grade

English 5, 6
    or
CC (SS 11, 12-E 5, 6)
Gym. (see bulletin for choices)

Art 5, 6
Chemistry
Consumer Science
Crafts 3, 4
Drama 1, 2
English 13, 14 (Journalism)
Homemaking 3, 4
Mathematics 5, 6 (Advanced Algebra)
Mechanical Drawing 5, 6, 8
Physics 1, 2
Pre-Flight Aeronautics
SS 9 (Ancient History)

SS 13, 14 (Present Day Problems)
SS 15 (Latin-American Problems)
French 5, 6
Latin 5, 6
Spanish 5, 6
Bookkeeeping 1, 2
Consumer Education
Commercial Geography
Salesmanship
Commercial Law
Shorthand 1, 2
Typing 3, 4
Trade Courses, Auto Trades, Bldg. Trades

Twelfth Grade

SS 11, 12 (American History) if CC (SS 11, 12-E 5, 6) is not taken

Art 7, 8
English 7, 8 (English Literature)
English 9a, 9b (Business English)
English 10a, 10b (Modern Literature)
English 11, 12 (Public Speaking)

Math. 7 (Solid Geometry & Spherical Trigonometry)
Math. 8 (Trigonometry)
French 7, 8
Latin 7, 8
Spanish 7, 8
Shorthand 3, 4
Office Practice

core curriculum (CC) classes and others. But—most important of all—the selection is to be made first in terms of a good general education rather than in terms of preparation for college or of future vocational plans.

Provision for Special Needs and Interests.—In the program of studies of the Highland Park High School, it is evident that there is a rich opportunity for pupils to specialize in different areas or to sample different fields in which they may be interested. The pupil could take considerable work in art or industrial arts, for example. He could find it possible to develop his talents in the field of music. Or he could specialize further in the fields of science, business education, or mathematics. Special work in drama or public speaking or language will meet other interests.

In all four grades, there is opportunity to elect courses that fit special needs. Pupils may often choose, under competent guidance, courses listed as electives for other grades as well. It should be noted in the above example that there are few common courses in the eleventh and twelfth grades. It is also obvious that pupils can select courses to fit many vocational or college preparatory needs from a program of studies of this type.

The Core Curriculum as a Basis for Common Learnings.—Over a period of years, a number of secondary schools have been developing a core curriculum in order to provide common learnings, using an experience approach. This is one of the most significant developments in recent years in the secondary school curriculum. It is not the final answer to provision for youth needs, for final answers are not characteristic of a democratic society. Some schools have abandoned its use after a trial. But where it has been gradually introduced and studied carefully by staff and administration and—most important of all—accepted by the teachers, it has generally succeeded and is being constantly improved upon. It is a hopeful development out of which the organization of the secondary school curriculum provides for better learning experiences.

The core curriculum as defined in Chapter 4 is a type of organization of school experiences in the school day. These experiences are regarded as important common learnings, certain ways of behaving that all should have. However, the core is not merely a "form" of organization; it has definite educational characteristics. In this section will be discussed the general characteristics and organization of the core; the experiences in core classes will be considered in Chapter 8.

1. The core curriculum is generally scheduled for a longer block of time than one period a day.

At the Ohio State University School, the core classes are scheduled for a three-hour period in the junior high school grades. In some schools, the core classes occupy half of the day in the seventh and eighth grades, two periods in the ninth and tenth grades, and only one period in the eleventh and twelfth grades. Admittedly, the purposes of the core curriculum cannot be adequately carried out if only one period is devoted to it.

2. The content of the core classes is drawn from more than one subject field to solve problems that meet the interests and needs common to all pupils at a particular maturity level. The experiences in dealing with these problems are those considered necessary to participate effectively in a democratic society.

In this plan, differentiation of materials and activities to suit individual needs is made within the class. Social studies and English are the areas most frequently drawn upon, but mathematics, science, art, music, and other areas are often sources of information and activities. Social studies, English, health, and general science are the subjects most often replaced by the core. Attempts to have the core take care of all experiences for mathematics, art, and music have not been very successful. It is not merely a matter of fusing subjects, however, but drawing upon any needed subject content in a problem situation. Outside of the core classes, opportunity for specialization in other areas is possible, including the areas of social studies and English.

The problem areas for the core curriculum in the senior high school grades of the Ohio State University School are illustrative of the types of content included : [7]

> School Living
> Problems of Healthful Living
> Problems of Living in an Urban Society
> Problems of the Family as a Basic Social Unit
> The Development of the American Scene
> Problems of Living in the Atomic Age
> The Problem of Establishing Beliefs
> The Problems of Making a Living (Exploring Vocations)
> Current World Problems
> Problems of Producer-Consumer Economics
> Implications of Scientific Advancement
> Major Conflicting Ideologies
> The Bases for Determining Values by Which We Live

3. Group and individual guidance functions are an integral part of the core curriculum.

Since pupils spend more than one period a day with the teacher, he will have many opportunities to study them as individuals and assist them with their problems. Records of the pupils are kept by the teacher, who is sometimes known as the core counselor. Aspects of group guidance, usually a part of the home room, are absorbed into the core class.

At Smiley Junior High School in Denver, Colorado, the general education course stresses group guidance. The general education teachers have a class for two periods in seventh or eighth grade, and one in the ninth grade, with the thirty-five pupils in the class as their counselees. They follow through the same group of pupils until they graduate and may again pick up one or two general education classes. Included in the units in this course are such phases of group guidance as orientation to Smiley Junior High School, how to study, and get-

---

Adapted from *Tentative Statements of Core Program for Grades 10, 11 and 12* (mimeographed), Columbus, Ohio: Ohio State University School, Ohio State University, p. 5.

ting ready for high school. Meetings with parents form a part of the program to understand the pupils and their problems.

4. The organization of the curriculum within the core is generally arranged in large units of the experience type.

The study of problems of pupils and of contemporary society, and the emphasis on guidance in the core curriculum, is in line with the experience approach to curriculum development.

Statements about the core procedure in Denby High School, Detroit, Michigan, and the contents of the ninth and tenth grade core courses [8] illustrate how schools using the core curriculum are tending toward the experience approach.

The essence of the method of Core teaching is the *arrangement of opportunities* for pupils to work in situations which seem fundamental to the education of an individual in a democracy, namely cooperative thinking and working and the ability to solve problems when they arise. This necessitates giving boys and girls as many opportunities as possible *to make decisions which are of importance to them* and which, because of this importance, seem to them worthy of their consideration.

1. The content of Core courses in the 9th and 10th grades is not predetermined with the exception of three units, an orientation unit and a unit on Democracy in the 9th grade, and a unit on English grammar in the 10th grade. With these exceptions it is determined by the pupils and is based on needs and interests as expressed by them. The subject matter is unlimited.

  a) The subject matter selected by Core classes to date has been largely of a personal interest type in the ninth grade. Toward the end of the ninth and throughout the succeeding grades the problems selected lean increasingly more toward larger social problems.

The core teacher and teachers from specialized areas spend considerable time planning together for each particular group of pupils. This is the type of planning that gives the teacher greater leeway and, at the same time, the confidence and background necessary for pupil-teacher planning of experiences in the classroom. In Smiley Junior High School, Denver, every teacher has one planning period a day; therefore, it is possible for teachers to plan together for specific groups of pupils and for counseling individual pupils. Planning meetings are held every two to three weeks.

5. In each core group are included pupils of varying abilities and interests.

---

[8] *Selected Aspects of the Denby Educational Program* (mimeographed), Detroit, Michigan: Edwin Denby High School, 1948.

The core curriculum plan is not likely to be accompanied by permanent grouping or to result in social segregation and undesirable distinctions on the basis of future occupations. In the secondary schools in which the core is carried on successfully, pupils are placed heterogeneously in core classes. Since the experiences in the core are supposed to be common learnings basic to all, grouping into classes on the basis of intelligence or future vocations would be out of place. One of the essential experiences of living in a democratic society is learning how to live with others different from one's self in abilities, vocational objectives, social level, ethnic grouping, race, or family background.

The core curriculum is still in its experimental stage in American secondary education. It may go through many modifications before it is generally adopted. Larger school systems or laboratory schools connected with universities and colleges have generally tended to be more receptive to the idea. In a study of common learnings in secondary schools of the United States, Umstattd found that among 267 schools reported to have some program of common learnings, 24 per cent used the core curriculum, or some other type employing the same principles but known by a different name, such as unified studies, general education class, common learnings course, core course, basic course, integrated course, or social living class.[9] This study dealt with a selected group of secondary schools. A study to determine how many high schools include a core type of course, made by the Office of Education in 1949, revealed that only 3.5 per cent of the high schools in the nation had some type of core.[10]

4. FIRST STEPS

Most secondary school leaders are agreed that the curriculum organization which represents compartmentalization and division rather than integration and unity is not in accord with principles of a good educational program. But the weight of tradition hangs heavily over the concepts of what a secondary school program should be like. Parents demand Latin for its prestige value; colleges ask for a pattern of subjects in the face of overwhelming evidence that no combination or pattern of subjects will assure greater college success.

---

[9] From a mimeographed statement, *The Common-Learnings Program in the American School,* furnished by J. G. Umstattd, Professor of Secondary Education, University of Texas.
[10] Grace S. Wright, *Core Curriculum in Public High Schools: An Inquiry into Practices, 1949,* Bulletin No. 5, Washington, D.C.: Federal Security Agency, Office of Education, Government Printing Office, 1950, p. 28.

The following recommendations relate to the initial steps that can be taken in moving toward the principles of curriculum organization discussed at the beginning of this chapter. Many of these steps can obviously be taken only by a school staff, not by the teacher alone.

1. A school staff might begin with the study of what courses individual graduates have taken, in order to determine how balanced a general education they have received. Such an analysis could lead into a consideration of what should be the nature of a basic general education for all pupils and how the program can be changed to provide for it.

2. Many schools that have used the multiple curriculum plan of organization are gradually abandoning the fixed curricula, and are instead providing a common program, first, for ninth grade pupils, with plans to extend the plan later if it proves successful.

3. A number of schools are requiring more subjects for graduation. This seems to be a step that can be taken without a great deal of fuss since it is not too difficult in most schools to convince pupils, parents, and teachers that the typical study hall is a waste of educational time, a place where bad study habits are developed. In this way, provisions can be made for additional areas of general education.

4. There is precedent in the junior high school grades for having all or at least several of the general subjects taught by the same teacher. Only as junior high schools sought to ape the senior high school did the extreme departmentalization begin. Again, the transition could be made beginning with the seventh, eighth, or ninth grade, with one teacher responsible for at least two subjects. The teacher can volunteer to take this step on an experimental basis.

5. Any teacher who believes in the principles of the core could ask to teach two subjects, such as social studies and English, to the same group of pupils. This is one of the best ways of beginning to move toward a core curriculum.

6. In other school situations, where a number of teachers are interested in a core plan, the school can begin with an experimental group of pupils under their direction, with the entire faculty participating in the study and its evaluation. Often such an experimental plan can be started by a few interested teachers.

7. A change from differentiation through addition of courses to differentiation by adapting materials within courses by each teacher would go a long way toward solving the problems of providing for common learnings. Such a change calls for co-

operative study by the staff to develop the "know-how." *It is one of the most significant "first steps" that could be taken to improve the curriculum of the secondary school.*

SELECTED REFERENCES

ALBERTY, HAROLD. *Reorganizing the High-School Curriculum.* New York: The Macmillan Co., 1947, chaps. 6, 8.—This is a well-illustrated discussion of the core curriculum and the nature of unit teaching. The entire book helps to clarify the point of view behind the core.

DOUGLASS, HARL R. (ed.). *The High School Curriculum.* New York: The Ronald Press Co., 1947, chaps. 9, 18.—Integration, fusion, and correlation of the curriculum are considered. The matter of differentiated and single curricula is discussed from a point of view different from that in this chapter.

EDUCATIONAL POLICIES COMMISSION. *Education for ALL American Youth.* Washington, D.C.: National Education Association, 1944, 421 pp.—Recommended as indispensable reading for a student of secondary education. Two hypothetical secondary schools and communities, Farmville and American City, are described, indicating how a more closely integrated curriculum organization is achieved. The core course here is termed "common learnings."

GILES, H. H., McCUTHCHEN, S. P., and ZECHIEL, A. N. *Exploring the Curriculum.* New York: Harper & Bros., 1942, chap. 11.—Discusses the core curriculum and other reorganization of subjects in the twenty-nine schools that participated in the Eight-Year Study of the Progressive Education Association.

GRUHN, WILLIAM T., and DOUGLASS, HARL R. *The Modern Junior High School.* New York: The Ronald Press Co., 1947, chap. 5.—Points out trends in curriculum organization in the junior high school. Contains additional sample programs of study.

KRUG, EDWARD A. *Curriculum Planning.* New York: Harper & Bros., 1950, pp. 121-33 and 142-51.—These pages supplement the present chapter on scope and sequence.

LEONARD, J. PAUL. *Developing the Secondary School Curriculum.* New York: Rinehart & Co., Inc., 1946, chaps. 12, 13.—A chapter on the core curriculum and one on units of work contain many examples from schools.

MUDD, DOROTHY. *A Core Program Grows.* Bel Air, Maryland: Board of Education of Hartford County, 1949, 138 pp.—Includes a complete description of how the core developed in this county and what records, materials of instruction, teacher-pupil planning, and other specifics are found in the core program.

THUT, I. N., and GERBERICH, J. RAYMOND. *Foundations of Method for Secondary Schools.* New York: McGraw-Hill Book Co., Inc., 1949, chap. 4.—This chapter by Vernon E. Anderson explores further the question of the kind of curriculum organization appropriate to a democratic school philosophy.

Chapter 7

CLASS EXPERIENCES—COMMON LEARNINGS

The previous three chapters have been concerned with the teacher's function in curriculum development, the approach that he makes to planning curriculum experiences, and the organizational setting for those experiences. This chapter and the two following will center on the curriculum as it is and as it should be developed in secondary school classes. Since the curriculum is defined in terms of experiences of pupils, these three chapters on the common and specialized learnings are a discussion of the kinds of experiences youth have and ought to have in their classes. These experiences are with subject matter, in the broader concept. However, a description of the subject content alone would fall short of indicating what the curriculum is like. The student is referred at the end of the chapter to other recent sources that summarize the trends in different subject fields of the high school curriculum, such as *The High School Curriculum*.[1]

As previously mentioned, when we speak of common learnings, we do not mean that all pupils should do the same thing or study the same books in their classes. Instead, we are concerned with developing some integrating experiences that build desired attitudes, skills, and understandings for democratic participation in the society in which these young people live. We want all youth to have in common an opportunity to share in planning classroom work and regulations, for example, or to experience the joy of creating something of their own. The teacher plans situations in which these things can happen. What happens to pupils is the focal point of our attention on the curriculum of the secondary school.

1. The Principles

The common, integrating experiences that all youth should have in the secondary school ought to include subject content, problems, and activities that challenge them to sincere and fruitful exploration of the world in which they live.

---

[1] Harl R. Douglass (ed.), New York: The Ronald Press Co., 1947, 661 pp.

In their courses that include the common learnings, youth should have an opportunity to explore the social and the scientific world of which they are a part. Youth are interested in the world about them, in the tremendous problems facing our society, and the fascinating advances in science. They are constantly in contact with these developments through newspapers, radio, books, and the community. It is the school's responsibility to see that many resources are at hand for further stimulating and widening those interests, and to guide those interests. However, these issues can be approached in a formal, impersonal manner that leads to rote memorization and copying materials from reference books instead of the investigating and seeking that come from a sincere desire to learn. The subject matter of these courses must come from the concerns and the lives of the American people in a world of today. But this world must be more than an adult society; it must be the world in which the young people live, their concerns for their own school and community as well as the larger focus. Only thus can the real challenge that arouses the spirit of inquiry be secured.

The common learning experiences should satisfy the needs and goals of young people which grow out of their own personal problems and interests concerning themselves and their relations with others.

In Chapter 3 it was pointed out that youth have a need for experiencing personal achievement, adjusting to the family group, being socially accepted, and the like. These are real life concerns. Any high school curriculum that neglects them is apt to be bogged down by some deadwood of adult interests. The above principle is complementary to the preceding one. Both are vital to a well-balanced education.

The secondary school curriculum needs to give adolescents a chance to deal with their problems : their health, mental and physical ; their relations with their peers and with adults ; their immediate social life. Do all secondary school pupils have these opportunities ? Do schools consider that the lives of pupils in their own society are as important and significant as their future adult lives ? We need to consider the number of pupils who are taking courses that are concerned with problems of home and family living, for example, or the amount of attention given to good grooming, sex problems, and mental health. These are certainly the concern of all young people, not of a selected few.

The common learnings should make provision for a variety of experiences adjusted to individual differences and appropriate to the maturity of the group.

What consideration is given to individuality in a curriculum made up primarily of reading books and verbalizing? In order to build on personal strengths and to develop to the fullest the potentialities of each individual, the curriculum needs to be rich in experiences in creating, constructing, meeting people, experimenting, dramatizing, organizing and evaluating, seeing, listening, and making direct contacts with the community. Secondary school classes that are the medium for general education might have a number of such different kinds of activities going on at the same time. There should be varied experiences that will develop the attitudes and understandings needed by an intelligent citizen in a democracy. Important among these, for example, would be the skills of living together and operating as a democratic group. Uniformity will not develop individuality or encourage the differences valued by a democracy.

This principle means, too, that when written materials are used they should be appropriate to the pupil's maturity and his ability level. A one-textbook curriculum to be studied by all in a group of pupils who vary six grade levels in ability is not a practical or realistic one. Anything that the particular group sets out to do, or has assigned to them, should be suited to their maturity and their interests. The choice of books for English literature would be vastly different in many high schools if this principle were followed.

Pupils in secondary schools ought to work on tasks in which they can succeed, the accomplishment of which will contribute to their security and respect for themselves and their capabilities.

This principle is closely related to the previous one, for success cannot be achieved unless the curriculum is adjusted to individual differences. The principle is, however, significant in itself for judging the kind of curriculum that actually exists in the day-by-day work in the classroom of secondary schools. It is a common experience that all pupils should have. If pupils are constantly given tasks beyond their abilities, they have a very definite kind of experience that results in a change in their behavior, but certainly not the kind of change that schools consider desirable. Any tasks pupils are asked to perform must be achievable in order to be integrating and satisfying. What happens to the individual who is continuously blocked and frustrated in an atmosphere of authoritarianism, failure, and fear?

On the other hand, where the pupil can make use of his talents and interests in contributing to the group, his experiences in the secondary school will strengthen his confidence in himself and his respect for himself as an individual. We need to examine seriously what is happening to individuals or groups of low academic ability in the secondary schools.

The secondary school must provide youth with opportunities for sharing in classroom experiences devoted to planning, developing, and evaluating.

The common learnings in the secondary school curriculum should give youth a great deal of practice in democratic procedures. To the extent that their maturity permits, they should have a part in managing their own experiences in the classroom, helping to make decisions governing what goes on in the class. The authoritarian classroom, where the teacher makes all decisions, does not serve the educational purposes of American schools. If pupils are to have the most effective learning experiences, they should be able to participate in setting their own goals, in planning with the teacher the activities and experiences to achieve those goals, and in constantly checking up on themselves to see if they are making progress toward their goals. It is inconceivable that teachers should make all these decisions in educating young people for democratic living.

In the classrooms of secondary schools that serve democratic purposes, pupils ought to do these things:

Make group decisions and carry them out
Express themselves freely without fear of recrimination by the teacher
Assume responsibility for the appearance of the room
Participate in making rules by which they live
Participate in orderly parliamentary procedure
Select leaders and serve as group leaders
Work in committee and small group situations
Practice techniques of group dynamics
Use the conference method of settling disputes
Exercise responsibility for their own and others' conduct.

In such a situation pupils would not be floundering around or creating chaos, but consciously and carefully planning their purposes and then working at their plan, ready to revise it when it proves cumbersome or unworkable. Cooperative study helps to solve the problem of motivation because pupils are working on their purposes. It is a much superior atmosphere for good mental hygiene, since teacher and pupils are partners in the classroom. The common experiences should be those that develop democratic values through a constant consideration of human values in both thinking and action.

The secondary school should give many opportunities for investigation of different points of view, sources of data, and factual information, and for making choices based on intelligent inquiry.

The undergraduate student of education would recognize at once the difference between a classroom in which this principle is put into operation and one in which the teacher is the hearer of lessons and the textbook the final word. We are all familiar with the teacher who stifles inquiry by having pupils repeat orally, or in a test, what the textbook says, or who squelches curiosity and initiative by taking an adamant position on controversial issues. Teachers in secondary schools who stimulate questioning, who lead youngsters to delve into new sources of information, and who welcome an opinion different from their own are the ones who help to develop the inquiring mind. In their classes, groups do research on different aspects of the problems studied. As a result, pupils learn how to question information and to seek the correct sources.

Cooperative study and investigation by young people should create opportunities for action.

Pupils who just study about things are apt to see little relationship between what they study and their own lives. True, many classroom topics have had little relation to contemporary life. However, many topics are closely related to the life about them, such as the study of intercultural education. Intergroup tensions exist in their own community, both in and out of school. Young people can be guided to decisive action for the improvement of the welfare of others. They need to see that these issues are related to themselves and their own school, and they need to be assisted in doing something about these problems.

Effective participation in a democratic society is a technique that needs to be learned through all avenues of the school, not just in extraclass activities. Right answers in written statements should no longer satisfy secondary school teachers as demonstrating the student's ability and willingness to take the right course of action. Research has pointed out that such an assumption cannot be made. As a part of living and planning together in the classroom on a

cooperative basis—particularly in the social studies and core classes
—youth, as they progress through secondary school, should become
more active participants in a gradually expanding community. Civic
skills are not something that can be expected to happen by magic as
youth leave school and enter civic life. Studies of high school and
college graduates have indicated that civic participation of young
people after they leave school cannot be taken for granted.

*The common learnings in the secondary school should include
varied experiences in creative self-expression.*

Pupils should be able to express themselves through many media:
art, crafts, dancing, dramatics and speech, music, creative writing.
Although there should be opportunities for them to pursue specific
interests and abilities in these fields, all pupils should have some
experiences in these areas of self-expression. The products of such
experiences do not need to meet the social standards of creativity.
However, the teacher needs to know the pupil well in order to help
him. The classroom in the secondary school that encourages individuality as a means to a more interesting and full life will be more
in the nature of a workshop in the broad sense, where teacher and
pupils live and work together in an atmosphere of mutual respect and
understanding.

Creativity has little chance to be nurtured in an atmosphere of
sameness, conformity, and meeting standards set for all. Creativity
refers to "a fresh response, unique to the creator," as defined in
Toward Better Teaching.[2] When the pupil's joys, sorrows, and
angers are repressed, when his individuality is not encouraged, then
his desire to express himself in new ways is dulled. Many an English
classroom, for example, has repressed creativeness through undue
stress on mechanics in all writing done by pupils.

*The secondary school curriculum should include rich and
continuous experiences in the skills of communication and the
necessary practice in computation skills needed by the citizen.*

The Three R's are communication and computation skills to which
modern schools have added many social and creative skills. There
is a need to continue improving skills in reading as well as in speech
and writing during the high school years. Secondary school teachers
have not generally been trained to assist pupils in the improvement

---

[2] Association for Supervision and Curriculum Development, *Toward Better
Teaching* (1949 Yearbook), Washington, D.C.: The National Education Association,
p. 121.

of reading skills, but there is a growing realization of the need. It is doubtful if much progress will be made if communication skills are considered as a prerogative of the English teacher. Every class in science or social studies, for example, is rich in opportunities for explaining, relating experiences, reporting, reading, and writing. Only in classrooms where learning the subject matter is the aim will these important skills be lost sight of. They can be improved in a good learning situation, one in which they are used for a specific and real purpose.

The fact that such opportunities have been continuously neglected is one of the reasons for the trend toward the core curriculum. Educators have long realized that communication skills may be taught more effectively in classes other than the type of English class where they become submerged in an ordeal of theme writing and speeches which lacks meaningful purpose and real life substance. Adding more English courses to the curriculum does not necessarily mean that pupils will have better experiences in communication skills.

In high school, the skills in arithmetic taught in the elementary school need "refreshing" and extending, particularly in their more complicated application to complex life situations. Pupils in higher mathematics courses, as well as pupils who take little or no mathematics in high school, have been found to be deficient in such skills. The improvement of these skills is especially important in the junior high school years. Personal affairs demand ability to deal with mathematical computations. Problems of modern society which are increasingly technical and quantitative need citizens who understand mathematical concepts. The maintaining of the skills, and improvement in cases where needed, might be done through volunteer classes or short-term courses in the upper secondary school rather than through full year or semester courses. Again, these skills need to be taught with meaning and in relation to real life situations inasmuch as possible.

2. Some Typical Practices

This section deals with the types of experiences found in some schools in those courses serving to provide the common learnings. To a large extent, these courses are English, social studies, science, mathematics, health, and physical education. To a much lesser extent, they include home economics (for girls), industrial arts (for boys), art, and music. In fact, in many communities, it is almost exclusively in the junior high schools that these latter courses are considered important enough to be included in the general education of the majority of the pupils. In the illustrations in this section, there is much that is sadly outdated, as judged by principles of a good learning situation and the adolescent's needs. These descriptions of practices are not intended to be average practices. They are, however, practices with which the beginning teacher may come in contact in schools. They are their curriculum, the experiences that a number of boys and girls have in American secondary schools. The following chapter presents the more hopeful side, or the trends toward which American secondary education seems to be moving. In a correct evaluation of what the secondary school is like, a picture of both sides is needed.

Experiences in Studying Problems of Concern to Youth.—In many a school, the observer has to look hard to find any discussion of the real concerns of young people. Often, these problems are relegated to the "extracurricular" area, but even there only a few can be considered. The conscientious, well-liked teacher in such a school probably talks to pupils about their homes, their friends, and, at times, their innermost troubles, but only when she sees them after school is over or between class periods. A great part, at least, of sex education is miseducation, received through friends, the school toilets, smutty magazines and books; sometimes, fortunately, a sounder and more sympathetic approach is achieved through the family doctor or understanding parents. Literature that is full of examples of social and psychological problems of young people may be discussed entirely for its literary merits. The knowledge needed as a consumer of goods, the knowledge about care of the pupil's own clothing, home duties and responsibilities, and home repair may be left to the vocational schools, to the home economics curriculum, or to the forward-looking high schools.

It appears that one of the characteristics of the usual American secondary school curriculum is the storing up of information for future use. There is a great deal of stress on facts that may be useful later, in quiz-program fashion. History classes have moved away from the detailed study of battles in the major wars, toward more of a consideration of the historical trends and political and social movements. However, the stress on knowing facts for their own sake still continues in some schools. The rather close adherence to subject matter organization as the design for curriculum experiences has tended to emphasize the remote and the past. The pupil lives in a fascinating world of scientific developments and world-revolutionary social changes, yet, he may spend most of his time on scientific formulas, outdated scientific principles, chronological history up to 1940, and mathematical abstractions for the specialist. He lives in a golden age of profusion of magazines and books; yet, in many schools, very little of his time is occupied with current literature. He is condemned for reading trash but nothing may be done to cause him or help him choose the good from the poor among current publications.

We need to ask ourselves seriously about the youth needs and problems discussed in Chapter 3. Should they be of no concern to the school curriculum? Is it only the things of concern to adults or to the past that will help youth acquire the desired skills, attitudes, appreciations, and understandings? Is the life of the adolescent period itself of less importance than that of any six years of adulthood?

The home room, core classes, home economics classes, general science classes (in the junior high school), biology classes, and often ninth grade general social studies classes, have been the spearhead for consideration of real youth needs and youth interests in the typical secondary schools. Girls—usually less than half of those in high school—have had a chance to study about care of clothing, good grooming, and personality problems. Biology and general science classes vary from those taught out of a book to those that consider scientific phenomena in everyday living, use the richness of the community and life about them, and consider personal health problems rather than classification of plants and animals as significant learnings for youth. For a number of years, secondary schools throughout the country have been shifting their emphasis in ninth grade social studies from the concerns of ancient Greece and Rome to those of high school youngsters and the social life of their community and their school.

Experiences and Skills Suited to Youth's Own Capabilities.— Although research has shown that differences in ability are great, no matter how pupils are grouped in any one grade, the single textbook for all has predominated in the scene. As a result, many pupils in English, social studies, science, and other general education classes have had the experience of studying books which they could not read with profit because of the difficulty of the vocabulary. Books usually above the average in vocabulary and academic interests have tended to be purchased for a mythical average pupil. At the same time, there has been almost no attempt to measure vocabulary difficulties of secondary school textbooks or to write them from this scientific approach. The usual textbook is a highly condensed account and, therefore, is more difficult reading than the general or "supplementary" books in the school library. The experience of many pupils has consequently been a frustrating one, for they could not possibly understand clearly what they read. Few classes in the common learnings areas have sets of texts suited to different reading ability levels.

More tragic, however, has been the failure in many cases to adjust materials in supposedly homogeneous groups. In some schools, all pupils in slow groups have been required to read Shakespeare's plays or *Ivanhoe* since it was required reading in the English course of study. Rather than choose from literature dealing with the life interests and a culture background the pupils could understand, some schools have resorted to simplified versions of the classics. Others vary the materials for the different groups but not within the group itself.

The belief that everyone should meet certain minimum essentials in each course is held by many teachers in secondary schools. These essentials might be a certain standard in English mechanics, specific minimums of factual knowledge in science or social studies, or a list of books to be read and tested upon. For the slow learner, these standards have been beyond his capability of attainment, or they have been placed so low that they were entirely unrealistic even for the "average" pupil. For the bright pupil, they have been standards of mediocrity that have kept him from doing his best. There has been neither challenge to him nor provision for him to use his capacities to the fullest. Stress on uniformity has created for pupils an experience in dulness and marking time, or has resulted in undesirable learnings of loafing and restless behavior. In most secondary school classes, we will find that pupils are all doing the same thing at the same time, all studying out of the same book on the same assignment, all writing a theme, or all working on certain mathematics problems. Grouping within a class, a practice successfully carried on in elementary schools, is found in few high school classes.

As a consequence, the pupil with special interests and a tremendous capacity and interest for learning is held back, with his curiosity dulled. There has probably been more done for the gifted pupil in special groups than in heterogeneously grouped classes in most schools; the tendency has been to "reward" the most capable teachers with the groups in the upper end of the academic ability scale.

As yet, secondary schools have been slow to provide special help for remediable cases, those whose difficulties arise from social, health, or emotional problems. These adolescents have either found school entirely unsuited to them and have dropped out as soon as possible or have become greater problems, often being grouped with pupils of low academic ability.

The slow-learning pupil, from the standpoint of verbal materials, has generally found his high school experiences a world of books that were hard to grasp, rather than contacts with people, with things, and with life about him, which he could understand and from which he could profit. In some schools, his life has been one of baffling parts of speech and algebraic symbols.

It is in the newer areas of music, art, physical education, home-making, and industrial arts, for example, that the adjustments have been made more readily to differences among pupils. These areas have been more apt to include projects or experiences which a pupil was capable of attaining. Those unable to play the clarinet could sing in large choruses, or listen to good music. The day of all pupils making tie racks in industrial arts classes is fast approaching a close. In physical education, too, there is a more rapid change to a realization that all are not similarly endowed, even to the point that some who need rest find that opportunity in those classes. In art, there is a fortunate trend toward self-expression through different media, rather than perfection, although it is still slow in coming in many schools.

Experiences in Developing Useful Skills and Habits.—One of the common learnings of the secondary school curriculum considered important by all educators is the building and strengthening of skills, most of which had their foundation in the elementary school curriculum. In the main, these skills have tended to be assigned to certain subject areas. For example, skills of speaking and writing have been placed in the English area, without much concern for them in other subject areas except incidentally or through correlation of subjects. Vocabulary study, although of vital importance in reading materials in any subject, has been primarily the concern of English teachers.

When pupils work to improve speaking and writing skills, they may frequently carry on the activities as isolated exercises unrelated to the subject matter in their high school courses or to their ongoing life activities. Speeches may be given simply to practice speaking, not to present important information or to sell a real idea of significance to the youngster. Long themes are apt to be an experience in copying or paraphrasing. Reading skills have received little attention until recently. Now some English teachers are including it in their programs, but few are trained to improve such skills effectively. The emphasis on the classics and literature which are beyond the pupil's reading comprehension has worked against an improvement of reading skills. Listening skills, which are becoming increasingly important, are practically ignored.

The junior high school in its mathematics courses stresses useful arithmetic skills. Except in a few cases, pupils have little opportunity to improve and maintain these skills during their senior high school years. Higher mathematics courses have not always recognized the need for maintenance of those skills. Pupils in commercial curricula or shop courses are more likely to receive additional practice in arithmetic in a practical situation.

Study skills and work habits have received a good deal of attention in recent years, although at times apart from the important question of the teaching procedures used in the class. While the teacher works for improvement in organization for study, the idea that so much ground must be covered in a year's course militates against good study habits. As a result of the haste to cover material without giving attention to how well the job is done, the habit of thoroughness has not been developed. Some teachers believe that it is essential to cover all the phases of a subject, fearing that the pupil may never have another opportunity to learn them!

Experiences of Pupils in Directing and Managing Their Own Activities.—One of the first questions that should be asked about the secondary school in a democracy is: "Do pupils have a chance to experience democracy?" This is not a teaching method but a fundamental principle that either does or does not permeate the classroom atmosphere. The skills and attitudes that grow out of such participation need continuous improvement and refinement from elementary school through college. Yet it is especially in high school and college that youth are regarded as inactive vessels designed to receive knowledge and wisdom. In some secondary schools, the more quietly the pupils sit and take orders from the teacher, the better the situation is regarded. In such an atmosphere, there is little opportunity to make choices in order to grow in the ability to exercise mature judgment.

Many pupils in secondary schools have a day-by-day experience of accepting without question the things that the teacher asks them to do. They do assignments that may appear to have neither meaning nor sense, but traditionally in school it has not been the practice for pupils to question what the teacher demands. More classrooms have daily assignments handed out to pupils than have cooperation in planning what the group is to do to achieve its purposes on a long-range basis. In the former case, few know or accept what the purposes are or what the group has set out to accomplish.

The use of the unit plan for organizing experiences is still in its infancy. The careful planning of a piece of work, carrying through the plan together, and stopping to see what progress is being made, is an infrequent practice, although it has gained more headway in social studies than in other classes in the academic areas. Industrial arts classes have long included more of this type of experience.

The opportunities for pupils to exercise leadership, to practice skills as chairman and as class leader, or to take part in a panel are found more often in English courses that emphasize speech, in some social studies courses conducted as laboratory situations, and in other courses through the making of oral reports.

We can ask, also, what experiences pupils are having in self-direction through managing their classrooms. The making of rules and regulations for classroom living seems to have been entrusted to the primary grades in the sequence of curriculum experiences. Too infrequently do pupils consider together with the teacher regulations concerning chewing gum, meeting visitors, leaving class, or assigning responsibilities for care of blackboards, heat, or light. A classroom in which pupils are learning self-direction can easily be spotted by observing what happens when the teacher leaves the room. Growth, or lack of it, is evident as a result of the kinds of group living and cooperation present. Teacher-dominated classrooms are not conducive to learning democratic skills.

Experiences in Analyzing Social Issues and Taking Action for Human Welfare.—The case cannot be made too strong for giving high school pupils continuing experience in critical study of the live social, political, and economic problems facing the world, the nation, the state, and the community. Practices such as the following— prevalent in a considerable number of secondary schools—are not conducive to intelligent inquiry and interest in current social problems:

1. History is studied as an end in itself. In other words, the stress is placed upon historical facts and events without any conscious attempt to bring those facts to bear on clarifying present happenings. The learning of innumerable dates is fortunately on the decline, for movements in history are regarded as of greater importance. The study of the history of the presidency of the United States to throw light on the presidential powers and relationships with Congress, or the study of the historical background of India to understand the turmoil in that country, is still a rare type of approach.

2. In American history classes, even though many of the pupils have not taken world history, little time is spent on the background of other countries to determine how their relations with and attitudes toward the United States have developed.

3. More recent developments, being left to the last, are often neglected or never reached at all in the history course. Some schools, in order to avoid this mistake, have instituted current events days once a week in history classes. Although the practice has brought contemporary material into the course, such content may still be fairly unrelated to the study taking place the remainder of the week.

4. Social problems courses have often become formalized, bookish, and out-of-date. While world-shaking events take place outside the school, pupils may confine their study to the textbook. The question of poverty is not real to pupils unless they investigate what the community and state do for people and what has resulted from poverty in their own community. Labor-management relations have many sources of learning in any industrial community.

5. Closely related is the study of controversial issues. In many secondary schools the teacher, for various reasons, is afraid to deal with such questions. In these schools, pupils are being deprived of the chance to learn how to examine critically all sides of the question. The study of the nature of communism, Russia, corruption in local politics, and even socialized medicine may be taboo because of the mistaken belief that keeping such facts from young people is the best way to help them develop into good American citizens. Communism cannot withstand critical analysis and thinking based on facts; we have but to note the thought control used in communistic countries, a practice that has no place in a democratic society or its schools.

The social action necessary to democratic citizenship is often missing as an outcome of secondary school social studies. Follow-up studies, such as the Regents' Survey in New York State [3] and other studies of graduates and dropouts, have shown that many youth do not participate actively in civic affairs after leaving high school. The type of experience that pupils have had in high school may have improved their ability to verbalize about the situation but not their skill in initiating and executing a course of action. In most schools, pupils have studied *about* social conditions rather than making plans of action to bring about improvement. Knowing how to give the right answers on paper is accepted as evidence that the pupil is willing to act effectively as a citizen, and knows how to do so. Action for improvement of human welfare in the community has been shied away from, and, more significant, the same type of action in the school community has never been fully utilized in social studies classes

---

[3] Ruth Eckert and T. O. Marshall, *When Youth Leave School,* New York: McGraw-Hill Book Co., Inc., 1938, 360 pp.

as suitable content. We are more likely to find futile mayor-for-a-day projects or mock elections than the careful study of real school elections or an examination of city government at first hand to discover what it is doing about community problems.

Experiences in Scientific Inquiry.—The careful examination of facts and the testing of hypotheses to arrive at sound conclusions should not be confined to the field of science. These are desirable skills and attitudes that apply to many areas of living. Yet, there are still too many classrooms where pupils have the kinds of experiences that cannot possibly result in these outcomes. In a visit to such a classroom, we would see the teacher leading the recitation from the front of the room with a book in hand, orally quizzing the pupils on page after page of the assignment, occasionally interspersing comments of his own to amplify the text. Pupils would raise their hands and give answers as they recalled them from the book. They would strive to figure out the teacher's "system" of calling upon pupils.

What is the curriculum for the pupils in this class? What is happening to them? Their experience is one of repeating information given in a book, memorizing facts, interpreting an author's meaning, outguessing the teacher, accepting the written word or spoken word as truth, and accepting one person's point of view as final. This type of curriculum would be a far cry from one that promotes scientific inquiry: weighing of information, suspending judgment, using many sources of data, reasoning from facts, and arriving at sound conclusions.

The use of sources other than the textbook is often confined to reports assigned by the teachers, for which the information is gathered from reference books and encyclopedias. Few people in the school or in the community are questioned as to their opinion on the problem. There is often more copying than weighing of information. In such a situation, the gathering of data is not an enterprise that grows out of planning together on a challenging problem. Laboratory work in the sciences may simply require following directions instead of scientific inquiry; filling in blanks in laboratory manuals on experiments already laid out for the pupil is a frequent practice.

Experiences in Enjoyment, Self-Expression, and Exploration of New Interests.—To what extent are high school classroom activities genuine, honest experiences in enjoyment? Let us examine practices found in some classrooms. In English classes, the trend is away from the minute analysis of literary selections, a practice that for many pupils ends forever the desire to read anything that smacks of the literary. Yet, the practice of including classics such as *Silas Marner, Macbeth, The Merchant of Venice,* and *Ivanhoe* as required study for everyone still has a firm hold on the English curriculum. Pupils may not enjoy them but at least they should be exposed to them, is the reason sometimes given for their inclusion. All pupils, whether or not they can read such selections with profit, or have the necessary background to enjoy them, are required to study them. Everyone reads the same thing. Hundreds of fascinating and illuminating books go unread on library shelves, or are unpurchased, because every classroom must have thirty copies of one book instead of thirty different selections. The few who read with enjoyment above the level of comics and pictorial magazines is striking testimony to the failure of these practices to promote real enjoyment for many pupils. The study of poetry has an even more dismal record, for what should be an enjoyable experience more often becomes a dreary exercise in analysis of meanings.

In the area of music, there are appreciation classes where popular songs are scoffed at, and the experience of analysis and identification of instruments becomes a chore that is far from enjoyable. Fortunately, in glee clubs more popular songs and folk music are being included. People like to sing for the sheer joy of singing, but many pupils are deprived of that experience. The bands, orchestras, and choruses are a unique contribution of American secondary education. In small secondary schools of a hundred pupils or fewer, however, young people seldom have the opportunity for participation in such musical activities. The discrimination against music as not being worthy of "solid" credits—whatever they are—has kept many pupils from this type of enjoyment.

In arts and crafts at the secondary level, emphasis frequently will be on perfection of the product judged by adult standards. This emphasis has enabled those with artistic abilities to derive enjoyment from this creative medium, but it has left out the majority of pupils. Where the stress has been placed on self-expression in the arts and crafts, all pupils have been able to participate with enjoyment.

Any subject taught in high school has opportunities for enjoyment, for stimulating and extending interests so that young people may learn to live a fuller life. In too many instances, however, pupils are glad to "get physics off." New avenues, new interests in science in the world about them, have failed to be stimulated in an area rich with possibilities. In other areas, too, the extending and exploring of new interests have been deadened by minimum standards and uniform assignments. Wide reading about the world of today in social studies, or extended participation, reading, curiosity, and investigation in any area has not been encouraged enough.

Experiences in Play and Physical Education.—The area of physical recreation and activity has continued to be neglected in the secondary school curriculum. In some cases, no facilities are available for indoor activities during the cold season; in others, no physical education classes at all are included; and in the majority of schools pupils do not receive adequate attention in this phase of their development during all three, four, or six years of high school. More frequently, the gifted few receive the greatest attention.

Physical education still does not have the prestige of other subjects, and schools give only half or quarter credits for an equal amount of time spent in class. In small high schools, untrained teachers often are assigned these classes in addition to their regular classwork. In such classes, pupils spend most of their time playing basketball or softball, and little attention is given to systematic development of recreational skills, bodily coordination, exercise, balanced physical development, and testing of growth. The fluctuation in emphasis from extremely formal to extremely informal activities has served to give pupils going through high school at different times a different type of experience. The physical fitness training institutes held during World War II served, through demonstration and emphasis on varied activities and testing of skills, to improve the physical education program in many localities.

The practice still prevails of giving a disproportionate amount of staff time to interscholastic teams, with relatively less time and effort spent on intramural activities. This situation is particularly true in smaller high schools. In other words, those pupils who need special attention the most receive the least. High school pupils are generally more familiar with group games that have little carryover value than with games that can be easily participated in by adults, such as tennis, golf, badminton, or handball. Dancing skills are more often acquired incidentally than through systematic instruction in school. Unfortunately, too many pupils still go through high school feeling awkward and clumsy and do not receive enough help in gaining recreational skills, or have the fun and recreation in the process of learning them.

Experiences in Achieving Self-Respect and Security.—In the secondary school society, many a pupil is bewildered by a premium on right answers, on academic ability, on outstanding talent, on conformity, and on verbalization. In such situations, a few pupils rebel, others drop out as soon as possible, but the majority accept. It is the pupil who has no outstanding verbal or academic ability who drops out of school the earliest and to whom these conditions have done the most damage. Experiences in satisfaction, security, and self-respect do not recognize any subject boundaries. Too frequently, the right answer is the answer given by the book or dictated by the teacher. Pupils are afraid to make mistakes; therefore, they fear talking in class or are not willing to explore new avenues. A premium is placed on a situation in which no mistakes occur, in spite of the fact that learning comes about more readily by making mistakes and profiting by them.

In typical classrooms, there is much more fear of ridicule and punishment than is generally apparent. The atmosphere in a classroom is a part of the pupil's experiences. In too many instances, the general feeling is one of repression, harshness, or sarcasm. The teacher in the secondary school is more likely to look at the externals in discipline than at the causes of the behavior. In a classroom environment of repression and punishment for infraction of rules which he had no part in making, the young person may develop frustrations, aggressions, and other types of undesirable behavior manifestations inimical to a healthy personality.

The rewards given for outstanding talent in any area, but especially in the academic field, are a constant threat to the security of a great number of youngsters. The best themes are read, the best art work is found on the bulletin board, and the best marks are posted in the halls and printed in newspapers. Honor societies are for those who make the top marks, in a marking system in which it is statistically impossible for all to reach that category of the elite. All this type of "motivation" is based on the theory that pupils need external rewards in order to do their school work. The effect upon all but a few is one of discouragement or a loss of interest in academic areas in favor of other life activities in which they can excel. As yet, secondary school teachers have not generally accepted the principle that every student is regarded as important. The contributions of those pupils who apparently lack special abilities—or reveal relatively minor capacities—are not sufficiently recognized. Full utilization of different types of abilities, such as the ability to meet and work with people, is often lacking.

When much emphasis is placed on learning subject matter and bringing pupils "up to standard," there is little time given to helping pupils to become accepted by others. Youth who desperately need to gain status, to have a sense of belonging, continue to stumble on reading materials, incomprehensible problems, and tasks that are generally beyond their maturity. If these are not accepted objectives of the teacher, pupils may continue to grow more insecure or become "disciplinary" problems. The pupil who constantly fails in high school—and there are many in this category among those who receive D's as well as those who receive F's—is not helped in his development of a rich and full personality. The scars that are left by failure and competitive marking are many and ugly.

Selected References

Aiken, Wilford M. *The Story of the Eight-Year Study.* New York: Harper & Bros., 1942, chaps. 1, 3.—Chapter 3 includes a brief survey of the changes in curriculum in the schools of the Eight-Year Study. In chapter 1, the failures of many secondary schools to meet the needs of youth are discussed.

Alberty, Harold. *Reorganizing the High-School Curriculum.* New York: The Macmillan Co., 1947, chap. 1.—This chapter presents several indictments against high schools that hold to traditional and outmoded practices.

Douglass, Harl R. (ed.). *Education for Life Adjustment.* New York: The Ronald Press Co., 1950, chaps. 5-10, 12, 14.—Various leading educators describe what the modern secondary school should do to attain life adjustment education through the areas of English, social studies, science, mathematics, music, industrial arts, home economics, and physical education. Along with *The High School Curriculum,* it supplements the information in this book by presenting desirable trends in the various subject fields.

Douglass, Harl R. (ed.). *The High School Curriculum.* New York: The Ronald Press Co., 1947, chaps. 12, 20, 21, 22, 24, 25, 27, 28, 29, 30, 31.—Students should supplement their reading of the two chapters on common learnings with the type of information given in this book. Each subject in the general education area is discussed separately, from the standpoint of trends in content and organization of courses.

Educational Policies Commission. *Learning the Ways of Democracy.* Washington, D.C.: National Education Association, 1940, 486 pp.—Many good descriptions of civic education in the common learnings are included. Chapter 2 contains challenging information on how pupils tend to interpret democracy as rights and privileges more often than responsibilities.

Gruhn, William T., and Douglass, Harl R. *The Junior High School.* New York: The Ronald Press Co., 1947, chaps. 5-8.—The junior high school curriculum is discussed largely from the standpoint of trends in the subject content in various fields to indicate prevalent practices in the schools.

Harap, Henry, et al. *The Changing Curriculum.* New York: Appleton-Century-Crofts, Inc., 1937, chaps. 9-11.—Contains descriptions as well as critical analyses of the curriculum in a number of selected secondary schools. Some of this material deals with curriculum organization.

Spears, Harold. *The Emerging High-School Curriculum.* New York: The American Book Co., 1948, chaps. 4, 5, 9, 13, 14.—Includes illustrations of programs in selected schools; somewhat outdated but still of value for information on curriculum practices. (Originally copyrighted in 1930.)

Chapter 8

CLASS EXPERIENCES—COMMON LEARNINGS
(CONTINUED)

While the descriptions of many of the practices just presented may cause the undergraduate student with high ideals to be discouraged, he can be encouraged by the fact that these practices are not typical of all secondary schools. There are many secondary schools, to be found in every state, that are genuinely concerned about improving the type of education they provide. There are administrators disturbed because these situations prevail in the classrooms of some of their teachers. And there are courageous, creative teachers whose primary interest is providing boys and girls with classroom experiences that will help them develop into well-balanced individuals. Their concern, first, last, and always, is *young people*. They are open-minded to change and new ideas. Some are labelled "traditional", others, "progressive", but fortunately they place low value on labels and have a high regard for the worth of each individual pupil with whom they come in contact. Examples are drawn from their classes. This entire book is written in the hope that it may help the future teacher to join their ranks and work for a live, growing, secondary education. It would be a serious mistake to assume that individual schools can easily be pigeon-holed among the "typical" or the "better." These practices may be found in individual classrooms in many kinds of secondary schools. It is hoped that the student will examine many classroom situations critically, asking himself: What kinds of experiences are being provided for the pupils?

After the student has read this book, he may conclude that the usual subject organization is the best way to organize the curriculum of the secondary school for all courses, or he may decide that the content of certain courses providing general education ought to be combined into core classes. This chapter is concerned with what happens to pupils, what they study, what they do, and how they live together, no matter what the organization. These experiences—the curriculum—may be worth while or wasteful in an English class, a science class, or a core class. Certainly, there are elements within an organization that may help or hinder them from being fruitful and satisfying to boys and girls.

3. PRACTICES IN THE BETTER SECONDARY SCHOOLS

The areas of experience from which this chapter draws its examples are those found in the conventional pattern of subjects as well as in the more recently developed core programs. Subject content is not neglected, but a listing of such content alone, we believe, is of little value in finding out what is the real curriculum for boys and girls in any school. The illustrations are taken from high school classes providing the common learnings; they are the living situations, not the dry seeds of the course of study, which come to life only as they are planted in the classroom. The student is asked to note especially what is done with the subject matter. The areas from which the illustrations are drawn are these:

Social studies	Science and mathematics
English	Practical arts
Core classes	Fine arts
Health and physical education	

Although music, art, homemaking, and industrial arts are not included as a part of the general education of most pupils, this fact does not mean that they should not be included here. We believe, with many other educators and lay people, that experiences selected from these areas *ought to be* an essential part of every pupil's general education.

The accounts are illustrative of good practices. No claim is made that they are the best practices or the only ones worth recording. The references at the end of the chapter contain descriptions of many more good school situations. It should be obvious that examples appearing under any one category may illustrate more than one type of experience, for varied kinds of experiences are an integral part of a specific situation. These types of examples take place in situations where subject matter is used as a means to an end; where purposes are clear; where the fundamental question that determines purposes is: "What kind of an individual do we want to develop in this group, this class, or this school?"

The Study of Problems from Current Life, Significant and Challenging to Youth.—In the classrooms of secondary schools where the best type of learning takes place, teachers realize that the adolescent's world is full of significant events, startling discoveries, and difficult problems. He lives in an environment of radio, motion pictures, music, a tremendous amount of written material, travel, the family, organizations, and expanding contacts with people. These teachers have learned to utilize this extraordinary potential for guiding learning in the right direction. They know that dreary drill on facts, continuous prodding, and the use of extraneous "motivation" are necessary only when the content has little or no relation to the lives of youth. They are aware, too, that real learning will result when pupils are concerned with the issues, the challenges, and the curiosities that come from their contacts with the world about them.

In social studies classes, core classes, science classes, and English classes, pupils in many secondary schools are studying content that is significant and meaningful. This content helps the pupils deal with the problems that must be solved, analyze the current social scene, and cope with the changing of their community and their environment. It forms a setting for developing skills of scientific attack upon problems, for these skills can be practiced only in a situation that has purpose and meaning for the pupil.

1. *Analysis of social issues and trends.* Classes in American history and world history begin with such problems as labor unions and their place in the improvement of living conditions, and go back into history to throw light on conditions that exist today. The geographical facts about such a country as China, for example, are brought in to help clarify the development of its peoples, its institutions, and its place among nations. The question of civil rights for all people in the United States involves a study of the Negro, his place in early southern society, the part played by Negroes in the reconstruction in the South, and additional facts which generally have to be searched out from sources other than textbooks.

Consumer education courses, representing a relatively new area in the social studies, deal with such real life problems faced by the citizen as instalment buying, wise selection of goods, aids to the consumer, and budgeting.

English classes, in studying literature, approach the core idea when they develop units around such topics as "Understanding Our World Neighbors," "Contributions of Science to the Welfare of Humanity," "Following the Progress of Science and Invention." Literature is read for the understanding of current life and at the same time for enjoyment. Greater emphasis is placed on the content than on literary form.

Units in current affairs in 1948 in the high school in Springfield, Vermont, included among others the study of issues before the Eightieth Congress, such as universal military training, housing legislation, and the outlawing of the Communist party. Pupils followed the 1948 elections, studying the policies of the parties and the speeches of the candidates. Among economic problems, crop price support and farm surpluses were studied, as were developments in the price situation and reasons for price increases. The group also followed United States foreign policy in such matters as the European Recovery Plan, our attitudes toward China, the work of the United Nations Commission in Palestine, and the political and economic policies of the Soviet Union. These were but a few of the live issues which confronted pupils in the news every day, but which were clarified through organized study in the classroom. A considerable amount of historical background necessarily was brought into the study of these questions.

Two of the units in a twelfth grade course in modern problems given in East Rockford High School, Rockford, Illinois, are problems of management and labor, and problems of racial and religious intolerance. Both are issues in youth's world of today. Unemployment, strikes, a comparison of the CIO and AF of L, government regulation of labor unions, all come in for discussion. The radio, current periodicals, newspapers, books, and pamphlet materials furnish the pupils with up-to-date information and background to current problems. In the study of racial and religious intolerance, pupils investigate the different racial and nationality minority groups, study intolerance and bigotry among religious groups, and apply the principles they develop to the situation found in the local community.

Core curriculum classes are primarily built around problems of the present day and adolescent concerns. At Highland Park, Illinois, High School, the core curriculum in the first year includes such topics as juvenile delinquency, housing, fear of war, social change, the newspaper in America, the effects of the machine age on society.

At South High School, Denver, Colorado, such units as propaganda, newspapers, and health and health services are developed. The analysis of radio and magazine advertising, political speeches, newspapers, and other sources gives pupils experience in evaluating what is propaganda and what is reliable information. Obviously, this type of instruction is aimed at behavior changes, such as suspending judgment and weighing evidence. Pupils study the common source of information, the newspaper, to select readable and reliable news and to improve their ability to read newspapers with understanding. They investigate local health services, sewage disposal, disease control, water supply, and other phases of community health with which the citizen needs to be familiar.

2. *Concern for one's own community.* A notable feature of the curriculum of the modern secondary school is the fact that problems of all kinds are brought home to the pupils through consideration of those problems in their own community. The above examples indicate that these classes did not divorce from the lives of pupils such issues as racial discrimination, but considered how these social problems affect them.

Pupils in secondary schools in rural areas of the South (discussed in Chapter 11) have worked closely with the community to study and improve living conditions. In these rural areas, where pupils may lack shoes or funds for adequate school lunches, school leaders with imagination have turned the situation into one of richer experiences for children than many well-to-do and self-satisfied communities have been able to provide.

When high school pupils own their own school bank, operate a farm, grow produce for the lunch program, make their own clothing, and plan their own community recreation, there is bound to be a growth in responsibility, cooperation, civic pride, and the respect for labor—qualities that our grandparents and great-grandparents valued as an essential part of their education which they gained through daily living, with its opportunities for responsibility and work experience.

The modern problems course at Rockford, Illinois, referred to above, deals with the topics of housing, recreation, and education, with specific applications to the community. Rockford housing projects are studied at first hand, and recreational facilities are surveyed. In an important area, often neglected entirely by the high school curriculum, pupils study cost of public education as it is related to the local situation.

3. *Exploration of the scientific world.* Forward-looking high schools have demonstrated that a field of study as fascinating as science does not have to be an experience gained vicariously by reading about science. Science—in those courses planned for general education purposes, such as general science, biology, and applied science— draws upon community resources: industrial plants, museums, persons with scientific interests, flowers, trees, animals, the stars, and geological formations of the surrounding area. Pupils chart the weather, study eroded areas, collect fossils, study at first hand the habitats of animals, grow gardens of their own, and investigate the application of science in everyday living. A course in general applied science at Manual Arts High School, Denver, Colorado, includes such areas as testing of consumer products, care of electrical appliances, analysis of modern advertising, and the study of scientific hobbies

In an experimental course in physical science at Bulkeley High School, Hartford, Connecticut, taught to a group of senior pupils who do not intend to go to college, the class through cooperative planning has selected such areas of study as these: atomic energy, the lowering of the water table, manufacture of glass. The methods of science, its potentialities and limitations, the social implications of scientific advancements, and other aspects of science in a person's life are important considerations in this course.

4. *Intelligent inquiry into problems to be solved.* Good teachers have recognized that having pupils listen to the teacher lecture or read from a book in order to repeat the information in quiz fashion is very likely to be an experience in docility and accepting statements without questioning their validity. Pupils value the experience of searching out, questioning, and sifting the facts. In the classes of teachers who understand the learning process and have set up ability in scientific inquiry as a definite goal for their pupils, we find groups working on different aspects of a problem. Pupils use library sources to gather data, interview people to get further information, and read from a number of sources to get different points of view. It is in these classes that pupils feel "we even have the freedom to question the teacher!" —something that will always offend the insecure teacher. These pupils are learning to make decisions based on fact rather than on propaganda and hearsay.

One of the "controversial" issues in the school curriculum is the study of the facts about communism. In the social studies classes of Arthur Goldberg at Norwich Free Academy, Norwich, Connecticut, where school people believe that youth should be encouraged to search out the facts for themselves, pupils investigate the topic. They do a tremendous amount of research in the different ideologies. The meaning and advantages of democracy are studied, and improvements needed in order to assure democracy for all peoples. The policies of Russia are examined far more thoroughly than merely the reading of daily newspaper accounts. The historical backgrounds of the Russian people, their experiences in thought control, the amount of democracy existing or lacking, and the present relations of our country with Russia form a part of the class research. Pupils who know the facts are not likely to be misled by propaganda and other methods used by followers of totalitarian ideals.

The course in problems of American democracy at Sequoia Union High School, Redwood City, California, includes such activities as research and discussion, trips, surveys, and other projects. Special community projects or investigations have been undertaken, such as traffic and housing surveys, surveys of working mothers and their need for a nursery school, a school lighting survey, and safety drives. Reference materials, observations, speakers, visual materials, and the community form the learning resources rather than a single textbook.

Attention to Personal Life Problems and Needs of Youth.— There are secondary schools throughout the country which believe that youth's own conflicts, life adjustment problems, and problems of growing up are of sufficient importance to merit a prominent place in the curriculum. These schools find that the here-and-now, the adolescent's own life, forms the best basis for motivation for writing, speaking, discussing, and developing the various skills. They are giving youth an opportunity to deal with their problems in an intelligent way. Coping with one's own problems is an experience far different from a desultory study of problems of the age of Charlemagne.

1. *Problems of health and the maturing body.* More and more youth are being given a chance to discuss with qualified teachers, school nurses, and doctors the results of medical examinations, diet in relation to health, questions regarding posture and appearance, clothing and health, body changes, and rest and sleep. They have open and frank discussions about sex and the sexual functions of the body. Some of these experiences are in health classes, others in combined health and physical education groups or in biology classes or core classes; still other opportunities are offered through physical examinations and through conferences. Well-developed physical education programs pay attention to individual needs for exercise, for group and individual recreation, and for rest.

Achieving physical fitness in these schools is not an absurd study of the structure of the body through learning "what the books says," but is accomplished through visits to health centers, diagnosis by doctor and dentist, consideration of school lunches, and investigation of information on diseases, on quack medicines, on one's habits of living, on the functioning of the body processes. It includes the viewing of health films, learning first aid, participating in healthful outdoor and indoor recreational activities, and testing one's progress in bodily coordination and muscular development.

These are examples of questions relating to healthful living considered by a class in the core program at the Ohio State University School:[1]

[1] Adapted from *Tentative Statement of the Core Program for Grades 10, 11, and 12* (mimeographed), Columbus, Ohio: The University School, The Ohio State University.

What is the significance of my personal vision, hearing, blood pressure, and other tests?

Will tea and coffee hurt me?

Do I need vitamins?

What is a healthy attitude toward sex?

What need I know about disease?

How should I select my physician?

How can I protect my personal health?

2. *Problems of home and family relationships.* In home economics classes, girls are studying a wide variety of home duties and family responsibilities. Pertinent topics considered are home management, child care, buying foods, preparing balanced meals, care and selection of clothing, health and care of the sick, and other definite problems encountered in running a home. In some schools, the girls actually receive experiences in cooperatively managing a practice home owned by the school, in decorating the rooms, and in planning, preparing, and serving meals to selected groups of outsiders. Frequently, too, we find that homemaking classes learn child care through conducting nursery schools for parents in the community.

In an increasing number of schools, boys participate in cooking classes or clubs, sometimes in camp cooking. In River Rouge, Michigan, High School, for example, boys and girls are together in a class in home planning. Here the problems studied deal with banking and insurance, broken homes, buying and furnishing a home, food preparation, child development, preparation for marriage, and other topics. Other schools give girls, as well as boys, experiences in home repair of electrical apparatus, care of household machines, and simple tool skills needed for the upkeep of the house. The Cloonan Junior High School in Stamford, Connecticut, provides such experiences for boys and girls.

It is through the core curriculum that high schools have been able to solve the knotty problem of how to include some aspects of home and family living in the program of general education of all pupils. Here adolescents can discuss freely the conflicts in brother-sister or parent-child relations that may arise in a home, or any other phases of family life. They may use typical case histories of families for discussion of their own problems. The Ohio State University School's core program has as one of its major units "Problems of the Family as a Basic Social Unit." In these classes pupils consider the causes of family tensions and how these conflicts can be solved, the family budget, adequate housing, and ways of making family living happier. These are real concerns of young people.

3. *Problems of personal and social adjustments to school and community life.* New courses in psychology, personal problems, and the core curriculum are naturally replete with topics that concern the adolescent. The areas of home economics, social studies, and English have, in many schools, begun to develop units around these basic problems. Three illustrations are given here to show how problems of the adolescent's adjustment to his own society are considered.

In the social studies program of the junior high school of the Wilson School, Wilson, Arkansas, the course is arranged around major areas of living. Included in the three years' course are units such as room beautification, hobbies, choosing a vocation, education, homemaking and community living, and developing personality and character. In all these units, pupils are definitely concerned with their own social and personal world, such as adjustments to be made to others, developing one's hobbies, and getting acquainted with the school.

Forward-looking high schools have found that English classes offer an excellent medium for study of personal-social problems through literature and that these problems in turn serve as a purposeful means for improving communications skills. In Orientation English in the ninth grade of North Phoenix, Arizona, High School, for example, pupils study the school's plant, its life, its procedures, and its activities. Group living in family, gang, school, and community forms another unit that assists pupils in analyzing their own group membership. Individual talents and skills are assessed and pupils consider how they can adjust themselves to new groups in school, make new contacts, and achieve the goal of "belonging." The development of a personal philosophy, study skills, vocational opportunities, and self-assessment of one's own abilities, interests, and health come in for consideration.

The General Education class at South High School, Denver, Colorado, includes the following problems for study as units in the course: orientation to South High, how to study, getting along with others, vocations, movies, radio, after high school, boy and girl relationships. All these represent interests of youth in their everyday living and their planning for the immediate future. The contrast with the typical problems that young people study in secondary schools is sharpened when we examine some of the work more closely. In the unit on boy and girl relationships, for example, the pupils consider together correct manners and social customs, moral standards for relationships with the opposite sex, conduct on dates, "going steady," and other questions that young people ask.

Opportunities for Practice in Democratic Living.—What experiences do youth have in secondary schools in managing and directing their own activities within classes? Is democracy confined to extra-class activities? Do schools recognize youth's need for progressively increasing opportunities to make decisions and to take responsibility for their own actions? Indeed, there are many schools that understand that the ability to live democratically comes through practice, not through reading about democracy. In addition, there are fearless teachers, who, in spite of an autocratic school atmosphere, give their own pupils rich experiences in democratic living. In these schools and in these teachers' classes, pupils share in making decisions according to their own maturity. It is realized that individuals who have not learned to live democratically cannot be given the responsibilities that could unhesitatingly be placed in the hands of pupils who have had continuous practice in these skills. In such cases, these responsibilities must be introduced gradually.

These are some of the things that are happening in an increasing number of high school classes:

1. *Pupils set up their own goals under the guidance of the teacher.* Instead of autocratic assignments in which pupils are told to do this or that, or "I want you to write a theme for me," they decide together with the teacher what they want to accomplish for the unit, month, semester, or year. In schools where pupils have for a number of years been guided in determining their goals, high school youth show unusual competency in planning what they need to study. It is not a situation of confusion or "doing what we want to do today," as some insecure or ill-informed teachers would have us believe. Instead, pupils usually select objectives that teachers think are important plus others that might have been overlooked in an entirely teacher-planned situation. Teachers are finding that the aims selected under guidance are realistic, are close to adolescent needs, and result in a greatly improved learning situation.

2. *Pupils plan and develop cooperatively the experiences to achieve their objectives.* As there is sharing in setting up goals in these classes, there is also sharing in deciding how to achieve those goals. Pupils and the teacher plan together what needs to be done by the group, how the work can be shared by individuals and by smaller groups in the class. The activities decided upon are generally more varied, more demanding of time, and often more difficult than those a teacher, planning the assignment by himself, hopes that he can get his pupils to carry out.

3. *Pupils evaluate their own progress toward their goals.* The final part of this educational trilogy is the appraisal to find out how far the group and individuals have progressed toward the ends in mind. Evaluation is a constant process in these classes. Pupils are continually checking themselves to see how they have improved, and discuss what they have accomplished to date and what they need to do to improve further. Anyone observing such a group long enough cannot help but be impressed by the difference between purposive, mutual evaluation and the more usual testing for the purpose of determining marks.

4. *Pupils have a part in drawing up their own rules and regulations for conduct and management of the class.* It is a more common thing to find children developing their own rules in the primary grades than in high school. However, in high school classes where the democratic atmosphere exists, pupils govern themselves through setting up regulations for their classroom conduct and share in the responsibilities for duties. Pupils in these classes carry on discussions by themselves if the teacher leaves the room, may have their own elected chairman conducting class discussion, and make it their responsibility to see that a visitor is escorted to a seat and told what the group is doing. These pupils are experiencing self-government and self-control.

5. *Pupils work together in small groups, in committees, and as a total group with selected leaders.* Pupils in democratic classes select leaders to represent them or to lead their class, serve as leaders themselves, practice parliamentary procedure, choose committees, arrive at decisions in committee work, and generally have a chance to function as a good citizen should function in our adult society. Arriving at solutions cooperatively in the give and take manner are important experiences in the day's activities.

Let us look at a more specific example of teacher-pupil cooperative planning in a classroom situation in which democracy operates. The Northeast Junior-Senior High School in Oklahoma City has a unified studies class, allied with some other school subjects, which takes up a double period. This particular eleventh grade group, allied with an American history class, chose to plan and stage an auditorium performance for Thanksgiving.[2] The idea of a Thanksgiving assembly was presented to the class for their acceptance or rejection. A student chairman first carried on the discussion of the question: Shall

---

[2] This account is condensed from a mimeographed bulletin, *An Educational Adventure in Auditorium Activities,* Oklahoma City, Oklahoma: Northeast Junior-Senior High School, 35 pp.

we give the assembly? Pupils discussed the things they might like about putting on an assembly, the talents in the group, and mistakes made by previous programs, and approved the project. The next question discussed was: What kind of a Thanksgiving assembly shall we have? With the teacher participating as one of the group, a decision was arrived at to call the assembly "Thanksgiving—A Ballad for Americans," contrasting life of the Pilgrim fathers and life today and emphasizing political, economic, and social aspects. The group then proceeded to allocate the work of production to committees on the script, costuming, music, staging, and dramatization, plus a general committee to work on details of the performance. Again, these matters were decided by the group.

In subsequent class meetings, the outline of the script was presented for discussion and criticism, the general committee reported on details of the production, and other committee reports were discussed. The casting of parts was done cooperatively. Pupils worked in the art laboratory in making costumes and painting properties. The stage group met at separate times to build the sets. Political problems of today and yesterday, our change in economy since the first Thanksgiving, UNESCO, and life in early colonial days came in for much investigation and some heated discussions. The performance itself was pupil-managed.

Following the production, the group conducted an oral evaluation of the assembly. Some weeks later, pupils were given an opportunity to evaluate the whole project through a questionnaire. Such questions were asked as: What ideas did you gain? What group change of outlook have you noticed since then? If you had the job to do over, what changes would you make in the planning? Questions dealt both with the pupils' evaluation of the project and with their ideas as to how they themselves might have profited or failed to profit from the activity. The teacher used the results as an evaluation of the pupils' growth, and as a basis for future improvement, important phases of classroom evaluation.

Pupil comments about their work furnish an excellent means of finding out how effective the class activities may be. Core groups generally have a good deal of pupil-teacher planning and cooperation. Seldom are autocratic assignments used in these situations. The core group in Fairview High School, Cullman, Alabama, gave these comments [3] that relate to their progress in democratic living:

---

[3] From *The Core Program as Students in Senior High School See It* (dittoed), Cullman, Alabama: Fairview High School, n.d.

We learn to plan and organize work together around common problems.

We learn to think for ourselves, to compare opinions of authors, other students, and teachers, and make up our own mind.

Our teacher is a member of our group. She learns with us.

We have a right to question each other or to be questioned.

Core classes are more like family living.

In the core curriculum groups at Highland Park High School, Highland Park, Illinois, students' comments [4] upon their own activities shed light both on what happened and how they felt they had advanced in democratic procedures:

I think group work is fine because while doing it everyone has a chance to participate.

In this unit I liked the way we did the work in groups and then had a round table discussion.

This helps people to work together and that's what I think the world needs.

When I first came to E2-SS2 I was very confused, because instead of having a teacher giving pupils assignments, the students themselves were not only planning the course of study, but were actually telling the teacher what to do and how to do it. My first thought was "How does anyone get anything done?" for it seemed to me that there was nothing but chaos in the room. However, I soon saw with amazement that everyone had a certain job and was doing it well and accurately. This unit which we have done has opened a new door for me . . .

Taking Action for the Social Good.—Education for citizenship that stops short of taking social action as a result of study about conditions in school or community is lacking in an important element. Teachers know that it is difficult to have the study of civic problems lead to some action. In a curriculum where school and community problems may never arise, and where the end is factual knowledge, action as an end result is inconceivable. But accounts of pupil activities initiated through classes show that going further than reading about a problem is not an impossibility, nor as infrequent as may be supposed. During the war years, community service activities were sometimes given school credit in the high school program. School work camps have been successfully placed in areas where the underprivileged could be helped or run-down buildings could be restored. At the same time, the pupils in the camp studied about the social

---

[4] From *Core Curriculum* (mimeographed), Highland Park, Illinois: Highland Park High School, n.d.

problems of the people and the institution or community with which they worked.

Pupils have worked with community government agencies and institutions to carry out some of the principles studied in classes. The experience of pupils in Skokie Junior High School, Wisconsin, in developing rules for bicycle riding that were accepted by the city council is well known. During the time of Japanese resettlement on the West Coast, when animosities were spread by hate-mongers, land-grabbers, and self-appointed judges, students in the International Relations Club at Commerce High School (now renamed Cleveland High School), Portland, Oregon, did something about their convictions in the field of intergroup relations. When a local roller skating rink refused to admit high school students of Japanese background, the student club members interviewed the manager of the rink, saying that their fellow students should be allowed to skate with them or they would boycott the place and work to convince other students to do likewise. Their action resulted in correcting the situation and extending human rights in the pupils' sphere of living.

Service activities to school and community often originate in classes through the insight of good teachers. School ground beautification projects are one example of this type. In Hanson High School, Hopkins County, Kentucky, a community recreation program developed from a discussion in the home economics class, as a result of which the girls realized the need for community recreational opportunities for themselves and adults. A recreation club was organized to develop a year-round recreational program. In Ascension Parish, Donaldsonville, Louisiana, pupils and teachers contributed jointly to an effort to have the city water supply extended to the area where the Negro population is concentrated. A description [5] of this activity states:

A social science class interviewed residents to determine their interest in the project; a science class made samplings of the water; a mathematics class measured the area over which pipes would have to be laid. Through cooperation of the school board, the churches, the parish health unit, and the water supply company, the connections were provided and in a short time two thirds of the families in the area were using city water. The same school children were able to arrange for garbage collection in this section of the town.

In West Junior High School, Kansas City, Missouri, the housing situation was surveyed through the core classes in the ninth grade.

[5] W. K. McCharen, *Improving the Quality of Living*, Nashville, Tennessee: Division of Surveys and Field Services, George Peabody College for Teachers, 1947, pp. 41, 63.

The classes took pictures of houses in the community, met with the congressman from the district, and furnished him with information to use in his support of the housing bill in Congress. Junior high school pupils in this case took action for improved social conditions on a national scale. In Watertown High School, Watertown, Connecticut, ninth and tenth grade pupils in civics classes investigated housing conditions in their own neighborhood in conjunction with the school-community survey conducted by the Watertown Fact-Finding Committee on Education. The results of the survey were reported to the Governor's Fact-Finding Commission.

Opportunities for Self-Expression and Creativeness.—We can find many examples of creative talents put to use in art classes and in creative writing in secondary schools with an enriched curriculum. In these classes, pupils produce remarkably good sketches, paintings, designs, or short stories. The opportunities for the less talented to express themselves through different media and to receive encouragement to be creative are not so abundant. The common learnings in forward-looking secondary schools and other classes in the hands of sympathetic teachers, do, however, include opportunities to be creative. Creativeness, in this sense, is not confined to particular subject areas. Rather, there is emphasis in many subjects on freeing the individual to express himself, to experiment, and to develop new ideas. A permissive atmosphere, found in such classrooms, gives the pupil a sense of security and a desire to explore, as contrasted with the deadening effect on creativity of the practice of rewarding pupils for giving answers the teacher wants. The opportunities that these schools have found are a result of the work of imaginative teachers themselves.

In schools where each child is considered unique, creativity is fostered in many ways. English teachers give due credit for any attempt at creativity, no matter how many mechanical errors there may be. They share the pupil's joy in creating something of his own in writing. Social studies teachers encourage pupils to develop original ideas for the solution of school and community problems and to use and develop whatever talents they have in contributing to a group project. In music classes, pupils write the words and compose the music for songs to be used in operettas. Art classes often join them in the staging and costuming, or English classes in writing the script. More value is placed on student creativity than on having a finished, ready-made professional production.

Original pageants or plays are produced by English classes or jointly by several groups. Dances and skits are developed by pupils.

Pupils receive the experience of leading the orchestra; vocal or instrumental groups arrange their own music and think out new ideas for performances. Home economics classes stress originality in making clothing, rather than merely copying patterns, or in arranging furniture and decorating the home. Physical education groups develop dances that express individuality. Pupils in crafts or industrial art classes are creative through the media of wood, leather, or metal, rather than being slavish followers of ready-made drawings.

Enjoying the Creations of Others.—In addition to experiences in creating, pupils in secondary schools enjoy the products of other imaginative minds. In another section of this chapter, we described the mediocre results that some schools obtain in developing appreciations, the rather dismal and dreaded experiences that some pupils go through in studying literature or music or history. There are many schools, however, in which real enjoyment in reading, listening, or observing is experienced.

In the better situations, teachers are concerned more with changing behavior and less with seeing that certain material is covered. The emphasis in art appreciation is upon the artistic and the beautiful in the adolescents' immediate environment as well as upon artistic products: the clothing he wears, the home in which he lives, his community, his school, the beauties of nature that surround him. Social studies teachers develop a lasting interest in social and world problems. English classes begin with appreciation on the pupils' own level and build on what is there instead of on the fond but unrealistic hopes of a teacher who feels that anyone who cannot see the beauty of Keats's poetry is an oddity. Pupils are encouraged to read literature that interests them, at their own maturity level, and a plentiful variety is available to cover a wide range of interests.

The ninth and tenth grade classes at Milwaukee, Wisconsin, organize the study of literature around the adolescent's interests in sports, in science and invention, in the world about him, in adventure, in the desire to know people and places, in an attempt to understand himself and his home and community. The pupils read different types of literature centered around such topics as "Enjoying Adventure," "Learning to Know One's Self," and "Following the Progress of Science and Invention." They discuss the problems and issues that are common to the selections read. Abundant reading materials on each topic are found in the classroom and in the library—novels, newspapers, magazines, drama, biography, poetry, travel books, and documents. Pupils have an opportunity to select from materials suited to their needs and interests. Pupil-teacher planning helps to discover the real interests that pupils have, as specific points in each center of interest are developed together.[6]

When experiences in the English class are organized in this manner, dramatization, lively discussions, quiet reading, and other activities grow out of the unit naturally. Adolescents are helped with their own problems through seeing how others deal with family conflicts, sacrifices, and friendships. As a consequence, they read more, and—what is most important—*they read*. Skilful guidance helps in the choice of continuously better literary selections. English courses also assist the adolescent to develop a more critical appreciation of movies, radio, and television programs. New avenues of interests in these cultural media are opened through group study.

In schools concerned about appreciation, music gives real enjoyment through participation and listening. Pre-service education students will undoubtedly be familiar with the enjoyment given thousands of high school youth through participation in bands, orchestras, other instrumental groups, and vocal groups, many of which are on a class basis. Not so common are the experiences in enjoyment through listening. However, teachers who recognize the importance of sheer delight in music include in their appreciation courses listening to music that youth enjoy, the popular as well as the more sophisticated types.

Using the Skills of Communication for Real Purposes.—When the activities of the class are centered around units of social and personal interests, these units are excellent vehicles for the development of communication skills. There are many occasions for reading, writing one's ideas, expressing one's thoughts orally, and listening with understanding. This is the functional approach to teaching English skills. In classes using this approach, there are informal class discussions of literature read or topics investigated. Panels and forums furnish plenty of opportunities for learning the skills of speaking. There is opportunity for oral reading in audience situations, for dramatization, for individual reporting, for conversation, and for planned programs given before school and community groups. Radio skits, minutes of class meetings, booklets, diaries, articles for the school paper, and summaries, all should form an integral part of classroom study. In these situations, the pupils dis-

---

[6] *A Literature Program for Grades 9 and 10*, Curriculum Bulletin, Vol. III, No. 1 (mimeographed), Milwaukee, Wisconsin: Milwaukee Public Schools, 1946, 23 pp.

cover together the difficulties of conquering the mechanics of writing or speech and make plans to improve them. They are learning with a purpose.

The chief reason why core classes or social studies problems represent some of the best situations for developing skills of communication is evident. The schools with core groups that have the responsibility for teaching English skills look for real life problems about which youth *want to* express themselves orally and in writing. The topic investigated must be organized, developed in writing, and presented as reports to the class. People must be interviewed, many kinds of books must be read, the class needs to listen to reports with understanding, explanations must be made, and letters must be written to gather more data or to thank visitors for speaking to the class.

In the ninth grade English class of Maurice Wohler in Red Wing High School, Red Wing, Minnesota, pupils learn writing skills in functional situations. An interest in correspondence with pupils in foreign countries grew out of a talk by a member of the community. The class received a list of boys and girls to whom they could write. A committee parceled out the names in accordance with the pupils' interests in certain countries or in certain hobbies. Before letters were written, a good deal of information about these countries was secured in order that intelligent questions might be asked. Business letters were used here to get free materials that would help supply such information. The pupils were concerned about correct spelling, punctuation, and sentence structure in these letters, class members often assisting each other in making these corrections. When letters were received in return, attention was turned to mechanics and to phrasing that might be different, leading to a study of sentence structure. This project resulted in other learnings about history, geography, customs of other countries, better attitudes toward other peoples, and an appreciation of their ways of life. Foreign students discussed in their letters such current social problems as the Berlin situation and difficulties in Palestine. Lasting correspondence friendships were formed.

Youth in a growing number of English classes are receiving specialized assistance in improving their reading skills and their speech habits. The improvement of vocabulary, speed, comprehension, and reading for specialized purposes is given attention. More teachers are attempting to find materials suited to the reading ability of different pupils. Many give pupils special assistance with speech difficulties, through working with them individually, using speech clinics where available, and giving them numerous opportunities to function in speech situations in a group.

Using Arithmetic Skills Functionally.—As mentioned previously, all youth in some high schools are given assistance in diagnosing and improving their skills in arithmetic. In these schools, arithmetic review may be merely drill or a functional purposeful drill to correct weaknesses. The same is true of general mathematics courses and commercial courses in junior high school. Where the functional approach is used, pupils are given experiences in making change, collecting money, and keeping records of their own budgets. Personal finances, banking for the average person, income tax reports, interpretation of time tables, measurement of rooms to be painted, and graphs on the student population constitute life problems for the improvement of fundamental skills.

In a twelfth grade arithmetic course of the Milwaukee public schools, personal finance problems such as these form the basis for study: budgets and records, instalment buying, social security, income taxes, savings, personal insurance, and home ownership. Pupils plan with their teachers the selection and organization of topics around such questions as "How much would it cost to run an automobile?" Problems are solved concerning the individual's recreation, education, budget, and other areas of living. The pupil prepares an individual budget, compares the cost of buying on the instalment and cash basis, determines the best type of life insurance for himself and his family, and investigates the cost of home activities.[7] Obviously, other important learnings result from this approach in mathematics.

Experience in Security and Successful Accomplishment.—This is one type of experience that is difficult to illustrate because it is an integral part of a total situation. Pupils have experiences in security and success in classes in which they are considered as individuals, in which they do not fear punishment, scorn, or a poor mark because of making a mistake. Fortunate indeed are youth who find themselves in a high school where there is freedom of expression, freedom of movement, and freedom from fear. This type of experience is one that leaves its definite mark on individual behavior.

In these classes, the pupil's individual progress is considered as most important. His personal strengths are sought out and stressed.

---

[7] *A Tentative Course in Twelfth Grade Arithmetic*, Curriculum Bulletin, Vol. IV, No. 2 (mimeographed), Milwaukee, Wisconsin: Milwaukee Public Schools, 1947, 22 pp.

One teacher searched for things that each child in the eighth grade could do better than anyone else, in order that she might instil in each one that confidence so necessary to a balanced personality. She almost despaired of one boy who could not compete in academic achievement and had no special hobbies or obvious talents. However, she found that he could drive a tractor, a skill which no other boy, nor even she, had mastered! The teacher who understands mental hygiene makes it evident that everyone's contribution is valued. How different an experience for the slow learner from constant failure and a feeling of dullness and inadequacy! Teachers in these classes guide the group so that all children feel that they belong, no matter what their race, religion, social status, or ethnic background. In such classes, living as a group is a democratic experience.

When teachers are conscious of the need for development of self on the part of each pupil, they use materials that are suited to varied abilities and interests. The books and pamphlets represent a range of reading levels as wide as reading tests indicate are present in the group. Besides, these teachers recognize that all children are not equally endowed with the ability to use books. Many types of situations are used, in which some can excel in dramatizing, others in meeting people, others in creating with their hands, and others through leadership abilities. These are the classrooms where adolescents have integrating and satisfying experiences because they are regarded as human beings whose welfare comes first and foremost.

4. First Steps

Class experiences must be the focal point of attack if we are to succeed in making any significant and lasting improvements in the secondary school. The defeatist attitudes of some professors of education, high school principals, and high school teachers toward changing classroom practices are an anchor on progress. Only as all concerned with secondary education begin to focus their attention on behavior changes that result from classroom experiences can we expect to make any real headway toward better life adjustment education. These are ways through which we may make a beginning toward developing the kind of a curriculum for the common learnings described in this chapter:

1. We can challenge at every turn people who talk about good secondary education but never have the courage to exert positive leadership in the direction of fundamental changes.

2. Secondary school administrators and supervisors can be on the alert to recognize the teacher with imagination and interest in experimentation, to give him every assistance and encouragement to succeed and to feel secure in his attempts to improve the experiences of youth in his classes.

3. Teachers can evaluate the kinds of experiences that pupils have in classes, with the aid of the pupils themselves; the experiences can be checked against such criteria as those listed in the principles of this chapter.

4. We, as school people, ought to make it a point to discuss with parents and pupils their reactions to what pupils are doing in classes at school. Such discussions may be the beginning of a more critical attitude toward the experiences that make up the curriculum.

5. In groups, or as individuals, we can focus our attention on the adolescents in our classes: on what they are like, on their adjustment problems, on what they think is important, on their homes, their ideals, and their fears.

6. As teachers we should always, upon completing a project or unit of study, have courage enough to ask our pupils what they thought of it. If we are afraid to do so, we ought to do some serious self-analysis as to the kinds of experiences we are providing for them.

7. In any subject, we can always ask the pupils about their particular interests in the area and in related phases of their school and community living. We will get possible leads to units and probably gain more confidence in ourselves in planning with pupils.

8. We can follow the newspapers, magazines, movies, and radio for opportunities to bring our own subjects up to date or to look for ideas on how to make use of real life situations.

9. Then, if we are really interested, we can try to find situations in the pupils' own school lives which need consideration as a group and which might furnish the basis for teaching communication or computation skills.

10. We can keep up with world and community problems, for only if we are well informed ourselves can we function effectively in guiding youth in the common learnings.

11. We can find out as much as possible about the failing pupils and look for strengths on which we can build. Perhaps they can draw, act, make costumes, sing, or contribute to the class in some special way. If we are creative teachers, we can use such contributions in any class. Then, too, we must see that any insur-

mountable obstacles that we have placed in the way of their succeeding are removed.

12. In getting away from the use of a single text, we can begin by building classroom libraries to supplement the text, borrowing from the library, asking for new purchases, and sharing our own and the pupils' store of books.

13. As beginning teachers, we may feel more secure in initiating teacher-pupil planning in such projects as assemblies, dramatizations, field trips, or culminating activities, and we can always use the more formal parliamentary procedure. Especially if we have not *experienced* cooperative planning in our high school and college classes, we may wish to be on surer ground at first.

SELECTED REFERENCES

ASSOCIATION FOR SUPERVISION AND CURRICULUM DEVELOPMENT. *Toward Better Teaching* (1949 Yearbook). Washington, D.C.: National Education Association, 282 pp.—This recent yearbook is filled with descriptions, written by teachers, of what is happening in their classes. The organization of the book around such topics as "Fostering Security and Satisfaction," "Fostering Creativity," "Providing Opportunities for Social Action," etc., lends itself well to descriptions of the curriculum in terms of the experiences of pupils.

COREY, STEPHEN M., *et al. General Education in the American High School.* Chicago: Scott, Foresman & Co., 1942, Part II.—Three chapters in this section on "General Education in Action" describe the programs in a number of schools. These descriptions give a good picture of worth-while experiences that youth have in secondary schools.

MACCONNELL, CHARLES M., MELBY, ERNEST O., and ARNDT, CHRISTIAN O. *New Schools for a New Culture.* New York: Harper & Bros., 1943, 229 pp.—Illustrates democratic techniques in action, particularly in the New School, Evanston Township High School, Evanston, Illinois. The student will find help in understanding the core program.

MORT, PAUL S., and VINCENT, WILLIAM S. *Modern Educational Practices.* New York: McGraw-Hill Book Co., Inc., 1950, Part III.—Presents a series of brief descriptions of current practices illustrating such activities as pupil participation, cooperative group action, use of a variety of materials, and use of community resources. Each is a description written by a teacher or an administrator. The school is not identified. The student will need to select examples critically, since many apply only to the elementary school and others are very sketchy and incomplete.

NOAR, GERTRUDE. *Freedom to Live and Learn.* Philadelphia: Franklin Publishing & Supply Co., 1948, 159 pp.—This is an excellent account of how pupils and teachers work together in a junior high school with an experience-centered curriculum.

OHIO STATE UNIVERSITY HIGH SCHOOL, CLASS OF 1938. *Were We Guinea Pigs?* New York: Henry Holt & Co., Inc., 1938, 303 pp.—In this unusual book, an account written by the pupils in University High School relating their experiences, the student can get a view of the curriculum for common learnings in action.

OLSEN, EDWARD G. *School and Community Programs*. New York: Prentice-Hall, Inc., 1949, chap. 9.—This chapter on "Service Projects" gives several illustrations of youth taking social action in their community. The book contains innumerable reports of significant experiences that pupils are having in using the community as a laboratory.

PROGRESSIVE EDUCATION ASSOCIATION. *Thirty Schools Tell Their Story*. New York: Harper & Bros., 1943, 802 pp.—The student will need to select his reading from this comprehensive book that reports what happened in the curriculum of the twenty-nine schools participating in the Eight-Year Study. This is a splendid resource for descriptions of the actual curriculum, experiences pupils had in classes and in school.

STILES, LINDLEY J., and DORSEY, MATTIE E. *Democratic Teaching in Secondary Schools*. Chicago: J. B. Lippincott Co., 1950, chap. 14.—Gives examples of how teachers and pupils plan together in the classroom in problem-solving situations.

Chapter 9

CLASS EXPERIENCES—SPECIALIZED LEARNINGS

Specialized learnings are distinguished from common learnings in that they provide skills, interests, and specialized knowledge that are not common needs for the individual in a democratic society. They are vocational skills that characterize the general occupational groupings. They are avocational pursuits that make for a richer life. They may be agriculture, baseball, science, drama, or painting, but they are an expression of individual personality needs and interests. We should not think of the specialized learnings as merely vocational in nature, for occupational activity is only one of the life activities that all people do not experience in common. This chapter deals with the specialized learnings found in the vocational areas of agriculture, business education, distributive education, industrial training, and home economics; in the advanced courses in science and mathematics; in foreign languages; in the creative and cultural areas of journalism, creative writing, drama, art, music, and literature.

Some of the same types of experiences outlined in the principles for the common learnings are certainly also needed in classes that provide for specialized learnings. Youth should have, in all classes, experiences with tasks in which they can succeed, experiences with cooperation and group responsibility, experiences with challenging problems for investigation, and experiences with activities that have a direct relationship to their own lives.

1. THE PRINCIPLES

The secondary school curriculum should provide opportunity for youth to discover and pursue their special interests, such as cultural, vocational, scientific, and leisure-time interests.

Although there are many opportunities for the exploration of individual interests in the elementary school, the secondary school should be an institution where these interests can be deepened and explored. During this period of formal education, youth should have an opportunity to discover what are their genuine interests that may be followed either vocationally or avocationally. The boy with a

scientific bent should find in the secondary school a sympathetic encouragement and definite guidance in pursuing this interest. The
girl who wants to dance should find in the curriculum a chance to
develop her talents. There should be no barriers to youth who have
a keen desire to invent, experiment, or explore some area of the
world's culture.

As soon as any high school restricts its program, either by reason
of its small size or through a highly prescribed curriculum for college
entrance, it fails to consider that young people differ in interests.
There must be opportunity for searching further than many will wish
to go into the areas of mathematics, science, languages, literature,
the arts, history, and current problems. Either through special
courses or through general courses in the field concerned, pupils
should find time and assistance in exploring those particular problems that appeal to them for further study. No highly regimented
atmosphere will suffice to give them these opportunities. Exploration of interests also lays the basis for an intelligent selection of an
occupation. Many high school courses can serve such an exploratory
function. Rigid college preparatory curricula permit little exploration of different skills or areas such as the crafts, art, home economics,
and business. Obviously, any plan of specialization must have its
basis in a good guidance program.

*Every youth in the secondary school should be encouraged
and assisted in developing his latent capabilities and potentialities
to the maximum.*

Do experiences that youth have in secondary schools serve to
bring out their potential abilities—yes, even develop their idiosyn-
cracies as strengths in their personalities—or do they bury these
potentialities in a mass production of mediocrity? Can a school that
stresses having all pupils doing the same assignments really further
individuality? There must be special attention and assistance given
to the gifted in speech, the gifted in mechanical ability, the gifted in
bodily coordination, and the gifted in mathematical reasoning. We
know that there are vast differences in abilities of individuals. We
do not seem to understand as well how to provide a curriculum that
will allow each individual to develop his abilities to the maximum.
What does our own experience in high school indicate? Have secondary schools really developed the know-how that encourages and
assists individuals to broaden and improve their own peculiar
potentialities?

A secondary school that considers the gifted in academic ability as the only group worthy of special attention is not meeting the needs of youth. The chance for the youth with mechanical abilities must be as real as for those with special ability in verbalization. In order to care for these varied needs, the secondary school must offer not merely a variety of courses but a greatly expanded flexibility within all courses. It does not make sense to circumscribe a course in chemistry so that for the brilliant academic student it may become an exercise in repetition and dulness and for the pupil with other talents it may be an experience in unreality, frustration, and defeat.

For the smaller high school, this principle means even greater flexibility within a number of courses, since the offerings must necessarily be fewer. It may be that for some pupils the school day should be altogether different from that of the student who might be taking courses as we now conceive them. Certainly, for the extremely maladjusted adolescent whose ability to learn is blocked by emotional difficulties, a half or full day in the shop or the arts and crafts room would be more appropriate than a program of the usual course work.

The creative secondary school teacher looks for ways to encourage the growth of individual potentialities. He does not have all pupils doing uniform assignments even in a "homogeneous" group. He does encourage the pupil with an unusual interest in the subject to go as far as he can; he sets up a learning situation in which he can help and guide different ones. He does not reward just the "student" who can easily work with written, abstract materials. He does give recognition to accomplishment in creative talents, social skills, manual skills, and physical skills. He knows that uniform requirements and competitive marking hinder rather than promote the growth of individuality, that they serve mediocrity better than they serve the development of special talents.

The specialized learnings in the curriculum should give youth experiences that develop vocational skills, understandings, and attitudes useful in a general occupation area.

It is the function of the secondary school to prepare youth for entrance into vocations, but the curriculum would be hopelessly regimented, and the costs tremendously high, if specific vocational education were given for the many types of occupations into which high school pupils are certain to go. Studies have indicated that specific vocational skills are common to many types of related jobs. Vocational education at the secondary school level should prepare for broad fields of occupations, in other words, develop skills useful in a variety of jobs. The vast majority of jobs require no preliminary formal vocational training. In one study it was found that in 2,216 occupations, 90 per cent required a training period on the job of only six months or less.[1]

Thus, while the secondary school can in its curriculum train for the basic skills of typewriting, filing, shorthand, and English mechanics, it would be impractical to give all pupils training in operating a wide variety of business machines. The occupational fields of agriculture, business, and industry are broken down into innumerable types of jobs. Youth in the secondary school can develop skills, attitudes, and understandings that will permit them to enter into any one of these many types. The more specific applications will be developed as a part of their experience on the job.

It is generally agreed by educational authorities and by employers that the vocational education offered by the schools should be of a broad nature, stressing attitudes and work habits as well as specific skills. Employers want people who can take responsibility, who are honest and industrious, who can get along with others, and who will be interested in improving themselves on the job. Good health and recreational habits and an understanding of working conditions are considered important. The skills demanded are those that belong to families of occupations, such as typewriting and shorthand skills for a large number of clerical jobs, or knowledge of farming and ability in farm practices for a large number of related jobs in the field of agriculture. Many employers and labor unions prefer to have the training in particular skills given on the job through apprenticeship.

It is the responsibility of the secondary school to provide the necessary work experience for youth in school and in the community as a part of their education.

Although work experience is a valuable part of anyone's education, youth who plan to go directly into community occupations from the secondary school should have some opportunity for work in the community as a planned part of their education for vocation. In the first place, these job experiences can give the training in skills that cannot easily be provided by the school. The necessary equipment is available in the shop or place of business. Moreover, the real situation is provided; in it, contacts with people must be made,

---

[1] Howard M. Bell, *Matching Youth and Jobs,* Washington, D.C.: American Council on Education, 1940, 58 pp.

production schedules must be met, or customers must be satisfied. Here proper work habits can be developed through actual performance.

When youth work part time and attend school part time, they are helped in making the transition from school to the job. Such an arrangement needs the cooperation of industry and business, and, at the same time, must be carefully planned and supervised. The experience itself must be educative. The right kind of relationships between school and the job—relationships to insure that values from work performed will actually prove a learning experience—can be secured through proper supervision by the school.

Vocational education in secondary schools should be given as near as possible to the time when the vocational skills will be used on the job.

The application of this principle will mean that much of the vocational education will be given in the upper years of senior high school or in an extended secondary school or junior college, as a greater number of youth continue their education over a longer period of time. Agriculture and homemaking are usually begun in the ninth grade, since they are both definitely related to the job from the beginning and, in the case of home economics, many of the experiences are considered as desirable common learnings. The assumption is that pupils will have some opportunity in these areas in case they drop out of school. However, it is safe to assume that social and industrial trends will further postpone the time of entrance into employment, and that more youth will continue through high school and into junior college education for life responsibilities as school facilities are extended.

The advance of the beginning-employment age is an important social trend. Employers prefer more mature individuals. Trade union restrictions as well as employment practices tend to raise the age of entrance into employment. These are but manifestations of social changes such as a gradual increase in the average age of the population and the mechanization of industry requiring fewer man-hours to perform a specific job. The restrictions on child labor through social legislation tend to prevent pupils from having these experiences before they are eighteen years of age. For youth, therefore, these experiences in learning vocational skills need to come near the time of transition from school to work. The young worker should be able to put them to use immediately on the job and receive further upgrading after beginning work through adult education programs conducted by high schools, junior colleges, or special adult schools.

As youth are placed on the job full time by a junior college or extended secondary school, the school still has a responsibility to assist these young people through evening classes, guidance services, and other means. Part of the experience of youth in education for vocation should be assistance in adjustment to the job and further skills training after full-time work has begun. To carry out such a program, a new concept of the secondary school is called for, one in which the transition from school to work may be a gradual process without emphasis on graduation.

Vocational education in the secondary school should be related to community needs.

The secondary school is the terminal point of formal education for the majority of young people, a number of whom will enter employment in their own community upon leaving school. In developing the kinds of vocational education to be offered, the school will need to survey the community needs and employment conditions. In some manner, the school should keep in touch with employers, labor unions, and independent workers in the community to secure their advice as to the types of experiences to give youth as job preparation. In an agricultural community, agriculture will find a place. In an industrial community, there will be other types of vocational needs. In other words, the community needs should help determine the type of vocational education. Constant contact must be maintained with employers to keep up with those needs. The community should be considered as the area served by the high school, regional school, or junior college. To a greater extent than any previous time in history, the school will also need to consider what types of occupations its former students have entered, for migration enters definitely into the picture today.

Specialized learnings, as well as common learnings, should be an experience in democratic living with consideration for personality and a sharing of responsibility and authority.

It should be quite obvious that such specialized learnings as higher mathematics do not lend themselves to the experience approach as well as do the common learnings. Yet, this should not be an excuse for day-by-day assignments in textbooks as a basis for the curriculum without any setting of goals or cooperative checking to see if they have been attained.

Work in the specialized areas also should give pupils a feeling that they are a definite part of the learning situation. There is just as much of a need in these areas for seeing that the materials and the learning activities are adjusted to the learner. There will be differences in temperament, ability, background, and maturity that will demand adjustments in what is done in the class. Democracy is learned by living it throughout the day, by being given something to say about one's own affairs, by opportunities to make decisions, by a chance to live in an atmosphere of respect for each individual and his contributions to the group. These experiences should be a part of every class in school.

2. Some Typical Practices

The typical practices discussed here are again those found in some—not all—schools. In examining practices in specialized areas in the secondary school curriculum, it is evident that the principles outlined in this chapter are applied to a greater extent in some areas than in others.

Schism Between Vocational and Academic Fields.—Throughout the history of secondary education, since such vocational subjects as agriculture, distributive education, and trade and industrial education have gained a foothold in the curriculum, there has been an unfortunate division between the academic subjects and the vocational subjects. Proponents of each have extolled the virtues of their subject areas and have overlooked the fact that subjects are a means to the development of children in a specific type of society. The academicians, aided by college entrance requirements of 1890 vintage, have scoffed at the vocational educators and to a large extent have managed to maintain their high post of superiority. Students have elected the academic subjects rather than shop courses, home economics, and business education, because of college preparatory curricula requirements, pressure of parents, and—sadly enough—often pressure from the school.

Moreover, this schism between two types of courses, both filling specialized needs and both serving as a part of education for vocation, has been reflected in the types of experiences given to pupils in the two areas. In the specialized academic courses, time has virtually stood still in many schools as far as implementing good learning practices is concerned, while the vocational courses have often forged way ahead in adapting instruction to individual differences and motivating pupils to real learning.

Little Adaptation to Individual Differences in Specialized Academic Areas.—Considered here are courses in physics and chemistry, in the foreign languages, in higher mathematics, and in advanced literature. Advanced speech courses and specialized courses in the social studies area, such as international relations, might also be included, although they are taught infrequently and generally have more flexibility and more of the characteristics of an experience approach than is indicated in this description of practices. All of these are considered as specialized learnings to permit individual pupils to pursue their special interests and meet their needs in specific fields. Many of them will contribute to vocational efficiency.

Most new teachers will find their first teaching position in a relatively small secondary school. In these schools, what can they look forward to in regard to specialized academic courses? How do teachers select the curriculum for these courses and what types of materials do they use? In the majority of these classes, the textbook is the course of study. The subject matter to be covered is selected entirely by the teacher with very few opportunities for pupils to participate. The class follows the logical arrangement in the textbook.

1. *Mathematics.* In mathematics texts, the problems are there to be worked, and all pupils do them at the same rate. There is often very little evidence of any knowledge on the part of the teacher that ability to do mathematics problems differs among pupils in these classes, even though they may be a selected group. Algebra classes have been an experience in dismal futility for many pupils who could not master the concepts. Little time has been spent on helping them understand the vocabulary and the concepts involved. Stress is placed on finding the right answers, not on understanding the processes. The inept and the skillful have sat down together, pursuing the same work at the same speed, much to the detriment of both. To capable students with an interest in mathematics, such an experience has been far from stimulating. The emphasis on rote memorization has been especially noticeable in geometry classes, where theorems are often learned to be repeated verbatim. Cases of students in junior college who have completed two years of high school mathematics in one semester of individual work are frequent enough to point the way as to what might be done if mathematics skills and concepts, instead of covering the text, were the goal of instruction.

2. *Physics and chemistry.* Physics and chemistry classes have permitted more individual participation on the part of the pupil. He actually carries out the laboratory experiments himself, often proceed-

ing at his own rate. Chemical processes, safety precautions, and attitudes toward care of equipment are learned through participation. However, the work of the course is still governed largely by the textbook, with but little variation. The learning of physical and chemical principles and laws is an end in itself. The laboratory manuals or workbooks set up definite steps for experiments and leave little room for scientific investigation in which the pupil must use his own originality and reasoning. Any real learning, we recall, must result in change in behavior—in attitudes, appreciations, skills, or understandings. What is learned of lasting value in the usual high school chemistry course? What real understandings resulted from our own experiences? An analysis of these questions should indicate to us which experiences in these classes resulted in the learning that we now value as a part of our education.

Some physics classes still do not use the airplane, jet propulsion, the diesel engine, or even the modern automobile to illustrate principles, or they may teach laws that the atom bomb has outmoded. In his reading on his own, the talented student is apt to go further and gain a deeper scientific understanding and interest than he does in connection with such a class.

3. *Foreign languages.* The above areas and the foreign languages are often the extreme of book learning, abstraction, and verbalization. Foreign language classes begin and often end with a study of the component parts and the grammatical structure of the language. The language may be read but is rarely spoken, or even used for any genuine purposes whatsoever. As we read the many defenses that have been written for the foreign languages, we could come to the conclusion that the purpose of learning a foreign language was not to learn how to use it readily in communication! Latin retains its place as one of the vestigial remains of an outmoded secondary school curriculum. There is little to bolster this subject except prestige value and college requirements.

Although—as many a student of a living language knows—learning a new language can be a most fascinating experience that opens for exploration new interests and new areas of culture, pupils may spend a good deal of their time translating laboriously and reading books that hold no interest to them or concern for their own lives. A favorable trend in Spanish classes toward the use of more up-to-date materials can be noticed in a number of schools.

Limited Opportunities for Creative Talents as a Part of Class Activities.—The small high school generally does not provide youth enough opportunities to explore their talents in art, creative writing, drama, speech, the dance, crafts, and, to a lesser degree, music. Music has found its way into most high schools, first coming in as an extraclass activity and then achieving more "respectability" by being accorded a regular place on the school schedule and being offered for credit, usually a trivial amount to be sure. Both instrumental and vocal groups have been accorded that privilege in many schools. In larger schools, pupils in various curricula are usually allowed to participate in music groups. There is a dearth of opportunity for special exploration in any of the other creative areas as a class activity, although many are often included in the extraclass activities. A few larger high schools offer courses in creative writing and drama where pupils may develop their talents in writing and acting. Creativity through the dance is seldom found in physical education classes, or elsewhere. The development of special talents in speaking is left largely to the extraclass category. Arts and crafts are more expensive offerings that have found room neither in the budget, in the curriculum, nor in the building of the usual small high school.

Large high schools that confine pupils to rigidly defined curricula only delude themselves and others when they profess that "any student may take art." In such a school, the curriculum may be as barren and void of art experiences for most pupils as in the small high school, for their program is filled up with required and recommended courses. We need to look at the course program that pupils *follow*, not what is offered in the program of studies, in order to get the real picture.

Opportunities for Vocational Education.—In the majority of secondary schools of the country, some type of vocational education is offered. Agriculture courses and farm shop work are found in many small rural high schools. Business subjects, such as typewriting, are quite common in all but the smallest schools where the expense of equipment has been prohibitive. Home economics courses are frequently offered. Less common are the vocational shop courses, such as printing, automotive mechanics, and the like. Distributive education in the business field is offered mainly in the larger high school, generally restricted to the eleventh and twelfth grades.

One of the main factors that has stimulated development of vocational education has been the underwriting of the program by the federal government brought about by the demands of the people for education suited to the times. Through the Smith-Hughes Act passed by Congress in 1917, the George-Deen Act, and other subsequent acts, grants of money were provided to the states for specific purposes of promoting instruction in agriculture, home economics, distributive education, and trades and industries. Depending upon the particular state plan developed, the local school receives money for a certain portion of the cost of conducting courses in these fields. In turn, the school must meet specified standards for its facilities and instruction. Certainly, thousands of youth have been given the opportunity of taking vocational work because of these provisions.

Barriers to Youth Securing Experiences in Vocational Areas. —In the total secondary school, high school through junior college, the proportion of youth who take advantage of courses in any one of these areas except business is small. This fact is not surprising when we examine the conditions. There is more than one barrier that stands in their way:

1. A student seeking admission to college usually must have a certain number of academic or "solid" ("academically respectable") credits. He is limited in the number of vocational subjects he can present for admission.
2. The college preparatory or academic high school curriculum in a multiple-curriculum type of school program has little or no room for electives from the vocational fields.
3. Few high schools have the facilities to accommodate a larger number of pupils in vocational courses. Additional equipment and space would require considerable expenditure.
4. The factors of prestige and tradition, mentioned above, have had considerable influence in maintaining the status quo.

On the other hand, some pupils are forced into vocational courses, since they do not have any academic abilities; others take these courses as the lesser of two evils.

Greater Use of the Community in Agriculture Courses.—In the vocational areas, there has been a much greater use of the experience approach than in the academic areas. The very nature of the course, plus the fact that it is not hampered by tradition and that a certain amount of actual experience is required by the federal acts setting up the program, has been conducive to pupil participation. For many, these courses have been an experience in learning by doing. Projects have been constructed with the hands, skill in the handling of tools has been learned through actual use, working plans have been made and put into action. Part of the vocational work has been experience on the job. The work in the school shop has been organized to resemble the situation in the industrial shop. There is more experimentation, closer touch with the community, and a closer relation to real life experiences than is true in the academic areas.

Contrast the types of experiences that pupils have in studying only from a book with those they have in an actual participation program. Teachers of agriculture use the pupils' home farms as a laboratory for learning good agricultural practices, for the federally aided program stresses a supervised farming program made up of a number of projects. The teachers under this program, ordinarily called vocational agriculture teachers, are employed full-time and spend the summer supervising the projects that the boys have selected to carry out on their home farms. The project becomes a year-round one, for which planning and gathering information is a part of the organized classroom work. Typically, agriculture classrooms are work rooms, with tables and chairs, an abundance of state and national agriculture bulletins, filing equipment, laboratory equipment such as a milk testing machine and a soil testing kit, and farm shop equipment.

In spite of these advantages, the monotonous question-and-answer recitation from a book sometimes persists, even more ridiculously out of place in this atmosphere. Agriculture teachers also can fail to see the inherent possibilities of a good learning situation. Some teachers, in a misguided attempt to maintain status and to gain respect for their subject, have resorted to the paper-and-pencil test as the chief means of evaluating progress on the part of the pupils. In these classes there can also be found little variation of the curriculum to suit individual abilities, little use of democratic practices, and but a minimum of attention to pupils' basic needs and adjustment problems. Fortunately, such cases are in the minority. Home visits and contacts, the ability of farmers to evaluate the work that is done by the agriculture department, and other factors have tended to keep these undesirable experiences at a minimum.

Failure to Use Work Experience in Business Classes.—There is a natural motivation for typing, and most of these classes are a scene of purposeful activity. Office practice classes, which are not typically found in the curriculum of the secondary school, are usually conducted on as high a level. Shorthand and bookkeeping, however, have not fared so well. There are teachers of shorthand who seem to have the capacity for making the class time as dreaded and unlifelike as any class in Latin or Greek might be under similar direction. Bookkeeping has become largely something taught out of a book, with practice exercises accompanying the text. It is an unusual rather than a typical commercial department that takes advantage of all the opportunities for handling real business transactions in the life of the school. Work experience as a part of business education is not typical of the majority of secondary schools.

The Experience Approach Ordinarily Utilized in Home Economics and Industrial Arts.—It is not the intention here to argue whether home economics and industrial arts are general education or vocational education. We have already discussed both under common learnings, for we believe that the two areas should contribute materially to the general education of every student. It is not an either-or proposition. For many students, both subject areas will fill specialized needs and interests. Certainly, for the vocation of homemaking, girls should go beyond the skills that all boys and girls need as a part of their education for home living. All girls will be homemakers, but some will desire more breadth or depth in homemaking. In industrial arts, many boys acquire skills that will be valuable in later work in trades and industries; these of course go beyond the common needs. Some phases of industrial arts, agriculture, and home economics in the early junior high school years, are commonly referred to as pre-vocational education.

The small high school's shop usually consists of only a woodworking shop, with perhaps a mechanical drawing room attached. As the size of the high school increases, metal, electrical, and machine shop work are more frequently included. Less frequently there is an auto mechanics shop, and sometimes a print shop is a part of the industrial education offered. The practice in some high schools of separating the curriculum into various courses, each confined to one type of shop, is an unfortunate one in view of the varieties of industrial production which require little pre-employment training of a specific nature. The general shop that includes experiences in various areas is gaining in popularity.

In the subject of home economics, teachers have gone further than in any other area in developing the unit plan for organization of the curriculum. The problems studied are generally those of real interest to the girls. Home management and decoration, clothing construction, food preparation and preservation, and child care are all phases of life that usually interest the adolescent girl. Yet, some courses are still conducted along the outmoded pattern of cooking and sewing classes, with separate teachers for each and with little attention paid to the broader aspects of homemaking. In such classes, the sewing projects may all be assigned, all girls making aprons according to specific patterns or doing other projects that make no provision for individual interests. The splendid opportunities for teacher-pupil planning are likely to go unheeded.

3. Practices in the Better Secondary Schools

Some of the experiences discussed here provide youth with education for vocation; whether they are in agriculture, art, or journalism makes little difference. Others enrich the possibilities for leisure-time hobbies and interests. Still others serve to develop the adolescent as an individual, giving him an opportunity to build up his special talents and to succeed in the eyes of his world.

Fruitful Learning Experiences in the Specialized Academic and Cultural Courses.—First, it should again be made clear that these so-called academic and cultural courses may also be education for vocation. Thus, mathematics is a foundation for engineering education and is used in business and many other types of work. The division made here is a rather artificial one, made for discussion purposes to show what is happening in different types of courses. Adolescents in various high schools are having worth-while experiences that lead to desirable goals; among these are the following:

1. The community is utilized for the study of advanced science courses through excursions to industrial plants, city sewage-disposal plants, electric power plants, and through the study of other industrial processes first hand.
2. Special application to real life situations is made in chemistry or physics: the study of soil fertility, plant foods, spray solutions and dusting powders for the garden, of patent medicines and cosmetics, of refrigeration and the making of ice cream, of rubber and other synthetic products, radio and television, aviation, photography, and the like.
3. Pupils develop concepts and understandings of the mathematical processes in addition to the skills. They learn to deal with mathematics as a means of communication through charts, tables, symbols, and measurements.
4. In a few secondary schools, considerable flexibility has been developed to allow superior pupils in mathematics or science to proceed at their own pace.
5. The use of home-made apparatus, constructed by students, has made science a more profitable experience for many. The making of objects to illustrate geometric forms and shapes has had the same influence in mathematics courses.

6. The study of a language through its use in the classroom in speaking, reading, and writing, with the emphasis placed on functional use, has opened up for many a student the possibilities for communication in another tongue. Obviously, this is quite a different outcome from learning how to conjugate verbs or translate sentences on paper. Lasting interests have been developed in the living languages.

7. Many pupils in language courses are reading books, newspapers, and magazines that deal with current happenings and life in the countries in which the language is used. In Spanish classes, for example, the life and culture of present-day South and Central America have become the focus of study, supplanting the reading of outdated materials concerning Spain.

8. Pupils in science, advanced literature, or other areas, have an opportunity for extensive reading in specialized topics that they want to investigate.

9. There is much practice in leadership in various classes through pupils taking charge of projects, field trips, and phases of dramatic productions; conducting the orchestra; leading musical groups; and the like.

10. Many different media or activities in arts and craft classes make it possible for youth to explore their talents: sketching, metal arts, clay, plaster, plastics, graphic arts, lettering, designing, commercial art, puppetry, stage settings, model making, map making, leather work, wood. Comprehensive arts and crafts offerings are being given more frequently and provide for a variety of types of expression.

11. Music courses and group meetings on regular schedule offer innumerable possibilities for pupils to develop proficiency in choral singing, solo singing, performance on various types of instruments, participation in instrumental groups, composing, orchestration, and experience in staging musical productions. Many high schools have highly developed music programs.

Newer Courses to Provide for Individual Needs.—These are courses that have been added to the secondary school curriculum more recently than such rather traditional courses as physics and chemistry in order to make provision for individual talents and interests. Included in this category are courses that are rarely found in small high schools, but may be added as electives when the size of the school increases. Although more likely to be found in the large city high schools, there are many schools with enrollments below a thousand pupils that have included them in their program of studies. The nature of the curriculum is indicated for each of these courses. This is a selective rather than an inclusive list.

1. *Journalism*. In this course, pupils often have the responsibility of producing the school paper or, in a few schools, a section of the local paper. In such cases, the course provides first-hand experience in managing, planning, and writing articles for the paper.

2. *Drama*. As their work in the course, pupils carry out the production and staging of plays. Besides the acting, there is practical experience in selecting the play, doing makeup, constructing scenery, lighting, costuming, directing, and managing the production. In better situations, pupils rather than teachers take much of the responsibility for these various aspects of presenting a play. In a few cases, pupils also write productions. Such an undertaking may be a cooperative venture with the music department, in producing an operetta, for example.

3. *Creative writing*. In this course, pupils who do superior work in English composition and show imaginative and creative abilities are given further opportunity to explore. The student's own writing, in the different literary forms, provides the basis for discussion and criticism. There is real purpose for the activities carried on. In a number of cases, students publish their writings in the school paper or magazine through the course.

4. *Speech*. The experiences in speech courses vary with the situation in the school and community. When the school operates a radio station or has access to local stations, speech work may be built around radio programs. Other activities of speech classes include panel discussions before local clubs, discussion groups, assemblies, and practice through various other avenues. Speech correction and training in enunciation, pronunciation, and articulation is given.

5. *Radio*. Theory is combined with practice, for students have radio sets for laboratory experiments and construction. Other similar specialized courses in physical sciences are aeronautics and electricity.

6. *Latin American history, Far East, international relations*. These are types of courses in social studies of a more specialized nature that permit students interested in this field to go further in their studies. They utilize a good deal of pamphlet and periodical material and many of the more popular nonfiction books.

7. *Commercial art, industrial design, applied arts*. These and other types of arts and crafts courses fill a vocational purpose which

may be closely related to other areas, such as business education and home economics. They also serve recreational and leisure time interest functions.

8. *Harmony, theory, applied music.* Advanced courses in music give high school youth advantages for intensive study in this special field.

These courses offer a natural setting for active participation by pupils. Should they grow into book courses, where the class studies about play production or about radio, they become less and less valuable for the development of individual abilities and interests. They are illustrations of courses that are fulfilling worth-while special needs in the secondary school curriculum. The education student can find others of a similar nature in bulletins on programs of studies, or handbooks, published by secondary schools.

Education for Vocation that Develops Basic Skills for Many Types of Specific Jobs.—Many excellent secondary schools, including high schools, junior colleges, extended secondary schools, and trade and technical schools, have applied the principles relating to vocational education as outlined at the beginning of this chapter. These schools are adjusting their programs of preparation for entrance into occupations to the realities of the modern economic world, and its conditions of employment, industrial processes, and labor organization. Agriculture courses are made directly applicable to a number of types of farming and other occupations related to farming. Bookkeeping, typewriting, and other secretarial courses train for many kinds of clerical or secretarial jobs. In the part-time cooperative education plans, discussed later in this chapter, schools are pointing the way toward a means of providing the broader training at school and the more specific skills on the job.

General shop programs are replacing the specialized shop courses in many high schools. In these schools, pupils get varied types of experiences in wood, metal, auto mechanics, drafting, and machine tools rather than specializing in one of these phases. This is a unified industrial arts program with more than one type of activity, and is considered by many educators as general rather than vocational education. In shop courses with vocational objectives, pupils make working drawings of their projects, learn to use hand tools and power machine tools in working with wood; make projects with sheet metal; learn how to use machine tools in constructing items of metal, such as hand tools; work with electric wiring, installation, and repairs; repair autos, often bringing their own to the school shop; do carpentry jobs in constructing actual houses. Blueprint reading, forging, and welding are less common types of experiences provided. The shop experiences are intended to give the pupil basic information, skills, and attitudes.

English, mathematics, science, and social studies are important phases of education for vocation. In addition to improving the individual's competency as a citizen, they often contribute directly to the vocational objective. In agriculture and distributive education programs, special efforts are made to relate these courses to that objective; for example, science is definitely related to the need for scientific knowledge in farming, and economics courses include discussion of employment, labor-management relations, and similar problems.

Stress Placed on Habits and Attitudes Necessary for Success in the Vocation.—The care of tools, thoroughness and accuracy in carrying out projects, careful planning of work, promptness, and the like are stressed in the instructional program in the shop, home economics laboratory, business education, and other classes. For example, secretarial training programs in junior colleges differ considerably in this respect from those in commercial business colleges. The latter teach the skills in the shortest period of time, while the junior colleges stress ability to take responsibility, attitudes toward employers, proper dress, background information, and skills in English. In related classes in distributive education programs, proper dress for work, relations with employers, and habits that contribute to success on the job are important problems discussed. In some schools the academic courses also deal with these problems.

Vocational Skills Placed in Upper Years of Secondary School. —In school systems that have a six-four-four plan of organization, or in those communities that are fortunate enough to have extended secondary school facilities available, much of the vocational work has been placed in the upper grades, particularly Grades 11 to 14. In Grades 7 through 10 pupils are given a well-developed curriculum in the various areas of general education considered essential to the life of every individual. Although the pupil may have had opportunity to explore his abilities and interests in general shop courses in the first years of secondary school, he does not begin to specialize until the later years, in some cases not until the thirteenth and fourteenth years. Some larger high schools receiving federal aid under the Smith-Hughes Act offer courses in skilled trades, such as the auto trades and building trades courses in Highland Park High School, Highland Park, Illinois. These are offered for juniors and seniors in a half-day of practical shop or trade experience.

The cooperative education plans discussed in this chapter are specifically limited to the upper years of the secondary school. Technical schools have many pupils enrolled who are high school graduates, and most of the others are older youth or adults.

Education for Vocation to Meet Community Needs.—Surveys are conducted to determine what are the community needs. A larger community with a number of business establishments, for example, finds that there is a need and a demand for trained stenographers. Communities like Rochester, Minnesota, have developed a program for training medical secretaries in the junior college, a definite need in that community. Agriculture courses are established in farming areas where boys have an opportunity and an interest in farming. Distributive education programs are begun in communities that have a number of retailing establishments which are interested in having the schools develop this type of education. The junior college or technical school often serves more specialized community needs for training at the post-high school level, offering courses such as carpentry, printing, airplane mechanics, and the like. Pasadena City College, for example, has among its terminal curricula, training for cosmetology, landscape design, painting and decorating, and stage technology. In San Francisco City College, a hotel management program and the training of cooks and bakers has been found suitable to the community, which has a large number of hotels.

In these cases, it is not a hit-or-miss matter. The vocational programs have advisory committees of community members from the employers and from unions. In other words, in the best programs of vocational education there is first an initial survey to determine the needs and then a constant working arrangement with the industry or business to keep the program functional and useful. The most successful semi-professional and other terminal programs in junior colleges are the ones that are planned and carried out cooperatively with community industries or business and professional establishments. They include considerable attention to attitudes, understanding the job, getting along with people, and a broad general education.

A New Concept of the School's Laboratory.—The entire community, as well as the school, is the laboratory in many phases of the specialized learnings. Especially is this true of some of the vocational programs. If we seek examples of a curriculum that is life-centered and holds the interests of youth, we should look at some of the work being done in agriculture, in homemaking, and in part-time cooperative education. We ought to examine the programs of secondary schools in which pupils perform work for the community as a part of their education.

The illustrations that are given in the following pages live up to the principles of good education discussed in the first chapter. They represent learning by doing. As we read them, we should note that they have these characteristics in common:

1. Pupils learn through real life experiences. It is not a matter of merely reading about a process; it is living the process. These are educative experiences of the highest order.
2. The experiences have meaning, for they concern the here-and-now problems that must be solved today. Contrast them with the practice of storing up knowledge that may be useful in the future.
3. The experiences are purposeful. Youth know why they are doing these things and do them because they want to. There are no assignments that must be done to please the teacher in these classes where the teacher is awake to the vast possibilities in his area of teaching.

Vocational Agriculture—An Experience Program.—In the vocational agriculture programs in secondary schools there are many examples of youth carrying on significant learning experiences. The student's home farm is his laboratory. Much of the investigation and study that he does at school is centered around acquiring information that will be helpful in carrying on his projects on the farm. These are not nine-month affairs. Instead, they are year-round projects that the farm boy carries through to completion. The teacher of agriculture works with him on the farm and at school. During the summer, the teacher spends his time visiting the farms of his pupils.

Production projects are of a common type, in which the pupil raises crops, cattle, hogs, or some other kind of farm produce. He often owns his projects himself or in partnership with his father. For example, a boy will buy some calves, make his plans for raising them, plan how to feed them, keep records of costs, and market them at the proper time. The supplementary farm practices that are a part of his experiences consist of learning, through the actual operation, such skills as caponizing chickens, shearing sheep, or operating an incubator. These again are done on the farm. The farm shop in connection with agriculture programs gives the pupil an opportunity to repair farm machinery that he uses and to learn skills useful to a farming career. Many schools have well equipped farm shops.

Another type of farm project, known as an improvement project, has as its objective improving the land, farm buildings, or stock. In one instance, farm youth might work for dairy herd improvement, keeping actual milk production records and feeding records. At Frost Community School, Navarro County, Texas, the agriculture teacher and the high school boys in his classes have cooperated with the boys' fathers to extend such improvement projects to a community-wide basis. They have built terraces for conservation of the soil, sprayed fruit trees, introduced new crops, culled poultry, and helped in other ways to make their agricultural community a better place in which to live.[2]

In response to a need for improvement in the breeding and care of poultry, the eighth grade of Plainview-Rover School, Plainview, Arkansas, constructed a poultry house and raised a flock of purebred chickens. In this community, the project supplied the lunchroom with eggs. It illustrates that in junior high school grades also, outside the federal vocational program, significant experiences in the area of agriculture are provided as an integral part of the life of the school.[3] In some sections of the country where forestry is a source of livelihood, the school may own a forest, or the state may lease land to the school for forestry instruction. Elma High School, Elma, Washington, for example, owns several tracts of forest land where youth acquire first-hand laboratory experience in forestry practices.

Real-Life Laboratory Experiences in Home Economics.—For many high school girls, home economics is a specialized phase of study. They may take courses for four years in order to develop their competencies as a homemaker. Here again in the well-developed programs, we find a wealth of first-hand experiences that are actually a part of the homemaker's life. Home economics teachers, too, work with their pupils for more than nine months of the year. The best programs are found where schools have more actual laboratory experiences than just in the areas of foods and clothing. In these schools, the girls take care of children; manage a house; prepare meals for outside groups; do upholstering, papering, painting, and the like.

---

[2] W. H. McCharen, *Improving the Quality of Living,* Nashville, Tennessee: Division of Surveys and Field Services, George Peabody College for Teachers, 1947, p. 52.
[3] *Ibid.,* p. 38.

In New London High School, New London, Connecticut, the girls operate a nursery school where parents send their children certain hours of the day. This experience is a part of the required homemaking course for all girls; in the senior year, a small group of girls specialize in child care. Invaluable experience is gained through observing the children, playing with them, and caring for them. At Weatherwax High School, Aberdeen, Washington, the home economics classes renovated a school room and established a nursery for children in the area.

While the writer was associated with the Portland public schools, Portland, Oregon, the Jane Addams High School operated a house owned by the school district. Under the direction of the teacher, who lived in the house, the girls redecorated rooms, planned the furnishings, and served luncheon to small groups of the school staff that scheduled meetings there. The girls planned the menus and bought and prepared the food. When the guests arrived, they met them at the door. Later they served them at luncheon. Such experiences are a far cry from answering questions on "a lesson assigned for today."

Home nursing classes, as well as the more common homemaking classes, use the homes of the community for laboratory experiences. The pupils learn skills which they practice in their own and other homes of the community.

Part-time Cooperative Work Programs.—One of the most significant developments in American secondary education in recent years is the part-time cooperative program in which the school and business or industry cooperate in providing the education for youth. The plan has been given an impetus through federal aid to the school under the George-Deen Act of 1936.

Pupils spend part of their time at school and part of the time on the job. In some cases, they alternate a few weeks at school and at work; in others, a half a day is spent at school and a half a day on the job. During the time at school, pupils receive training related to the job and take other related courses. For example, in retailing programs the related work may consist of show-card lettering, salesmanship, and other skills useful to the job. Related study may include employer-employee relationships and conditions that promote successful employment. A coordinator employed by the school supervises the pupils on the job and serves as contact person with the employers. At the school, he gives the related training courses. Here we can see the experience-centered curriculum operating. Pupils and teacher plan their work together to fit the needs of the particular job. Each pupil will have individual goals, for no two jobs will be exactly alike.

In this type of plan, the school gives the general education and the broad, general vocational training, while the community provides the laboratory for actual work experience. It is fundamentally an educational program, for no employer is obligated to hire any of the trainees as his regular employees after they have completed training. It is realistic, for it meets community needs and is set into the community rather than apart from it. It holds promise for the future, since it does not require huge outlays of funds for equipping elaborate school shops designed to give training in specific skills.

Cooperative Programs in Distributive Education.—One type of federally aided program, known as distributive education, deals with retailing and other distributive occupations. The school and the place of business cooperate in the education program. In Sulfolk High School, Sulfolk, Virginia, the pupil works at the store, which serves as his laboratory for vocational education, fifteen to twenty-five hours a week. He learns the different aspects of the work and is supervised by the coordinator from the school. At school, he studies salesmanship, advertising, display, business English, store and stock keeping, and related work as a part of a course in retail selling.

The cooperative retail selling program at Springfield High School, Springfield, Vermont, is planned by the coordinator and the merchants of the community. Pupils work afternoons in the stores during their senior year for fifteen to eighteen hours a week. They are at school during the morning for English, social studies, physical education, and the related subjects. Apprenticeship wages, determined cooperatively by the school and a merchants' advisory committee, are paid to pupils for their work. The merchant trains the pupil in various phases of retail selling as a part of his experience on the job. For example, this training includes use of the cash register, the writing of sales slips, wrapping, filling orders, marking merchandise, inventory, store arrangement, window display, sales technique, and the like. The store reports to the school coordinator on the student's progress.

Cooperative Programs for Various Occupations.—Another type of rather common vocational program is cooperative training for specified occupations, in some states called a diversified occupations program; this is a form of part-time education adaptable to smaller communities, since no elaborate equipment is needed in the school. It again involves a cooperative arrangement between the school and local businesses and industries. In this plan, there is a variety of types of jobs in which the pupils may receive their training, such as foods, printing, electrical work, auto-body repair, cleaning and pressing, jewelry repair, shipping clerk, general store work. In the related course at school, there are usually many types of jobs represented in one group of pupils. Its purpose is to prepare youth who are sixteen years or over for jobs available in their own community. A school coordinator makes the contacts in the community and supervises the work of the pupils.

For example, Sewanhaka High School, Floral Park, New York, includes in its cooperative training for specified occupations program, auto mechanics, plumbing, machine shop, printing, beauty culture, banking, office practice, and retailing. The pupil spends alternate weeks at work and in the school. The director of placement supervises the pupils on the job, contacting the employers each week. Although pupil learners must be paid the rate set by either the minimum wage law or union regulations, a number are paid more than the minimum.

Springfield High School, Vermont, has a variety of cooperative programs. In the cooperative course, a trades and industries cooperative plan, pupils receive training in machine shop, pattern making, carpentry, cabinetmaking, sheetmetal work, electrical work, and auto mechanics. For example, in the tenth grade, pupils spend half their time in the school machine shop learning to operate the machines used in local industries, alternating every five weeks in the shop and in taking other school subjects. Pupils interested in other trades are placed in various trade shops on the same basis. In the junior and senior years, pupils selected enter local shops, garages, building trade companies, and other local contracting firms and serve as apprentices in the community, alternating every five weeks between school and shop. One year of post-graduate work completes the apprenticeship period. Wages are set at a figure suitable to the occupation. Students receive the high school diploma at the end of their senior year.[4]

Office Practice Work.—In many instances where secondary schools may not have a part-time cooperative education program under the federal plan, they have established cooperative working relations with the business offices of the community. The office practice course, usually offered in the senior year to pupils preparing for stenographic work, often is an example of that type of plan. In the office practice class, pupils may receive work experience on the job, either

---

[4] "Vocational Education at Springfield High," *The Green Horn* (student newspaper), May 11, 1942; New England School Development Council, *Effective Practices in New England Schools,* Cambridge, Mass.: Peabody House, 1947, pp. 16-17.

through part-time work or work in an office over an extended number of days, such as during vacation periods. Often, experience is obtained in the school offices as well. Where the most successful programs are carried on, the teacher maintains a close contact with the business establishment to assure that the experience might be a profitable one for the pupil.

The School as a Community.—We have seen that some high schools plan the curriculum with just a token recognition that youth lives in a world of ongoing activities. Others take full advantage of the marvelous opportunities for learning that exist in every school. In this community of young people, they make use of the lunchroom, the accounting of funds, and the planning and executing of pupil safety programs. They experience learning situations in books that must be checked and distributed, supplies that must be sold, and equipment that must be constructed. Often, these activities are tied in with the classroom work.

An example of training in the handling of money is found in Weatherwax High School, Aberdeen, Washington, where the bookkeeping classes take charge of activity accounts. The classroom here has become an integral part of the ongoing life of the school community. In other places, the commercial classes run the school bank, as at Windham High School, Willimantic, Connecticut.

Art classes and music classes, instead of resenting "intrusions," welcome the privilege of preparing stage sets for dramatic productions, posters for many types of events, and music for different school functions. It is in these subject areas that we often find an integrated plan for cooperative production of operettas or other musical productions. In these classes, the productions may become the major project for the classes for a period of time. Industrial art classes also participate in such types of coordinated all-school projects.

Again we turn to some of the southern high schools for examples of building a curriculum around the school's activities in the various specialized classes. These schools have turned necessity into opportunity. It is difficult to determine where classwork ends and extra-class activity begins. All of these activities are an integral part of a worth-while program of experiences, but they are examples of work experiences that are varied and individualized. Pupils run the school store, run the feed and grist mills, work in the cannery, work in the slaughterhouse, or maintain the school grounds. A number of such examples are given in Chapters 10 and 11. Care is taken that pupils are not exploited and that such experiences are not merely drudgery and hard work.

Baxter Seminary, a private secondary school in Baxter, Tennessee, is a living example of a school community that furnishes all types of work experiences. Service and work experiences are combined. The buildings have been built by pupils, furniture has been constructed by them, and a good share of the food is raised and prepared by them. The main difference between this and many other schools is that here all who can do some form of work participate; work experience really becomes a part of everyone's general education, except in the case of some pupils who have difficulty in arranging schedules in traveling to and from school. The entire school plant and campus serves as a laboratory.

Classes go to some building or repair project for two hours a day to learn jobs such as bricklaying, plastering, carpentry, cabinetmaking, concrete mixing, and the like. It is evident that these work experiences furnish specialized vocational skills. Students are also employed by the school or by local business places as apprentice trainees in a part-time cooperative program.[5]

4. First Steps

Many of the first steps that were mentioned in the preceding chapter on common learnings, apply to specialized learnings as well. Any school that is genuinely concerned about adjusting its curriculum to the needs of youth and to community needs will in some organized fashion work toward improvement. Results cannot be expected overnight but cooperative study will result in progress. These suggestions assume that teachers and citizens are examining their secondary school program together to fashion a growing, functional curriculum.

1. All teachers can give attention to specialized interests of students in their courses, seeing that they are given every possibility to develop and expand those interests.
2. The beginning teacher who makes broadside assignments to all pupils has taken his first step *away from* the principle of developing individual potentialities. It is tragic to see students of outstanding ability sit through class after class answering questions on the textbooks, when the library, the rest of the school, and the community are so full of possibilities for learning. As a new teacher, if we must ask questions of the entire group day after

---

[5] See Jeanne Kellar, "When the Roof Leaked," *World Outlook,* 37 (April, 1947), 144-46.

day, we can at least plan independent study programs for those pupils.

3. It would be sensible also for us to use these pupils as leaders, as committee chairmen, as class chairmen, and as committee members to assist other pupils with their learning problems.

4. We will have taken the first long step if we will resolve not to teach any class in such a manner that all pupils pursue the same activities. When we have done that, we will find it possible to let pupils explore certain interests as far as they wish to go, and to assist them in doing so.

5. Teachers should ask themselves: do the courses that youth elect develop interests that are lasting, skills that are useful, and attitudes that will make them better workers and producers? What do youth do with their leisure time outside of school? Are they successful in their jobs? What happens to them after they leave school? A real searching analysis, open-mindedly approached, should be revealing.

6. Most important of all, we can diligently search for the potentialities of each individual and find something that he can do better than others. Democracy holds that every individual has a contribution to make. We can help him make it.

7. It would be helpful if every teacher had some opportunity to work at different kinds of jobs and gain a better understanding of work conditions and the culture of other groups than the middle or professional class.

8. We can bring our influence as faculty members to bear on providing flexibility for some pupils with outstanding capabilities along certain lines—music, art, crafts, mechanics, science, or any other type. Such a pupil *could* be given the privilege of meeting with different classes, in addition to the four or five regularly scheduled for his program. Perhaps at times he might remain in the shop for a half a day. Only if we are concerned with covering subject matter rather than developing potentialities of people, will this suggestion seem objectionable.

9. A survey of the community, in which youth, the school staff, and lay people all participate, can reveal how adequate is the education for vocations offered by the school. The kinds of skills and attitudes wanted by employers, the community needs for vocational training, and the opportunities for work experience as a part of education should be explored. An honest evaluation of the present program for vocational education can only be secured if the employers, labor unions, and other citizens participate.

10. If vocational education is to continue to be realistic, advisory committees of lay citizens should constantly appraise the needs and search for additional possibilities.

11. The teacher who is working in the vocational area must keep up such contacts himself in order that he might adjust the curriculum in his courses to changing needs.

12. If a school were just beginning to examine how effectively it provides for the specialized needs of youth, it could profitably study the programs of courses that pupils have pursued in high school, weighing them against the interests and special abilities shown in the individual pupil records. In effect, this is a type of case study in which the guidance workers should participate. Have different pupils with varied abilities actually pursued any special interests, or have fixed curricula limited them to much the same kind of program? Were capable students allowed freedom to explore? Do the records show that the school helped pupils to build upon whatever strengths they had? Of course, adequate records of growth are necessary to the most effective type of study of this nature.

13. In the case of a small high school, such a study might be a strong factor in the realization of a need for expanded school facilities through consolidation. Teachers and lay people ought to consider whether the curriculum that it is possible to offer with existing resources is the best for the youth of the community. Local pride and intercommunity animosities must be weighed against what is good for the children. However, someone must have the foresight and vision to begin such a study.

14. Where financial resources are limited, the human resources of imagination, ingenuity, and a deep concern for children should not be overlooked. As we have seen in this chapter, some of the areas in the South, poor in the former but rich in the latter, have built for themselves some outstanding secondary school programs. Are there possibilities for acquiring a school farm? What does the community offer as resources? How can the people work together to build a school curriculum that utilizes all of the splendid laboratory that the community offers for education?

SELECTED REFERENCES

Administration of Vocational Education. Federal Security Agency, Office of Education, Vocational Education Bulletin, 1948, No. 1, General Series No. 1, Washington, D.C.: Government Printing Office, 1949, 112 pp.—Presents a brief, convenient description of the various kinds of federally aided vocational education programs.

CASWELL, HOLLIS L. (ed.). *The American High School* (Eighth Yearbook of John Dewey Society). New York: Harper & Bros., 1946, chap. 9.—This is a chapter on the problems and possibilities of vocational education.

DOUGLASS, HARL R. (ed.). *Education for Life Adjustment.* New York: The Ronald Press Co., 1950, chaps. 7-13, 18.—These chapters also contain information on specialized learnings in the various subject fields: science, mathematics, music, industrial arts, business education, home economics, and the general area of vocational education and work experience.

DOUGLASS, HARL R. (ed.). *The High School Curriculum.* New York: The Ronald Press Co., 1947, chaps. 13, 14, 22-29.—Different chapters are written by specialists in science, foreign languages, mathematics, home and family living, business education, music, industrial arts, and art. Includes some discussion of education for vocation. The student will need to select those portions of the chapters concerned with specialized learnings.

EDUCATIONAL POLICIES COMMISSION. *Education for ALL American Youth.* Washington, D.C.: National Education Association, 1944, chaps. 3, 4.—Select portions of these chapters for the proposals for specialized education in "American City" and "Farmville."

McCHAREN, W. K. *Improving the Quality of Living.* Nashville, Tenn.: Division of Surveys and Field Services, George Peabody College for Teachers, 1947, 67 pp.—This is a fascinating pamphlet on the story of how various southern communities have provided opportunities for specialized learnings by making use of the community as a laboratory.

NATIONAL SOCIETY FOR THE STUDY OF EDUCATION. *Vocational Education* (Part I, Forty-second Yearbook). Chicago: Department of Education, University of Chicago, 1943, chaps. 1, 2, and Section III.—This comprehensive reference will be useful for further information on various types of vocational education programs, the purposes of vocational education, and its relation to general education.

OLSEN, EDWARD G. *School and Community Programs.* New York: Prentice-Hall, Inc., 1949, chap. 10.—Presents a number of specific illustrations of work experience, including experiences at school, on the farm, and in community industrial and business establishments.

PIERCE, PAUL R. *Developing a High-School Curriculum.* New York: American Book Co., 1942, chap. 9.—An account of community and school work experiences is included in this interesting report of the development of a functional curriculum in Wells High School, Chicago.

PROGRESSIVE EDUCATION ASSOCIATION. *Thirty Schools Tell Their Story.* New York: Harper & Bros., 1943, 802 pp.—The accounts of the schools in the Eight-Year Study will be especially useful for getting further information on specialized learnings in the academic fields.

Chapter 10

EXTRACLASS EXPERIENCES

"Extracurricular" activities are by no means new in the program of the secondary school. Literary societies and debating societies were very common in the academies that preceded the high school, as well as in the early high schools. The daily chapel period, so prevalent a century ago, was the forerunner of the modern school assembly, while essay and poetry contests had also been a common form of extracurricular activity for many years. Commencement exercises, with speeches by the class valedictorian and the salutatorian, were likewise found in the early high school.

In the last twenty-five years a considerable change has taken place in our point of view concerning "extracurricular" activities. More and more we have come to see that these activities have a significant contribution to make in the educational growth of the child. For instance, the child may make far more growth in effective speech skills through participation in debate than in an English class; the school band may contribute more to growth in music appreciation than the more formal music class; the school paper may give much more opportunity to develop writing skills than the English class; and growth in certain citizenship qualities may result from school clubs as well as from the social studies class.

The realization that these activities have significant educational values has encouraged educators to attach greater importance to them. It is now believed that these activities should not be considered "extra," but that they should form a well-integrated part of the school curriculum. This principle is in harmony with the present thinking that the curriculum includes all the educational activities provided under the supervision of the school. In harmony with this point of view we shall call these activities "extraclass" rather than "extracurricular," to distinguish them from those activities which form a part of the usual classroom program.

1. The Principles

There are certain principles which are basic to a forward-looking and effective program of extraclass activities in the secondary school.

These principles are appropriate to all the different types of activities. They apply at both the junior and senior high school levels.

The extraclass activities should be developed and carried on in terms of well-formulated and worth-while educational goals.

This principle is as essential for the extraclass activities as it is for any other aspect of the instructional program. There are many schools in which this principle is not applied. All too often the extraclass activities grow by accretion, with no clear-cut understanding of the contribution which they should make to the educational growth and development of the child. However, unless the extraclass activities contribute directly toward realizing the ultimate goals of education, there can be little justification for expending on them the public funds of the community, the time and attention of the teachers, and the energy of the children.

It may be helpful to give the important immediate objectives that may be served by an effective program of extraclass activities. These objectives may be summarized as follows:

1. To help pupils develop qualities of leadership, group cooperation, and other qualities essential to effective democratic living.
2. To help pupils acquire certain personal and character qualities, such as self-confidence, poise, initiative, resourcefulness, courtesy, and self-control.
3. To help pupils explore various interests, talents, and abilities, in a manner which would be difficult in the usual classroom program.
4. To assist pupils to be active and creative, and to gain the satisfaction that comes from accomplishing things that to them are interesting and worth while.
5. To give pupils an opportunity to apply many of the fundamental skills and much of the knowledge which they acquire in other ways in the classroom program.

It is true, of course, that these same purposes may be achieved in part through the usual classroom activities. The fact remains, however, that in extraclass activities there is much more freedom for pupils to carry on projects in terms of their own interests and preferences. It is this freedom for pupils to plan and carry on various projects and activities that gives much value to the extraclass program.

The extraclass activities should be well integrated with other aspects of the school's instructional program.

When extraclass activities were first introduced into the secondary school program, they were clearly "extra" in every sense of the word. Usually participation was confined to a few pupils, the activities took place after school, and in other ways they were treated as nonessentials in the educational program. Educators today believe that the instructional program of the school should be planned as a whole, with every phase closely correlated with every other in so far as that is possible. For instance, the various clubs, classes, and home rooms should prepare and present assembly programs; the English and social studies classes should prepare pupils for responsibilities in clubs and on the student council; the home rooms, homemaking classes, and English classes should give pupils backgrounds in etiquette and social practices for more effective participation in school parties; and in other ways the various classes and pupil activities should contribute to each other.

The program of extraclass activities should be sufficiently broad and varied to provide for the needs, abilities, and interests of all the pupils.

If the program of extraclass activities is to serve the purposes for which it is intended, it is essential that there be clubs which will interest every child in school, sports activities for every boy and girl, music organizations that provide for pupils with various talents, and assembly activities that appeal to every interest. This indeed presents a challenge to every teacher and administrator in the secondary school. That it can be done is evident from the practices found in many junior and senior high schools today, some of which will be presented later in this chapter.

The management of extraclass activities should provide for much pupil participation and responsibility in their control, administration, and planning.

Pupils should participate in developing the extraclass program as a whole. For instance, they should be consulted when the offering of club activities is decided upon; they should participate in planning the assembly activities for the year; and they should have a voice in suggesting the nature of the social functions. What is more, the pupils should have a considerable part in planning and carrying on the specific activities once the extraclass program is under way. In the clubs, the pupils should plan the activities, the projects, and the meetings. They should also plan the school parties, make decisions concerning school publications, and in other ways assume responsibility for carrying on the various activities. Of course, this pupil participation should take place under the careful supervision of competent faculty sponsors.

These activities provide an excellent laboratory for skills in democratic living. As pupils assume responsibility for the various activities, they learn how to make and carry out decisions, to organize group activities, to work democratically with their fellows, and to evaluate their successes and failures. Student participation in the government of the school should involve real responsibility, not merely such "clean-up" tasks as the administration may want to have done. Only if that is done will pupils experience the satisfaction of making a significant contribution to the life of the school and thus have enthusiasm for further participation.

The pupil's school experience outside class should be planned as carefully by administrators, teachers, and pupils as any other phase of the instructional program.

The idea that these activities were "extra" has had considerable bearing on the attention which has been given to planning and organizing them. There is a tendency to plan for them after the "regular" school work is done. As long as this attitude persists, much of the educational value of these activities is lost. The principal and faculty should plan the entire program of extraclass activities for the school, having pupils participate in so far as their time and ability permit. Faculty sponsors working with pupil officers and committees should prepare carefully the program and organization of each individual activity. The same principles of organization and planning which pertain to English, the social studies, and other classes are equally appropriate for the activities in the extraclass program.

Extraclass activities should be carried on largely during school hours.

Until this principle is applied, the values of extraclass activities cannot be realized to the fullest. As long as pupils must remain after school hours to participate in these activities, that participation will necessarily be limited. After school there will be interferences for many pupils, such as the departure of the school bus, after-school employment, and duties at home. One would hardly expect pupils to make much progress in history or English if these courses were taught after school hours. Likewise, growth in leadership, citizenship, personality, and other qualities is most likely to result for all the pupils if the extraclass activities are carried on during the regular school day. In some schools, the school day will need to be lengthened to provide the time needed for these activities.

The extraclass activities should be evaluated continually in terms of the educational goals they are to achieve.

Continuous evaluation is essential to the success of any part of the educational program. The evaluation of extraclass activities should answer such questions as : How well are pupils realizing the ultimate aims of education through the extraclass program? What activities are particularly effective in contributing to the growth of children? What activities apparently are making little contribution to the educational growth of the children? How well are the principles for an effective extraclass program being implemented in the various activities? In what specific ways can the effectiveness of the various activities be improved? What new types of activities should be added to the program? What proportion of the student body takes part in activities? All groups who are in any way concerned with the extraclass activities should participate in evaluating them, including the principals, supervisors, teachers, parents, and pupils. Pupils particularly should have a significant part in evaluating the effectiveness of the various activities.

The interests and needs of individual pupils should be the only prerequisites to participation in extraclass activities.

If extraclass activities provide desirable learning experiences for pupils, the prerequisites for participation that are typical in the secondary school cannot be justified. The pupil with poor speech habits, little music talent, or mediocre athletic ability as well as the talented youth, should have the opportunity to make growth in the areas in which he is interested. This does not mean that all interested pupils should play on the first team, represent the school in interscholastic debate, or have the lead in the class play. That is obviously impossible, as well as undesirable. But it does mean that a place should be provided for the child in every aspect of the extraclass program where his limited talents may find expression, that he should have the privilege of participating in assemblies, clubs, journalism, and other activities to the extent that his abilities permit, and that he be given help in improving himself so that his level of participation in the various activities may be improved as he proceeds through the secondary school. The practices of electing members to "elite" social clubs and of requiring passing marks for participation in activities are not in accord with this principle.

The entire school community should serve as a source of learning experiences.

In a number of the other principles already stated, the thought has been expressed that extraclass activities provide just as important learning experiences as the classroom phases of the instructional program. There are numerous opportunities in the total school community for worth-while learning experiences. For example, assemblies offer leadership experiences; the school library, the cafeteria, and intramural activities present service opportunities for pupils; corridors, playgrounds, and study halls present situations in which pupils can participate in managing the school; and activity finances, the care of school supplies, and safety precautions are rich in learning opportunities. Not only may pupils have significant experiences in various phases of the life of the school community, but they may also have the satisfaction of performing a service for that community. The entire program of the school should be fully explored if we are to discover all the learning experiences it may provide for pupils.

The extraclass activities, like other aspects of the educational program, should be provided at little or no cost to the pupil.

If extraclass activities provide significant learning experiences for pupils, there is no more justification for imposing costs on the participants than in the mathematics or English classes. The cost of equipment for football, instruments for the band or orchestra, supplies for clubs, and other similar items should be assumed by the school much like the expense of purchasing textbooks. Furthermore, the cost of such items as dues for club membership, club pins, school parties, attendance at athletic contests, subscription to the magazine and newspaper, and the school yearbook, should be kept to a nominal sum so that pupils will not be prevented from participation for this reason. The fact that pupils vote such expenses does not justify them, because the pupils who find them prohibitive are not likely to express themselves on the subject. There should be an established policy in the school to keep the costs to pupils of extraclass activities to an absolute minimum.

2. Some Typical Practices

Extensive Club Activities—Particularly in the Junior High School.—In both junior and senior high schools, pupil clubs are a significant part of the extraclass program. Practices governing these activities vary widely from school to school. In junior high schools, it is common to offer a considerable variety of club activities so that every child may find an interest in them. In these schools, clubs usually meet during an activities period which is part of the regular school day, every pupil is expected, though not required, to belong, and the fees and other costs are held to a minimum. There are seldom prerequisites for membership, other than the pupil's interest in the club. In the junior high school, election to membership by the present club group is rare.

One characteristic of club activities common to both junior and senior high schools is the attempt to meet the interests of all pupils. Half a century ago, clubs consisted primarily of debating and literary societies. Today, many large schools have a club for every conceivable interest of boys and girls. In a study made some years ago it was found that one fourth of the schools with enrollments exceeding 750 pupils had more than fifty different clubs.[1] A list of various types of clubs found in secondary schools, with sample clubs in each group, is as follows:[2]

All-school clubs: booster, cafeteria, girl leaders, leadership, pep, safety patrol, school service, traffic

Foreign language clubs: French, German, Latin, Spanish

Physical education clubs: aesthetic dancing, archery, first aid, folk dancing, gymnasium leaders, hiking, life saving, posture, riding, rifle, social dancing, tap dancing

English clubs: biography, book design, debate, dramatics, impromptu speaking, journalism, library service, magazine, oratory, poetry, short story, story telling

Civic-social-moral clubs: friendship, Girl Scouts, historical fiction, Hi-Y, Indian lore, Junior Red Cross, personal improvement, travel

Art clubs: basketry, block printing, cartoon, chalk talkers, clay modeling, commercial poster, greeting card, leather craft, paper novelties, portrait, pottery, sculpture, soap carving, water color

Science and mathematics clubs: astronomy, bird, camera, field and stream, mathematics, puzzle, microscope, nature study, radio, science news, telegraph

Domestic arts clubs: baking, candy making, cooking, embroidery, 4-H club, gift, home entertainment, home nursing, hostess, knitting, needlework, personal appearance, rag doll, rag rug, tatting, toy cloth animal

---

[1] William T. Gruhn, "The Administration of Club Activities in the Junior High School," *The Elementary School Journal,* 35:107-14 (October, 1934).

[2] A much more complete list of clubs is available in William T. Gruhn and Harl R. Douglass, *The Modern Junior High School,* New York: The Ronald Press Co., 1947, pp. 355-57.

Manual arts clubs: airplane, automobile, birdhouse, boat, book mending, electricity, handicraft, house plans, jig saw, kite, marionette, scenery, model house, printing, saw club, stagecraft, toy making, wood carving, yacht

Commercial clubs: advertising, bankers, business practice, secretaries, thrift, typewriting, vocations

Music clubs: band, chorus, drum-and-bugle corps, glee, harmonica, marimba, minstrel, music appreciation, piano, popular songs, singing, ukelele, violin

Miscellaneous clubs: anagram, bachelors, beauty culture, believe-it-or-not, Braille, bridge, campcraft, checkers, chess, circus, jokesters, knot tying, magicians, party planners, puzzle, stamp and coin, table tennis, usher

Practice governing club activities in the senior high school is rather different from that in the junior high school. Club activities are carried on largely after school hours; they tend to be divorced from, rather than integrated with, the other aspects of the school program; the cost of dues, pins, and other items is frequently so high as to exclude some pupils from participation; and the percentage of pupils who belong is too small. Furthermore, in some senior high schools, membership is restricted by tryouts and election by present club members. Any device that restricts the freedom of a pupil to join clubs and other activities, except to limit the number in which he may participate, tends to defeat the educational purposes which these activities should achieve. Election to the club by present members, though now practiced in only a few schools, is a particularly undemocratic procedure.

Fraternities Discouraged in Secondary Schools.—One of the most difficult problems for the faculty and administration of a secondary school in dealing with extraclass activities is the fraternity and the sorority. Often they are secret, meeting away from the school building, with no supervision from teachers or parents. Not only are they undemocratic in their selection of members, but it is doubtful that they serve any worth-while educational purpose. Still, they have existed for years in many secondary schools, and continue to exist despite objections from school administrators, teachers, and parents.

In some states, a definite stand has been taken to abolish fraternities and sororities in secondary schools through statutes passed by the legislature. Courageous school administrators and interested parent groups have also attacked the problem with varying degrees of success. One positive approach is to have an excellent program of club activities and social functions which will appeal to every pupil who might have an interest in belonging to a fraternity or sorority. Under intelligent supervision from faculty and parents, clubs and social activities can do much to counteract the appeal of these societies.

Speech Activities Often on a Formal Basis.—The speech activities in the secondary school usually include debate, oratory, interpretative reading, and extemporaneous speaking. In the junior high school, these activities tend to be conducted on an informal basis, with much emphasis on wide pupil participation, noncompetitive activities, and activities confined largely to the regular school day. These speech activities are carried on in assemblies, club meetings, English and social studies classes, and similar groups. In some communities, there is interschool competition in speech activities at the junior high school level, although it is usually between schools in the same system. Some junior high schools, however, have interscholastic competition in speech activities, much like the senior high school speech program. Such competition in the junior high school is indeed to be discouraged. In such a program, the emphasis on winning is likely to interfere with the realization of worth-while educational objectives.

The situation governing speech activities in the senior high school differs sharply from that in the junior high school. There the speech activities are usually carried on in a much more formal manner with participation limited to a few able pupils; there is considerable interschool competition in such activities as debate, oratory, and declamation; and much attention is given to the audience situation. Such a formal speech program is difficult to justify in a democratic secondary school. Dozens of pupils who have an interest in these activities and need the educational opportunities which they provide are deprived of the privilege to participate. The four-year and senior high school could profit much by studying the various informal speech activities —with a place for every child—that are now fairly common in the junior high school.

Athletics Provided for Few Pupils.—The athletics program is more controversial than any other extraclass activity. It attracts more interest among the student body and the public than any other group of pupil activities, and it has great potentialities for worthwhile learning experiences. At the same time, it is probably the subject of more abuse than any other phase of the educational program in the secondary school.

The program of athletics at the senior high school level may be characterized as follows:

1. It is primarily an interscholastic program, with most of the interest and energy of faculty and students directed toward developing winning teams.

2. Participation is limited to a small part of the student body. If there are teams other than the varsity, they tend to exist to prepare material for the first team rather than to give the participating youth a wholesome educational experience.

3. The program of athletics is largely divorced from other aspects of the educational program, instead of being closely integrated with them. In fact, it is frequently as unrelated to other phases of health and physical education in the school curriculum as it is to such subjects as English and mathematics.

4. There is much less attention given to sports which are likely to be enjoyed in adult life, such as tennis, golf, and swimming.

5. Much attention is given to the spectator situation and the support of sports fans in the community. Sports which are emphasized most are those, like football and basketball, which have the greatest spectator appeal.

The only justification for the inclusion of any activity in the curriculum of a secondary school is that it contributes to the educational growth and development of youth. Measured by this criterion, the athletics program in most senior high schools is indeed found wanting. It is true that more and more schools are developing broad intramural programs. Too often, however, the facilities provided by the school are not adequate for an intramural program that meets the needs of a considerable majority of the youth. The demands of the varsity teams on the faculty and the physical facilities usually are so great that little time is left for the intramural activities.

In the junior high school, there is a greater tendency than in the senior high school to provide a sports program to meet the needs of all youth. At this level, intramural activities tend to predominate, with competition carried on between grades, home rooms, or physical education classes. Usually these activities are carried on in the afternoon rather than the evening, participation by many pupils is considered to be more important than to have winning teams, and the evils of interschool competition usually are not a problem. Many junior high schools, however, do not have staff or the facilities to provide sports activities for every physically able child.

In both junior and senior high schools, girls are badly neglected in the sports program. In many schools, there are no activities at all for girls, except in the physical education classes. Furthermore, the gymnasium, swimming pool, and playgrounds frequently are just not available for a girls' sports program. Girls of secondary school age, like boys, should have some sports participation. It need not be as extensive or as strenuous a program as that for boys, but there should be some sports activities which meet the needs and interests of secondary school girls.

A particularly obnoxious practice, from an educational standpoint, has been that of demanding "eligibility" in scholarship as a prerequisite for participation in athletics. To deprive the child of one educational experience because he has failed to do well in another surely cannot be justified on educational grounds alone. In the intramural program, there is little justification for the eligibility requirements that are so common in the senior high school, and also are found occasionally in the junior high school. In interscholastic competition also, such requirements are not justifiable. They are maintained largely because of the undesirable features of interscholastic athletics cited above.

Pupil Participation in Administration.—The participation of pupils in the administration of the school is most commonly provided through the organization of a student council. The council is usually a representative pupil body elected by grades or home rooms and serves under a constitution which defines its duties and responsibilities. As a rule, its authority is limited to such activities as (1) the direction of corridor traffic, (2) cafeteria supervision, (3) supervision of pupil elections, (4) the sponsoring of assembles, parties, and field days, and (5) service as an advisory body to the administrative authority of the school.

The effectiveness of the student council is limited in many schools because there is a lack of understanding of the functions of a council and how it should be set up. Some of the more serious shortcomings of student government organizations are the following:

1. The responsibilities of the student council are not clearly defined, with the result that neither students nor faculty know precisely how it can make a significant contribution to the life of the school. In some schools an aggressive council may assume that it has authority over all school functions, while in others it may find nothing significant to do. Frequently, the council is given the feeling that it has no real authority except in unimportant matters. Often, it is not given genuine responsibility for student affairs and activities.

2. There is not sufficient time for student council meetings to study thoroughly the problems that may come before it. Frequently, the

council meets before or after school, during the noon hour, or at some other time when its deliberations are likely to be hurried.

3. There is often a lack of forward-looking and effective leadership among the student body. This is true in part because few schools have a program of leadership education to develop the potentialities and skills of pupils to administer positions of leadership.

4. A capable, tactful, well-prepared, and interested faculty sponsor for the council is difficult to find. Upon such a sponsor, more than any other one factor, the success of the student council will depend.

In some schools, the student council has been given considerable responsibility for school discipline. In the majority of schools, however, pupils have little opportunity to participate either in formulating a policy for discipline or assisting in carrying out that policy.

Pupil Publications Not Always Integrated with the School Program.—The most common pupil publications in the secondary school are the school paper, yearbook, magazine, and pupil handbook. These publications are usually prepared by editorial staffs composed of pupils working under the close supervision of a faculty committee or adviser. In the larger schools, the paper and the magazine are issued regularly, but in the smaller schools a regular publication schedule is less common. In some schools, the paper and the magazine are the work of the English classes, while in others they are carried on as extraclass activities with an editorial staff chosen from the student body. Particularly in the senior high schools, the latter practice is common.

The pupil handbook is different from the other publications because it is not always published at regular intervals. Usually there is one issue a year, while in some instances the same handbook is used for several years. Frequently, the handbook is prepared by the faculty or the principal purely as an administrative device to help orient new pupils to the school. If that is done, the school is losing a fine opportunity to give pupils a worth-while educational experience. Sometimes the student council prepares the handbook, making this one of its major projects for the year. Other pupil groups that prepare the handbook are a citizenship club, a school service club, an English class, or a social studies class.

Pupil publications at present do not make as much of a contribution as they should to the educational program of the school. This is true in part because participation is usually limited to a small group of pupils. Furthermore, there is usually a lack of correlation between these publications and the work in the various subject areas, particularly in the English classes. Sometimes these activities are hindered by a lack of funds, especially if they must be entirely self-supporting from subscription fees. Faculty domination is also an adverse factor in providing the best learning experiences from these activities, especially if the faculty sponsors are so concerned with literary perfection that they discourage natural pupil expression. These publications should be planned as part of a well-integrated program of written expression, giving many pupils opportunities for applying the skills developed elsewhere in the school program.

Social Activities Can Be More Effective.—The social functions in the secondary school are frequently thought of as entertainment activities for the pupils, and nothing more. As such it would be difficult indeed to justify the time and attention which they often receive. Actually, these activities may provide excellent opportunities for the educational growth of the boy and girl in such areas as personality development; skills in music, art, dramatics, and cooking; confidence, poise, and skill in adjusting to various social situations; and wholesome boy-girl relationships.

In many schools, the program of social activities is much too limited and not sufficiently varied to provide the experiences that adolescents need to develop personality, poise, and self-confidence. These activities often consist of two or three evening dances which are attended by the pupils who are least in need of social development. There are many opportunities for informal activities which are overlooked, such as parties during the club and home room periods, informal dancing during the noon hour and after school, and social activities for such special groups as the athletic squads, play casts, and the student council.

The effectiveness of social activities depends to a large extent on the manner in which they are planned and carried on. There should be considerable preparation of pupils for participation in these activities. For instance, there should be discussions of various aspects of the social graces—how to ask a girl for a "date," courtesies toward one's "date," courtesies toward the chaperones, etc. In the junior high school, some attention might be given to table manners, what to wear, and how to conduct oneself at a party. If there are dancing parties, there should be instruction in social dancing. Few schools, however, provide this preparation for social activities anywhere in the school program. As a result, pupils often have a good time at social functions but make little educational growth from participation in them.

Dramatics Limited to a Few Major Productions.—The presentation of a junior class play and a senior class play has become the accepted practice in most four-year and senior high schools. In most schools, however, this is the extent of the dramatics activities. Occasionally there is a dramatic presentation for a school assembly or social function, but these activities are so few that they have only a small place in the extraclass program. Such limited dramatics activities are inadequate for meeting the needs of youth to participate in this type of learning experience. The shortcomings of the dramatics program in the four-year and senior high schools may be summarized as follows :

1. The activities are too few to give more than a very limited group of pupils opportunities to participate.
2. There is a tendency to be more concerned about presenting a finished production than giving pupils the best learning experience. Frequently, this means that the leading parts repeatedly go to the same pupils, that an undue amount of time is given to work on the production, and that the pressure on pupils to perform well is carried so far that emotional upsets result.
3. Time to prepare for the production is not recognized in the total instructional program.
4. The dramatics productions are frequently used as a means of raising funds for a class memorial, a junior-senior prom, or some other purpose. Although the raising of funds by this means is not necessarily objectionable, it may overshadow the educational objectives for this type of activity.

In the junior high school, the situation with respect to dramatics differs considerably from that in the four-year and senior high school. In few junior high schools does one find major productions corresponding to the junior or senior class play. Rather, the dramatics activities tend to be much less formal, with emphasis on presentations in club meetings, at school parties, and in school assemblies. Sometimes these activities are centered primarily in a dramatics club, although in some schools they grow out of oral work in the English classes. Even in the junior high school, however, there are not a sufficient number of dramatics productions to provide for participation by all pupils who should have such experience. It is probably true that, in both junior and senior high schools, teachers and school authorities have neglected to explore all the possibilities for pupil growth which are inherent in dramatics activities.

Music Activities Greatly Expanded.—In the secondary school, music activities have been greatly expanded during the past two decades. That is especially true in the Middle West and the Far West. The music organizations which are most generally found in the secondary school include band, orchestra, chorus or choir, and glee clubs. In some schools these activities have been incorporated into the instructional program much like the regular subjects, but more often they continue to be offered on an extraclass basis.

Although the music program in the secondary school has been much more fully developed in the last two decades than some other types of extraclass activities, it still does not provide educational experiences for pupils to the extent which is desired by leaders in music education. The most serious shortcomings in the program of music activities include the following:

1. Individual instruction in instrumental and vocal music is not provided in many schools for pupils who participate in the music organizations. Such instruction is essential if pupils are to have the help they need to develop their individual talents.
2. Inadequate time is provided for meetings and practice by the music groups. In many schools, they meet largely or entirely outside school hours, while in others the time during the school day is far too limited to provide adequately for the needs of these activities.
3. Many pupils are excluded from participation because of the cost of instruments and instruction.
4. The music activities tend to be teacher dominated, with the faculty director planning the concerts, directing the music groups, and doing other planning with little or no pupil participation.

In the junior high school there has been more of a tendency than in the senior high school to make the music activities a part of the regular school program. Frequently, time for these activities is arranged in the daily schedule as it is in classwork in English, mathematics, and social studies. Consequently, pupils in the junior high school have the opportunity to participate in these activities more fully than do senior high school pupils. But in the junior high school the instrumental groups are not as fully developed as in the senior high school, the greater emphasis being given to chorus and glee club. Furthermore, these groups are not given as much of an opportunity to perform as might be desired. They tend to be overshadowed by the senior high school organizations to the point where invitations from outside agencies and support from citizens in the community are directed more toward the groups of older pupils. The authorities in the junior high school, however, are not always as aggressive as they might be in developing opportunities for the music groups to present programs both within the school and in the community.

3. Practices in the Better Secondary Schools

Pupil Activities an Integral Part of the School Program.—The faculties of some secondary schools are making an effort to integrate pupil activities with other phases of the instructional program. Some of the things being done to achieve this purpose include giving credit toward graduation for participation in activities, having the **activities** included in the regular school day, giving more thought to planning the activities, and correlating the various activities with classwork in the subject fields.

The activities program at the Oakland High School, Oakland, California, is an example of close integration with the other aspects of the school's program. The student council at Oakland meets daily during a regularly scheduled period as a class in leadership, with the pupils studying ways of planning and directing various phases of student life. The student council has some responsibility for the conduct of pupils in the neighborhood of the school, and it participates in planning and presenting assembly programs.

Another group at Oakland High School that meets like a regular class is the youth council, composed of class and club officers, officers of a school service club, and other leaders of pupil activities. Like the student council, this group meets daily with a faculty sponsor, who is in turn responsible for directing and coordinating the program of pupil activities in the school. Giving pupil groups regular school time for their meetings, as at Oakland High School, does much toward making these activities a well integrated part of the instructional program.

One step toward integrating the various pupil activities with the rest of the school program is to provide school time for all or most of the activities. In quite a few junior high schools and some senior high schools, a period each day is set aside for this purpose. For example, in one school using this plan, the activities period on Monday, Tuesday, and Wednesday is used for guidance and other home room activities, Thursday is club day, and Friday is devoted to assemblies. Meetings of officers, committees, and other similar groups are scheduled early in the week, while the student council meets during the club period on Thursday. In some schools, the music organizations meet during the activities period. That is not a desirable practice because the music activities require more time than is available in most schools during the activities period.

A particularly effective plan for integrating pupil activities with the rest of the school program is the core curriculum arrangement in which pupils spend several consecutive periods each day with one teacher. In schools with this plan of curriculum organization, the home room, clubs, and certain other activities are frequently brought into the core program. They can therefore be closely integrated with the work in English, social studies, and other subjects, as well as being well coordinated with all aspects of the program of extraclass activities.

Pupil Activities Provided at Minimum Cost.—In quite a few secondary schools, the various pupil activities are being offered at little or no direct cost to the pupil. Until that is done, pupil activities cannot be considered a well-integrated part of the total instructional program because some pupils will not be able to participate in them. The tendency is for schools to provide equipment and to reduce incidental costs, but to have pupils pay for some of the materials they use. Several different practices are being employed to accomplish this purpose, among them the following:

1. The board of education provides for much of the expense of the various activities by an appropriation in the school budget.
2. School authorities and faculty sponsors carefully plan to keep down the cost of the various activities by establishing policies limiting the amount that may be spent for pins, dues, social functions, and other items. In some schools, club pins and dues are not permitted, and the amount spent on parties is limited.
3. In many schools activity tickets are sold at a reasonable cost early in the school year. These admit pupils to athletic events, concerts, plays, and other performances and entitle them to the various school publications. The activity ticket permits better budgeting by the pupil in his personal finances and enables many pupils to attend more activities by reducing the unit cost.

Credit Given for Participation in Activities.—One way of making pupil activities an integral part of the total school program is to give credit toward graduation for participation in these activities, as is done with English, mathematics, and other course work. Such a policy tends to give the same prestige to these activities as to other aspects of the curriculum. Central High School, Aberdeen, South

Dakota, has had such a plan for many years, pupils there being required to earn seventeen units for graduation. Sixteen units are earned through regular course work, while the seventeenth unit is for participation in extraclass activities. A point system has been formulated to compute credit toward the seventeenth unit, giving points for holding certain pupil offices and for participating in activities according to the amount of time which such participation requires. For instance, the editor-in-chief of the school paper would earn more points than one of the reporters. Pupils have three years to earn the seventeenth unit.

At Oakland High School, Oakland, California, pupils are required to earn twenty-four units, instead of the usual sixteen, for graduation. They receive credit for any activity that is carried on during the school day, which is six periods long. This includes study hall as well as extraclass activities. Thus, over a period of four years, the pupil may earn twenty-four units, six for each year.

It is perhaps unwise to attach too much importance to the giving of credit for participation in extraclass activities. Such a practice does not necessarily lead to better integration of pupil activities with the rest of the instructional program. School faculties should therefore explore other means for making these activities in every sense a part of the educational program of the school.

Participation Distributed Among Pupils.—The faculty and administration in some secondary schools have taken steps to distribute participation in activities among as many pupils as possible, as well as to limit the participation of individual pupils so that they will not become involved in too many activities. If there is to be wide participation by all the pupils, it is essential that there be activities that appeal to the interests of everyone. In some schools, the sports program, the club activities, assemblies, speech activities, and pupil publications are so planned that every interested pupil can find an opportunity to participate.

The trend toward such broad offerings of activities has made it increasingly important that the participation of the individual pupil be limited. The oldest practice limiting participation is the point system, under which a pupil is permitted only a certain number of points prescribed in advance by the faculty, the principal, or some other school authority. In some schools, such as the Central High School, Pueblo, Colorado, the point system was developed by the student council, which is likewise responsible for its administration and enforcement. It has proved to be an appropriate responsibility for the student council.

In schools where the activities are carried on largely during school hours, or where they are part of a core program, there is a less serious problem in distributing and limiting pupil participation. Since certain groups of activities, such as clubs, meet at the same time, a pupil could not belong to more than is advisable, nor could he hold too many offices in such organizations. Consequently, in these schools the control of pupil participation is largely automatic, at least for certain groups of activities.

Preparation of Pupils for Leadership.—Activities designed to prepare pupils for responsibilities of leadership in pupil organizations have been developed in some secondary schools. Parliamentary procedure is frequently studied in English and social studies classes, sometimes with considerable opportunity for pupils to gain actual experience in conducting meetings. The home room is also used for leadership education, pupils there studying parliamentary practice, the duties of pupil officers, and the qualities of good leaders.

In some schools, student officers meet regularly to study leadership problems. The youth council and the student council at Oakland High School, previously described in this chapter, meet daily with a faculty sponsor to study problems of leadership, much like a class in any other subject. At the Sheridan Junior High School, New Haven, Connecticut, pupil officers are organized into councils according to their responsibilities, such as presidents' council, secretaries' council, and treasurers' council, which meet regularly to study the work of these officers.

A handbook for pupil officers has been prepared in some schools. The junior high school at Minot, North Dakota, has such a handbook which describes the duties and responsibilities of various student officers and gives suggestions for performing that work effectively. The National Association of Secondary School Principals has published several handbooks for student council officers which are proving helpful in preparing students for work on councils.[3] Practices such as these are increasing the effectiveness of extraclass activities in preparing youth for democratic leadership responsibilities.

Pupils Participate in School Government.—In some secondary schools, pupils have assumed considerable responsibility for certain aspects of the government of the school, usually through the student council or a similar group. The activities include control of pupil elections, providing safety patrols on streets adjoining the school,

---

[3] An example is *Student Councils Handbook, 1949,* published by the National Association of Secondary School Principals, Washington, D.C.

regulation of corridor traffic, supervision of playgrounds, control of pupil conduct in the cafeteria, making of policies for extraclass activities, and study hall supervision. The extent to which pupils assume such responsibilities varies greatly from one school to another. In some schools they formulate policies and make regulations, while in others they merely assist in enforcing faculty-made rules.

In schools where youth are given the best experiences in democratic participation, the student council or some other student group both makes and administers policies and regulations. An example of such a school is the Woodrow Wilson High School, Middletown, Connecticut, which for some years has had considerable pupil participation in the government of the school. Every pupil at Woodrow Wilson High School automatically becomes a voting member of the student association, with the student council serving as the representative group for the student body. The council, which consists of twenty members representing the various classes, determines policies in those activities of direct concern to pupils, supervises pupil elections, plans and finances assembly programs, and sponsors an annual scholarship for a worthy senior.

In addition to the student council there is a student advisory board at Woodrow Wilson High School which is responsible for supervising pupil conduct in corridors, study halls, and the cafeteria. The advisory board is parallel to the student council in its authority; like the council it is directly responsible to the officers and executive committee of the student association. The board formulates policies and makes regulations concerning pupil conduct, and, through the pupil squads in charge of study halls, the corridors, and the cafeteria, it is responsible for enforcing the policies and regulations. Uncooperative pupils are referred to the advisory board by the squad members responsible for pupil conduct. The advisory board is not a disciplinary body, but instead uses a counseling approach to help pupils develop a more cooperative attitude toward the policies and regulations established by their elected representatives.

Pupils who persistently violate the conduct regulations at the Woodrow Wilson High School are referred by the advisory board to a student court, which is composed of a student judge, jury, and prosecutor. The student court, whose sessions are open to the student body, is the only student group that imposes penalties. These include removal from study hall, depriving the offender of school privileges, or placing him in the custody of a member of the advisory board. The pupil's parents are informed of any penalty imposed by the court and it is placed in the pupil's cumulative record. Only a few cases are referred to the student court, most of them being cared for on a counseling basis by the advisory board. The mature behavior of pupils in this school can be attributed in large part to the sense of responsibility which pupils acquire from participation in the management of their own conduct.

The plan for control of pupil conduct at the Woodrow Wilson High School is similar to those found in some other secondary schools. Usually the student council is the legislative body which formulates the policies and makes the regulations. Other schools have also had considerable success with such plans for pupil participation in the control of pupil conduct.

Pupil Control of School Elections.—An exceedingly valuable form of pupil participation in the administration of the school is in the control of pupil elections. At the Woodrow Wilson High School, Middletown, whose plan for student government is discussed in the preceding paragraphs, the student council is responsible for supervising and administering the election of pupil officers. The election is planned and conducted according to regulations prescribed by the council. There are parties which meet to nominate candidates, there is a campaign for the various candidates, and there is a carefully supervised election. In order to avoid loss of good leadership, the defeated candidates for the major offices become members of the governing group in which they sought office. Quite a few secondary schools have this type of pupil participation, with the student council most frequently being in charge.

Pupil Administration of Finances.—In a few secondary schools, the pupils participate in the administration of finances for extraclass activities. One of the oldest forms of such participation is to have pupils in the bookkeeping class or other business courses share in the accounting work for the activities funds, usually under the supervision of some teacher who has been assigned this responsibility by the administration. At the Windham High School, Willimantic, Connecticut, this participation is provided through a school bank operated by pupils who are taking the business education curriculum. All purchases made by pupils in school are paid at the school bank, including dues for clubs and classes, cafeteria tickets, activity tickets, and similar items. Pupils serve as tellers, check the cash, keep records, and bank the funds.

In a few schools, pupils participate in preparing the budget and in making other decisions concerning the raising and spending of activities funds. The student council is usually the group which has this responsibility. The most common practice is to have each pupil organization prepare a budget which is submitted to the council for approval. The council then prepares a composite budget for all the activities and supervises the expenditure of funds by the participating activities. Responsibility such as this provides excellent preparation for democratic living in the community outside the school.

Athletics Provided for All Interested Pupils.—Some progress is being made in the secondary schools toward providing a program of athletics which meets the needs of every interested and physically able pupil. The practices which tend particularly to accomplish this purpose include these:

1. Broad intramural programs in certain sports are being introduced. Frequently these programs include both junior and senior high school pupils, with the younger and smaller senior high school pupils competing with the larger ones in the junior high school.
2. In the larger schools, there are sometimes several teams in interscholastic competition, with teams other than the varsity competing with smaller schools.
3. The scholastic prerequisites for intramural competition are quite informal or there are no such prerequisites at all. For interscholastic competition, the eligibility requirements of the interscholastic athletic associations must, of course, be observed.
4. More sports appropriate for adult life are being included in secondary school programs: volley ball, softball, tennis, golf, swimming, riflery, and archery. These sports are in addition to the usual offerings, which include football, basketball, baseball, and track.
5. Sports programs for girls are being developed, though not on as extensive a basis as for boys. Furthermore, the sports competition for girls is largely on an intramural basis.

For some years, the junior and senior high schools at Aberdeen, South Dakota, have had an extensive athletics program for boys which is characterized by the trends mentioned above. This program gives every interested and physically able boy an opportunity to participate in every sport. For example, in football the senior high school has a varsity team which plays in interscholastic competition with the large schools in the state, a second team which competes with teams from medium-sized schools, and a third team with meets those from the smaller schools. In addition, for all other interested boys there are teams which play in intramural competition. The intramural league includes the upper junior high school and the senior high school pupils, providing for a series of games according to a well-planned schedule much like the interscholastic program. A touch football league in the fall gives an opportunity for all boys to participate. During the winter there are bowling leagues for all boys and girls. In basketball and track, the Aberdeen senior high school also has several teams that play in interscholastic competition, with intramural leagues for other pupils in the senior and the junior high schools. The sports program at Aberdeen is a broad one, including tennis, golf, and other sports appropriate for adult life, as well as the team sports ordinarily offered in secondary schools. A competent coach is provided for every squad, whether it plays in intramural or interscholastic competition, this assignment being considered a part of the teacher's regular load.

At Windham High School, Willimantic, Connecticut, there is a similar program for girls which provides every interested pupil an opportunity to engage in one or more sports. The program is developed on an intramural basis, with scheduled periods in the gymnasium, swimming pool and other facilities. Teams usually represent the various classes, although for such activities as riflery there are clubs which cut across grade lines. The program is well planned but flexible, both in its organization and in the activities that may be included. The sports include softball, basketball, swimming, field hockey, volley ball, badminton, riflery, and others in which there may be an interest.

Music Activities Given Class Status.—The music activities in the secondary school are being placed on a basis that recognizes the contribution they offer for the cultural development of the pupils. In some schools, they are given as important a place in the school program as any regular class activity. The following indicate the practices found in the music programs of the better schools:

1. It is begun in the elementary school, with thorough instruction in music in all the grades. Instrumental instruction on a small group basis is offered beginning in the third or fourth grade. In some elementary schools there are organized music groups, but in most cases the work is carried on in the regular classes.
2. In the junior and senior high schools, there are organized music activities for pupils from various grades, these organizations including band, orchestra, chorus, and glee club. The practice periods for these organizations are scheduled during the regular school day. In some schools they meet during a scheduled activities period, but in others they have regular class periods.

3. Credit toward graduation is given for music participation, the amount of credit depending upon the amount of class time devoted to the activity.
4. Music materials and instruments are furnished by the school. Although pupils frequently buy their instruments, they are furnished for those pupils who would find it difficult to purchase them. The more expensive instruments are usually provided by the school.

As with its program of athletics, Aberdeen, South Dakota, offers a splendid example of a school system that provides a well-rounded music program for its youth. The music activities in the secondary schools at Aberdeen are scheduled like other classes, all meeting for one full period daily; there is a competent instructor for each type of activity, in which he is a specialist; credit is given toward graduation; and there are music organizations for every interested pupil. At the present time there is a band, orchestra, a cappella choir, second choir, and glee club in the high school. Each junior high school has vocal groups as well as instrumental instruction for those desiring it. In a program such as this, the outcomes of the music activities are likely to be very significant, indeed, in the total educational growth of the child.

Evaluation of Activities Programs.—In the statement of principles given earlier in this chapter, it was suggested that there should be continued evaluation of the effectiveness of the extraclass program. Although few secondary schools have adequate evaluation of these activities, some devices are being employed for this purpose. The teachers in some schools are being asked to evaluate the activities program, usually at the end of the year. Sometimes this evaluation covers the entire program of activities, but more often it concerns only certain activities in which the teacher has engaged. For example, in the Middlebury High School, Middlebury, Vermont, at the end of the year every teacher evaluates the activity for which he was the sponsor. The device used for this purpose is a two-page questionnaire in which such information as the following is requested:

1. What were the main objectives of the group?
2. What principal projects did the group engage in?
3. What major difficulties did the group encounter in meeting its objectives?
4. What were the chief accomplishments of the group during the year?

5. What suggestions do you have for improving the activities of the group in another year?

In some secondary schools, pupils participate in the evaluation of the activities. Sometimes the evaluation is made by pupil members of an activity group and in other cases by the entire student body. In Central High School, St. Joseph, Missouri, the student council prepares a list of activities in which it has engaged during the year, with the request that each member indicates which activities should be continued another year. Before the close of school, the outgoing officers and cabinet have a meeting with those elected for the coming year to discuss, among other things, the results of this survey.[4] A similar evaluation of student council activities is made at the Jesup W. Scott High School, Toledo, Ohio, where the members of the council fill in a questionnaire at the end of the year giving their evaluation of the council's work, including their own contribution as individual members of the group. They also give suggestions for improving the work of the council in another year.[5] In other schools, similar evaluations are made, usually by questionnaires which apply to certain groups of activities, particularly clubs, assemblies, and the home rooms. These evaluations are exceedingly helpful in improving the effectiveness of the activities concerned.

4. First Steps

The program of extraclass activities can be improved in all secondary schools if the administrative authorities, faculty members, and pupils work consciously toward that end. In some schools, rather drastic steps will need to be taken to develop a more effective program, but in others an improvement may be effected without major changes. The following are some of the first steps that should prove helpful in developing a more effective program of extraclass activities in any secondary school:

1. The faculty should formulate a philosophy and objectives for its program of extraclass activities. If it has already formulated such statements, these should be re-examined in the light of current thinking on extraclass activities. Until statements of philosophy and objectives are formulated and are accepted by most of the faculty, little can be done to develop an effective and forward-looking program of extraclass activities.

---

[4] National Association of Student Councils, *Student Councils at Work,* Washington, D.C.: National Association of Secondary School Principals, 1945, p. 108.
[5] *Ibid.,* p. 110.

2. The program of extraclass activities should be evaluated in terms of the accepted philosophy and objectives. Administrative authorities, teachers, pupils, and parents should participate in that evaluation. As a basis for that evaluation, the faculty might well formulate a statement of criteria which indicate the standards that are considered desirable for a program of extraclass activities. The literature on extraclass activities and the principles presented early in this chapter should prove helpful in formulating such a statement of criteria. This evaluation should reveal the strengths and the weaknesses of the present program as a basis for improvement.

3. The time devoted to extraclass activities might be studied to see how well the needs of the various groups of activities are being met. If the time available for certain activities does not seem satisfactory, then the daily schedule of the school should be analyzed to see if additional time can be made available for pupil activities. If necessary, the school day should be lengthened or time provided by making basic changes in the plan for the daily schedule.

4. If the school does not have a director of extraclass activities, the need for competent leadership in the direction and planning of the extraclass program should be studied. The principal alone cannot provide that leadership. The possibility of having faculty members devote part time to the direction of the club program, home room activities, school assemblies, and other activities, should be considered. Competent leadership is essential if significant progress is to be made in improving extraclass activities.

5. A survey of pupil interests in the various groups of extraclass activities can be exceedingly helpful. For example, the results of such a survey may prove of value in expanding the club offerings, in developing different types of assembly programs, and in other ways. The advisability of making such a survey should be considered.

6. Because of the importance of the sponsor in the extraclass program, considerable thought should be given to in-service education activities to help teachers improve their effectiveness in supervising extraclass activities. Some in-service activities can be carried on by the faculty group as a whole, while the individual teacher may engage in professional reading, take extension and summer courses, and find other means to improve himself for extraclass responsibilities.

Selected References

Douglass, Harl R. (ed.). *Education for Life Adjustment*. New York: The Ronald Press Co., 1950, chap. 17.—Presents a discussion of extraclass activities in the secondary school, with particular reference to an educational program emphasizing life adjustment for secondary school youth.

Educational Policies Commission. *Learning the Ways of Democracy*. Washington, D.C.: National Education Association, 1940, chaps. 4, 5.—In Chapter 4, there is a discussion of the place of extraclass activities in the program of education for democratic living, while Chapter 5 deals with school activities that are carried on in the community. Both chapters give many examples of things that are being done in secondary schools to prepare youth for democratic living.

Fedder, Ruth. *Guiding Homeroom and Club Activities*. New York: McGraw-Hill Book Co., Inc., 1949, chap. 5.—Presents the story of two school clubs—a leadership council and a boys' pep club—with an interesting discussion of their activities. This chapter is helpful to teachers in planning the activities in which a club may engage.

Forsythe, Charles E. *The Administration of High School Athletics*. New York: Prentice-Hall, Inc., 1948, chaps. 13-16.—Presents various aspects of a program of high school athletics, especially intramural athletics, athletics for girls, junior high school athletics, and trends in athletics.

Gruhn, William T., and Douglass, Harl R. *The Modern Junior High School*. New York: The Ronald Press Co., 1947, chap. 13.—Gives an overview of the program of extraclass activities in the junior high school, including the principles underlying such a program and the organization of the various types of activities found in the junior high school.

McKown, Harry C. *Extra-Curricular Activities*. New York: The Macmillan Co., 1948, 734 pp.—Presents a comprehensive discussion of the program of extraclass activities, including the principles that should underlie such a program, the more common practices in schools, and suggestions for organizing and carrying on the various types of extraclass activities.

McKown, Harry C. *The Student Council*. New York: McGraw-Hill Book Co., Inc., 1944, 352 pp.—Covers all important aspects of student council organization and activities, with practical suggestions for teachers in secondary schools.

National Association of Student Councils. *Student Councils at Work*. Washington, D.C.: National Association of Secondary School Principals, 1945, 199 pp.—This is a handbook of policies and practices of student councils as reported from 154 schools which are members of the National Association of Student Councils. It covers such topics as aims and functions of student councils, constitutions of student councils, how councils report to the student body, the council meeting, qualifications, election and duties of officers, council projects, finances, and the relation of the council to other student organizations.

National Association of Student Councils. *Student Councils Handbook, 1949*. Washington, D.C.: National Association of Secondary School Principals, 1949, 128 pp.—Besides such information as a report of the annual national conference, the directory of student council associations, official organ and insignia for student councils, and the directory of the National Association of Student Councils, it gives suggestions for planning and carrying on student council activities. Sponsors of student councils will find this handbook exceedingly valuable.

Pierce, Paul R. *Developing a High-School Curriculum*. New York: American Book Co., 1942, chaps. 2, 3, 8.—This book describes how the educational program at Wells High School, Chicago, Illinois, was brought into being. The chapters indicated suggest how the various aspects of the activities program were developed.

Chapter 11

THE SECONDARY SCHOOL AND THE COMMUNITY

The school should be a vital force and factor in every community, serving all youth and all the people. The community truly provides a rich learning laboratory for the school, which in turn seeks to interpret, serve, and improve community life. The modern secondary school is a community school in that it makes a real difference in community living; serves the children, parents, and other community members in many ways; extends its borders into community industries, business places, organizations, and institutions; and clarifies its purposes through a close working relationship of community members and educators. In this chapter are discussed the ways in which the secondary school provides useful, challenging experiences to youth and adults through its partnership with the community.

1. THE PRINCIPLES

The facilities of the secondary school should be used as educational, recreational, and service centers for the entire community.

The school belongs to the entire community; its physical plant should be utilized to improve and enrich the personal and social living of children and community adults. Far too many valuable school plants operate upon an eight-hour day, forty-hour week, and nine-month year. One school in a large midwestern city actually has a "STAY OFF—POLICE ORDER" sign on its playground! The school plant and staff should provide both formal and informal adult educational opportunities for its citizens. After-school, evening, and Saturday classes should be organized to meet the varying interests and needs of adults in the community. Adult education classes in modern languages, art, music, arts and crafts, current affairs, current literature, world history, chemistry, general mathematics, home economics, agriculture, and commercial subjects have been popular in a large number of different communities. The United States Veterans Program under the G. I. Bill has proved the popularity of adult education when properly organized, staffed, and financed. In some cases, the school library also serves as a library for the town.

239

Many of the educational classes named above serve useful recreational purposes as well. In fact, it is often difficult to distinguish between the work and play aspects of these courses in "community-centered" adult evening classes. The attendance at any such center always attests to the value and interest which adults find when their needs are being met. In addition to the recreational classes in arts and crafts, music, shop, physical education, and the like, many secondary schools, especially in rural areas and small towns, are rendering a real service through organizing evening social events for the entire community. The current revival of interest in square dancing, even in cities, has shown that the secondary school can meet a vital social and recreational need for its community if it will but plan carefully and work diligently.

Youth and children will participate naturally in many of these adult recreational activities. Secondary schools have also recently turned their attention to planning and organizing social and recreational activities directly for youth of the community. This movement received great impetus during the war years with the operation of "Teen-Towns" for and by adolescents. They served a vital purpose during the war, and many schools and communities have found it desirable and possible to continue their operation. School boards, park boards, and other recreational agencies, by using school and community facilities, are successfully operating supervised summer play programs for thousands of children and youth. Communities have learned that money spent upon summer recreation is a wise expenditure for the future health, happiness, and citizenship of their youth. School and community summer camping programs are rapidly increasing to provide further recreational opportunities for all youth.

Many types of services should be operated cooperatively by the school and other community agencies.

During the war years, the community found that the school could render many valuable services. Teachers, administrators, and custodians joined ranks with local and federal agencies to assist in issuing ration coupons, in collecting and processing Red Cross supplies, in providing bomb shelters, and in coordinating civilian defense activities. It was generally agreed that the teaching profession gained considerable recognition and status for this leadership and service to the community and nation. The secondary school has much to gain by continuing to provide social services to the community on the same scale as during the war period.

In the area of economic and consumer services, there are promising fields of cooperative endeavor. Under partially federal auspices, some rural secondary schools operate summer food processing plants, hybrid seed plots, school forests, dairy herds and cattle breeding facilities, and repair centers for farm machinery. For an idealistic picture of possibilities in this area, the reader is referred to the co-operative services operated by the "Farmville Community School" in *Education for* ALL *American Youth.*[1]

The secondary school should discover and utilize the interests, resources, problems, and needs of the community in building its curriculum.

The secondary school can be a "community-centered" school that uses people, organizations, institutions, and industries, as well as books, for sources of information, instead of a "book-centered" school which relies primarily on books. Youth can study natural resources directly, rather than just studying about them. As was indicated in Chapter 1, learning is far more meaningful when it is based first upon concrete experiences and then later related to other vicarious experiences. The community in its total physical, social, and economic setting provides a rich learning laboratory which should be used in developing the curriculum of the modern secondary school.

Secondary schools can determine the resources, needs, and problems of their communities through community studies and surveys. Teachers and students sometimes make these studies independently, although they always need the assistance of certain community agencies and personnel. Examples of the more simple type are surveys of traffic hazards, of areas needing landscaping, and of breeding grounds of flies and mosquitoes. More comprehensive types may involve careful planning and cooperation with the agricultural extension agent, health department, safety department, police department, planning council, Chamber of Commerce, courts, automobile club, unions, highway department, and various state and federal agencies.

In addition to or in connection with community studies and surveys, secondary schools are utilizing a great variety of other curricular and community study techniques. Resource visitors (individuals of the community who have valuable information to present) are brought into the school to make special contributions. Students go out into the community to interview other resource people and bring

---

[1] Educational Policies Commission, *Education for* ALL *American Youth*, Washington, D.C.: National Education Association, 1944, chap. 3.

back much valuable information. Many types of pertinent local documentary materials are collected, organized, and interpreted. Audio-visual teaching materials pertaining to community resources and problems are obtained from a variety of local agencies and industries or, in some cases, are produced by the school.

Secondary schools vary markedly in their use of community resources in the curriculum. Some use these materials only to invigorate traditional programs. Others attempt to relate community problems and resources to their social studies and science classes. A relatively small number of modern high schools actually base a considerable part of their learning experiences directly upon community problems and needs.

Many opportunities for vital work experiences should be provided jointly by the secondary school and the community.

This important principle has been previously stated and illustrated in Chapter 9. We repeat that it is a necessary function of the school to provide work experiences for those of its youth who will go directly into community employment. It is, moreover, exceedingly important that all youth have such experience, both the paid and service types. Again the reader is referred to "Farmville" and "American City" to visualize the possibilities of such a program of work experience.[2]

Leadership should be given by the modern secondary school in coordinating the total educational efforts of the community.

It is widely recognized that the school is only one of many educative agencies in the community. Youth were educated directly in the home before they were of school age, they receive many valuable educational experiences outside of school, and they will all continue to learn after formal education has ceased. Home, church, job, club, gang, movies, radio, playgrounds, restaurants, and pool rooms all serve positively or negatively in furthering the desirable education of youth.

It is not enough to leave such necessary educational coordination to the chance participation of school teachers and administrators in community clubs, agencies, and social institutions. The school may serve the community effectively by coordinating the efforts of many of the community's educational agencies. The success of the school's leadership in such a free community situation will depend largely upon the initiative and personality of the school superintendent, the

---

[2] *Ibid.,* chaps. 3, 4.

principal, and the teachers. In an ever-increasing number of cities, both large and small, the schools are joining with other community agencies and organizations to form a community coordinating council. This is a cooperative organization of groups and individuals who join together to work to improve the total welfare of all persons within the community. Such a council may represent homes, churches, welfare organizations, police departments, courts, clinics, labor unions, veterans organizations, schools, and service clubs. It serves primarily as an advisory rather than as an administrative agency, and fosters cooperation and coordination in sponsoring studies of community needs and resources. It may aid in securing needed youth recreational facilities, improving health and safety programs, seeking employment for youth, providing adult education, and promoting new organizations to meet local needs. *Education for* ALL *American Youth,* presents a picture of such a coordinating council actively planning for an improved educational program for youth.[3] School personnel who serve on the council have special training and unique opportunities to give advice on youth needs, interests, and problems, as well as to secure the active participation of youth within the coordinating council.

2. SOME TYPICAL PRACTICES

The beginning teacher may find that the school in which he secures his first teaching position does not apply many of the principles which characterize the modern community school. He may also discover that the only time there is any active community interest in the school is during a drive for a bond issue, a flare-up concerning a teacher or a school policy, or during a school board election in which there is a real issue.

Many different factors tend to operate to prevent high schools from serving maximum educational functions within their communities. Tradition is perhaps the single strongest factor; the typical high school has been subject-centered rather than life-centered. School buildings are rarely planned and constructed to serve broad, community functions. High school teachers are generally trained to teach subjects, not to aid in solving community problems. The large high school with more than a thousand pupils does not serve a community of people in the sense that they have many interests and activities in common. In order to carry out community studies and surveys suc-

---

[3] *Ibid.,* chap. 3.

cessfully, more time is required than the usual fifty-minute period; many teachers and administrators are reluctant to disrupt the regular schedule of classes, as would be necessary to meet this need. Relatively few communities have had experience in coordinating their total educational facilities and resources; hence, they are reluctant to give this leadership function to the school. Finally, the whole school and community often demonstrate the policy of laissez-faire in relation to curriculum change; they usually either accept the high school program as it is or vigorously oppose any great or sudden change in it.

Community Resistance to a Changing Curriculum.—Since the time of its first dominance over the academy, the high school has largely been a college preparatory institution with an academic, subject-centered curriculum. Its function in 1900 clearly was to educate the selected minority for entrance into higher education. English, mathematics, foreign languages, the sciences, and various social studies were "solid subjects"—highly respected within the school, community, and college, and universally taught in high schools large and small. This program satisfied parents who had had the same type of education if they attended secondary school, or who had ambitions for their children to attend college.

It has been a slow, difficult process to change the academic curriculum of the secondary school. For the first two decades of the twentieth century, the high school remained largely college preparatory, still teaching the academic subjects to a relatively selected student body. Slowly the required college preparatory subjects were reduced in number, such independent subjects as ancient and medieval history were combined into world history, and new studies, such as vocational education, problems of democracy, and general science, were added to the curriculum. Only as school people worked closely with communities in studying and evaluating the purposes and program, were changes readily brought about.

The building of a modern secondary curriculum, based upon personal and social needs of youth and the expanding community, has been an especially slow development. Inertia, lack of security, lack of leadership, fear of reprisal, and insufficient training have all jointly operated to prevent secondary school teachers from building vital programs of community-centered education. In many cases, the community, not understanding the purposes school people had in mind, has resisted the change.

Limited Use of School Buildings and Facilities.—The use of the typical high school building, in either a city or small town, is almost exclusively limited to the school program and activities between the opening and close of the school day, and occasional evening school functions. The building is often empty shortly after the closing bell. A few conscientious, hard-working teachers always remain an hour or more after school to prepare the next day's lessons, to rearrange their rooms, or to counsel students. A few may remain to work upon committee assignments, while another small group—especially the athletic coaches, music teachers, and dramatic teachers—usually have regular after-school duties with various types of extraclass activities. The trend in large cities, however, is to pay these teachers a special compensation for their regular extraclass responsibilities. It remains, nevertheless, a fair statement to say that in the typical high school today the building is unoccupied and unused by a large majority of the pupils and faculty after 4:00 P.M. from Monday through Friday, and on Saturday.

It is the universal pattern that the high school operates upon a five-day week. Since this is becoming the pattern for industrial, service, and governmental employees, it may only indicate that the school is in line with the national trend. However, home responsibilities have decreased markedly for most youth, while there has been a lessening of part-time employment and a corresponding increase of leisure time. The serious student of secondary education may well raise the question of the responsibility of the modern high school for some part of the youth's after-school, evening, and week-end recreation and education.

A large majority of high schools are closed tightly almost every evening, with no indication of school or community activity. During the fall months, the larger schools use the athletic field and shower rooms for football or baseball practice. For the four winter months, practically every American high school makes intensive use of the gymnasium either in the afternoon or early evening for that nationally favorite indoor game of basketball. Yet, again we must recall that perhaps only 20 per cent of the boys of a small high school, and as few as 10 per cent in a large high school, turn out regularly for these varsity and reserve teams. Intramural sports which could serve a majority of high school youth are largely limited to the regular school day or late afternoon.

Five or six home football games each fall may attract either huge or meager crowds of pupils and adults, depending upon the size of the town and school and the traditional emphasis given to athletics. Home basketball games may number up to ten or twelve, drawing varying sized crowds on Friday or Saturday nights. The size, equipment, and seating facilities of modern high school gymnasiums attest to the relative emphasis given to interscholastic athletics today. The community quite obviously wants, enjoys, and will adequately support this aspect of the program of the school.

School dramatic productions, musical programs, dances and parties are given perhaps an average of once monthly during the school year. Some of these are restricted to the pupils; others, frequently attract hundreds of adults as well. These programs and social events serve vital functions for pupils and parents alike, indicating that a real social need is being met for the school and community. Parent-Teacher Association meetings are held ordinarily bi-monthly on the high school level. Attendance ranges from good to very poor, with usually not more than a fourth of all parents attending regularly. P.T.A. open-houses and social parties usually attract larger numbers of parents.

These practices describe fairly well the *average* range of the utilization of the high school plant for the education, recreation, and welfare of the youth and community adults. Although the number is growing, relatively few secondary schools use their buildings regularly for adult education classes or recreation groups. During the summer vacation period of three months, the usual high school building is devoid of pupil activity and community adult participation. In a few cities and towns, the athletic fields are being used for youth recreational programs, which we shall describe in the following section. In the typical American high school building from June until September, the custodian, engineer, and superintendent reign supreme! Should we not ask again the question of whether this summer inertia is justified in a modern high school which seeks to meet the needs of its youth in all phases of community living?

Guidance and Education Services Provided for a Limited Number of Out-of-School Youth and Adults.—Some high schools regularly give valuable services directly to their communities; these will be described in the following section. There are more high schools, however, that do not render a large number of vital services *directly* to the community, other than the more or less formal schooling of its youth. For example, few schools follow up their graduates as they become employed, and fewer still provide placement services for them. Services to out-of-school youth other than graduates are rarely offered, except in the case of a few community or junior colleges. Not many high schools assist social welfare and service agencies within the community. Some high schools seem totally oblivious to safety hazards, littered streets and alleys, and general lack of an attractive community environment.

Athletic, recreational, musical, and dramatic programs are regularly given for the community by the typical high school today. These events, discussed above in some detail, represent both a service to youth and to community adults in the nature of education, recreation, and entertainment.

Although adult education programs are being offered increasingly by secondary schools, they are still limited mainly to the larger communities and, in smaller communities, to agriculture classes. Not many high schools regularly give other services to their communities. Among those services which may be found are: providing entertainment or speakers for service clubs and religious groups; aiding in clean-up campaigns; soliciting in Red Cross, Community Chest, Christmas Seal, and other campaigns; raising funds for public libraries, parks, and museums; maintaining minimum repairing services for home appliances.

Occasional Field Trips and Excursions.—In the typical high school of today, we find field trips and excursions being taken by some classes. The ninth grade civics class and twelfth grade problems of democracy class may visit the local town or city council chamber. These classes may also journey—rarely—to the state capitol to watch the legislature in session. History classes frequently visit local places of historical interest and importance. Museums are often centers of some intensive study. These excursions are usually limited primarily to social studies classes, although many such classes are given no opportunities to go on field trips.

Vocational agriculture and home economics classes often have excellent programs of field trips and excursions. They are generally well planned, efficiently organized, related to other fields of learning, and evaluated. In the fields of science and English, few high schools maintain regular community study. The general science class may occasionally visit a power plant or dam; the biology class sometimes goes afield for specimens or to note erosion or flood control. The typical physics, chemistry, or English class rarely leaves the security of its classroom to study real life situations under the skillful guidance of a teacher.

Administrative inertia, the failure to see the educational value of excursions, and rigid adherence to fixed class schedules combine to make field trips difficult if not impossible in many secondary schools. Some boards of education actually do not permit them. While some administrators and teachers are able to work out the necessary co-operative details of time, finance, safety, and transportation so essential in planning vital community excursions, in other schools, this friendly and helpful attitude is lacking and neither class schedule nor school day can be kept flexible enough to provide for these concrete learning experiences.

Outside Speakers Most Frequently Serve Assemblies.—Perhaps every high school in the nation has some resource visitor or "outside speaker" each year. In some cases, these guests are forced upon the school by pressure groups or are wholly accidental visitors, for whom little planning can be done. Most of these speakers perform in assembly programs, school or community drives, or in some aspect of vocational guidance. Some assembly speakers do an effective job, but few teachers relate their contributions to the class work. Career days and vocational guidance conferences for seniors typically use many community leaders, but the follow-up is not always made.

Many modern secondary teachers of social studies, English, health, and business education use planned resource visitors in vitalizing their curriculum. Such visitors are carefuly selected, pre-interviewed, oriented to the class project, and used to help the class in some special problem or interest area. Although this practice is increasing, it is not common.

Community Survey and Planning by Individual Classes or Organizations.—One of the most important, yet difficult and consequently neglected, techniques of community study is the survey. It requires trained, technical leadership, intensive preplanning, wide-scale cooperation with other community agencies and institutions, schoolwide participation, adequate finance, widespread publicity, and careful appraisal and follow-up. Consequently, community and resource-use surveys are few and far between in our high schools today. Since surveys require school and community-wide planning, participation, and support, they usually represent large-scale projects. Some individual classes have organized and carried out small and limited surveys. Business education departments, especially in junior colleges, have been most active in making surveys of business establishments.

Almost every high school principal and many teachers belong to a service club, if one exists in their community, where they often serve on committees which plan and administer worth-while community educational and recreational projects and services. Teachers and administrators perform similar leadership functions in clubs, churches,

and other community agencies. Different service, church, and frater-
nal groups in the community may cooperatively plan parks, playgrounds, programs, health and safety campaigns, and the like for
youth. These groups sometimes compete directly for youth participation or provide duplicating facilities and services. Perhaps the typical pattern is nearer to independent planning and duplicating services
than to cooperative group planning on service projects. Careful
group action through coordinating councils has proved its value in a
few dynamic communities.

3. Practices in the Better Secondary Schools

In the earlier sections of this chapter, reference has been made to
ways in which a high school may serve as a real community school.
Here we shall describe a number of practices which illustrate in some
detail the principles given at the beginning of this chapter. These
actual practices will illustrate phases, as well as total school programs,
which are based upon community study, service, and improvement.

The entire plant and facilities of the modern high school are used
as educational, recreational, and service centers for the whole community. Pupils, parents, and other community adults are benefited
by the school facilities. Educational, recreational, and service functions are provided after school hours, evenings, week-ends, and
throughout the summer months.

Adult education in some communities is frequently organized
independently from secondary education, while other cities have
developed evening classes, community colleges, and vocational schools
as an integral part of secondary education in order to meet the educational needs of adults. Veterans' classes under the G.I. Bill, and
vocational education under the provisions of the Smith-Hughes and
George-Barden Acts, are other programs well developed in many
cities. (See Chapter 9.) Particularly in southern rural communities,
high schools today are providing vital learning experiences for adults.

High Schools in Rural Areas Are Centers of Community Life.
—Hanson High School in Hopkins County, Kentucky, is in the center
of the coal fields of the state. It was selected in 1942 for a school-
community improvement center sponsored by the state department of
education and by Western Kentucky State Teachers College. It has
improved its campus, added buildings, vitalized its instructional program, and improved total community living. It serves as a center
for the adults of the surrounding community, and its plant facilities
are used several nights each week for club and association activities,

adult evening classes, and recreation. Adults often spend considerable time at the community cannery assisting neighbors in the processing of food.[4]

The Bruton Heights School near Williamsburg, Virginia, operated as a community center since its opening in 1938, has served the needs of Negro youth and adults alike through the provision of educational, recreational, and health services and facilities. Activities of the school throughout its total facilities are almost continuous during the week and throughout the year. Its doors are open from early morning to almost midnight. Many thousands of youth and adults use its staff and resources each month. As a result, the total community living has been improved year by year.[5]

Holtville High School, in the Alabama cotton area, has since 1938 built a community school under the leadership of a five-year Southern Association Study. It has a fifty-acre campus with twenty buildings, including a home economics cottage, agriculture building, cannery, frozen-food locker plant, poultry house, and a large specialized shop building. It offers a broad variety of recreational activities for children, youth, and adults. Every Saturday night, for a very low admission fee, a full-length feature motion picture is shown with newsreel and short subjects. Farmers and their wives come to the high school every Wednesday night to play volley ball and ping-pong, to bowl, and to engage in many other recreational activities. The school also circulates magazines, books, and home games widely throughout the community.[6]

City High Schools Serve as Educational and Recreational Centers for Adults.—In Minneapolis, Minnesota, for the past few years, the public schools have operated two community centers for adult education and recreation. Each center is located in a junior high school building, one serving a community area in north and one in south Minneapolis. Classes are given four evenings per week, from 4:00 to 9:30 P.M. On Friday evenings, square dancing regularly attracts large numbers from all over the city. Instruction is provided by regular faculty members, who receive extra compensation for their services, and by other trained leaders. The two centers serve approximately five thousand different community adults each year. The

---

[4] W. K. McCharen, *Improving the Quality of Living*, Nashville: Division of Surveys and Field Services, George Peabody College for Teachers, 1947, pp. 40-41.
[5] *Ibid.*, pp. 64-65.
[6] Whilden Wallace, James Chriestzberg, and Verner M. Sims, *The Story of Holtville*, Deatsville: Southern Association Study Staff and Holtville High School Faculty, 1944, 191 pp.

following list of classes [7] shows what one of these community centers offered for adults in the spring of 1950:

JORDAN COMMUNITY CENTER

MONDAY
Clothing
Dresden
Furniture Upholstering
Landscape Gardening
Short Cuts in Clothing
Shorthand
Speech
Tailoring
Woodwork, Men

TUESDAY
Ceramics and Oil Painting
First Steps in Clothing
Managing Your Finances
Millinery
Novelties-Needlecraft
Typewriting
Woodwork, Men

WEDNESDAY
Dresden, Beginning
Draperies and Slip Covers
Family Life and Its Problems
Furniture Refinishing
Furniture Upholstering
Speech, Advanced
Textile Painting
Woodwork, Women

THURSDAY
Cake Decorating
Clothing, Advanced
Correct English
Furniture Upholstering
Better Hostess
Interior Decorating
Lampshade Making
Rug Hooking
Woodwork, Women

FRIDAY
Peasant Painting
Peasant Painting, Beginning
Photography

Rochester, Minnesota, employs almost all of its teachers on a twelve-month basis and utilizes their services in part for community recreation and education during summer months. Recreation pro-

---

[7] From descriptive literature distributed to the public by the Minneapolis Public Schools, Minneapolis, Minnesota.

grams are sponsored jointly by the city park board and the board of education. Physical education teachers, coaches, and other teachers with recreation experience and interest coordinate and supervise the extensive summer recreation program for youth and young adults. Recreation activities include library services, movies, crafts, as well as sports and outdoor activities. School buildings, athletic fields, and other facilities are extensively used for a wide variety of activities. Teachers not doing summer school teaching or recreational work serve in local workshops, attend summer school, or travel while on regular salary.

The Indianapolis public schools provide extended school services for an increasing number of adults and out-of-school youth each year. More than four thousand enroll in evening high schools, in addition to adult programs in apprentice training, distributive education, Americanization courses, home economics for adults, and practical nursing. High school pupils have a wide range of interscholastic and intramural sports and extraclass activities under trained leadership during late afternoon hours each day. W. S. Barnhart, Director of Extended School Services, reported that more than sixteen thousand children and youth engaged in summer school educational activities in 1950 as follows:

	Enrollment
Classes in all subjects, 9:00-12:00, five days per week in elementary schools, 28 schools	3,284
Speech and dramatics class, two days per week	150
Art centers, morning classes one or two days per week, 38 schools	1,516
Music centers, one or more days per week, 63 schools	5,300
Summer orchestra	65
Foods and clothing under 4-H standards, 44 schools	2,298
Garden clubs, 17 schools	346
Shop classes and related concrete work, 12 schools	180
High school summer schools, conducted for eight weeks in 7 schools	2,933
Classes for veterans in special trades, Crispus Attucks High School	82
Grand total in summer activities	16,154 pupils

San Francisco has developed an outstanding community-centered educational and recreational program for adults and out-of-school youth. It is directed by a coordinator of adult education of the San Francisco Unified School District and has largely abandoned the night school concept of adult education. More people attend adult classes during the day than in the evening, and there is a larger attendance in nonschool than in school locations. More than eighty thousand adults regularly enroll each year in this program, representing approximately 30 per cent of the adult population of San Francisco. The following is a general description of this outstanding program of community-centered education: [8]

To work with the community in such a way as to meet the educational needs of all adults is the objective of the Adult Education Division of San Francisco's public school system. In 200 locations throughout the city, at every hour of the day and evening, classes are held to serve the people of the various neighborhoods. Thousands of adults in San Francisco learn during their leisure—for their leisure.

Parents of the community, fathers and mothers, are given an opportunity for direct training in home and family life. Adults who are planning to travel may acquire a conversational knowledge of Spanish, French, Russian, Italian, or other foreign languages. Forums and lecture series on current topics of interest are always available.

In shop and in studio, adults work on projects for the home—polishing stones in the lapidary class, fashioning mounts in the jewelry group, throwing pottery, weaving cloth, and so on. A husband and wife may join to reupholster their living room furniture or even to build a new breakfast set. Home gardening and vegetable gardening are activities in which hundreds participate. Photography classes are crowded.

Men and women come together in great numbers to learn folk dancing or badminton; and women, particularly, work to develop poise and posture and confidence in personality development classes.

Civil service classes and instruction in all commercial fields train and upgrade workers for San Francisco's offices. Those who wish to complete high school, or even elementary school, may do so by attending classes leading to a certificate of graduation.

In half a dozen different locations activities especially designed for adults over 50 years of age are operating enthusiastically. Elsewhere, seeing persons come together to learn to write Braille and prepare books for the blind.

For the person who is interested in learning to speak to groups, to write, to act, to sail a boat, to drive a car, there is a course.

The Secondary School Improves Community Living.—The Allen-White School is the only senior high school for Negroes in Hardeman County, Tennessee. Since 1923, nine buildings have been constructed, mostly by the high school students. The school provides evening classes for many adults who have only a fourth grade education and helps them plan to improve their homes, farms, health, and livestock. Most families are share croppers. Students made a com-

---

[8] Taken from a folder describing classes for adults, winter term, 1950, San Francisco Unified School District, San Francisco, California.

munity survey to determine food and clothing needs and necessary home repairs. As a result, homes were screened; a tuberculosis isolation house was built and is in operation; sanitary toilets and a community slaughter pit were constructed.[9]

In the small northern Minnesota town of Floodwood, the school has provided many vital community services. A high school agriculture class a few years ago started an artificial insemination program for dairy herds which has helped change the area from a marginal lumbering town to a fairly prosperous dairy community. A school science survey revealed sources of water pollution which marked the beginning of a city water supply system. A seventh grade core class recently made a complete census survey of the community, including population, employment, and housing. A ninth grade core class made a survey of opinion and support for a projected community hospital. A home economics class recently held weekly nursery school sessions for young children while the teacher gave the mothers instruction in child care. The school now operates a nonprofit community cannery in which pupils do considerable work. The school provides meeting places for scouts, civic club, veterans' organizations, child study groups, sewing, and adult farming classes.

The Benjamin Franklin High School, New York City, is an example of a community school in which pupils, teachers, and community adults serve on the East Harlem Community Council, a coordinating council of community agencies with subcommittees on child welfare, housing, intercultural education, recreation, and education. Students help prepare materials on budget needs for the local board of education. They participated in a school-community campaign to clean up vacant lots, streets, sidewalks, and homes and to improve garbage disposal. In this drive both landlords and tenants were contacted by letter from the Children's Division of the East Harlem Sanitation Council. It was a cooperative action program of young people and adults to improve their community. The school has a staff member who serves as a community coordinator with two periods in the school schedule assigned for this purpose.

Secondary School Youth Serve the Community.—In some places, high school pupils serve on committees of service clubs, community recreation councils, and coordinating councils, or in other ways help to plan and carry out community service projects. In these cases, pupils are actually receiving an "apprentice" type of training in civic participation.

---

[9] McCharen, *op. cit.*, p. 26.

In Hartford, Connecticut, students from the high schools have a part in the city government through the Hartford Junior City Council organized to work with the city manager and the Hartford City Council. Through their Junior Council, youth have a chance to voice opinions on educational and civic matters. A charter, drawn up by a committee of students, was ratified by all senior high school students in the city. The Junior City Council meets in the office of the mayor once every month during the school year and works with the city manager of Hartford, a school coordinator, and a faculty adviser in each of the city's three high schools. It initiates and submits to proper authorities suggestions pertaining to the welfare of youth. The preamble to the charter for the Council reads as follows : [10]

We, the youth of Hartford, in order to provide a medium through which we and municipal authorities may exchange suggestions and advice on matters of mutual concern, promote awareness of city problems, and arouse active interest in city government, do hereby establish this Charter for The Hartford Junior City Council.

Field Trips Supply Real Life Experiences.—In the senior high school of Kirksville, Missouri, practically every department and many extraclass activities each year join in a cooperative study of racial relationships in community, state, and nation. Social, economic, religious, political, cultural, and aesthetic problems, needs, and contributions are studied—both directly and vicariously. On the local community level, much of the study is carried out through excursions, field trips, and surveys. Students spend several days visiting and observing in Negro schools; committees attend Negro churches on Sundays; an entire class visits the state university for Negroes. Student committees survey local population and housing data, occupations, business conditions, savings, welfare activities, churches, schools, and recreational facilities. These data are collected, tabulated, and interpreted in the form of a report which is given to the community through programs in clubs, churches, and civic organizations. Negroes participate jointly in these programs. Community interest and participation indicate the value of these studies in improving the culture of the minority group in Kirksville.[11]

In furthering the study of the history and archeology of the

---

[10] From a reprint from the *Hartford Courant* section, "The Parade of Youth," of July 3 and 10, 1949, distributed for use in the Hartford Public Schools. See also J. Ralph Spalding and Paul W. Coons, *Our City Government: A Manual for Hartford High School Students,* Hartford: Board of Education, 1950, 25 pp.

[11] Edward G. Olsen (ed.), *School and Community Programs.* Copyright 1949 by Prentice-Hall, Inc., pp. 198-202.

Southwest, classes in the Albuquerque High School have organized an archeology club which owns and is excavating the ruins of an abandoned city. The club works throughout the year at the nearby ruins, excavating a village that flourished before the first crusade. Dwellings, council rooms, burial grounds, pottery, and even charred corn have been dug out by these youthful scientists. They have made maps and charts of their discoveries as they read history from ruins rather than from books.[12]

The School Surveys Its Community.—A group of ninety-five seniors in four social studies classes of Anoka, Minnesota, High School recently made a study of their community in its total social and economic setting. Each class took a major topic: history, social activities, economic affairs, and government. The students gathered their information through personal interviews, questionnaires, documentary sources, newspapers, local historians, and visits to the state historical museum. Their study is now published in a booklet entitled, *On Both Sides: A Study of the Community of Anoka, Minnesota.*[13]

A class of seventh and eighth grade children in Glencoe, Illinois, assisted their community coordinating council to make a survey of the human resources of their community. In order to determine how each citizen could help improve the community, a committee of the council had constructed a questionnaire to ascertain individual interests, collections, travel, hobbies, etc. In making the survey, the pupils planned their interviews, organized survey districts, gathered and tabulated the data, wrote stories of the survey for the newspaper, and constructed a mural showing the occupations of the citizens of the community. The pupils had many valuable experiences making the survey, and the entire school now has a vast reservoir of classified resource visitors, speakers, entertainers, and special talents to vitalize the teaching of almost any topic, problem, or area.[14] The material has been kept up to date by a P.T.A.-school committee. The League of Women Voters later carried out a new survey in which children helped, and the teachers add current information by including questions on resources in their parent conferences each fall.

Community People Used as a Resource.—Recently, the social studies classes of the Wilbur Wright Junior High School in Cleveland had distinguished auditorium visitors in the persons of the president

[12] *Ibid.,* pp. 202-4.
[13] *Ibid.,* pp. 229-33.
[14] Miriam Sutherland, "A Survey of Personal Resources," *Educational Method,* 18 (March, 1939), 275-78.

and five other members of the city council. Each of the thirty social studies classes had carefully prepared for their coming by studying ward maps and the organization and work of the council. The councilmen outlined their responsibilities and committee activities to the pupils, and a lively question period followed. The school considered this one of their most effective community learning experiences.[15]

Recent graduates of Elkridge High School, Baltimore, no longer fear their initial vocational interview, for each senior has a practice interview with some business executive or industrial personnel manager as a part of the senior guidance program. At the beginning of the school year, the senior class made a survey of local job possibilities through a simple questionnaire; they also asked permission for a practice interview. Prior to the individual interviews, the pupils prepared an outline of occupational questions for their guidance. The businessmen were cooperative and helped the pupils to overcome their nervousness during the interviews. Each pupil wrote a report of his interview findings, which were discussed in future classes. These experiences have proved highly valuable in the counseling program of the school.[16]

Work Experience Furnished by the Laboratory of the Community.—Work experience or cooperative part-time programs are excellent illustrations of using the community as a learning laboratory. In these programs, the school takes the initiative in planning with business and industry the individual pupil programs in which they work, both in school and on the job. Practically every large city in the nation now has these cooperative programs in operation.[17]

Community Coordination for Improved Education and Community Life.—The statement of principles at the beginning of this chapter emphasized that the modern high school should assume a definite responsibility for leadership in coordinating the total educational facilities and activities of the community. Since youth spends so much of their time living, working, loafing, and playing in the community, the school cannot ignore these highly significant influences upon the personality and behavior of their pupils. Throughout this chapter, we have considered various aspects of the direct educative influence of the culture of the community. A few situations have revealed some degree of community cooperation in providing

[15] Olsen, *op. cit.*, pp. 149-52.
[16] *Ibid.*, pp. 147-48.
[17] See Chapter 9 for a detailed discussion.

educational functions for youth. The following is an example of a high school's leadership in developing the coordination of a community program of recreation.

The village of Frost in Navarro County, Texas, has developed a community planning board to help plan the program of the Frost Community School and to relate it to the community. The community planning board works with the school board, the Parent-Teacher Association, and civic clubs to develop a school-community program.

The school has an enrollment of three hundred in grades one through twelve, and the village has a population of seven hundred. It is located in the cotton land of east Texas. The school campus contains a central building, a gymnasium, a homemaking cottage, a lunchroom, and a farm shop.

Residents of the community are frequently called into classes to demonstrate skills and activities to the pupils. The school facilities are used regularly for community-centered activities of many kinds. The community planning board and the school jointly promote many vital services to improve the community. Pupils have assisted in conservation projects, poultry improvement, veterinary work, social entertainment, beautification projects, and health improvement programs. Valuable work experiences are given pupils throughout the community. In all these activities, the community planning board helps to coordinate the educational program of the school as it seeks to improve living in the community.[18]

California Promotes Adult Education.—For the past few years, California has promoted a program of adult education through state reimbursement to the public schools which is an outstanding example of the recognition of the principle of state and local community responsibility for adult education. In this program the state department of education accepts three hours' attendance at evening or night classes as being equivalent of one day's attendance for the purpose of state remuneration. This means that for each three hours of adult night school attendance, the local school receives the same payment from the state that it received for an entire day's attendance of a high school pupil.

At Acalanes High School, Lafayette, California, for example, during the school terms of 1949-50, there was a total enrollment in the adult education program (night classes) of 2,020 as compared with the high school day enrollment of 960. Classes were held each

18 McCharen, *op. cit.*, pp. 51-53.

night, Monday through Friday, of the school year. The adult program was discontinued during the summer months, though the school's recreational facilities are widely used by the public during the summer vacation period. Courses offered adults included ceramics, woodworking, bookkeeping, typing, music appreciation, child care, adolescent problems, folk dancing, automobile shop, arts and crafts, and many other similar courses, largely of a recreational nature. These courses are financed jointly by funds from the state department, the local school district, and by a small fee for each course.

School-Community Library Cooperation.—Athough school library service is primarily a responsibility of the board of education, many communities have developed cooperative programs between their schools and their public libraries. It is desirable that each high school have its own library, serving as a coordinated unit of a central school library system working in close cooperation with the public library. In some communities, however, school library service is provided entirely or partly by the public library. For example, in Faribault, Minnesota, a city of approximately fifteen thousand, there is a long-standing written agreement between the schools and the public library providing for a cooperative plan for school library service. This plan provides,[19] among other items, for:

1. School librarian to be selected by the public librarian and superintendent of schools and to be employed and paid by the school district.
2. School librarian to render part-time service at the public library building.
3. School library a branch of the public library.
4. Public library to lend its resources to the school branch . . .
5. School library books purchased by the school district to be shelved at public library, except those for the high school, and shall be subject to community use when not in actual school use . . .
6. Public librarian to render such personal oversight and service to the public schools and the teachers in the line of library work as conditions may require.

In many areas of the nation, library services have been provided rural school pupils through county libraries. In some places, school leaders have initiated programs leading to the organization of county libraries where such facilities were lacking.

---

[19] Joint Committee of the National Education Association and the American Library Association, *Schools and Public Libraries,* Washington, D.C.: National Education Association, 1941, p. 34.

Public libraries regularly lend books, films, records, and exhibits to high schools through loans to individual teachers. School and public libraries often cooperate in observing book week, in presenting radio programs, in making displays of pupils' work, and in working with parent groups. Public libraries sometimes reserve facilities during certain hours exclusively for high school pupils and classes. In addition, they sometimes provide excellent books for a parent and teacher room, work directly with curriculum committees, and provide professional reading for teachers.[20]

4. First Steps

If the future teacher accepts the principles given at the beginning of this chapter, he can be expected to move in the direction of some of the practices described in the better schools. Much will depend upon the kind of high school in which he teaches—the staff, administration, and the community itself. If the entire school faculty and administration work cooperatively with the community, however, the following steps will lead toward the development of a real community school.

1. A policy should be developed which recognizes and encourages the use of the school to interpret, serve, and improve the community. Educational experiences need to be recognized as being far broader than textbooks. The school must see that the whole community is its learning laboratory. It must develop school policies growing out of a philosophy which actually encourages community service and improvement, field trips, surveys, resource visitors, interviews, school camping, and community coordination. The first step might be to have teachers meet with the board of education to discuss the educational significance of these types of experiences.

2. The administration of the high school must implement this policy by giving definite assistance to teachers who seek to provide for community service, improvement, and understanding in their classes. The principal can help provide flexible daily class schedules to secure a two or three hour block of time for field trips. He can assist in supplying transportation for excursions. He can secure outstanding resource visitors. The teacher should actively seek this assistance.

[20] *Ibid.*, pp. 8-16.

3. The high school staff can make a cooperative study or survey of the local community resources, needs, and problems. This survey could be made either by the staff, or by the pupils as class projects. Community services, government, industry, housing, welfare, recreation, and the like can be assessed to determine their use in the curriculum. The human resources—the travel, hobbies, nationalities, experiences, and interests of the *people* of the community—should be classified for possible use in learning activities. An individual teacher can often stimulate such a study by offering the resources of his class.

4. Any high school teacher can take limited field trips, within a single period if necessary. He can combine his class period with an early morning hour, noon period, free period, or after-school hour in order to double the time available for an excursion. He can invite resource visitors to come to his classes. He can send his pupils to make simple community studies and interviews. He can bring samples of community and natural resources—such as rocks, soil, lumber, flowers, plants, plastics—into his classes for observation, study, and analysis.

5. Any energetic teacher can persuade at least *one* other teacher to join in such projects. Another teacher in his department, one in the adjacent home room or whose field is closely related to his own, may be influenced to join forces in planning field trips, sharing speakers, gathering local soil or rock specimens. Such cooperation doubles the effectiveness of the project.

6. After two or three teachers learn how to study, to use, and to serve the community effectively, it should become possible to direct the total school gradually toward larger projects. For example, building a school camp, developing a school reforestation project, or landscaping the grounds can become cooperative projects eliciting the efforts of every department, teacher, and pupil.

7. In the vocational areas and special fields of the high school, a work experience program can be developed slowly on a small scale without federal aid. A teacher of business education might begin to develop plans with the administration for work experience in business offices or service organizations.

8. Secondary school teachers and administrators can develop a school speakers and service bureau for the community. The special abilities of teachers, such as singing, speaking, and organizing square dances, can be determined and classified to serve community agencies and organizations. Pupils in music classes, debating, public speaking, and physical education can similarly be classified

for community programs. Service clubs and women's organizations are always interested in discovering sources of programs.

9. The total school staff, with the leadership of the principal, can begin to develop adult education and recreation by having an occasional Parents' or Students' Night. Even without special equipment, extra teachers, or increased salaries, the high school can have at least one or two parent recreation nights per year.

SELECTED REFERENCES

COOK, LLOYD ALLEN, and COOK, ELAINE FORSYTH. *A Sociological Approach to Education.* New York: McGraw-Hill Book Co., Inc., 1950, 514 pp.—The study of American community life as it relates to the school is presented through a number of cases. Cooperative procedures and human relations are stressed. Deals with many problems discussed in the text besides being a valuable source book for information on school-community relations.

DOUGLASS, HARL R. (ed.). *The High School Curriculum.* New York: The Ronald Press Co., 1947, chap. 8.—This chapter contains an excellent discussion of the principles and place of the community in the curriculum of the modern secondary school.

EDUCATIONAL POLICIES COMMISSION. *Education for ALL American Youth.* Washington, D.C.: National Education Association, 1944, chaps. 3, 4.—Contains a recommended program for American high schools, including a detailed description of how a functioning program could operate in a rural and urban community.

HANNA, PAUL R., and RESEARCH STAFF. *Youth Serves the Community.* New York: Appleton-Century-Crofts, Inc., 1936, 303 pp.—This was the pioneering study in the area of the community school, and is still valuable. It contains several hundred examples of schools working to interpret, serve, and improve their communities.

McCHAREN, WILLIAM K. *Improving the Quality of Living.* Nashville, Tennessee: Division of Surveys and Field Services, George Peabody College, 1947, 67 pp.—This is an excellent pamphlet on twenty-two school programs in the South which are serving the needs of the people in their communities, describing in greater detail some of the illustrations given in this chapter.

McCHAREN, WILLIAM K. *Selected Community School Programs in the South.* Nashville, Tennessee: Division of Surveys and Field Services, George Peabody College, 1948, 216 pp.—Presents a more complete description of outstanding selected community school programs and their work in improving living in the South.

OLSEN, CLARA M., and FLETCHER, NORMAN D. *Learn and Live.* New York: Alfred P. Sloan Foundation, Inc., 1946, 101 pp.—This fascinating account shows how elementary and secondary schools participating in the Sloan Foundation Experiment in Applied Economics geared their program to community needs. These were schools serving low-income groups. The project, under the direction of the Universities of Florida, Kentucky, and Vermont, centered around the economic necessities of food, housing, and clothing.

OLSEN, EDWARD G., and OTHERS. *School and Community.* New York: Prentice-Hall, Inc., 1945, 422 pp.—This book is the best basic standard reference on the community school. It contains a comprehensive statement of philosophy, goals, and techniques, and separate chapters dealing with the use in schools of documentary materials, audio-visual aids, resource visitors, interviews, field trips, surveys, extended field studies, camping, service projects, and work experience.

OLSEN, EDWARD G. (ed.). *School and Community Programs.* New York: Prentice-Hall, Inc., 1949, 510 pp.—"A casebook of successful practice from kindergarten through college and adult education" (subtitle). This book contains a large number of excellent community-school programs compiled and edited largely from current periodical articles. They are classified in general around the major study techniques given in Olsen's book above, *School and Community.* Many of the illustrations in this chapter are given in greater detail here.

Chapter 12

EVALUATING AND REPORTING PUPIL PROGRESS

Evaluation is the process of gathering and interpreting evidence regarding the progress and problems of pupils in achieving desirable educational objectives. An evaluation program is far more comprehensive than a "measurement" or "testing" program, since it is based upon the assumption that the *values* of the curricular experiences are to be determined. Various types of tests are but one of the many kinds of appraisal instruments and techniques used to secure data in evaluating the curriculum of a modern school.

The program of evaluation in a modern school functions within the framework of the educational philosophy of the particular school. It derives its guidance from the statement of purpose, which determines the curriculum of the school. These educational objectives (discussed in Chapter 2) are cooperatively determined by pupils, teachers, and community adults. Objectives represent the kind of changes in the behavior of the pupils which these groups have deemed desirable. Evaluation, therefore, must determine the degree to which the school is fulfilling its responsibility in changing society through modifying the behavior of its pupils. Hence, evaluation operates as an integral part of the process of purposeful learning, and not in isolation from it.

1. The Principles

The evaluation program seeks to determine the degree to which the objectives of the school or the particular group are being attained, for each pupil and for the group.

The faculty and pupils must constantly keep in mind the goals of the school. All activities and experiences selected for the curriculum should help pupils develop the kind of behavior which represents progress toward the desired goals. Evaluation requires that valid, reliable, and objective evidence be collected regarding the ways in which boys and girls are changing their behavior in the directions indicated by the school's objectives. In other words, all evaluation in a class is done in terms of the goals set up by the teacher and pupils. Any evaluation that merely seeks to determine how much a pupil has learned of the material covered in a book is not sound.

Evaluation recognizes the concept of the "whole child" in the learning process.

The program of evaluation in the modern school curriculum is based upon the organismic concept that the individual learns and grows as a whole in interaction with his environment. At the same time, however, it recognizes that the "whole child" cannot adequately be evaluated at any one time by any one appraisal instrument, score, or symbol. Pupil behavior and growth are far too complex and inter-related to lend themselves to such analysis. Evaluation attempts to secure as complete a picture of the individual as possible, but must necessarily operate through sampling different aspects of behavior at different times in a variety of learning situations. Interpretations of different aspects of behavior are made in terms of the total personality of the child, even though single phases of growth need to be examined for the purpose of diagnosing learning difficulties.

Evaluation is an integral part of the learning situation, a con-tinuous, cumulative process.

Evaluation is rooted into the philosophy of society, the nature of the individual learner, and the goals of the school. Hence, it is never an isolated process nor an end-point—something to be done at the end of a unit or semester. It is not a goal in itself—a mere test to be passed. Evaluation is a continuous, cumulative process, a part of all functional learning serving to diagnose difficulties and guide child growth and development. Evidence of pupil growth and progress should be gathered daily in reference to goals established by teacher and pupil. Tests are used to determine how much a pupil knows be-fore he begins the work and to diagnose difficulties. Self-appraisal is an important part of the work of pupils during the course of a unit. One cannot teach for a month and then appraise with validity desirable growth in a test lasting for one hour.

The pupil plays a vital part in the evaluation program.

The individual learner has an important function in modern eval-uation. First, he must accept each goal as being vital to himself before it will serve as motivation for his learning. Second, he helps define accepted goals in terms of his own behavior. Third, he helps suggest experiences in reaching these goals. Fourth, he may co-operate in determining situations in which to appraise his growth.

Fifth, he will aid in securing records of his growth and progress. Sixth, he will finally assist in interpreting this behavior, determining what it means in light of the desired goal. Thus, self-appraisal is a vital part of modern evaluation.

Effective evaluation requires the cooperation of pupils, teachers (including all professional personnel), parents, and other community adults.

Evaluation, being an integral part of modern education, must be in harmony with democratic principles and procedures. Since many persons jointly share in determining purposes and in planning learning experiences, they should also cooperate in appraising the learning process. This procedure insures efficiency, yet provides both for individual differences and for sharing common social purposes. Teachers who share the planning of a course, and make it a regular practice of meeting together, also evaluate cooperatively the progress made in the course. Evaluation of a school program, on a broader base, is a cooperative job for administrators, teachers, parents, and pupils.

The evaluation program should be a comprehensive one that appraises pupil progress in achieving all the significant goals of the school.

Since modern secondary schools are attempting to promote many kinds of pupil growth, it is therefore imperative that the school systematically gather evidence regarding a variety of desired behavior changes. Too frequently, schools test only for the retention of information and use of skills, and *assume* that other goals are likewise being attained. This is a dangerous practice. When teachers try to help pupils develop desirable attitudes, functional skills and information, and vital understandings, a broad program of appraisal is needed to guide learning in all these areas. To secure evidence of growth, or of difficulties, within these wide areas of significant learnings, a great variety of appraisal instruments need to be used. Essay examinations and standardized objective tests alone are not adequate for valid evaluation.

The assigning of marks in the process of reporting is but one aspect of evaluating the total growth of an individual pupil.

Many parents, teachers, and pupils still consider evaluation primarily as a means of assigning marks. Reporting to parents on this basis is the relatively simple process of sending home a mark for each school subject. Not only is such a system wholly inadequate as an evaluation program, but it also has serious implications for the learning process: pupils tend to work for marks rather than for real achievement. This becomes a menace to the development of self-direction on the part of the pupil and to his continued self-education beyond the years of formal schooling. Marking is only a narrow phase of the total evaluation of growth. In most instances, marks give but an extremely limited picture of what is happening to the child in school. Much more evaluation than is used for marking purposes must go on in the class room.

Marks, in order to show progress, should reflect individual growth. Competitive marking and relative ranking deny known psychological facts regarding individual differences in ability, interests, and home background by assuming that all types of pupils learn the same things in the same way and at the same time. Each child should be evaluated in terms of his own abilities and interests rather than compared with others who may differ markedly. Equal achievement does not necessarily indicate equal abilities or effort. Undue emphasis upon competitive marks also frequently results in bad morale and conditions of poor mental hygiene in the classroom.

The interpretation of evaluation data must be meaningful and consistent with a democratic philosophy of education.

Many modern schools no longer use a single mark to appraise pupil growth. Teachers increasingly feel that a single mark or numerical score may by failure to show variations in behavior conceal more than it reveals. Such a procedure offers little diagnostic guidance. The mark itself frequently becomes the only interpretation given. Hence, pupil growth needs to be described and summarized in terms meaningful to pupils, parents, and teachers. Such interpretations should be based primarily upon the individual pupil's own abilities, interests, and background rather than upon reference to group or national norms, although the latter are sometimes useful and necessary. Evaluation of an individual's growth in terms of his own progress and within the limitations of his own ability is consistent with democratic principles outlined in Chapter 1.

2. Some Typical Practices

In many high school classes, one is likely to find that several of the principles of evaluation given above are not applied. Partially, this condition results from a lack of understanding of the true nature of modern evaluation and also from certain misconceptions. All too frequently, evaluation is considered as being something apart from the curriculum rather than an integral part of learning. Tests are often given *after* units or books have been completed, primarily for the purpose of reporting to parents rather than to diagnose learning. Students typically have little active part to play in evaluation, serving only as recipients of marks. Schoolwide standardized testing programs are often administered uniformly to all students without reference to pupil or teacher objectives. Little remedial work follows the standardized testing program.

The student has little role to play in helping develop a functional and useful record system. In fact, the record system is often sadly neglected or, at best, poorly coordinated. Each teacher keeps a record of his "grades," but there is little cooperative gathering of data pertaining to all the school's goals. Records do not follow the student; there is little in the way of cumulative records. The evaluation program has little if any direct or functional relationship to the school's guidance program. Teachers make their own objective tests crudely and use essay tests with little reliability.

Common Misconceptions in Evaluation.—Two extreme positions regarding evaluation may be found in high schools today. One group —decidedly in the minority—has practically abandoned all appraisal as a result of the abuse of objective and standardized tests. Since these tests have overemphasized the mastery of isolated facts and skills, some schools have gone to the other extreme and use practically no tests. This practice is unfortunate, for it results in a failure to gather evidence systematically regarding student growth.

Another common fallacy is to assume that a teacher can measure certain facts, skills, and information accurately and use these data to predict the achievement of other desired outcomes. A history teacher, for example, may give tests in American history dealing with important events, administrations, and dates, and base much of his evaluation of progress upon this single test. Such a practice assumes that there is a close relationship existing between the mastery of the factual knowledge of the test and other significant goals. If the teacher holds effective citizenship, cooperation, social sensitivity, and intellectual understanding as goals of the social studies, then the mere mastery of the facts of American history is not a valid index of the student's achievement of these other socially important objectives. It is necessary to gather evidence directly concerning the achievement of each objective within a subject or area.

Periodical Rather than Continuous Appraisal.—We have indicated that evaluation or appraisal is an essential aspect of the learning process that should operate continuously in the program of a school. Teachers may teach intensively for a month or six-week period, and then give an hour test or fifteen-minute "quiz" assuming that this represents satisfactory appraisal. Obviously, it is a poor practice, for it violates most of the principles of learning developed in Chapter 1. Evidence of problems, learning blocks, and difficulties needs to be collected daily in order to diagnose and guide learning effectively. Some teachers in high schools base a large part of the student's marks upon a monthly or term examination. If the student makes a high score on this test, he is given a high mark in the course. Again, the assumption is that the pupil has made satisfactory growth in all the goals of the course. Other teachers give regular weekly objective and essay tests and short quizzes. Although this is a better practice than monthly testing, it still raises questions of how adequately *all the significant objectives* of the course are being evaluated.

Testing for Marking Rather than Evaluating for Diagnosis.— Many high school teachers still conceive of marking as the primary function of testing. Not only do they overemphasize marking, but frequently marks become ends in themselves. Students and parents also accept this limited conception of evaluation, and marks become symbols of great significance. Marks or "grades" are not goals to be achieved for themselves. Teachers and parents often fail to see that marks in and of themselves have little significance in the learning process. They sometimes do not understand that marks serve primarily the function of *recording and reporting* student growth, problems, and progress to the student himself, to parents, to the community, and to the college. The report, therefore, need not necessarily be a mark, but may be any symbol or technique which carries meaning. If marks are meaningful, and are readily recorded and interpreted, then they may serve a useful function in evaluation.

Tests Used as Incentives for Learning.—Tests are also related to motivation in the learning process. In Chapter 1 we pointed out the value of intrinsic incentives as against extrinsic. Marks are obviously extrinsic—that is, they have little value in themselves. It is probably true that competition with other students for marks is a motivating factor of great significance for many students. For some few individuals, it may even have desirable effects within limits. Yet, for most students such competition for marks is not desirable, for it discourages the slow student, promotes cheating, and detracts from the learning process itself. As mentioned previously, competitive marking in the general education program of secondary schools is unrealistic, for it runs counter to the psychology of individual differences. Competitive marking and grade standards also deny many of the values of democratic education outlined in Chapter 2.

Testing is but one important aspect of evaluation, one technique for gathering evidence of pupil progress or learning difficulty. It does give the teacher valuable clues and evidence of factors which impede learning. Tests used as diagnostic tools can and do serve vital functions in modern high schools: they help to reveal errors, problems, difficulties, prejudices, handicaps, emotional blocks, maladjustments, as well as satisfactory growth, learning, and achievement. Such diagnostic and prognostic tests are invaluable in helping to guide learning and to plan remedial instruction. There is a good deal of testing by standardized instruments done in high schools today, although considerable progress needs to be made in using these tests for diagnostic purposes.

Misuse of Standardized Tests.—Standardized achievement tests are widely used in secondary schools. Some measure facts, skills, and understandings within a single field, such as the Cooperative Chemistry Test. Others, such as the Iowa Every-Pupil Tests of Basic Skills, attempt to appraise basic skills in many fields. A third type, such as the Progressive Achievement Test, tries to measure both facts and skills. These tests are standardized with large populations and provide grade and age norms.

Standardized tests can be either helpful or harmful in a high school, depending upon the nature of their use. Often such tests are given for the purpose of attempting to promote uniform achievement throughout an entire school or school system. Some principals and superintendents seek to bring every ninth grade English class up to the "grade standard" in spelling, punctuation, or grammar. Administrative pressure is frequently placed upon teachers to bring *all students* up to the national grade norm, a concept which represents a basic psychological fallacy. Teachers in turn employ undue pressure upon their slow and retarded students, thus aggravating their problems, frustrating them, and causing them to become even more handicapped and maladjusted.

Another serious abuse of the standardized test is the tendency of the teacher to overemphasize the importance and place of skills and information in the curriculum. Since teachers know their pupils will be tested regularly by standardized tests, they sometimes tend to "teach for the test"; that is, they may spend far more time than necessary upon formal grammar, spelling, vocabulary, dates and places, computation, and the like, and neglect the more intangible results. This practice is especially true in schools where a teacher's competence is judged rather largely in terms of the success of his students with standardized examinations and tests. We shall describe in the next section the proper place and use of standardized tests and scales. They can serve a desirable function in a modern evaluation program if they are used to appraise those objectives which the teacher and school hold to be important.

Many Significant Objectives Neglected in Evaluation.—Numerous kinds of important growth in adolescent behavior previously discussed are not directly evaluated. While many modern high schools state objectives relating to attitudes, ideals, appreciations, and understandings, and plan pupil experiences relating to them, few teachers attempt to evaluate those behaviors directly. Teachers either take for granted that those objectives are being attained, or else believe that the achievement of skills and facts indicates satisfactory growth in the more intangible goals. Consequently, progress in learning many significant objectives is slow, confused, and highly inefficient since teachers lack valid and objective data with which to guide their pupils' learning.

Although this condition is largely due to a failure to see evaluation in terms of appraising growth toward objectives, it must also be attributed to the fact that few written appraisal instruments have been developed for measuring effectively attitudes and appreciations. The training many teachers have received in measurement has tended to develop the concept that evaluation, in order to be objective, can only be done through measuring instruments which have been standardized and found highly reliable. The improvement of competency in evaluation, through sharpening observation powers and techniques, is just gaining hold in education. Careful observation can yield objective evidence of growth, especially in behavior indicating attitudes and habits.

Failure to Use Self-Appraisal.—The typical high school teacher tests periodically. He usually gives all the tests, records all the scores, places the marks upon the report cards, and judges whether his pupils pass or fail. Pupils occasionally discuss goals and objectives with teachers and frequently help plan some of their work, but rare indeed is the teacher who permits the pupils to participate democratically in the evaluation of their growth and achievement. "Trading papers" for marking errors is commonly the maximum participation students enjoy in appraisal. Some teachers even go so far as to withhold test scores and marks, making of the marking and reporting a highly secret process.

Pupils can help collect much valuable data regarding their own progress and problems if given opportunity and encouragement. Parents, too, can share in the process. After the student leaves the protection of the school, his learning should continue, largely self-directed. He should, therefore, receive maximum training and experience in self-appraisal during school in order to insure independence and continuity of learning in his later life experiences as a citizen.

Undue Stress Placed on Marks.—In schools where evaluation of all the objectives of a modern school is not understood or accepted as a principle, the evaluation done is generally for the purpose of determining the pupils' marks. When marks, in and of themselves, become an end of learning, permanent and significant learnings suffer. There is perhaps no other practice that so glaringly belies the evidence concerning how learning takes place. The mark, rather than progress toward important educational goals, is made the chief purpose for the pupil. Measuring time by "marking periods," labeling reports "marking period reports," jotting down a mark in the record book for each contribution by the pupil, and constantly using marks as incentives for doing the assigned work are evidences of the excessive emphasis on marks in secondary school classes. A vicious practice is the threatening of possible failure of the pupil who may have no reasonable chance of success in the work assigned.

Marks are mainly of a competitive nature in the large majority of secondary schools. The A, B, C, D, F symbols, based upon the statistical concept of the normal curve, are most widely used. A surprisingly large number of secondary schools still use the numerical system of marking, usually 65 or 75 to 100 being the range of passing marks. This practice, which is unsound mathematically, assumes that one has been able to measure 85 per cent, or any given per cent, of something. The question is, percentage of what?

Sketchy Reports to Parents.—The present-day marking and reporting system in most secondary schools is better suited for the purpose of record keeping and transferring marks to other institutions than for reporting information to parents. The traditional card illustrated on pages 274-75 actually furnishes little information. There is no indication of the phases of a subject with which a pupil may be having difficulty, for example. In such a subject as English, the work in literature, spelling, letter writing, punctuation, and speech may be lumped into one mark. No indication is given of progress in attitudes, health habits, or social skills. The report indicates what the school believes is important in a pupil's growth.

3. Practices in the Better Secondary Schools

We have previously pointed out many desirable practices which will improve the evaluation program in a modern high school. Some of these practices are relatively widespread; others are still limited to a few of the more outstanding secondary schools. In this section, we shall describe some of these recommended practices and give illustrations of their use in selected secondary schools.

A Wide Variety of Appraisal Instruments Used.—In order to have a satisfactory evaluation program, teachers cooperatively need to collect and develop a large number of appraisal instruments and techniques to evaluate all the significant goals of a school. The following are some of the newer types of appraisal instruments in use in the best learning situations in secondary schools: check lists; diaries; sociograms; anecdotal records; interest questionnaires; aptitude tests; social acceptance scales; personality inventories; self-portraits; self-direction inventories; attitude indicators; tests of clear thinking, social sensitivity, skills, achievement, and appreciations; and identification of values scales. Some of these types are illustrated in the rest of the chapter.

A Modern High School Plans Its Evaluation Program.—The following evaluation plan is one developed by the staff of the University High School at Ohio State University: [1]

Evaluation should be focused upon the important values which underlie the program of the school, and the success or failure of the school should be judged in terms of how well it meets the values held.

A long-range evaluation program should be so planned that no one year would involve the school in a complete study of every aspect of its work.

The University High School has set up a long-range five-year evaluation program [2] in which:

. . . it is proposed that we collect, organize and interpret information about changes taking place in our students. The basis for this study should be our

---

[1] Geneva Hanna, chairman, *Evaluation Committee Report, 1946-47* (mimeographed), Columbus, Ohio: Ohio State University, 1947, p. 2.
[2] *Ibid.*, p. 3.

REPORT TO PARENTS

Grades Seven to Twelve

Pupil_____

Year_____ Grade_____

School_____

Teacher_____

Principal_____

Superintendent_____

In order that your child may have the best possible opportunity

for his richest and fullest growth it is of prime importance that

his parents and teachers keep closely in contact. The school will

send you this regular report once every six weeks throughout the

school year. It will indicate to you some of the things which we

consider important in your child's development. If deficiencies

are apparent you are urged to confer with teacher and principal

so that all factors in the case may be thoroughly understood.

SUBJECTS	First Semester				Second Semester				Year
	1	2	3	S	1	2	3	S	

EXPLANATION OF MARKING

A—Superior work.　　　　B—Good, above the average.

C—Average work.　　　　D—Work below the average,
　　　　　　　　　　　　　　　unsatisfactory but passing.
F—Failure.

If no mark is given, it indicates either that the pupil has not completed the required work in the subject or that he has not been present enough to merit a mark.

ATTENDANCE RECORD

	1	2	3	Sem.	4	5	6	Sem.	Year
Days Absent									
Times Tardy									

PARENT'S SIGNATURE

Your signature indicates merely that you have examined the report; not that you approve or disapprove.

Period	Parent's Signature
1	
2	
3	
4	
5	
6	

statement of continuous curriculum experience. We should collect the following information:

3. Junior High School (grades 7, 8, and 9)
    a) Intelligence test scores
    b) Achievement in reading
    c) Arithmetic achievement
    d) Library skills
    e) Identification of values
    f) Vocational interests

4. Senior High School (grades 10, 11, and 12)
    a) Intelligence test scores
    b) O.S.U. Psychological
    c) American Council Psychological
    d) Achievement in reading
    e) Arithmetic achievement
    f) Library skills
    g) Identification of values
    h) Vocational interests
    i) Aptitude tests

Anecdotal Records Evaluate Behavior.—Many teachers are beginning to record pertinent behavior of pupils in anecdotal form. This is a type of record that will reveal progress through objective accounts of what a pupil has said or done. In most instances, no special form is used. However, the report on page 277 is an interesting example of a newer type of form for recording data about certain intangible objectives.

Pupils Appraise Themselves.—Self-appraisal plays a vitally important part in good evaluation programs in secondary schools. These schools understand that learning is an active process and that the learner must recognize goals which are important to himself and determine his own needs with respect to them. Such appraisal includes: (1) cooperative determination of goals, (2) cooperation in determining status with respect to these goals, (3) cooperation in the activities required to secure the desired growth, and (4) cooperation in securing evidence of progress. In these classes, the pupil is an active participant in the program of evaluation. In this capacity, under teacher guidance, he discovers his strengths, weaknesses, problems, and special abilities. Through daily sharing and participating in the total learning process, he uses the evidence collected in the evaluation process to guide more effectively his progress toward significant personal and social goals. It is not necessary for him to wait for a

APPLETON HIGH SCHOOL

Anecdotal Record of Student

Teachers: From time to time, you observe acts and attitudes of students characteristic of them. These are invaluable in knowing personality and character.

Please jot down such incidents on this form at the time. Place same in principal's box.

Be objective, please. Jot down exactly what took place. In the lower half, give your judgment or subjective interpretation, if you wish.

Name of Student   Date

Objective Event:

Name of Teacher

Subjective Judgment:

The Appleton, Wisconsin, Anecdotal Record.

monthly or quarterly report card in order to determine his progress. He is a functioning partner in the planning, directing, and judging of his own growth toward the goals of the modern school.

The self-appraisal technique on page 278 is part of an achievement test on a junior high school teaching unit.

Continuous and Cooperative Evaluation of Individual Progress. —The modern secondary school places emphasis upon the growth of the individual, his own progress during a unit, semester, year, or longer period of time.   We find teachers and pupils who keep progress records of each pupil's improvement in such skills as speed of reading, spelling, or typewriting.   Such evaluation is done, not by the teacher at the end of the work, but continuously by teacher and pupil working together.   When groups have set up their own goals, under the teacher's guidance, they constantly check themselves to see how well those goals are being attained.   There may be group goals, such as gathering specific information, but the teacher in the kind of classroom de-

TEST ON OUR WATER SUPPLY

Burdick Junior High School, Stamford, Connecticut

Part I General Self-Check

Key

1—not at all; 2—small; 3—medium; 4—great; 5—greatest
In answering the following questions, use the numbers in the key.

To what extent
1. Did I participate in the listed activities? _____
2. Did I participate in class discussion? _____
3. Did I improve my ability to form my own conclusions? _____
4. Did I depend on others? _____
5. Did I increase my willingness to respect the opinions of others? _____
6. Was I critical? _____
7. Was I interested in my own growth? _____
8. Was I interested in the growth of others? _____
9. Did I employ my time well? _____
10. Did I do a thorough piece of work? _____
11. Was I interested in gaining knowledge? _____
12. Did I gain knowledge? _____
13. Did I increase confidence in myself? _____
14. Did I present my material clearly? _____
15. Did I observe self-control? _____
16. Did I respect authority? _____
17. Did I achieve a greater community spirit? _____
18. Did I recognize my own responsibility to maintain
    Stamford's healthful water supply? _____

Pupil Self-Appraisal Form.

scribed here does not expect all pupils to attain a certain set standard. Instead, there are different standards for pupils of different abilities.

Teachers Evaluate Pupil Behavior.—In addition to other kinds of evaluation techniques and records, teachers use rating scales or evaluation sheets, such as the following, on which they appraise a pupil on such behavior as social adjustment, attitudes toward work, ability to get along with others, leadership, and the like. Shorewood, Wisconsin, High School has developed the form on page 279 for the cooperative use of teachers and counselors.

PUPIL EVALUATION SHEET *

Shorewood High School, Shorewood, Wisconsin
Evaluation of Individual Growth and Development
(In terms of present grade-growth levels)

Counselor_____ H. R._____ Student_____ Grade____
Teacher_____ Subject_____ Date_____

	High	Aver.	Low	COMMENTS
RESPONSIBILITY AND DEPENDABILITY				
1. Sees a job through under all conditions........				
2. Uses time effectively......................				
3. Uses good judgment......................				
4. Participates well in class activities.............				
SOCIAL ADJUSTMENT				
1. Gets along well with people..................				
2. Understands and accepts authority.............				
3. Considerate of others and their opinion........				
4. Shows satisfactory self-confidence.............				
5. Refrains from attention-getting................				
INFLUENCE AMONG HIS FELLOWS				
1. Manifests constructive leadership among peers..				
2. Recognizes and supports democratic leadership..				
3. Develops a spirit of friendliness in the group...				
4. Stands for socially and morally sound principles.				
WORK HABITS				
1. Sets standards in line with ability.............				
2. Follows directions ably......................				
3. Works independently........................				
4. Organizes work well........................				
5. Has tools at all times.......................				
6. Gets work in on time.......................				

1. Has at present a grade of approximately A B C D F Incomplete
2. Works at ABOVE_____ BELOW_____ EXPECTED_____ level.
3. Comments on health and physical status.

* The master copy of this report can serve as a summary for each pupil. On the reverse side of this sheet, the counselor will record the significant facts of each conference, which he will want to refer to from time to time. Among recorded items will be the program for the coming year.

Form for Evaluation of Behavior.

Individual Records as a Basis for Evaluation.—Many high school teachers keep an individual evaluation folder for each pupil for whom they are primarily responsible. In this folder the teacher and pupil regularly collect and interpret evidence relating to the personal and social goals of the individual. Samples of answers to essay examinations, written papers, objective and standardized test scores, ratings, questionnaires, records of free reading, samples of creative writing, samples of progress in various skills, anecdotal records, etc., are added periodically. Other teachers who work with the pupil add further data to the individual folder. The teacher collecting evidence is responsible for indicating the objectives to which it is related, and, if possible, the stage of progress as revealed by the evidence. This procedure facilitates the task of the home room teacher by broadening the basis of interpretation, and also guards against the inefficient accumulation of evidence unrelated to school objectives.

All these data are carefully interpreted by the teacher in the light of what he knows about the pupil and summarized in a short coherent picture of individual growth toward the objectives of the school. This summary is not made in marks or any stereotyped classification of evidence, but in paragraphs immediately intelligible for professional use and available with as little translation as possible for any reports which the school has to make to other agencies. It is written in terms of the objectives of the school, supplemented when necessary by a statement on other aspects of development not covered by specific objectives.

Improved Report Cards.—Secondary schools are improving their reporting to parents by including an appraisal of pupil traits and behavior in addition to the mark in each subject. This movement represents progress in attempting to broaden the basis of evaluation to include all goals which the school holds to be significant. When such reports are carefully constructed to include all important objectives, they are far more meaningful than the subject mark alone. These report forms are usually ratings, however, and are consequently open to criticism for certain weaknesses. Teachers frequently rate the traits from memory rather than from records, are influenced by the recency and intensity of the situation, and consider each trait as an isolated factor. Such forms, too, require interpretation to parents in order to overcome the common tendency to give little attention to trait ratings when marks are also included.

An example of a report that gives more information on attitudes and habits than does the traditional type is shown on pages 281-83.

KALAMAZOO PUBLIC SCHOOLS

———————————————————————————Junior High School

Report of_____Grade_____

Homeroom Teacher_____

EXPLANATION:

In some instances words will be inserted.
ONLY outstanding characteristics will be checked.

———————

To Parents:

The Kalamazoo Public Schools try to furnish experiences and opportunities that will contribute to the educational growth of your child.   This card serves as a means for reporting the teacher's best judgment on the student's achievement.

Items 1, 2, and 3, under scholarship, will inform you whether the student has shown good, fair, or unsatisfactory attainment in each subject carried.   An attempt is made to mark the child in terms of his individual abilities and capacities except in the case of Latin and Algebra.

Outstanding characteristics will advise you of the reasons why achievement is good, fair, or unsatisfactory.   Character deserves comment, and space is provided for it.   You are urged to study the notations under this section of the card.

This card will come to you twice each semester.   The second checking includes the first, and therefore, is a full report for the semester.

Superintendent of Schools

Date_____

Kalamazoo Report Card, Front Page.

Name___ SCHOLARSHIP	GRADE	ENGLISH	MATHEMATICS	SOCIAL STUDIES	GENERAL SCIENCE	JUNIOR BUSINESS TRAINING	TYPE PRE-LANG. LATIN	ART	MUSIC	INDUSTRIAL ARTS HOME ECONOMICS	PHYSICAL EDUCATION	
1. Shows good attainment												1.
2. Shows fair attainment												2.
3. Is unsatisfactory												3.
OUTSTANDING CHARACTERISTICS												
Shows improvement												
Completes assignments												
Works up to ability												
Does neat work												
Does accurate work												
Responds, contributes freely												
Is industrious												
Reads understandingly												
Too many casual absences												
CHARACTER DEVELOPMENT												
a. Shows good leadership												a.
b. Is reliable												b.
c. Is co-operative												c.
d. Shows initiative												d.
e. Is courteous												e.
f. Has respect for property												f.
g. Respects the rights of others												g.
h.												h.
Initials of Teacher:												
TEACHER COMMENTS												

Kalamazoo Report Card, Inside Pages.

Name_____

        Attendance
          Half days absence
        Punctuality
          Times tardy

Estimate of homeroom teacher on scholarship and character growth_____

_____

_____

_____

Remarks by parents_____

_____

_____

_____

                           Signature of Parent

Full promotion to_____

Partial promotion to_____

Subjects to repeat_____

_____

Kalamazoo Report Card, Back Page.

Faribault High School in Minnesota has issued the following statement to aid teachers in supplementing marks in order "to describe more correctly the work the student is doing in this subject."

COMMENTS

1. Should use a positive statement in preference to a negative one.
2. Should use terms and vocabulary all parents are able to understand.
3. Should be in good taste and not insulting to parents and students.
4. Should be a statement and not another substitute for a letter grade.
5. Should be written with the goals of the course in mind and indicate the student's accomplishments in relation to those goals.
6. Should indicate student's basic strengths and weaknesses in the subject as well as indicate growth.
7. Should show whether student accomplishments are in line with his abilities or not.
8. Should contain an explanation of the type of work the student is doing and how he can improve it if it is unsatisfactory.

Reporting Through Letters to Parents.—An increasing number of schools are reporting to parents in letters which summarize pupil progress in the school's objectives. These letters require careful thought and expression to insure their serving as functional instruments in the evaluation program. Teachers, however, frequently complain that writing such letters requires an excessive amount of time. It must be granted that this form of reporting does require considerably more time than "marking the grades," but this factor must be weighed against their relative value in interpreting pupil growth to parents. Some schools issue reports of this type fewer times a year and give teachers more time to do a better job. All reports do not necessarily go out at the same time.

The following letter is a sample of progress reports sent to parents from the University School, Ohio State University:

1. JUNIOR HIGH, DECEMBER REPORT

Dear Mr. and Mrs. Blank:

School has been in session eight weeks. The ninth grade staff at University School has had an opportunity to work with your daughter and to be impressed by her work. The staff has taken this opportunity to state their impressions regarding the quality of work done, and to include other factors which are of concern to both parents and teachers.

CORE

Ruth's enthusiasm for her core project and her special interest in the housing problem in Columbus have revealed her capacities rather well. She has been patient with suggestions about her writing and spelling difficulties, but has been far more preoccupied with the "idea" aspect of her work than with the skills necessary to an effective presentation of her results. Her work is sincere, but she gets crowded for time, and the effect of this is to sometimes leave the mistaken impression that she has been over hasty. Ruth is to be commended for her naturalness in working closely and cooperatively with one of our finest Negro students, and for showing others, by her example, that she instinctively knows the meaning of truly democratic human relations.

MATHEMATICS

Ruth could make more rapid progress in mathematics if she thought she could. She attacks her work with a feeling of insecurity. I recommend that she spend more time on her assignments at home. Too frequently they are not complete when the group is discussing them and, therefore, she does not derive the value from the discussion that she otherwise would.

PHYSICAL EDUCATION

Ruth has been participating in soccer, hockey, and fencing for her physical education activities this fall quarter.

In fencing Ruth has been very interested in improving her skill and has succeeded in doing so. She has made some contributions in class but at times I feel she is holding back. She should express herself more often for I believe her contributions would be valuable to the class as a whole.

Ruth has participated regularly in hockey and soccer. She has an average skill in these activities but I have a feeling that she can do better. She has contributed little to the class but with a little more "self-pushing" or self-confidence she could contribute a lot more. She is very cooperative.

RELATED ARTS

Ruth is making quite a satisfactory adjustment to the work and personnel in this area. It is obvious that she is relatively unfamiliar with many of our methods of work and many of the opportunities available. It seems at this stage that with more time she should have no difficulty in making a creditable adjustment.

At present, she seems quite dependent upon the instructors and has a marked tendency to value the advice of others more than her own judgment. This, we feel, is a factor related to her unfamiliarity and will probably eliminate itself. We could, however, suggest that Ruth explore many of the other opportunities for work in the area.

Frequently it is difficult to arrive at a satisfactory judgment regarding the ability, rate of progress, and amount of adjustment to new situations, of a student after a short period of eight weeks. If you feel that this report is incomplete or unsatisfactory we would welcome a conference at your convenience.

Sincerely,

Reporting Through Parent Conferences.—The most effective method of reporting, which some schools combine with letters to parents and other forms, or use independently, is the personal conference, highly valuable because it provides face-to-face contacts with parents. When teachers use these personal conferences, they generally hold one early in the school year, one at midyear—if possible—and a final one toward the end of the school year. These conferences do not, of course, eliminate special parent contacts when unusual problems arise, but they may operate to prevent certain crises from developing.

In the parent-teacher conferences, some schools give pupils the responsibility for making the necessary appointment. The pupils frequently participate in the conferences, although there are times when it is expedient to exclude them temporarily. Special efforts are sometimes necessary to secure the attendance of both parents; here again the pupil can be effective in securing the necessary cooperation. In a friendly social atmosphere, parents, teacher, and the pupil may examine records, test data, and examples of pupil work, discussing all the significant aspects of the child's development and growth problems as they are observed at home, in the community, and at school. Such conferences held regularly are a vital force in promoting the kind of home and school solidarity so necessary in providing better learning experiences for the boys and girls.

4. First Steps

Evaluating and reporting student progress toward the goals of the schools is an important aspect of modern secondary education. It is an essential part of the learning process and the curriculum, for it determines the values of curricular experiences. Evaluation aids in diagnosing learning difficulties, in guiding student progress and growth, in checking the validity of educational hypotheses, in reporting to parents, and in interpreting the school to the community and general public. The way a teacher evaluates has a great deal of influence on the experiences pupils have in the school.

Many modern secondary schools are gradually developing satisfactory evaluation programs. The following are suggested ways in which any secondary school can move toward the establishment of a valid and comprehensive system of evaluation.

1. The staff of the school cooperatively, and teachers individually, can state their goals clearly and define each in terms of student behavior. This does not mean that many months need be spent in discussing philosophy apart from the ongoing school problems. Each teacher can simply state what kinds of changes in pupil behavior he desires to bring about. This is essential in

order to have a basis for the collection of evidence of the degree to which desirable changes are occurring.

2. The school staff can cooperatively plan an evaluation program to extend over a two or three-year period. All phases of the school program need not be appraised in detail each year. Areas of greatest need and concern should be attacked first.

3. A teacher can inventory existing satisfactory evaluation procedures, techniques, and instruments. If there are satisfactory mental and standardized achievement testing programs, for example, these should be utilized and continued.

4. One or two additional schoolwide objectives, such as reading comprehension, social participation, or health, can be selected for intensive appraisal during a school year. Staff meetings should clarify the kind of student behavior desired, the kinds of experiences needed to promote it, and the opportunities throughout the entire school for observing this behavior function.

5. Ways and means should be developed for gathering and recording this information regarding the objectives under consideration. A committee may attempt to construct experimental tests, scales, and other techniques. All teachers can share in gathering these data. Students and parents can also collect information, keep records, and observe behavior changes. A teacher can begin by keeping objective anecdotal records on certain pupils.

6. A record system must be devised in order to bring together in one place all significant information relating to the development of the desired behavior. This can be a cooperative task shared by students, teachers, administrators, and parents. The home room or core teacher is the logical person to act as record-keeper for a given group of students. He should periodically summarize these data in meaningful terms or symbols.

7. Any teacher might well keep a manila folder record on each pupil which can be used for keeping records of work completed, check lists, tests taken, and other data. This can be a job shared by teacher and pupil, since in most cases high school teachers will have more than a hundred pupils in their classes.

8. All the collected data, after being summarized, can be interpreted in the light of the desired student behavior. Staff meetings—often with students and parents participating—should be held to discuss the interpretation of the collected information, followed by more individualized analysis.

9. Interpretation is a part of reporting progress to students, parents, colleges, and community agencies. If the above steps are fol-

lowed, reporting is an integral part of the learning process. More often it will become a separate function, at least in the beginning, and pupil progress will be interpreted directly to the parents. Marking must not become an end in itself; it must serve to promote further learning. Descriptions, letters, and personal conferences are favored techniques of reporting progress to parents.

10. The curriculum of the school and the work of each pupil can be continuously revised in light of the evidence gathered and interpreted through a comprehensive evaluation program. So will the high school better serve the needs of youth and community.

SELECTED REFERENCES

ASSOCIATION FOR SUPERVISION AND CURRICULUM DEVELOPMENT. *Fostering Mental Health in Our Schools* (1950 Yearbook). Washington, D.C.: National Education Association, Part III.—This Part, "Knowing and Helping the Child," is an excellent presentation of methods for securing valid information about pupils and specific suggestions for fostering their mental health.

ASSOCIATION FOR SUPERVISION AND CURRICULUM DEVELOPMENT. *Toward Better Teaching* (1949 Yearbook). Washington, D.C.: National Education Association, chap. 8.—Entitled "Helping Pupils Evaluate Learning," this chapter is a very helpful presentation of the use of informal evaluation techniques as an integral part of the learning process in the classroom.

BURTON, WILLIAM H. *The Guidance of Learning Activities.* New York: Appleton-Century-Crofts, Inc., 1944, chaps. 17, 18, 19.—These chapters discuss evaluation, diagnosis, marking, and reporting, and their relationship to the learning process.

PRESCOTT, DANIEL A., and CHILD DEVELOPMENT STAFF. *Helping Teachers Understand Children.* (Prepared for the Commission on Teacher Education.) Washington, D.C.: American Council on Education, 1945, 468 pp.—An excellent research study, interestingly written, telling how teachers actually studied and interpreted the causes of the behavior of children.

SMITH, EUGENE, TYLER, RALPH W., and STAFF. *Appraising and Recording Student Progress.* New York: Harper & Bros., 1942, 550 pp.—This is the report of the Evaluation Staff of the Eight-Year Study of the Progressive Education Association. It contains a clear statement of the purposes of evaluation and sample items from many of the instruments developed to appraise a wide range of objectives of secondary schools.

THUT, I. N., and GERBERICH, J. RAYMOND. *Foundations of Method for Secondary Schools.* New York: McGraw-Hill Book Co., Inc., 1949, chaps. 5, 8, 11, 14.—Discusses the appraisal of pupil progress from the standpoint of three methods, or philosophies, the daily assignment method, the subject matter unit method, and the experience unit method.

TRAVERS, ROBERT M. W. *How to Make Achievement Tests.* New York: Odyssey Press, 1950, 180 pp.—Contains a clear statement of the principles of evaluation and their application to the construction of objective achievement tests. It shows how to define goals for evaluation purposes and gives many examples of different types of test items.

WOOD, BEN D., and HAEFNER, RALPH. *Measuring and Guiding Individual Growth.* New York: Silver Burdett Co., 1948, 535 pp.—Deals with individual differences, measuring instruments, guidance, and their interrelationships. Much of it is presented in an interesting discussion form.

PART III

GUIDANCE ACTIVITIES OF THE SECONDARY SCHOOL

GUIDANCE ACTIVITIES OF THE SECONDARY SCHOOL

In Chapters 13 and 14 the reader is given a picture of the total program of guidance in secondary schools and the teacher's part in this program. The point of view is expressed that guidance will be effective to the extent that the teacher participates in and has responsibility for guidance activities. The place of specialists in guidance is considered, showing their relation to the teacher. Actually, many of the activities discussed in this section are a part of the class and extraclass experiences of pupils, and thus are a part of the curriculum. The discussion of guidance is, however, placed in a separate section for both emphasis and clarity.

Chapter 13

THE GUIDANCE PROGRAM

The guidance activities in the secondary school have become increasingly important during the past three decades. There are a number of reasons for this. First, the world in which we live has become increasingly complex, making it more difficult for youth to make intelligent decisions and satisfactory adjustments. Second, the secondary school has been retaining a much larger percentage of our youth than was true early in the present century, many of them with little academic ability and interest. Third, the program of the secondary school has itself become increasingly complex. When there was only one curriculum for all pupils in the secondary school, there was no problem of educational guidance in so far as program planning was concerned. Today, the large school has many elective courses, as well as a broad offering of extraclass activities. Fourth, we have learned much in recent years about the psychology of the adolescent child, the nature of learning, and the mental and emotional development of children. This information has not only emphasized the need for more guidance activities, but it has also given us a basis for more effective counseling. Fifth, the emphasis in the secondary school in recent years has been on the growth of the individual child, the child-centered school, and an individualized program of secondary education. This trend has tended to emphasize the need for more effective guidance activities in the secondary school.

Guidance in the secondary school is not at all new. As long as we have had secondary schools, there have been principals and teachers who have concerned themselves with the decisions and adjustments that have to be made by youth and have given them such help as they could. With the recent emphasis on guidance, however, these activities have been greatly expanded. Guidance specialists have been added to our school staffs, and time for guidance has been provided in the regular schedule of the school. It is the provision which is being made in the secondary school for these activities on a well-organized basis that is designated as the guidance program. A discussion of these activities is the purpose of the present chapter.

1. The Principles

The guidance program should be well integrated with all other aspects of the educational program of the school.

Especially in schools that are developing a core curriculum or an experience-centered curriculum, it is essential that the guidance program be a well-integrated part of a total program of education. Too often there is a guidance department which is somehow set apart from the rest of the school. Where that situation pertains, the guidance activities lose much of their effectiveness. This program should extend into every classroom, every pupil activity carried on under the supervision of the school, and all school activities that are part of a larger community program.

The guidance program should draw on all the resources of the school and the community which may contribute to the guidance services.

Both in the school and in the community there are unlimited resources, both material and human, which may contribute materially to the effectiveness of the guidance program. Furthermore, it is in part through the use of these resources that the guidance program becomes a well-integrated part of the total program of education. In the school, the human resources include the physician, the nurse, the psychologist, the librarian, the principal, the superintendent, the coaches, the secretaries, and every member of the teaching staff. Each individual should be studied for the particular contribution that he can make to the guidance services, whether that contribution be a formal or an informal one. The director of guidance should be sure that the talents of all are utilized.

In the community, there are also many human resources that may contribute to the guidance program. In guidance on vocational problems, persons engaged in almost every profession and occupation may be of service; in guidance concerning post-secondary education, local graduates of various colleges, universities, business colleges, trade schools, and other post-secondary schools are valuable resource people; and in guidance concerning mental and emotional adjustment, many professional people in the community may be helpful.

The material resources in the school which contribute to the guidance program include books in the school library, films, film strips, and recordings. Such agencies as the public library, Chamber of Commerce, government agencies, business firms, factories, transportation companies, and the service organizations can provide a wealth of information that will be useful in the guidance program. These resources should be located through a careful community survey; they should be studied for their contribution to the guidance program; they should be classified and catalogued; and they should be utilized whenever they may be appropriate.

The guidance program should utilize all avenues and channels for guidance, both in the school and in the community.

Almost every activity in the school program may serve as an avenue for guidance. In the curriculum, such subjects as English, social studies, business, industrial arts, homemaking, and the vocational subjects are particularly appropriate for exploratory activities and for the dissemination of information that is basic to effective guidance on educational, vocational, and personal problems. In the extraclass program, clubs, the school newspaper and handbook, and the school assemblies also provide opportunities for exploration and for helping pupils obtain information as a basis for guidance. The home room is another avenue which may be employed effectively for both group and individual guidance activities.

In the community, the local newspaper may serve as an avenue for bringing information to pupils which will be helpful for guidance. Various business and industrial firms, as well as other community agencies, offer opportunities for work experience which help pupils explore interests and talents as a basis for making intelligent educational and vocational decisions. The effective guidance program utilizes to advantage all these school and community activities and agencies to provide pupils with the most appropriate guidance services.

Adequate information and records for all pupils are essential as a basis for individual counseling.

Adequate information about every child is absolutely essential to the success of a guidance program. That information should be readily available to all members of the staff who participate in any way in guidance activities. There should be information about the pupil's home and family background; out-of-school activities; vacation and part-time work experience; intelligence; educational, vocational, and avocational interests; previous achievement in school activities; social and emotional development; and any unusual problems, difficulties, successes, and failures of the pupil, both in school and out. Furthermore, there should be a system of records which will permit the accumulation, in a systematic manner, of information about each individual child.

Provision for guidance activities should be made in all areas where adolescents need to make decisions and adjustments.

In the discussions on guidance early in the present century, so much emphasis was placed on vocational guidance that, in the thinking of many educators, this was the sole purpose of the guidance program. Today, it is generally recognized that guidance concerning vocational decisions, planning, and adjustments is only one aspect of a broad guidance program. In addition to guidance on vocational activities, there is guidance concerning such problems as educational decisions and planning; social, emotional, and personality development; and health, citizenship, and character growth. In other words, today the guidance program in the secondary school is concerned with any decision, problem, or adjustment which must be made by the boy or girl.

Adequate information should be available in the school concerning vocational and educational opportunities beyond the secondary school.

There should be a complete file of catalogs, bulletins, and other informational material for universities, colleges, junior colleges, business schools, trade schools, and other post-secondary schools that might be of interest to the pupils. There should also be an occupational file in which pamphlets and bulletins are accumulated for every conceivable occupation that might be attractive to youth upon leaving the secondary school. These files should be available for frequent and ready reference by pupils and the members of the professional staff. There should also be many books on vocational life, both fiction and nonfiction, preferably on an open shelf where they may be easily examined by pupils.

It is important that time for group and individual guidance activities be provided in the school program.

It is essential that there be time for guidance activities in the regular daily schedule. A period, daily or several times weekly, may be set aside especially for that purpose, or time may be designated for guidance during the year when problems present themselves. For instance, at the time of year when pupils are planning their programs for the next semester, certain class periods may be set aside for group discussions on the choice of curricula and courses. These discussions may serve as a basis for counseling individual students with respect to their educational programs. The important thing is to have time definitely specified for carrying on guidance activities in a well-planned manner.

An effective placement and follow-up service for pupils leaving school or graduating is a part of any well-rounded guidance program.

The responsibility of a secondary school does not end when the pupils graduate or drop out of school. In the senior high school, there should be assistance in helping them to find employment and to succeed on the job. Furthermore, the school should assist its graduates in locating better positions as they gain experience and competence. This means, of course, that there should be an aggressive placement service in the senior high school and a competent staff to follow up the pupils with the thought of giving them advice and assistance in their first positions. Another essential phase is the follow-up on the success of graduates at universities, colleges, and other post-secondary schools to obtain information which may be used for counseling pupils. Both dropouts and graduates should be included in the placement services and follow-up study.

Specialists should be available to assist with planning and organizing guidance activities and with difficult guidance problems.

Expert advice and assistance are essential to the success of any guidance program. Whether full-time specialists are employed by the school or are available only on call is not of particular importance. It is essential, however, that the administrative officers and the faculty of a school be able to request the services of different specialists as they are needed. The specialists most often needed are counselors, a physician, nurse, psychologist, psychiatrist, and a specialist in measurement, evaluation, and statistics.

These specialists should also understand the peculiar problems of secondary school youth, they should be informed regarding the purpose and nature of a secondary school program, they should know the demands which are made on the physical and emotional growth of youth by such a program and by the normal activities of youth outside the school, and they should have a sincere interest in youth and in the guidance activities and program of the secondary school. In other words, every physician, nurse, psychologist, or psychiatrist is not necessarily qualified to assist with the guidance activities and program of the secondary school. These specialists should have training and experience which qualify them particularly for the responsibilities of a guidance program.

There should be competent leadership for the guidance program in a secondary school.

Although this principle is mentioned last, it is probably the most important. Without it, the other factors needed to develop an effective guidance program would indeed be unlikely to succeed. Leadership is needed to give direction to the program, to develop and carry on the various guidance activities, to assist with the in-service education of the participating staff members, and to evaluate continually and improve the program.

The principal of the school must, in any case, participate in providing that leadership, since he is responsible for the total program of education in the school. He should be thoroughly sympathetic with the purpose and nature of guidance in the secondary school and he should be well informed regarding guidance practices and programs. It should not be expected that the principal, however, will be sufficiently competent in guidance to provide the specialized and technical leadership to develop and carry on an effective guidance program. For that purpose, a specialist in guidance with broad experience in education and thorough preparation for guidance and counseling is needed. In a large secondary school, it is essential that a staff member devote full time to this responsibility, while in a small school a part-time professional worker in guidance is desirable. The selection of leadership for the guidance program should be given careful consideration, because upon it the effectiveness of the guidance program will largely depend.

The main functions of the guidance specialist are to provide leadership for the program and to assist teachers to become more competent in guidance and counseling. Since it is the teachers who frequently come into contact with the pupils, it is they who must do most of the counseling. The effectiveness of the specialists in the guidance program will depend largely upon their skill in working with teachers and other members of the professional staff.

2. Some Typical Practices

Principal Frequently Provides Leadership for Guidance.—There is some variation in the type of leadership for guidance which is provided in secondary schools. Large schools usually have a director of guidance. In some schools, he devotes full time to guidance activities, while in others he may be a part-time teacher. It is increasingly the practice to employ a person for this position who has preparation in psychology and in the philosophy and organization of guidance activities, as well as some experience in teaching at the secondary school level. In fact, some states today require that the director of guidance have a certificate, which is granted only after specialized education and experience have been gained.

In some large schools, the position of director of guidance is combined with one of the administrative positions, such as vice principal. Because of the many responsibilities which should be assumed by the director of guidance, combining this position with an administrative one is not recommended. In such an arrangement, the administrative details are likely to take an undue share of the time of the person assigned to this position.

In the small schools, it may be difficult to justify employing a full-time director of guidance. The most common practice is to have the principal provide the leadership in the guidance program. In the very small schools, those with a faculty of not more than five or six, the principal is usually the only member of the staff who has any background for this responsibility. Obviously, the best practice is to employ a person as director of guidance who is specially prepared for that work. The principal has neither the time nor the preparation to provide the leadership that is needed for a modern guidance program in the secondary school.

Inadequate Specialized Assistance for Guidance.—There are few schools indeed that have adequate specialized help for guidance. In fact, there are many secondary schools that do not have even one person with adequate preparation in guidance to serve as the director of the program. A few of the very large schools, those with two to three thousand pupils or more, have a full-time nurse and a full-time psychologist, as well as a director of guidance. They may also have ready access to the services of a physician, dentist, psychiatrist, and a specialist in evaluation and measurement. In addition, they may have a dean of boys, a dean of girls, and a staff of counselors.

In the small schools, specialized guidance services are sometimes provided on a county or state basis. For instance, there may be a school nurse and physician who serve a number of schools in a given area. But very few small schools have the services of a psychologist, a psychiatrist, a testing expert, and certain other specialists, either subject to call when needed or on a more regular part-time basis. It makes little difference on what basis these services are provided, just so they are available when there is a need for them.

Lack of Definite Organization in Small Schools.—In small schools, the typical practice is to have little or no organization for guidance. Especially in schools in rural communities with only four or five teachers and a hundred pupils or less, it may seem that this is not a serious matter. Possibly it is not. There is danger, however, that all guidance will become an incidental affair with little planning and little delegated responsibility for seeing to it that certain essential things are done. For instance, the giving of various tests, the accumulation of accurate data on permanent pupil records, and the planning of pupil programs are not likely to be done well if left to chance. The lack of delegated responsibility for certain aspects of guidance becomes, therefore, a serious handicap to the planning and carrying on of an effective guidance program in the small school.

The large schools frequently have a definite organizational plan for their guidance program, although it varies greatly from school to school. A typical plan of organization in large schools is outlined in the diagram below.

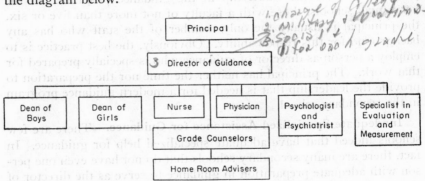

Typical Guidance Organization in Large High Schools.

In medium-sized schools, it is rather common to have some definite organization in the guidance program. In these schools, the line of responsibility usually proceeds from the principal to the director of guidance, and then to the home room advisers. Not many medium-sized schools today have a staff of guidance specialists, other than perhaps a nurse and a physician on a part-time basis.

Cumulative Records Provided in Most Schools.—The usual practice in the secondary school today is to have some type of cumulative record in which significant information about pupils is kept in convenient form. The cumulative record often includes the pupil's achievement record, test record, home and out-of-school record, health record, extraclass participation record, and anecdotal record. In too many schools, however, the cumulative record still is confined largely to the pupil's marks, his attendance, and few personal and family items such as date of birth, home address, and names of parents. That information, desirable though it may be, is seriously inadequate in meeting the needs of an effective guidance program.

In most schools the cumulative record is kept in the principal's office, while in others it is in the guidance office. Frequently, the two offices are adjacent so that the records may be used conveniently by various professional staff members. It is not a common practice to place the cumulative record or a duplicate in the hands of the home room teacher or other key teacher in the guidance program. In a few schools, a summary of that information is given teachers for all pupils under their supervision, but this desirable practice is the exception rather than the typical one.

The exact nature of the cumulative record form varies from school to school.[1] It is considered the best practice to have the pupil's entire school record, elementary as well as secondary, on the cumulative record. In many secondary schools, however, only information about the child from the time of entrance into the secondary school is included. The cumulative record ordinarily does not give complete information concerning the various backgrounds of the pupil. Instead, it gives the most pertinent information in each instance, with more complete information on the records in the offices of the various guidance specialists, the home room teachers, the classroom teachers, and the sponsors of extraclass activities. In schools that do not have specialists in guidance, the detailed information about pupils necessary for effective counseling is usually lacking.

Variety of Cumulative Record Forms.—There is a wide variety of cumulative record forms in use in the secondary schools of the United States. In small schools, as well as in some of the medium-sized and large ones, the single-card type prevails. If the card is a small one, it is usually unsatisfactory as a record form for the complete data about the individual child needed in a guidance program. A large card, approximately 8½ by 11 inches, does provide sufficient space so that considerable data about the child may be recorded.

Although the single-card type is still predominant, other forms are used so widely that they are now accepted as typical practice in the

---

[1] Samples of various types of cumulative records may be found in *Handbook of Cumulative Records,* A Report of the National Committee on Cumulative Records, U.S. Office of Education Bulletin, 1944, No. 5, Washington, D.C.: Government Printing Office, pp. 90-104.

secondary school. The different cumulative record forms, including the single-card type, may be briefly described as follows:

The packet type—this type of record form consists of a large envelope in which are kept cards that carry various types of pupil information. Each card has a different type of information. It may be removed from the packet for use by teachers, counselors, and guidance specialists.

The envelope type—this type of cumulative record form provides for space for most of the information on the outside of the form. Since it consists of a large envelope, probably 9 by 12 inches, various anecdotal items, record cards, and other forms may be retained in it.

The folder type—this is similar to the envelope type, except that the ends are not closed. Like the envelope type, anecdotal items and information cards may be kept in the folder.

The folding card type—this type of cumulative record form consists of a large folding card, usually of three or four sections, which provides space for all types of pupil information. As in the envelope and folder types, anecdotal items may be accumulated in the folder.

The single-card type—this consists of a single card, frequently 9 by 12 inches, but often smaller. All basic information is kept on this card. Anecdotal items cannot readily be kept with this form. It is the least useful type for guidance purposes but is the one most frequently found in secondary schools.

The loose-leaf type—this form may be kept in loose-leaf record books. The record may be one or more pages long, depending upon the amount of pupil information that it is intended to contain. Like the card form, it does not lend itself readily to keeping anecdotal information.

Cumulative Records Not Always Satisfactory.—Although we have had many years of experience in keeping cumulative records in the secondary school, these records are still far from adequate in the typical school. This is unfortunate, indeed, because adequate cumulative records are absolutely essential to the effectiveness of a guidance program. The most serious shortcomings of the cumulative records in the typical secondary school are the following:

1. The information contained in the record is frequently inadequate for guidance purposes. In many schools it is limited to the pupil's achievement and attendance record, with little or no information about his interests, extraclass participation, personality and char-

acter development, home backgrounds, and other items essential to guidance activities.

2. In many schools, a definite policy and adequate instructions for recording information on the cumulative records are lacking. Consequently, the records are not properly kept and the information is not uniformly recorded.

3. The information on the cumulative records is not used by the home room and classroom teachers as extensively as desired because often it is not conveniently available. For the teacher, the central office is not, as a rule, a convenient place for these records.

4. Teachers are not adequately prepared to use the information on the cumulative records as a basis for counseling. They lack skill in interpreting the data and in using all the data to gain broad perspective concerning the pupil's backgrounds, abilities, and needs.

Orientation Activities More Common in Junior High Schools.—
In the junior high school there are numerous activities to help pupils become oriented as they enter from the elementary school. After a study of these activities, Gruhn and Douglass report that a majority of the junior high schools have developed specific helps for pupils in becoming oriented to the philosophy, program, activities, and practices of the school. The more common orientation activities for entering pupils in the junior high school include the following: [2]

Handbooks and mimeographed materials on the program and activities of the school given to entering pupils.

Talks by the principal, director of guidance, or other staff member to the entering pupils in the semester before they leave the elementary school.

Orientation discussions in elementary school classes by the elementary school teachers.

Visits by elementary school pupils to the junior high school.

Discussions on school traditions, the curriculum, extraclass activities, and rules and policies held during home room periods for entering pupils early in the year.

Assignment of entering pupils to older pupils to help them become acquainted in the new school.

These activities are found less frequently in four-year and senior high schools. Entering pupils are too often left to shift for them-

---

[2] William T. Gruhn and Harl R. Douglass, *The Modern Junior High School,* New York: The Ronald Press Co., 1947, p. 287.

selves, with little direct help in becoming acquainted with the traditions of the school, the policies and regulations, the teachers, and other pupils. The most common practice in the senior high school is to present new pupils with a printed or mimeographed handbook to inform them about the school. Frequently there is an assembly program early in the year to welcome the new pupils, or a party to help them get acquainted. In some schools the student council assumes some responsibility for helping entering pupils become readily adjusted so that they are more likely to enjoy high school and succeed in their work.

Assistance to Pupils in Planning School Programs.—In most secondary schools, pupils are given some help in educational planning, though it is usually much too limited in its scope. Most often it is concerned with the choice of curricula and the planning of elective programs. The most common activities for helping pupils in educational planning are the following:

> Handbooks, mimeographed materials, the school paper, and school assemblies give pupils information about the curricula and courses in the secondary school, requirements for graduation, and prerequisites for college admission and for certain vocations.
>
> The home room periods are used for discussions of curricula and courses and the types of secondary school programs that lead to various educational and vocational goals.
>
> Individual counseling is provided at those times in the year when pupils are planning their secondary school programs, with home room teachers, the counselors, the director of guidance, and others participating.
>
> Group and individual guidance activities are provided for pupils concerning college and other post-secondary schools. In some schools, there is a file of catalogs and bulletins from universities, colleges, commercial and vocational schools, and other post-secondary schools, which are made available to pupils.

Even though many schools have activities to assist pupils with their educational planning, much more needs to be done to make these activities as helpful as they should be. For instance, in too many cases the home room teachers are not adequately informed concerning such things as college entrance requirements and prerequisites for admission to certain vocations. They tend to advise pupils on the basis of their own experience in college, which is usually limited to one institution and which may no longer represent campus conditions. Although the counselors may assume some of the responsibility for guidance on admission to post-secondary schools, the home room teachers usually have many more incidental discussions with pupils on such problems. Especially in the small schools, teachers do not have the help they need from specialists to prepare suggestions for pupils in planning their educational careers and to give pupils information concerning post-secondary education. Furthermore, the small schools often lack the secretarial help to maintain an up-to-date file of catalogs and bulletins for colleges and universities, business schools, technical schools, and other post-secondary schools.

One of the most serious handicaps to guidance in educational planning is the lack of school time available for individual conferences with pupils concerning their educational careers. Counseling on such matters cannot be hurried. In some schools, a period daily or several times weekly is set aside for home room and guidance activities. If the planning of pupil programs is begun early enough in the year, such a home room period helps considerably to provide time for assisting pupils with this problem. Few schools, however, have adequate time in the home room for this purpose, nor do they provide time for it elsewhere in the school day.

Some Activities to Help Pupils Succeed in School.—The activities to help pupils succeed in school are largely of an incidental nature. The home room or classroom teacher "talks" to the pupil who is failing or is not working to his full capacity. Sometimes this "talk" consists of little more than a scolding for not working harder, but in other cases the teacher makes some effort to diagnose the pupil's difficulties and to assist him in solving them. Although such incidental counseling concerning the pupil's progress in school is helpful, it is hardly adequate to assist pupils to overcome serious learning difficulties.

Some schools have activities for this purpose on a more regular and organized basis. For instance, one practice is to have home room teachers each marking period confer with pupils whose marks are low. In large schools, the counselors assume this responsibility. Such conferences can be exceedingly helpful when they are based on a careful case study of the individual pupil concerned.

Some Provision for Occupational Information.—In the past, exploratory courses in the secondary school have been the chief avenue for providing pupils with occupational information. Since this aspect of the guidance program is one for which teachers are primarily responsible, it is discussed more fully in the next chapter. Even in

schools with excellent exploratory courses, however, other means of
bringing pupils into contact with adequate occupational information
should be provided.

At present, too few schools are using effectively the various means
that are available for helping pupils become informed about the opportunities, the qualifications desirable for success, and the preparation
demanded in the various occupations. Very few schools have adequate occupational files, and these are limited to the larger schools
with the better guidance programs. Career days also are employed
effectively in some schools. If they are used as part of a larger program, they are fine indeed, but they will contribute little to the thinking of pupils concerning their vocational futures if career day is the
only time in the year when they give serious attention to vocational
planning. More schools need to have a broad program for helping
pupils become informed about the various occupations that are open
to them.

Incidental Placement and Follow-Up Services.—Many secondary
schools, especially the senior and four-year high schools, try to give
some assistance to pupils and graduates in finding positions. Usually, however, this placement service is likely to be haphazard, with
the principal or vice principal recommending pupils and graduates for
employment when requests are made by local employers. The typical
school does little, if anything, to locate positions and to encourage
employers to contact the school authorities when they want to fill
positions. In other words, in the typical secondary school the placement service is largely an incidental one provided by a busy principal.

This situation is changing, however, in those schools that are employing a director of guidance, particularly in the large schools. In
such schools the director of guidance or someone in his department
has the responsibility for contacting local employers to encourage
them to list positions with the school placement service, for listing
part-time and vacation employment opportunities, and for keeping in
touch with present and former pupils on employment problems. Seldom are placement services extended to dropouts and other youth in
the community.

Only a few schools have an organized plan of follow-up for graduates and former students. The follow-up usually consists of a record
of the pupil's first position or the college or post-secondary school that
he entered. Lack of adequate clerical and secretarial help usually prevents a systematic and continuous follow-up of former pupils. The
follow-up record of pupils entering college is likely to be more com-

plete than for others because many colleges keep the secondary schools informed of the success of their graduates, year by year.

Limited Guidance Concerning Physical and Mental Health.—For many years the secondary school has given some attention to the physical health of its pupils. In most medium-sized and large schools a nurse is available on a regular basis, either part or full time, while in the smaller schools there is frequently access to the services of a nurse and physician on a town, county, or district basis. The health services which are most commonly provided include:

1. Periodic health examinations.
2. Reports to parents on the results of these examinations.
3. Assistance to poor families in providing corrective measures for children with health problems.
4. Counseling of pupils with health problems.
5. Examination of pupils who have been absent because of illness.
6. Discussions with pupils concerning health matters that concern adolescents, usually carried on in physical education classes, home rooms, homemaking classes, and health classes.
7. Physical education and health classes, on a required basis in the junior high school, but often on an elective basis in the senior high school.

With our long experience in health education, it would seem that the health guidance provided in the secondary school should be adequate for the needs of secondary school youth. The truth is that the effectiveness of health guidance and health instruction is discouragingly limited. The shortcomings of health guidance in the secondary school may be summarized as follows:

1. Health examinations are so hurried that they reveal only the most obvious health deficiencies. Frequently the physician examines the pupils at the rate of one every minute or two, hurrying them along so that he may return to his office or the hospital.
2. There is insufficient follow-up with parents to be sure that they understand the results of the examination and do something about the child's health deficiencies.
3. The results of the health examinations often are not made available to teachers, except for pupils who have particularly serious health problems. Frequently teachers are not even informed about pupils who have sight and hearing deficiencies.
4. There are not sufficient funds to assist needy pupils with corrective health measures. Often the only funds for this purpose come

from welfare agencies upon the request of the principal, nurse, or physician.

5. Health services are frequently set apart from the rest of the school program, instead of being closely integrated with physical education, homemaking, the health classes, and the school lunch program.

6. There is little health counseling. The nurse and physician often devote much of their time to health examinations and the keeping of records, but little to counseling pupils and parents about health problems. Furthermore, they do too little to assist teachers in developing guidance activities in the area of health.

The secondary school today does too little to safeguard the mental health of its pupils. In fact, many of the practices of the secondary school actually lead to tensions and emotional upsets among pupils that may result in serious mental health problems. In his book, *Mental Health Through Education,* W. Carson Ryan points out that such practices as rigid and formal discipline, final examinations, and excessive home work create tensions which are not conducive to the development of the best mental health among growing adolescents.[3] These facts should not be a surprise to experienced secondary school teachers, since many of them have seen pupils seriously upset when school tensions become too great. Because these practices are of direct concern to the teacher, they will be discussed at greater length in the next chapter.

The surprising thing is that so little is being done to relieve these tensions in school and provide help to pupils in developing the best mental health. In fact, except in those few large schools having psychologists and psychiatrists on the guidance staff, guidance on mental health problems is almost nonexistent in our secondary schools. Many teachers, experienced in working with children, do excellent work in this area in so far as their time and training permit. But counseling on mental health problems is still not recognized as sufficiently important to justify staff, time, and attention in the program of most secondary schools.

Counselors Responsible for Large Numbers of Pupils.—In some medium-sized and large schools, it is the practice to have certain teachers with some interest and preparation in counseling designated

---

[3] W. Carson Ryan, *Mental Health Through Education,* New York: The Commonwealth Fund, 1938, chap. 4.

as part-time counselors. These counselors usually teach half or more of the school day, but have two or three periods free for counseling. They may be assigned an entire school grade or a given number of pupils in various grades. They serve as the official counselor for the pupils to whom they are assigned.

In a school that has just established a guidance program, this plan may have some advantages, as it is likely that few teachers will be qualified to assume responsibilities for guidance. The objection to having a few counselors in a large school is that each one has the chief responsibility for too many counselees—frequently several hundred— to become well acquainted with them. They see their counselees a few times each year when specific problems arise, but they lack the intimate day-by-day contact with the pupils which is essential in establishing mutual understanding as a basis for effective guidance. They do not work through teachers who have the responsibility for guidance of a small group of pupils.

3. Practices in the Better Secondary Schools

Guidance Integrated with Other Aspects of School Program.— Earlier in this chapter it was emphasized that guidance activities should be closely integrated with all other aspects of the educational program, rather than being set apart as separate services. Some schools are developing their guidance program to achieve that integration. An example of an integrated program is the one in the five high schools of Evansville, Indiana. When a guidance program was first introduced in the Evansville high schools, some years ago, one counselor was placed in each school. It soon became evident that this practice would not be satisfactory as a means of providing comprehensive guidance activities that were integrated with the entire instructional program. Furthermore, it seemed advisable to have the classroom and home room teachers become key persons in the guidance program and to correlate guidance activities with various individuals and agencies in the community. As a result the requisites for a comprehensive, well-integrated guidance program [4] were developed as follows:

---

[4] These requisites are outlined in some detail by Daniel W. Snepp, Director of Guidance in the Attendance and Guidance Department of the Evansville Public Schools, Evansville, Indiana, in an article "An Integrated Guidance Program in the High School," *The Bulletin of the National Association of Secondary School Principals*, 43 (May, 1950), 116-23.

1. A cumulative record system available to all teachers, which includes social, personal, educational, and health data.
2. A suitable testing program, as follows: (*a*) in the eighth grade, as an aid to proper placement of pupils in high school subjects; (*b*) in the ninth grade, to ascertain reading needs and to test achievement; (*c*) in the twelfth grade, for guidance concerning college and for locating pupils who need review in mathematics before graduation; and (*d*) in Grades 10 to 12, as a basis for vocational guidance.
3. Group and individual counseling by classroom teachers, home room teachers, class sponsors, and other guidance personnel.
4. Desirable integration between Grades 8 and 9, high school and college, and high school and employment.
5. Orientation procedures for all students new to high school.
6. An effective in-service training program for all teachers and home room advisers.
7. Coordination of the high school guidance services with related community organizations.
8. Provision for placement service by enlisting the aid of departmental staff members and becoming acquainted with local employers.
9. Provision for special studies, such as follow-up survey of graduates, employment survey of present pupils, and survey of pupil dropouts.

Broad Guidance Activities for Total Pupil Needs.—In many schools the guidance program is being developed in a broad, well-planned manner with definite attention being given to the various guidance needs of the pupils. Such programs are found not only in the large cities, but occasionally in a medium-sized or small community. The program at Evansville, Indiana, described in the preceding paragraph, is one that has broad guidance activities. Another program emphasizing broad aspects of guidance, but serving a smaller community than Evansville, is the one in the high school at Keene, New Hampshire, which offers the following services: [5]

A cumulative inventory, for analyzing the individual and his potentialities.

Educational counseling, for relating curricula to individual needs, providing remedial work, and advising pupils on extraclass activities, out-of-school activities, and post-secondary education.

Vocational counseling, for matching youth and jobs.

[5] From *Report of the Guidance Director, 1947-48* (mimeographed), Keene, N.H.: Keene High School, 6 pp.

Placement, for specific job counseling, arranging interviews, and job placement.

Work experience, for diversified occupations and distributive education activities.

Follow-up program, for follow-up of former pupils on jobs and in post-secondary schools.

Specialists Provided in Guidance Program.—Perhaps the most significant development in the organization of the guidance program in the secondary school during the last decade is the trend toward employing competent guidance specialists. Among large schools particularly, a number have a staff of specialists that includes a director of guidance, adviser for boys, adviser for girls, counselors, nurse, physician, psychologist, psychiatrist, specialist in speech, reading specialist, and a specialist in statistics, evaluation, and measurement. Even the smaller schools are making some progress in the employment of specialists, although these persons usually devote part time to teaching. The employment of guidance specialists is doing much to give purpose and effectiveness to the guidance activities in secondary schools.

Pupil Data Provided as Basis for Guidance.—The importance of having adequate information about individual pupils as a basis for guidance has already been mentioned. The adequacy of that information is determined largely by the pupil records which are kept in a school. In those secondary schools which have well-developed guidance programs, the following types of records may be provided:

Achievement records—these are records of the marks which pupils have earned in school. The best practice is to have them cover the pupil's entire school career, beginning with kindergarten or first grade.

Test records—these are records of the pupil's standing on various types of standardized tests. Usually the more permanent records include the pupil's standing on mental tests, interest inventories, and achievement tests. Results of diagnostic tests are available for current use, but they are not kept over a period of years.

Health records—these records are based on the pupil's health examinations given periodically in the school. In some schools such examinations are given once a year, while others have them only every two or three years but give them more thoroughly. The health records also give information concerning the pupil's illnesses, corrective measures that have been taken, and protective measures that the teachers should observe for the individual child.

Home and out-of-school backgrounds—these records give various types of pertinent information about the child's life outside the school. Information about the home and family constitutes a large part of these records, ordinarily giving such information as socio-economic status, education of parents and older siblings, nationality, language spoken in the home, and whether or not it is a broken home. Other information includes travel experience, church affiliation, participation in such community activities as Boy Scouts, Girl Scouts, YMCA, and YWCA, part-time and vacation work experience, and juvenile court record.

Extraclass participation—these records give information concerning school offices the pupil has held and his participation in all extraclass activities. In some schools the records give information on participation in major activities only; in others, the record of such participation is very detailed, including all activities in which the pupil has participated.

Anecdotal records—anecdotal information is being kept increasingly in the secondary school. The anecdotes may cover a variety of things: successes or failures of the child in school, difficulties he has encountered, relationships with teachers and other pupils, and contributions to the program of the school. Those anecdotes are kept which, in the estimation of teachers and other staff members, will give a better understanding of the child as a basis for future counseling activities.

Attendance records—this record includes, as a rule, information on both attendance and tardiness.

Social, character, and citizenship records—in some secondary schools there are records of ratings by teachers of the social, character, and citizenship qualities of pupils. This rating may consist of a summary mark on conduct or citizenship, but in many schools it is rather detailed so that there is some information on specific pupil qualities that may serve as a basis for guidance and counseling activities.

College or vocation entered after leaving school—this record is being kept in an increasing number of schools. Its chief value for guidance is for follow-up purposes and for assisting former pupils to obtain better positions.

Special abilities—not many secondary schools maintain this type of record, but it is available in some. It includes special abilities and talents in such fields as art and music. In some schools the records of interest inventories and extraclass participation provide such information.

Well-Developed Cumulative Records.—Some schools have developed comprehensive cumulative record forms that provide an excellent summary of the types of information about pupils discussed in the preceding paragraph. The better cumulative record forms have the following characteristics:

1. They provide a continuous record from kindergarten or first grade through the twelfth grade.
2. They provide a summary of all essential information about pupils needed for guidance.
3. They are readily available to classroom teachers, home room advisers, and others concerned with assisting pupils.
4. They are simple and easy to administer in recording information, filing cards, and interpreting the information they contain.

The State of Vermont has such a cumulative record form, called the Vermont Educational Development Record. It was prepared after much study by a committee of superintendents of schools and other educators. The record is in the form of a folder with three parts, each 9 by 12 inches. It provides a complete record of the pupil's school career from kindergarten through high school. Besides such essential information as family background, marks, and test results, it provides space for an appraisal of personality for each year, a record of post-secondary school attendance, and a post-school employment record. Liberal space also is provided for notes, anecdotal items, and explanations, so that the record may be made as meaningful as possible. For guidance and counseling purposes, this cumulative record form is exceedingly useful.

The Planeview, Kansas, public schools have a cumulative record form reproduced on pages 312 and 313 similar in completeness to the one being used in Vermont. Under both the elementary and secondary school sections, there is space to record each year the pupil's recreational interests, work experiences, and participation in school activities, as well as for a record of achievement and attendance. In addition, there is provision for a record of family background, health, tests, citizenship report, special achievements and honors, special guidance and counseling services, final recommendation by the counselor, and follow-up. Like the Vermont form, the Planeview form is of the folder type so that anecdotal items may be filed. It is complete, concise, and easy to use for counseling.

One of the important needs in a cumulative record system is a mimeographed or printed statement which defines policies and gives instructions for maintaining, interpreting, and using the data it

Form 100

Planeview Public Schools
CUMULATIVE RECORD

Name				Address		Phone
	Last	First	Middle		Street Number	

Birth Date			Place of Birth		Proof		Race	Sex

Entered				Grade	From			
	Month	Day	Year			Dist. No. or Name	City	State

Father or Guardian   Mother or Homemaker

No. Children In Family	Rank In Family	Physical Disability	Precautions Necessitated By Physical Disability

ELEMENTARY SCHOOL RECORD

KINDERGARTEN	Teacher	CODE
19 19		Circle the proper letter indicating the students Strength
Comments:		H — Above Average Grade Level
		M — Average Grade Level
		L — Below Average Grade Level

FIRST	SECOND	THIRD	FOURTH	FIFTH	SIXTH
19 19	19 19	19 19	19 19	19 19	19 19
Teacher	Teacher	Teacher	Teacher	Teacher	Teacher
Class Standing	Class Standing	Class Standing	Class Standing	Class Standing	Class Standing
Reading H M L	Reading H M L	Reading H M L	Reading H M L	Reading H M L	Reading H M L
Spelling H M L	Spelling H M L	Spelling H M L	Spelling H M L	Spelling H M L	Spelling H M L
Math Concepts And Skills H M L	Math Concepts And Skills H M L	Math Concepts And Skills H M L	Math Concepts And Skills H M L	Math Concepts And Skills H M L	Math Concepts And Skills H M L
Individual Growth H M L	Individual Growth H M L	Individual Growth H M L	Individual Growth H M L	Individual Growth H M L	Individual Growth H M L
Comments:	Comments:	Comments:	Comments:	Comments:	Comments:
Attendance Regular Irregular	Attendance Regular Irregular	Attendance Regular Irregular	Attendance Regular Irregular	Attendance Regular Irregular	Attendance Regular Irregular
	Kind	Type and Extent of Participation			
School Activities					

SECONDARY SCHOOL RECORD

SEVENTH				EIGHTH				NINTH				TENTH				ELEVENTH				TWELFTH			
19 19				19 19				19 19				19 19				19 19				19 19			
Subject	1	2	Cr	Subject	1	2	Cr	Subject	1	2	Cr	Subject	1	2	Cr	Subject	1	2	Cr	Subject	1	2	Cr
Attendance Regular Irregular				Attendance Regular Irregular				Attendance Regular Irregular				Attendance Regular Irregular				Attendance Regular Irregular				Attendance Regular Irregular			

SCHOOL ACTIVITIES

HEALTH RECORD

PHYSICAL EXAMINATIONS

CODE	DATE								
	Age Years and Months								
O - No Defects	Height								
	Weight								
X - Defects	Normal % plus % —								
	Physical Development-N or R								
T - Immediate	Posture								
	Deformities								
A - Action	Eye Right								
Important	Eye Left								
P - Parent Notified	Ear Right								
	Ear Left								
C - Correction	Teeth Temporary								
Made, Date	Teeth Permanent								
	Skin								
V - Doctor-Dentist	Nose								
Consulted	Throat								
Date and	Lungs								
Advice Given	Heart								
	Nerves								
N - Normal	Lymph Nodes								
	Endocrines								
R - Retarded	Digestive Organs								
	Kidneys								
Phy - Physician	Others - Name								
Nr - Nurse									
	Examiner - Phy. Nr. T.								
T - Teacher									
	Family Physicians and Dentists								

	Name	Address		Phone	
	Name	Address		Phone	

IMMUNIZATIONS

Date	Age	Disease

COMMUNICABLE DISEASES

Date	Age	Disease

OPERATIONS

Date	Age	Kind

ACCIDENTS

Date	Age	Kind

COMMENTS or RECOMMENDATIONS

Date	COMMENTS or RECOMMENDATIONS	Signature

RECORD OF TESTS

APTITUDE OR INTELLIGENCE

Name of Test	Date	C.A.	M.A.	I.Q.

EDUCATIONAL

Name of Test	Date	C.A.	Score	Norm	Rank

EDUCATIONAL

Name of Test	Date	C.A.	Score	Norm	Rank

INTEREST

Date	Occupational Interest	Aptitude	Preparation	Counselor's Recommendation

SCHOOL

Date Graduated			
Date Dropped	Reason		
Higher School Entered	Name	Date	Course
Employed by	Address		
Married	Date		

provides. That is essential if the records are to be properly maintained, the data are to be uniform, and there is to be some assurance that the pupil data will be used effectively in the guidance program. A few schools provide such a manual of instructions. Among these are the junior high schools of the City of New York, where a sheet of instructions to teachers shows, item for item, how the form is to be filled in. In Stamford, Connecticut, a printed booklet is provided which gives teachers suggestions for filling in and using cumulative records.

Orientation to Assist Pupils in Adjustment to School.—Excellent orientation activities are being carried on in some junior high schools. For instance, in the Colin Kelly Junior High School of Eugene, Oregon, the orientation program begins in the spring semester while pupils are still in the sixth grade of the elementary school. The principal and pupil leaders visit the elementary schools to discuss the junior high school program with the sixth grade pupils. Later, these pupils visit the junior high school where they are entertained by the Girls' League and the Boys' Club. In the fall semester, orientation activities include a "Hello Week" to greet newcomers, a special assembly, an all-school party, and discussions in the social living classes.[6]

The better four-year and senior high schools also carry on orientation activities, frequently in cooperation with the junior high school. East Rockford High School, Rockford, Illinois, begins activities in the ninth grade of the junior high school, where throughout the last semester one period weekly is devoted to discussions about the senior high school. Pupils also plan their three-year educational program for Grades 10, 11, and 12.

Attractive booklets describing the high school program are used in some schools to help new pupils become acquainted. The Rockland High School, Rockland, Maine, has an attractive printed booklet entitled, "What About High School?" which answers such questions as: How can I tell what to take? What are the various curricula and courses like? What steps should I take to plan my program? The junior high schools of Appleton, Wisconsin, have a well-organized printed booklet entitled "Futures: Your Need of the Senior High School." It was prepared by the principal and teachers of the Appleton Senior High School to explain to junior high school

---

[6] Lester M. Beals, "The Guidance Program in Colin Kelly Junior High School," *The Bulletin of the National Association of Secondary School Principals,* 34 (January, 1950), 250.

pupils the values of continuing in school, the relation between the various curricula and certain vocations, the purposes and content of various courses, and graduation requirements. Booklets such as these are exceedingly helpful in the orientation of pupils to the program of a new school.

Various Activities for Educational Planning.—An increasing number of schools are giving thought to the planning of pupil programs on a long-term basis. The junior high schools at Aberdeen, South Dakota, devote the home room periods for several weeks early in the second semester to helping pupils plan their programs of curricular and extraclass activities for the following year. In the seventh and eighth grades there are talks by teachers on elective subjects, discussions in home room groups, and counseling of individual pupils by the home room teachers. In the ninth grade, six weeks of the social studies course are devoted to vocational study and planning. Pupils are given interest and other tests as a part of this work. At the conclusion of the unit, the senior high school principal and vice principal come to the junior high school and explain the handbook and plan book used in the senior high school. They have an individual conference with each pupil, set up a tentative plan for his three years in high school, and register him for the tenth grade.

In schools with programs such as these, the planning discussions and activities are carried on over a sufficiently long period so that pupils and parents have ample opportunity to study various aspects of the school program and to consult with the principal, counselors, and teachers before choices of curricula and courses are made.

In the Central High School at Aberdeen, pupils for some years have used an educational plan book covering their program for Grades 10, 11, and 12. It provides for a statement of the pupil's educational goal and an inventory of his interests and needs. There are spaces for the pupil's program for each year, with several additional pages for revisions of the original plan. An accompanying handbook gives school regulations and policies, and describes the curricula, courses, and extraclass program of the school. The pupil's three-year plan is prepared before he enters the senior high school and is revised as desired each year. It is important that pupils be encouraged to plan the program for their entire secondary school career, as is done at Aberdeen and in some other secondary schools.

Health Guidance Integrated with Total School Program.—In some schools the health services are closely integrated with other aspects of the school program. Such a practice is in harmony with our present thinking concerning a well-integrated curriculum and, more particularly, the experience-centered curriculum. The Gallatin County High School, Bozeman, Montana, has a program of health education and health guidance which extends into all phases of the school program. In a bulletin [7] prepared by the staff of the school, there are detailed suggestions for bringing health education units and health guidance activities into the courses in home economics, biology, physical education, and social studies. The booklet also contains suggestions on health guidance for boys and girls, the relation of health guidance to attendance, health in the part-time cooperative classes, health regulation for the custodian service, health activities through the hot lunch program, and health specialists and services available to the faculty of the school.

In the Phoenix, Arizona, secondary schools, health education and guidance extend into most areas of the curriculum. A recent survey [8] showed that the following health areas are covered: nutrition, personal hygiene, scientific health attitudes, public health, personal health and human relations, physical activities, safety education, and sanitation. The subject areas in which instruction and guidance activities are carried on in a planned manner include biology, chemistry, physical education, homemaking, English, physics, home nursing, driving, economics, mathematics, civics, industrial arts, and agriculture. The survey showed that all pupils received much health instruction and guidance because a considerable amount of time is being devoted to them in such required courses as English, science, and social studies. Programs such as these need to be developed in secondary schools as they point toward the core curriculum and the experience approach.

Availability of Occupational Files.—A definite attempt is being made in some schools to provide more complete and adequate occupational information for pupils as a basis for planning their educational and vocational careers. An adequate occupational file is one means that now is being used to provide such information. The occupational file consists of a classified collection of bulletins and pamphlets describing the opportunities and activities of various occupations. The materials are obtained at little or no cost from colleges, vocational

---

[7] *Policies, Gallatin County High School, Health Service and Guidance Program* (mimeographed), compiled by Clifford D. Knapp, Health Coordinator and Biology Instructor, Bozeman, Montana, February, 1948, 20 pp.

[8] *Survey of Health Education* (mimeographed), by the North Phoenix High School Health Committee, Office of Research Services, Phoenix Union High Schools and Phoenix College, Phoenix, Arizona, March, 1948, 12 pp.

schools, industrial and business firms, professional organizations, labor groups, and community agencies. The materials are made available to pupils and teachers who have reason to investigate particular occupational activities. Usually the file is kept in the office of the guidance director or in the school library, with provision made to have it so placed that it will be readily accessible to both teachers and pupils.

Career Day Provides Occupational Information.—Career days are also being used more effectively to provide occupational information for secondary school youth. The plan for Career Day varies, of course, from school to school. Usually the day begins with an address on some aspect of vocational activity at a general assembly of the student body. The student body then divides into small groups according to vocational interests to participate in discussions led by speakers from outside the school. Ordinarily the program for the day is so arranged that pupils may attend two or three discussion groups. Career Day not only brings occupational information to pupils, but also brings them into contact with local leaders in the various occupations who may be available for further help in making vocational decisions. Then, too, it emphasizes dramatically for a day the importance of studying the various occupations as a basis for making intelligent vocational decisions. If teachers and pupils work cooperatively in planning Career Day and in carrying on its activities, it can be a truly significant experience in the educational program of our youth.

At the Oak Ridge High School, Oak Ridge, Tennessee, in a recent vocational conference there were forty-nine discussion groups with an outside speaker for each, a student chairman, and a faculty host. Occupations for which there were discussion groups included: machinist and machine designing, telephone operator, secretary, recreation worker, careers in government service, laboratory technician, dramatic artist, dietitian, electrician, minister and religious education, engineer, occupations in radio and television, lawyer, medicine (doctor, surgeon, psychiatrist), office receptionist, accountancy, marriage as a career, librarian, photographer, interior decorator, chemist, journalist, draftsman, forestry, teacher, occupational therapy, personnel director, dentist, careers in music, fashion designing, opportunities in the Armed Forces, business, research scientist, aeronautical occupations, coach and professional athlete, nurse, architect, pharmacist, commercial art, salesman, FBI and law enforcement, social work, building trades and construction, and psychologist.

Organized Placement Services.—In a few secondary schools, placement services are being put on a well-organized basis. In these schools a staff member is designated as the employment counselor to keep in touch with local employers, to list part-time jobs for pupils and full-time jobs for those leaving school and graduating, and to assist pupils in obtaining employment. Frequently, he is also in charge of the vocational guidance activities, including vocational counseling, maintaining the occupational file, and assisting teachers with vocational exploration and guidance activities.

East Rockford High School, Illinois, has an employment counselor who devotes half time to this work. He carries a large share of the responsibility for occupational guidance. He assists in the collection of occupational information, assists teachers and counselors with locating and using occupational information, counsels pupils on vocational problems, assists pupils in obtaining part-time jobs, and supervises the placement of pupils who leave school or graduate.

Increased Provision for Follow-Up of Graduates.—Some secondary schools are realizing the need for the follow-up of graduates and pupils who leave school before graduation. In these schools, this service has several purposes: (1) it keeps the school authorities informed of the success of their graduates, (2) it enables the school to assist its graduates and former pupils in obtaining more desirable jobs, and (3) it gives the school an opportunity to assist former pupils and graduates to succeed in their jobs. It is the last purpose, particularly, which is important, because so many pupils need help in becoming adjusted to the world of employment when they leave the secondary school. The school authorities know the pupil—both his abilities and his shortcomings. Frequently they can offer suggestions which may mean the difference between success and failure.

At the Torrington, Connecticut, High School, a brief questionnaire is sent to every graduate each fall to obtain information concerning his location, employment, and other pertinent information. This provides the school with excellent information concerning its graduates without excessive cost. Most secondary schools could develop similar activities for keeping in touch with their graduates as a basis for providing a more complete guidance service.

Use of the Community in the Guidance Program.—Some schools are capitalizing on the talents of local citizens and the services of civic, business, and industrial agencies to improve the effectiveness of the guidance program. The Career Day programs are one of the more dramatic examples of the contribution which the community can make to the guidance activities of the school. In the Career Day program at the Oak Ridge, Tennessee, High School (referred to above), fifty or more citizens from the local and neighboring communities participated, most of them professional, business, and industrial leaders of some reputation in their respective fields. In the high schools of Evansville, Indiana, one of the requisites of the guidance program is the coordination of guidance services with related community agencies.[9]

More specifically, some ways in which secondary schools draw upon community agencies and leaders for the guidance program are as follows:

1. Educational, civic, professional, business, labor, and other leaders are invited to the school to assist pupils in obtaining information as a basis for making educational and vocational decisions.
2. Pupils talk with leaders in various vocations concerning the qualifications, responsibilities, and opportunities in their respective vocations.
3. Pupils visit business firms, industrial establishments, hospitals, government offices, and civic agencies to gain information as a basis for making educational and vocational decisions.
4. The school authorities use the services of such local specialists as physicians, psychologists, psychiatrists, personnel managers, and social workers to assist with difficult pupil adjustment problems and to contribute to in-service educational activities in guidance for teachers.
5. School authorities work intimately with employers in the community in the placement and follow-up of graduates and pupils leaving before graduation.

4. First Steps

There are some things which should be done immediately in secondary schools as first steps in developing a guidance program which will function more effectively to help pupils with the various decisions, adjustments, and problems that they face. The following first steps are important:

1. Every secondary school should employ a competent person with preparation in guidance and experience in teaching to provide leadership in developing an effective guidance program. In large

---

[9] Snepp, *op. cit.*, p. 121.

schools this should be a full-time person, while in small schools he must undoubtedly devote some of his time to teaching. The small schools should not, however, rely upon the principal alone for this leadership.

2. Every secondary school should have available a staff of competent specialists in such areas as psychology, psychiatry, health, evaluation and measurement, reading, and speech. In small schools, these specialists will necessarily have to be employed on a part-time basis or on a cooperative basis among the schools of a town, district, or county.

3. The school should organize guidance and counseling activities so that each member of the staff knows his responsibilities for guidance and his relation with other members of the staff in planning and carrying on these activities.

4. The school should survey its staff to locate those persons who have special talents that might be employed in the guidance program.

5. The school should survey the community to locate persons and agencies who may contribute to the guidance program; to obtain information concerning education, vocation, and recreation opportunities in the community; and to obtain information about the social, economic, and cultural backgrounds of the community.

6. The school should survey its own student body to obtain information regarding the pupils, to ascertain their guidance needs, and to obtain information from pupils concerning the types of guidance services which they would like.

7. The school should study its system of pupil records to find out how they may be improved as a basis for more effective guidance.

8. The schedule of the school should be studied to ascertain whether adequate time is provided for guidance and to provide more time, if that seems desirable.

9. A survey should be made of the entire instructional program, including both class and extraclass activities, to find out what guidance activities are now being carried on and to see how various aspects of the instructional program may contribute more to the guidance program.

10. The teachers should be encouraged to undertake in-service education activities to improve their understanding and skills in guidance through such activities as independent reading in guidance, summer session and extension courses, and assistance from the director of guidance and other guidance specialists.

Selected References

ALLEN, WENDELL C. *Cumulative Pupil Records.* New York: Bureau of Publications, Teachers College, Columbia University, 1943, 69 pp.—Presents a plan for staff study and improvement of cumulative records in secondary schools.

AYER, FRED C. *Practical Child Accounting.* Austin, Texas: The Steck Co., 1949, chaps. 3, 7.—Chapter 3 provides an overview of the purposes of child accounting, with the teacher's part in it. Chapter 7 presents a discussion of cumulative records at the secondary school level.

BEALS, LESTER M. "The Guidance Program in Colin Kelly Junior High School," *The Bulletin of the National Association of Secondary School Principals,* 34 (January, 1950), 248-57.—Presents an overview of a forward-looking guidance program in a junior high school, based on principles resembling those outlined in this chapter.

DOUGLASS, HARL R. (ed.). *Education for Life Adjustment.* New York: The Ronald Press Co., 1950, chap. 16.—Presents an overview of guidance in the secondary school with particular reference to an educational program emphasizing life adjustment for secondary school youth.

ERICKSON, CLIFFORD E. *A Basic Text for Guidance Workers.* New York: Prentice-Hall, Inc., 1947, 566 pp.—Presents an overview of the entire guidance program in the secondary school in a readable, practical way.

GRUHN, WILLIAM T., and DOUGLASS, HARL R. *The Modern Junior High School.* New York: The Ronald Press Co., 1947, chap. 11.—Gives an overview of the guidance program as it has been developed in junior high schools throughout the country.

JONES, ARTHUR J. *Principles of Guidance.* New York: McGraw-Hill Book Co., Inc., 1945, 592 pp.—Presents a comprehensive discussion of the principles and point of view that are basic to the entire guidance program.

McELHINNEY, ROBERT S., and SMITH, HENRY L. *Personality and Character Building.* Winona Lake, Ind.: Light & Life Press, 1942, 345 pp.—Offers many practical suggestions for activities that lead to the development of effective pupil personality qualities and character traits. Written particularly for elementary and secondary school teachers.

TRAXLER, ARTHUR E. *Techniques of Guidance: Tests, Records, and Counseling in a Guidance Program.* New York: Harper & Bros., 1945, 394 pp.—As the title indicates, this reference emphasizes the use of tests and records in the guidance program.

Chapter 14

GUIDANCE BY THE TEACHER

In the previous chapter, attention was given to the organization of the guidance program as a whole. Little was said about the part that the individual teacher should take in the various guidance activities. It is the teacher, however, who ultimately must bear the brunt of any activities in the secondary school that are of direct concern to the pupil. That is true of guidance activities fully as much as any other aspect of the secondary school program. In the present chapter, we shall concern ourselves with the place of the teacher in the guidance program.

1. THE PRINCIPLES

The teacher is the key person in the guidance program in the secondary school.

The significance of this principle, already suggested in the paragraph above, cannot be overstressed. A guidance program can be effective only to the extent that it has the enthusiastic and intelligent support of every teacher in the school. The director of guidance and the other specialists should provide the technical backgrounds and skill needed in planning and conducting the various guidance activities. It is the teacher, however, who has the intimate contact with pupils which is highly essential in guidance. The teacher meets the pupils daily in home room and classes, he has them in clubs and other extraclass activities, and he has opportunities to meet their parents and to become acquainted with their home and out-of-school backgrounds. The teacher, therefore, is in an excellent position to locate pupils who are in need of guidance services. Furthermore, he can gain the confidence of pupils which is essential as a basis for effective counseling. Consequently, the effectiveness of a guidance program will depend largely upon the interest, the understanding, and the skill of the teacher in guidance activities.

The teacher should have some preparation in the psychology of adolescence, mental hygiene, and the theory and practice of guidance and counseling.

322

If the teacher is to participate in guidance activities, he must have some preparation for it. Much of the same preparation is also essential, of course, if he is to teach effectively. His understanding of adolescent children should be broad and thorough, including knowledge about their emotional problems, how they learn, their physiological development, their social relationships, and other aspects of their psychological growth and development.

The teacher should have some preparation in the area of mental hygiene. Although the interpretation of severe maladjustment problems should be made by a specialist, the teacher must assume responsibility for assisting pupils with the problem of understanding themselves, their fears, and their worries. In order to give effective guidance, he must understand the real causes of behavior of various types, such as shyness, aggressiveness, stealing, lying, and the like.

The teacher should also have some understanding of the organization and administration of a guidance program, the types of specialized services that are available, the types of problems that demand the services of specialists, and the techniques of counseling. Although the teacher need not have the preparation demanded of specialists in guidance and counseling, he should have sufficient preparation to discharge his guidance responsibilities with the utmost effectiveness.

The teacher should be assisted in improving his effectiveness for guidance and counseling through a continuous program of in-service education.

The organization of a program of in-service education in guidance for teachers is one of the major responsibilities of the director of guidance and other guidance specialists. Such a program should be carefully planned, it should be continuous, and it should be concerned with all the guidance activities of the teacher. Since his pre-service education ordinarily provides little experience in guidance, particular attention should be given to the beginning teacher. The in-service education program should be directed particularly toward objectives such as these:

1. It should give purpose and direction to the guidance activities of all the faculty members.
2. It should keep teachers informed of the available guidance services and the manner in which these services may be employed to greatest advantage.
3. It should inform teachers of new developments in guidance and thus prepare the way for the introduction of these developments in the local school program.

4. It should encourage and assist teachers to capitalize on various class and extraclass opportunities for exploratory activities, for giving pupils information as a basis for guidance, and for encouraging pupils to utilize available guidance services.

5. It should encourage and assist teachers to locate pupils with unusual guidance problems and to refer them to the appropriate specialist.

6. It should provide for the coordination of the various guidance activities and services so that they may form one unified and effective program.

7. It should help teachers in the use of effective guidance techniques.

A variety of approaches should be employed in the program of in-service education, including meetings of the entire faculty, individual conferences with teachers on guidance problems, the preparation of bulletins to assist teachers with guidance activities, and demonstrations of guidance activities. Film strips, recordings, motion pictures, discussion groups, lectures by guidance specialists, and publications in the school's professional library are all aids that may be employed effectively in the in-service education program.

The teacher should have adequate information available concerning the backgrounds, abilities, interests, and achievement of every pupil under his supervision.

In the previous chapter, reference was made to the importance of having adequate information and records concerning every pupil in school. Since the teacher is so important in the guidance program, it is essential that that information be readily available to him. It is not sufficient that teachers have the privilege of coming to a central office to study the records. Teachers are busy people and may neglect to study pupil records as frequently and thoroughly as they should. In an effective guidance program, ways must be found to place significant information about pupils in the hands of all the teachers who supervise those pupils in either class or extraclass activities.

The teacher should consider every contact with pupils an opportunity for guidance—in the home room, the classroom, and extraclass activities.

The teacher's value in the guidance program lies primarily in the fact that he sees the pupil frequently in various types of learning situations. It is important that the teacher take advantage of the guidance opportunities which these various contacts present, else much of his contribution to the guidance program will not materialize. The home room, particularly, is one avenue for guidance where the teacher's contribution can be a significant one. In fact, this is one of the purposes for which the home room was originally established. But there are also many situations in the classroom and in extraclass activities where the teacher can be of help to pupils in exploring their potentialities, in making adjustments to new situations, in making significant decisions, and in improving their educational progress.

There are numerous guidance activities that may be carried on by the teacher in these places in the school program, among them the following :

1. He can help them explore potentialities and interests in various educational, vocational, and avocational areas.
2. He can help pupils obtain information which may serve as a basis for educational, vocational, and avocational decisions.
3. He can accumulate information concerning the pupils under his supervision which will be of help in later guidance and counseling activities.
4. He can locate pupils with adjustment problems who need the help of specialists.
5. He can assist the guidance specialists in "following through" with counseling activities for individual pupils.
6. He can do much formal and incidental counseling of pupils. In fact, this may well be the most effective guidance which he does.

The teacher should have frequent, planned conferences with every child under his supervision concerning his educational, vocational, avocational, and personal problems.

Usually teachers have conferences with pupils when they are in difficulty. Although such conferences are important, teachers may be able to help pupils avoid difficulties through conferences held periodically even though they may face no serious problem. In fact, the best conference situation between teacher and pupil is likely to exist when the pupil is apparently getting along well. Furthermore, the teacher frequently is not aware of maladjustments on the part of pupils and of problems with which they need help until they are revealed through a routine conference. That is especially true in schools where the pupil load per teacher is heavy.

The arrangements for teacher-pupil conferences must necessarily vary from school to school. In any situation, however, they should be held during the school day, they should begin early in the year, and they should be held under conditions that assure privacy. In most schools, these conditions will be difficult to achieve. Even so, every effort should be made to arrange these conferences under the most favorable conditions possible.

The teacher should establish contacts with the home of every pupil under his supervision.

Home visitation by the teachers is essential as a basis for effective guidance activities. In a junior or senior high school with a core program where the teacher has contact with only a limited number of pupils, the teacher should visit the homes of all his pupils. In a departmentalized school where the teacher meets several different groups of pupils daily, the home visitation by the teacher may have to be limited to his home room pupils.

Home visitation is not at all a new practice. In the early schools in America, it was expected that the teacher would become acquainted with the parents of all his pupils and that he would occasionally visit them in their homes. As schools became larger and pupil loads per teacher heavier, home visitation became more difficult. Furthermore, home visitation in the cities created problems that did not exist in the early rural communities in America. Consequently, home visitation by teachers gradually decreased, particularly in the heavily populated centers, until it practically disappeared. In recent years it has been encouraged, especially for teachers in home economics and vocational agriculture. Among other teachers it remains a rather infrequent practice.

There are, of course, some serious obstacles to home visitation today, especially at the secondary school level. In some urban neighborhoods, teachers, especially the women, would probably be reluctant to visit the homes of some pupils. In rural communities, the homes may be so widely scattered that the transportation problem would obviate extensive home visitation. In spite of these obstacles, teachers should be urged to visit homes, in so far as that may be reasonably possible, as a basis for more effective guidance and counseling activities.

Basic to effective guidance is a situation in which the teacher can become intimately acquainted with the interests, backgrounds, previous achievement, and personal qualities of every pupil under his supervision.

Although this may be implied in several of the principles previously stated, it is so basic to the part which the teacher plays in the guidance program as to justify it as a separate statement. Effective guidance demands that the teacher know the individual child much more intimately than is possible from simply studying the cumulative records and examining test results. He must know much about the child that cannot be reduced to an office record form. Such information would include the child's relationships with his fellows, his attitude toward various types of school situations, his reaction toward both success and failure, his receptiveness to help and suggestions, and many other similar types of information.

In small schools, teachers see their pupils frequently in various situations, both in school and in the community outside the school. Consequently it is easy to become well acquainted with them. In large schools, it is difficult indeed to get to know pupils because the classes are frequently large and the teacher may have little or no contact with his pupils outside the classroom.

The departmentalized system, where the teacher has 150 or more pupils in five or six different groups throughout the day, has made it particularly difficult to implement this principle. The opportunity it gives teachers to know pupils is one of the strongest arguments that can be presented for a type of program, such as the core curriculum, which permits teachers to remain with the same group for a considerable part of the school day. Until some way is found to keep teachers in contact with smaller numbers of pupils for much of the day, the individual teacher will be seriously handicapped in the effectiveness with which he can participate in guidance activities.

2. Some Typical Practices

Special Subjects Provide Exploratory Experiences.—For many years, some subjects in the secondary school have been employed as avenues for exploratory activities to provide pupils with information and backgrounds as a basis for guidance. That is especially true in the junior high school, but also, though less commonly, in the senior high school. Exploratory activities enable pupils to obtain information concerning educational and vocational opportunities, to find out what preparation and backgrounds are desirable for success in those opportunities, and to try out their individual potentialities. They are, therefore, exceedingly important as a basis for counseling activities. In the junior high schools, subjects which traditionally have been used for exploratory purposes are industrial arts, homemaking, general science, and general language. In the senior high school, the vocational subjects are the ones where exploration has received most emphasis, especially business, industrial arts, and home-making.

Unfortunately, many teachers assume that the mere offering of courses in these subjects will result in satisfactory exploratory experiences for pupils. That is certainly not true. Teachers of these subjects often overlook the fact that pupil interests and talents are individual in character. If they are to explore those interests and talents, the pupils must have much freedom to decide upon the projects on which they are to work. Pupil participation in the selection and planning of learning activities is therefore an essential step toward providing effective exploratory experiences. Courses in such subject areas as industrial arts, business, general science, homemaking, and general mathematics often are too rigidly organized in content and method to permit adequate pupil participation in planning as a basis for exploratory activities. The teachers of these subjects should show leadership in developing the exploratory opportunities inherent in these subjects.

Little Exploratory Experience Provided in Regular Classes.— In the previous paragraph, it was suggested that courses in certain subject areas have been developed with exploration as a definite purpose. Teachers frequently overlook the fact that opportunities for the exploration of pupil interests and talents exist in every subject in the curriculum. English and social studies, for instance, can provide exploratory activities through the reading, the oral work, and the written projects which pupils do. For example, for their "outside reading" in English, pupils may read biographies of leading lawyers, statesmen, doctors, nurses, professional athletes, labor leaders, and others. For their written and oral activities they may investigate opportunities in certain vocational fields, entrance requirements for certain colleges and professional schools, post-secondary school opportunities of the noncollege type, and numerous other questions that may provide information that will help them make intelligent educational and vocational decisions.

Not many teachers see these opportunities for exploration in their own subject fields. All too often, they have narrow objectives that are concerned primarily with the accumulation of subject matter. Furthermore, teachers of all subjects, like those in the special subjects, tend to do the planning of courses, units, and daily activities, with little or no participation by the pupils. Because teachers lack sufficient imagination, desire for flexibility in course content and activities, and willingness to have pupils participate in planning, the op-

portunities which the various subjects offer for exploration are not
being fully realized.

Unused Potentialities for Guidance in Extraclass Activities.—
Extraclass activities serve exploratory purposes in some secondary
schools, especially in the junior high school. Clubs are one type of
pupil activity particularly appropriate for exploration. For example,
the speech and dramatics clubs permit pupils to explore interests and
talents in certain areas which have a bearing on educational and vocational planning; the various hobby clubs have a bearing on the pupil's
avocational interests; and clubs that emphasize social, personality,
and citizenship qualities have some relationship to emotional, personality, and character adjustments. These are only a few examples
of the opportunities provided by club activities for the exploration of
pupil interests and talents.

Similar opportunities for exploration as a basis for guidance and
counseling may be found in numerous other extraclass activities for
which teachers are responsible. They include journalism, athletics,
student council, music organizations, and the school publications.
Each of these activities may, under the supervision of an able sponsor,
provide pupils with many experiences to help them explore their
potentialities and interests and to evaluate their abilities as a basis for
educational and vocational planning.

It is unfortunate, indeed, that many teachers fail to capitalize on
the opportunities for exploration and guidance which these activities
afford. In the senior high school, particularly, the exploratory opportunities in the extraclass program are neglected. Frequently the
activity is an end in itself, serving no long-term purpose in the educational growth of the child. The faculty sponsor often does not understand the exploratory opportunities provided by the various extraclass
activities, he does not capitalize upon the opportunities to help pupils
analyze their own interests and abilities, and he fails to advise pupils
to engage in activities that will help them evaluate their interests and
potentialities. The teacher with resourcefulness and imagination can
make a truly significant contribution to the guidance program
through his work with pupils in extraclass activities.

Occupations Courses Provide Pupils with Information.—For
some years, a course in occupations has been employed to provide
pupils with occupational information as a basis for educational and
vocational planning. This course has been particularly common in
the junior high school, usually being offered in the eighth or ninth
grade. In some schools it is combined with the work in social studies,

several units or a semester being devoted to what is sometimes called occupational civics. It is not often taught above the ninth grade.

The course in occupations has met with only limited success as a means of providing pupils with occupational information. The following are some of the shortcomings schools have encountered in this course:

1. They have had difficulty finding teachers with sufficiently broad experience backgrounds to teach the course. The typical teacher is a college graduate with his occupational experiences limited to summer or part-time employment. Furthermore, his contacts with individuals in diversified occupations are also limited. He, therefore, relies largely on reading to become acquainted with occupational information.

2. Only a limited number of vocational areas can be covered in a semester, or even a year. Often these areas tend to be the ones with which the pupil is most familiar through his life in the community outside of school. Therefore, he does not gain sufficiently broad occupational information from the occupations course.

3. The course tends to be "textbookish." Although field trips are employed in some schools, these must necessarily be limited to a few in any one semester. Motion pictures, film strips, recordings, and other audio-visual materials are also used in some schools. But the fact remains that the occupations course, like other courses in the secondary school, is centered in reading materials to such an extent that its effectiveness in providing pupils with broad occupational information is limited.

Emotional Problems Aggravated by Some Classroom Practices. —It has been suggested elsewhere in this book that many practices in the typical secondary school, particularly in the senior high school, aggravate rather than relieve emotional maladjustments among pupils. This is especially true of some instructional practices for which the teacher is primarily responsible. Instructional practices which have a bearing on emotional maladjustments in the typical secondary school are as follows:

1. The policy concerning discipline, with its emphasis on quiet and order rather than on an atmosphere that is free from tension.

2. The marking system with its uniform standard of achievement for all pupils regardless of ability, its emphasis on subject matter mastery, and its encouragement of competition among pupils.

3. The practice of awarding such honors as valedictorian, saluta-

torian, and other scholastic recognition of standing in class based on marks.

4. The practice concerning final examinations, counting them as a major basis for the assignment of final marks and the recommendation of pupils for college.

5. The emphasis on assigned home work, depriving pupils of needed relaxation and recreation outside school hours and demanding late hours of study which interfere with the rest needed by growing adolescents.

In the junior high schools, some progress is being made toward modifying these practices to bring them into harmony with our understanding of mental hygiene problems among secondary school youth. For instance, final examinations in the traditional manner and the requiring of home work in excessive amounts are the exception in the junior high school today. In the typical senior high school, little is being done to modify these practices. There is a tendency to consider any effective change in them as a step toward reducing scholastic standards. Consequently, in the senior high school such instructional practices continue to be a serious handicap in providing for the best emotional adjustments among pupils.

Personality Development Opportunities in Extraclass Activities.—In the secondary school today, many opportunities are provided in extraclass activities for developing poise, self-confidence, and other personal and social qualities. The activities which contribute much in this respect are social functions, assemblies, speech activities, clubs, and the student council. In the typical school, however, the achievement of such objectives is incidental rather than adequately planned. Pupils are given insufficient help in preparing for these activities and in participating effectively in them. Adequate study of social manners, social dancing, leadership qualities, and other qualities basic in the acquisition of poise and self-confidence are frequently lacking. Although pupils acquire much in poise and personality from participation in these activities, more careful planning will make them increasingly effective for this purpose.

In the classroom, however, little attention is given to these aspects of a child's educational development. Secondary school classes are centered in subject matter to a point where this is the major if not the sole objective of all learning activities. As a result, reading the textbook and other references, written work, and recitation activities dominated by the teacher constitute the major part of all classwork, with little time allowed for oral activities developed from pupil interests and for group activities planned and carried on under pupil leadership. In the junior high school, some progress has been made toward modifying classroom methods so that child growth and development in its broader aspects can be emphasized, but the senior high school tends to rely largely on the program of extraclass activities for developing personality qualities.

Inadequate Recording and Use of Pupil Information.—In the typical secondary school, teachers have inadequate information about individual pupils as a basis for effective guidance activities. Usually, such information as is available is found in the office of either the principal or the director of guidance, where it may be obtained if requested by the teacher. It is seldom placed directly in the hands of the home room advisers and classroom teachers. Consequently, much of the value of the cumulative records in the central office is lost, at least in so far as their use by the individual teacher is concerned.

Teachers do not always use the devices at hand to obtain information directly from pupils as a basis for guidance. For instance, few schools have an established policy for home room teachers to visit the homes of their pupils. Also, school time for individual teacher-pupil conferences is seldom available. Some teachers arrange for such conferences after school, during study periods, and during the noon hour, but these arrangements are the exception rather than the rule. Autobiographies by pupils and informal questionnaires prepared by teachers are used frequently as means of obtaining information about pupils, particularly in the junior high school.

It is perhaps no exaggeration to say that relatively few secondary school teachers are well informed concerning the use that may be made of various types of information about pupils. In most teacher education programs, so little time is devoted to various techniques of studying pupils that beginning teachers do not know how to employ these techniques effectively. In larger schools which have an adequate guidance staff, teachers are given assistance in studying their pupils, but the great majority of secondary schools do not have a guidance staff adequate for this purpose.

Limited Opportunity for Teachers to Get Acquainted with Pupils.—It has just been suggested that teachers do not have as much information about pupils as is desirable for guidance. This problem is intensified by the organization in the secondary school which gives teachers very limited contact with their pupils. The typical teacher of English, for instance, may have five classes with an average of 30 pupils in each. Sometimes he has, in addition, a home room group which does not duplicate the pupils in these classes. Obviously, a teacher cannot become well acquainted with 150 to 175 different pupils, especially if he sees them for only one forty-five-minute period daily. Several weeks may pass before he even learns the names of all, to say nothing of establishing with them that feeling of mutual interest and respect which is essential for effective guidance.

Home Room Guidance Activities Are Limited.—It is a common practice in the secondary school to have pupils assigned to a home room group with a faculty adviser responsible for assisting them in making adjustments, advising them concerning personal and educational problems, and helping them with educational and vocational decisions. In many schools, however, the home room has become an administrative device for checking attendance, making announcements, keeping pupil records, and preparing reports, with insufficient emphasis upon the guidance functions for which the home room was established. Since the home room group usually meets for only a few minutes in the morning, there is not enough time to carry on group discussions which may serve as a basis for guidance or to have individual conferences with pupils about their problems.

The junior high school has made considerable progress in developing the guidance functions of the home room. In many schools there is a daily period, or several periods weekly, set aside for home room activities, most of them of a guidance nature. Even in the junior high school, however, there is not enough attention given to individual counseling, much of the home room time being devoted to group guidance activities.

Teachers Lack Preparation for Guidance Responsibilities.— The typical secondary school teacher today is not adequately prepared to participate in the guidance program. In his pre-service education, only a limited amount of attention was given to guidance, often only a unit or two in a general course in secondary education. Study in such areas as the psychology of the adolescent, mental hygiene, the psychology of abnormality, tests and measurements, and counseling techniques is limited indeed. It is true, of course, that in a four-year program of teacher education there is insufficient time to give adequate attention to subject matter preparation and all aspects of professional education. It may be that the program of pre-service education for secondary school teachers must be extended beyond four years to permit sufficient preparation for effective participation in the guidance program. The reader is referred to Chapter 18 for further discussion of teacher education.

3. Practices in the Better Secondary Schools

Guidance Provided Through the Core Program.—In the statement of principles for this chapter, it was stated that the teacher is the key person in the guidance program of the secondary school. Furthermore, it was suggested in the previous chapter that the guidance activities should be well integrated with classroom instruction. Both of these objectives are accomplished through the core program, discussed in Chapters 6, 7, and 8. Usually the teacher has the core group in a home room, so that the pupils may spend a major part of the day under his supervision. For this group, the teacher serves as teacher, counselor, and friend, assisting them in making adjustments, meeting learning problems, making important educational and vocational decisions, and solving personal problems.

Having the core teacher serve as the key person in the guidance program is practiced more widely in the junior than in the senior high schools, partly because this approach to both guidance and curriculum development lends itself more readily to the junior high school program. It is appropriate also, however, at the four-year and senior high school level. Colin Kelly Junior High School, Eugene, Oregon, provides an example of this approach to guidance activities. According to Lester M. Beals, principal of the school, the core teachers are the center of the guidance program.[1] In this school, the core program, called "social living," includes language arts, social studies, and some science and art. In the seventh and eighth grades, three periods daily are devoted to it, and in the ninth grade, two periods. Since the home room activities at Colin Kelly Junior High School are included in the core program, this is where the guidance activities also are centered. In schools such as this, where certain subjects are combined into a core program, it is much easier to have guidance activities that are well integrated with other aspects of the instructional program.

At East High School, Denver, Colorado, the guidance activities are closely integrated with the rest of the instructional program through the general education classes which are offered in the tenth grade. The general education teacher, who is the key person in the guidance program, is assigned two classes of thirty to thirty-five pupils each. In the tenth grade he meets these classes one period daily,

---

[1] Lester M. Beals, "The Guidance Program in Colin Kelly Junior High School," *The Bulletin of the National Association of Secondary School Principals,* 34 (January, 1950), 248-57.

in which such topics are covered as how to study, vocational opportunities, an analysis of the pupil's individual abilities, educational planning, current affairs, driver safety, and other problems selected by the pupils. The general education teacher, who does much individual counseling of his pupils, continues with the same pupils in the eleventh and twelfth grades, having one period daily for counseling purposes. When his counselees graduate, he usually begins with two new classes in general education at the tenth grade level.

The core program is one of the most promising developments for improving the teacher's effectiveness in guidance. It enables the teacher to spend a sufficient amount of time with the same pupils each day so that they can get well acquainted and develop sufficient understanding of one another to provide the basis for effective counseling. At the same time, it reduces the number of different pupils with whom the teacher has daily contact, thus improving even more his opportunity to know them intimately. Furthermore, under the core program the guidance activities can become well integrated with the rest of the school program instead of being set apart as a special service. This is especially true in schools where the home room becomes in effect a part of the core program, with the home room activities closely integrated with all other aspects of the curriculum that are under the supervision of the "core teacher."

Guidance Provided Through Many Subjects.—In a number of secondary schools, materials and activities related to guidance are included in many subjects in the curriculum. This is true of schools that do not have a core program, as well as those with this type of curriculum organization. Frequently, units of study that provide information which serves as a basis for counseling are included in English, social studies, homemaking, and industrial arts. An example of such materials is the unit on "Problems Concerned with Current Living" which is included in the sophomore English course at East High School, Rockford, Illinois. This unit deals with such topics as individual differences, conflicts of personalities, controlling emotions, learning to think straight, analyzing personality, choosing a life work, recreational interests, growing up, the "age of romance," and getting along with others.

A similar practice is followed in the high school at Winter Haven, Florida, where the social studies and English classes serve as avenues for bringing educational, vocational, and other information to pupils as a basis for counseling and guidance. In Grades 9 and 10 in this school, units for this purpose are included in the human relations classes, which are part of the social studies program. In Grades 11 and 12, units on vocational and educational problems are studied in the English classes. These units are illustrative of the way in which information bearing on the guidance problems of youth are incorporated into various courses in the curriculum. Every teacher should explore his subject for opportunities to include in it such units as a basis for guidance activities.

Guidance Provided Through the Home Room.—In many secondary schools the home room is the center of guidance activities in fact as well as in theory. At the Norwich Free Academy, which serves as the public secondary school at Norwich, Connecticut, a full sixty-minute class period is set aside each Friday for guidance activities in the home room. In some schools there is a daily activities period for club meetings, assemblies, and home room activities. Such is the case in Norwich Free Academy, where one of these periods is devoted to home room activity. The home room activities in these schools are largely of a guidance nature, providing information and background that will be helpful to pupils in making adjustments in school, participating more fully in various school activities, planning their high school programs, meeting personal problems, and making educational and vocational decisions.

In the home room, guidance activities are carried on in two ways. There is counseling of individual pupils on different problems by the home room adviser, and there is a study of problems by the group as a whole which serves as a basis for making intelligent decisions and ready adjustments in various situations. Some idea of the types of problems studied by home room groups in some schools may be gained from the following list of topics included in the suggestions for group guidance in the home room for the junior high schools of Brockton, Massachusetts: [2]

TOPICS FOR SEVENTH GRADE

    I. My New School
   II. Are Your Study Methods Up to Date?
  III. My Home-Room Organization
  IV. How to Become Well-Known and Liked in Junior High School
   V. My Responsibilities as a Pupil
  VI. What I Do Outside of School

---

[2] This material is summarized from three mimeographed publications of the Board of Education, Brockton, Massachusetts: *Suggestions for Group Guidance: Grade VII*, 1943, 65 pp.; *Suggestions for Group Guidance: Grade VIII*, 1944, 48 pp.; *Suggestions for Group Guidance: Grade IX*, 1945, 40 pp.

TOPICS FOR EIGHTH GRADE

   I. What Are My Interests and Abilities?
  II. After Grade Eight, What Then?
     A. What Am I Going to Be When I Grow Up?
     B. What Courses Are Offered in Grades IX-XII?
     C. What Course Shall I Elect for Next Year?
     D. What Extracurricular Activities Are Open to Me?
 III. How May I Appear at My Best?
 IV. What Can I Do This Summer?

TOPICS FOR NINTH GRADE

    I. Knowing How
   II. Living With Others
 III. In High School I Shall Take . . .
 IV. When I Go to High School
  V. When I Go to Work

Home room activities such as these have been developed particularly in the junior high school, many schools having extensive mimeographed or printed suggestions of this type for the home room adviser. These materials are almost always in the nature of suggestions, seldom prescribing the content or the form of the activities. Pupils are expected to suggest appropriate activities for the home room and to participate in planning them. Although these activities at times may seem somewhat foreign to the purposes of a guidance program, it is usually the intention to integrate them closely with some aspects of guidance and counseling.

Assistance Given Teachers with Guidance.—If the teacher is to be the key person in the guidance program, it is essential that he be given much help to improve his background and skills in guidance. Various approaches to such in-service help are being used in the better schools, including local guidance workshops and study groups conducted by the guidance director. In some schools, the guidance specialists prepare bulletins on various types of pupil problems which may require counseling by the teacher. The physician, nurse, psychologist, psychiatrist, and director of guidance, as well as home room advisers and teachers, participate in preparing these materials. Another practice is for the guidance director, or someone on his staff, to prepare periodic bulletins, perhaps weekly or monthly, to assist teachers with the guidance activities that are being emphasized during that period. Sometimes these bulletins outline activities to be carried on during the home room periods, with suggestions for doing them most effectively, while in other instances they provide suggestions to teachers for developing these activities cooperatively with the pupils.

The series of bulletins prepared by a guidance committee for the junior high schools at Kalamazoo, Michigan, is an example of in-service education materials on guidance for teachers. These bulletins present material on aspects of guidance for which teachers have a primary responsibility, including such as the following: (1) suggestions for orientation, (2) suggestions for home rooms, and (3) suggestions for individual interviews. The committee which prepared these suggestions included teachers, principals, the director of secondary education, and the director of research and guidance.[3] Materials such as these can be very helpful to teachers in improving their effectiveness in the guidance program.

Pupils Given Assistance with Study Skills.—One of the major responsibilities of the teacher in the guidance program is to assist pupils to succeed in school. One approach to this problem is to develop effective study skills and procedures so that they will be able to do their school work efficiently. In some schools, the problem of developing effective study skills is the basis for a series of home room activities in which various topics on how to study are discussed. Another approach is to include in all classes activities designed to assist pupils in improving their study skills, and to integrate these activities closely with the work pupils do in the various subjects. The latter approach is the more effective, particularly if it is carried on by the teachers in a well-planned manner.

A program for teaching pupils how to study which extends into every class in school was developed some years ago at the Simmons Junior High School, Aberdeen, South Dakota. The faculty there prepared a list of study skills which pupils ordinarily use in the various subjects at the junior high school level, and then prepared suggestions for helping pupils acquire each of those skills. The skills emphasized in the Aberdeen program include the following: (1) how to use the textbook, (2) how to use the library, (3) how to use the dictionary, (4) how to use and prepare a newspaper, (5) how to prepare and use graphic materials, (6) how to take dictation, (7) how to take notes, (8) how to outline, (9) how to prepare written work, (10) how to solve problems, (11) how to prepare oral reports, (12) how

---

[3] Kalamazoo Public Schools, Junior High School Guidance Committee, *Suggestions for Homerooms*, Guidance Bulletin No. 2, February, 1947, 10 pp.; *Suggestions for Orientation*, Guidance Bulletin No. 3, September, 1947, 19 pp.; *Suggestions for Individual Interviews*, Guidance Bulletin No. 4, September, 1947, 15 pp. (mimeographed), Kalamazoo, Michigan: Superintendent of Schools.

to prepare debates, (13) how to prepare projects, (14) how to prepare assignments for class discussions, (15) how to memorize, (16) how to drill, (17) how to prepare for tests, (18) how to engage in committee work, and (19) how to interview.[4]

Information About Pupils Readily Accessible to Teachers.—It was mentioned in Chapter 13 that the better secondary schools have cumulative records in which they accumulate much information about individual pupils as a basis for guidance. In some schools, this information is placed directly in the hands of home room teachers, and sometimes other classroom teachers as well, so that they may have convenient access to it as the need arises. For instance, such procedures as the following are employed to place pupil data in the hands of the home room teachers:

1. To have the cumulative records kept by the home room teachers rather than in the central office.
2. To have cumulative records maintained in duplicate, with one kept in the central office, the other by the home room teacher.
3. To summarize the basic information on the cumulative records and to have the summary retained by the home room teacher. The summary may be prepared by home room teachers or by the staff in the office of the principal or the director of guidance.

In a departmentalized school, it is difficult to give classroom teachers the pupil data on the cumulative records because each teacher has so many different pupils. In some departmentalized schools, a summary of data on the cumulative records is prepared for classroom teachers for the pupils under their supervision. In schools with a core program, it is much easier to give teachers the information on the cumulative records because they have the same group of pupils for much of the school day. For instance, in the Colin Kelly Junior High School, Eugene, Oregon, which has a core program, the cumulative record folders are retained by the core teacher for all pupils in his group. Thus he has convenient access to all available information concerning each pupil under his supervision.

---

[4] William T. Gruhn and Constance Conner, "Planning a Program for Teaching Pupils How to Study," *The High School Journal*, 23 (February, 1940), 61-65.

Books useful in planning activities for teaching pupils how to study include the following: R. W. Frederick, *How to Study Handbook*, New York: Appleton-Century-Crofts, Inc., 1937, 442 pp.; Forrest E. Long and Helen Halter, *Social-Studies Skills*, New York: Inor Publishing Co., 1942, 117 pp.; Arthur E. Traxler, *The Improvement of Study Habits and Skills*, New York: Educational Records Bureau, 1944, 39 pp.; J. Wayne Wrightstone, Dorothy Leggitt, and Seerley Reid, *Basic Study Skills: Finding, Evaluating, and Using Information*, New York: Henry Holt & Co., Inc., 1945, 182 pp.

Information About Pupils Secured by Teachers.—The resourceful teacher finds many ways of obtaining helpful guidance information in addition to that which is available on the cumulative records. Activities for this purpose, carried on by teachers in some of the better schools, include the following:

1. Visits to the homes of pupils are made by the home room teacher, the core teacher, and the teachers of such subjects as homemaking, health, and agriculture. In a few small schools, teachers visit all pupils under their supervision. The home visits are usually informal social calls for the purpose of getting acquainted with the pupil's parents, rather than for making a systematic survey of his home background.

2. Formal and informal testing activities are carried on, either as part of an all-school testing program or by the teacher for his own classes, in order to obtain information about the pupils' achievement and to diagnose their learning difficulties.

3. Conferences are arranged by home room and classroom teachers with pupils under their supervision, including periodic, planned conferences as well as informal ones. These conferences not only provide much information about the pupils unobtainable in other ways, but they also give the teacher an opportunity to establish an effective counseling relationship with his pupils.

4. Careful observation is made by the teacher of each pupil under his supervision. Such observation gives the teacher much intimate knowledge about his pupils and furnishes items for the anecdotal records.

Wholesome Classroom Atmosphere Relieves Tensions.—In some schools, teachers are making a considerable effort to establish a classroom atmosphere which is free from tension, and consequently is conducive to the wholesome emotional development of the pupils. The following are some of the things being done by teachers to develop wholesome classroom situations:

1. They try to develop a working relationship with pupils based on cooperation and friendliness, one in which pupils respect but do not fear the teacher.

2. The relationships among pupils are suited to the needs of the learning situation, with much freedom to work together in some situations and to do individual work in others.

3. Disciplinary measures are, when they are necessary, carried out on a constructive rather than a punitive basis. Teachers en-

courage pupils to conduct themselves in such a way that they contribute to, rather than interfere with, the learning of other pupils. A conference with a pupil about his conduct is considered preferable to keeping him after school, requiring extra work, or the many other punitive measures that are sometimes imposed.

4. Teachers help pupils think of examinations as means of evaluating progress instead of using them as "clubs" to get pupils to work. Frequent informal tests are used to make continuous evaluation of the pupil's growth; this helps to avoid placing undue emphasis on "final" examinations covering a semester or a year of work.

5. Teachers have a policy concerning home work which is in harmony with modern educational thinking and the best health interests of the pupils. Some teachers have pupils complete all or most of the work under the teacher's supervision. In any case, they limit the total amount of work to be done out of school so that pupils have enough time for relaxation and rest, for responsibilities at home, and for Boy Scouts or Girl Scouts, music lessons, church activities, and other community activities.

Activities to Develop Personality and Character.—The teachers in some schools plan many activities to assist pupils in developing effective attributes of personality and character. While these qualities are emphasized especially in extraclass activities, it is even better if they receive attention in the various classes as well. Activities which teachers are planning in order to assist pupils in acquiring the most wholesome aspects of personality and character include the following:

1. Teachers plan and carry on discussions and activities in their home room groups on various facets of personality, social, and character qualities.

2. Before school parties, they provide for a study of various aspects of social etiquette in the home rooms and in English, social studies, and homemaking classes.

3. They plan activities for developing leadership qualities, including a study of parliamentary procedure, the personal qualities desirable for leadership, and skills in working effectively with others.

4. Various types of oral and group activities are planned by teachers and pupils in English, social studies, and other subjects as a means of helping pupils develop poise, the ability to work with others, and other desirable aspects of personality and character.

5. Teachers assist pupils in gaining experiences through clubs, assemblies, the student council, and other extraclass activities which will lead to a more effective personality and character.

Teachers Assist Pupils with Health Problems.—In some secondary schools, it is being recognized that the classroom and home room teachers have the major responsibility for observing the health qualities of their pupils and for assisting them with their health problems. In many schools, teachers of physical education and homemaking are particularly interested in helping pupils in matters of health, but in a few schools all teachers share in this responsibility. For instance, in some schools the home room teacher is expected to make a rapid daily inspection of pupils in his group to detect evidence of communicable diseases: fever, colds, skin disease, and vermin in hair or clothing. He also is expected to be on the alert to recognize cases involving cleanliness, nervousness, listlessness, emotional upset, and other problems of health. The home room teacher refers pupils with such problems to the nurse or physician and assists in taking corrective measures.

Classroom teachers also recognize their responsibility for helping pupils in maintaining good health, giving attention to proper ventilation, the seating of left-handed pupils, the seating of pupils with sight and hearing deficiencies, pupils with posture problems, pupils with emotional problems, and pupils with other health problems. Teachers observe their pupils so as to locate those who need guidance in health matters, they solicit the aid of specialists in diagnosing and solving those problems, and they assist with remedial measures.

4. First Steps

There are a number of things which may be done immediately in most schools to improve the effectiveness of the individual teacher in the guidance program. Some of these steps should be taken by the teacher-education institutions, others by the secondary schools, and still others by the teachers themselves.

In teacher-education institutions, the following steps should lead to more effective participation by the teacher in the guidance program:

1. These institutions should examine their programs of pre-service education to find out how effectively they are preparing teachers to understand adolescent children, to help pupils with wholesome emotional development, to evaluate the achievement of pupils and diagnose their learning difficulties, and to be competent in guidance

and counseling activities. They should strengthen the pre-service programs in those areas in which they are found to be weak as a first step in preparing teachers who are well qualified in guidance and counseling.

2. These institutions should study their observation and student teaching programs to ascertain how practical experiences in guidance and counseling can be given to pre-service teachers. They should introduce such experiences in actual school situations in so far as that is possible. For instance, student teachers can be given opportunities to observe and participate in home room guidance activities.

In the secondary schools, these first steps may be taken to improve the teacher's effectiveness in the guidance program:

1. In every secondary school, the place of the teacher in the guidance program should be clearly defined so that he knows what responsibilities he is expected to assume in helping pupils make adjustments and decisions on various educational, vocational, and personal problems.

2. The director of guidance and other guidance specialists should study the needs of the teachers for help with their guidance responsibilities, as a basis for planning a program of in-service education in guidance. They should have teachers participate in such a study and in setting up an in-service education program.

3. Guidance authorities and the faculty should study the schedule of the school to plan a definite time for guidance in the home room, for individual counseling, and for other guidance activities by the teacher. The time provided should be adequate for the guidance needs of the pupils.

4. Guidance authorities and the teachers should examine the courses of study in the various subject areas to ascertain what materials and activities may be included in the various courses to assist the pupils to explore their interests, abilities, and potentialities, as a basis for making educational and vocational decisions.

5. Guidance authorities and teachers should formulate a definite plan for providing teachers with adequate information about the individual pupils under their supervision. They should make a careful study of the cumulative record system in the school, the procedure for keeping and using those records, and the availability of those records to the teachers.

6. The faculty should study the possibility of reorganizing the curriculum in such a way that teachers can spend more time with

their pupils each day, and that they may have a smaller number of pupils, as a step toward more effective guidance. The core program, which enables a teacher to spend several periods daily with the same group of pupils, provides such a possibility.

Individual teachers should also take some steps to improve their contribution to the guidance program, among them the following:

1. Teachers should improve their preparation for guidance by including it in their plans for in-service education. They should provide for a better understanding of adolescents, developing skills in evaluation and measurement, gaining skill in remedial activities, and acquiring backgrounds in guidance and counseling. Such study should be included in the in-service programs planned within the secondary school, in the teacher's professional reading, and in the advanced study that he may do at a university or college.

2. They should formulate plans immediately for becoming better acquainted with each individual pupil under their supervision. This may be done by each teacher through such planned activities as individual conferences with pupils, a careful study early in the year of the cumulative records of the pupils under his supervision, and visitation of the pupils' homes.

3. The teachers should examine their methods of teaching to ascertain how well they are providing for exploratory opportunities for their pupils. They should know, for instance, whether their methods of teaching permit sufficient pupil participation in planning learning activities, how much pupils may pursue their individual interests, and to what extent they are capitalizing in their classes on the talents and potentialities which the pupils possess. They should then introduce activities which extend the opportunity for pupils to explore their interests and potentialities as a basis for making intelligent educational, avocational, and vocational plans and decisions.

SELECTED REFERENCES

BAXTER, EDNA DOROTHY. *An Approach to Guidance.* New York: Appleton-Century-Crofts, Inc., 1946, 305 pp.—A discussion of guidance by the teacher presented in narrative form, with considerable interpretation. It is readable, practical, and interesting.

DETJEN, MARY E. and ERVIN W. *Home Room Guidance Programs for the Junior High School Years.* Boston: Houghton Mifflin Co., 1940, 509 pp.—Gives a complete outline of activities for the home room in Grades 7, 8, and 9, with suggestions for planning and carrying on those activities. Should be particularly helpful to teachers with little or no experience in home room activities.

DUNSMOOR, CLARENCE C., and MILLER, LEONARD M. *Guidance Methods for Teachers in Homeroom, Classroom, and Core Program.* Scranton, Pennsylvania: International Textbook Co., 1942, 382 pp.—The entire volume presents many practical suggestions on guidance methods, particularly from the teacher's standpoint. Every beginning teacher should become familiar with it and use it frequently.

FEDDER, RUTH. *Guiding Homeroom and Club Activities.* New York: McGraw-Hill Book Co., Inc., 1949, chap. 4.—Gives a lengthy, detailed discussion of the activities in which a ninth grade home room engaged over a period of time. It begins with the first meeting of the home room and shows precisely how the group was organized and how it carried on its activities.

GRUHN, WILLIAM T., and DOUGLASS, HARL R. *The Modern Junior High School.* New York: The Ronald Press Co., 1947, chap. 12.—Presents a comprehensive discussion of the home room in the junior high school, including its functions, organization, pupil participation, the adviser's preparation, and activities.

MATTHEWS, BLANCHE. "The Classroom Teacher and Guidance," *The Bulletin of the National Association of Secondary School Principals,* 34 (May, 1950), 124-34.—Summarizes the results of a study of the nature and extent of the classroom teacher's contributions to the guidance program.

McKOWN, HARRY C. *Home Room Guidance.* New York: McGraw-Hill Book Co., Inc., 1946, 521 pp.—Presents a complete discussion of all aspects of home room organization and activities, with particular emphasis on guidance. It has many helpful suggestions for home room teachers.

PRESCOTT, DANIEL A., and CHILD DEVELOPMENT STAFF. *Helping Teachers Understand Children.* Washington, D.C.: The American Council on Education, 1945, 468 pp.—The entire volume presents practical suggestions for helping teachers understand pupils as a basis for guidance and for more effective individualized instruction.

RIVLIN, HARRY N. *Education for Adjustment: The Classroom Applications of Mental Hygiene.* New York: Appleton-Century-Crofts, Inc., 1936, 419 pp.—Presents a discussion of classroom problems in teaching, management, and human relationships that have a bearing on the wholesome emotional development of children and youth.

STRANG, RUTH. *The Role of the Teacher in Personnel Work.* New York: Bureau of Publications, Teachers College, Columbia University, 1946, 497 pp.—Presents a discussion of the teacher's part in various aspects of the guidance program, including the classroom, the home room, and student activities. It gives suggestions on various guidance techniques that the teacher may employ.

PART IV

ORGANIZATION AND ADMINISTRATION
OF THE SECONDARY SCHOOL

ORGANIZATION AND ADMINISTRATION OF THE SECONDARY SCHOOL

The organizational pattern of the secondary school and its administration and supervision are important factors in determining the nature of the secondary education youth will receive. The three chapters in this section deal with the ways in which the principal administers his school and gives leadership to teachers through supervision, curriculum work, and types of in-service professional study. It is contended here that, to a large extent, the forward growth of modern practices in secondary education will depend upon its leaders. The relationships of the secondary school to the elementary school and the college are discussed from the standpoint of how they affect the secondary school. The scope of secondary education is considered as junior high school through junior college.

Chapter 15

LEADERSHIP FOR LEARNING

If our secondary schools are to help youth understand, preserve, interpret, and improve the American way of life, then it obviously becomes essential that such schools reflect democracy in every aspect of their organization and program. Many earlier chapters have discussed and illustrated in detail the application of basic democratic principles to the curriculum in all its aspects. Since we hold that the curriculum is the center of the school and that all other functions must relate directly toward improving the learning experiences provided, we shall focus in this section upon the organization and administration of the secondary school.

The crucial problem in school administration is that of leadership. Since its rapid growth late in the nineteenth century down to the present time, the American high school has never fully reached the goal of being organized and administered democratically. True, many individual secondary schools have been and are now operating democratically, but many schools past and present exemplify autocratic practices in operation. Why are so many high schools throughout the nation still functioning more or less autocratically even today? Must leadership be nondemocratic in order to be efficient? Must the beginning teacher be prepared to find that his principal may talk democracy but practice little of it day by day?

Perhaps the answer to some of these questions lies in an examination of what democracy *really means* in modern high school administration. Teachers and administrators may think that they understand the meaning of democracy; they often give lip service to many of its tenets and ideals, but still they fail to practice and live it in their daily relationships with pupils, colleagues, and community adults. A writer in school administration has recently emphasized the responsibility of the principal in developing a democratic school.[1] He believes that the principal

. . . must possess a firm conviction that the ultimate purpose of the school is to build democratic characters in children, and that the quickest and most

[1] Wilbur A. Yauch, *Improving Human Relations in School Administration,* New York: Harper & Bros., 1949, p. 11.

effective method is for him to devote his major concern to securing these characteristics in teachers. With this as a fundamental prerequisite, his further convictions must include an abiding faith in the democratic process and a willingness to follow consistently wherever it may lead.

1. The Principles

Educational leadership is most democratic when it frees the creative talents of all who work in the school.

The most crucial aspect of democracy is that of establishing and maintaining desirable human relationships. The high school principal has to work closely with his teachers, office staff, custodians, cooks, and maintenance personnel to help them reach their basic common goal of improving instruction for youth. He can do this best when he makes it possible for each person on his teaching and service staff to be free to make his unique contribution to the total educative process. Democratic administration, therefore, becomes a shared and sharing venture. When teachers and other personnel are free to make their own particular contributions and when they cooperate to improve their high school—then administration is truly democratic. This concurrent blending of individual freedom and collective effort is the essence of democracy.

There are many aspects of the administration of a modern high school. Some of the more significant are the administration of the curriculum, the physical plant, pupil personnel, and faculty relationships. Human relations, the way people live and act one with the other, are at the very heart of all these administrative responsibilities. For example, changing the curriculum is basically a social process— that of changing people. In order to bring about desirable changes in the behavior of pupils and staff, the high school administrator must practice good human relations. He can do this best by giving each person with whom he works the freedom and the motivation to make his own individual contribution to the welfare of the school.

Leadership is more effective when it is shared among the group.

The secondary school principal is the administrative leader of his school as a result of an appointment and a delegation of responsibility from the superintendent of schools. The superintendent in turn has a legal responsibility directly to the board of education. Therefore, one might correctly assume that the high school principal has direct "authority over" the teachers of "his school." Legally this line and staff organization (borrowing a concept from business and the army) still exists in American school administration. But this autocratic, or elite, concept is being challenged daily in our better secondary schools; administration based upon shared leadership is proving its worth in contributing more directly to the basic goals of a democratic society.

Leadership based upon delegated legal authority is called status leadership. The high school principal is a status leader because of his legal or appointive position within the school system. As a status leader he can improve human relations among the teachers, provide certain types of expertness, and promote and coordinate leadership within the faculty. While he cannot legally delegate his basic responsibility for administering his school, he may in practice permit his many leadership functions to be shared.

Shared leadership is based upon the democratic theory that the ultimate authority resides in the group, although it may be delegated when necessary. Thus in planning a Christmas program, the principal may temporarily relinquish the major leadership responsibility to the music teacher. The athletic director is largely responsible for all the details of the football games. Parent recreation nights may be delegated to a committee of teachers who are interested, experienced, and who work well with community adults. Leadership is thereby distributed among the total faculty and shared as situations arise in which different teachers have qualities of expertness to contribute. Such shared leadership may be highly efficient if the principal is an expert in dealing with people.

All individuals affected by school policies or practices should share in their determination.

This principle is basic to the cooperative aspect of democratic school administration. It means that democratic verbalization and philosophy must be translated into democratic methods and practices. The high school principal should not independently plan a curriculum, an assembly program, or even a change in the daily schedule until basic policies have been determined by the group affected. If this principle were accepted fully, it would markedly change secondary school practices. When it is necessary to make a change in the administration of the noon luncheon period, for example, pupils, teachers, parents, dietitians, cooks, and custodians, should all share directly in making the necessary decisions, if the change affects them. Curriculum change should be carefully planned by teachers, pupils, administrators, and community adults. In this way, common educational problems can best be solved through cooperative effort. Once the policy has been determined cooperatively, the status leader is the one to administer the policy to the best of his ability. However, if he finds that it is unworkable, he has an obligation to bring the matter before the group for clarification and revision.

The administrative unit best adapted to democratic leadership and control is the single high school faculty.

In very small cities and in all villages and reorganized school districts, the single high school is naturally the one and only administrative secondary school unit. But in cities having more than one high school, the practice is increasing to have policies determined in the central administrative office for all high schools within the system. This policy has resulted from an ever-increasing complexity of administrative details and pressures, as well as from false assumptions regarding efficiency. It has brought about a hopelessly undemocratic division between policy making and the carrying of the program into action. In Chapter 5 it was pointed out that this centralization is not desirable in the area of curriculum development. The basic responsibility for building a curriculum should be that of the individual faculty of a given high school. This is essential if the curriculum is to be adapted to local and community needs, individual differences of pupils, and to the varying experiences and abilities of the local faculty.

The same factors pertain to all other administrative aspects of secondary education. Democratic administration is based upon maximum individual participation in face-to-face relationships. The sharing of common experiences in a common school environment is highly conducive to understandings which lead to cooperative administration. Yauch emphasizes these points further:

The single school, with an organically functioning faculty, provides the best hope for the achievement of these requisites to democratic action. It has its own identifiable community of people, institutions, and organization. It has a unity of membership and common educational responsibility. . . . In every aspect, the hope of true democratic action lies in dealing with the single school as an organic whole, interacting with other organic wholes, to make up the administrative unit of the school system.[2]

Democratic high school administration practices and extends techniques of group process.

Some of the principles given in earlier chapters illustrate the urgency of utilizing group action rather than individual dictation. Not

---

[2] *Ibid.,* pp. 13-14.

only must secondary schools avoid such elite leadership, but they need to learn how to synthesize the various individuals of the faculty into a new kind of dynamic, interactive group. Effectively functioning groups reveal ample evidence that they are far more efficient than any other combination of individuals.[3]

Any leader in the school, therefore—the principal, the guidance director, the teacher who is chairman of a committee—needs to be expert in techniques of group process and action. He needs to use these tools for general teachers' meetings, for committee meetings, and for community meetings. When the teachers find such techniques valuable, they will employ them with their pupils in solving learning problems.

At the heart of group action is the attempt of an interested group of individuals to identify a problem or problems which they are motivated to solve through cooperative effort. Techniques of group process will be discussed in detail later in this chapter.

The primary function of educational administration is the improvement of the learning process.

The high school principal and faculty should keep firmly in mind that the school is organized and functions primarily to promote pupil growth and learning. The curriculum should be the center of the school. Unfortunately, however, many high school administrators spend much of their time with problems of building maintenance, attendance, textbooks, schedules, and the like. These matters are all important, but most of them are mechanical and can be routinized. They exist only to promote the curriculum of the school and should never become ends in themselves. The modern secondary school principal expends his major time and effort in giving leadership toward improving the instructional program for youth. All other functions are secondary.

Supervision should be a democratic process for the improvement of instruction.

Supervision is an aspect of administration and therefore must serve to help bring about desirable changes in the behavior of secondary school youth. In small high schools, there will frequently be no direct supervision other than that nominally given by the principal or

---

[3] See Association for Supervision and Curriculum Development, *Group Processes in Supervision,* Washington, D.C.: National Education Association, 1948, 130 pp.

superintendent. In large city school systems, however, the beginning teacher may find himself supervised by his principal, assistant principal, department head, and central office supervisor.

The trend in modern supervision is to provide friendly and helpful consultive service to teachers when they want and seek it. The old-fashioned supervisor who dropped into classrooms unexpectedly to rate teachers is fortunately disappearing rather rapidly. The modern supervisor may await a classroom call or at least announce his coming in advance. He has met the teacher previously and usually asks permission to visit the class. Some supervisors never visit classes in the older sense of the word, but drop in to talk to the teacher when he has a free period. Other supervisors consider themselves consultants or resource persons who are ready to help teachers whenever their assistance is requested. Some supervisors render most of their services to teachers through committee work.

Modern secondary schools, therefore, are improving their learning programs through democratizing supervision. A beginning teacher in such a modern high school should welcome and not fear supervision, since it is provided to help him become a more effective teacher. Such a plan recognizes the uniqueness and special talents of each teacher; it attempts to encourage and develop these individual teaching abilities rather than to make all conform to a common, stereotyped standard. Such supervision will assist the building of a more vital educational program in a modern high school.

2. SOME TYPICAL PRACTICES

When we look at some high schools today, we do not find many of the foregoing administrative principles functioning. Conditions of course vary from school to school, but American secondary education on the whole has not been characterized by democratic leadership of its educational program. Within the past two decades, secondary education has been brought to a large majority of American youth, although economic barriers to this education still exist and are a serious factor in eliminating many able young people. Legally and externally, American secondary education is democratic; yet in its organization and administration it frequently fails to meet the ideals which a free people expect from their schools.

Evidence of the lack of democracy in American secondary schools may be found in the slowness with which they have improved their instructional program, their inability to hold a larger percentage of youth through graduation, the unrealistic number of pupils guided into the professions, the dominance of college preparation, and the slowness in development of community schools.

These problems result in part from a lack of leadership by the administrators of our public high schools. It should be recognized that they are not entirely responsible. Public apathy, inadequate financial support, poorly educated teachers, college domination, and teacher inertia, all are contributing factors. But school administrators have the major responsibility and the authority to overcome most of these factors impeding educational improvement. Their very position as administrators confirms their leadership responsibility to a society which has faith in education to improve democratic living. The type of training given secondary school administrators by colleges of education has been an important factor in this situation.

The High School Principal at Work.—Townville Junior-Senior High School has an enrollment of 250 pupils. It is Friday at 9:15 A.M. and the student body marches into the auditorium under the watchful eyes of the faculty. They find seats quietly as the principal comes to the center of the stage—alone. Whispering and giggling cease as he stands waiting attention. He then gives a series of announcements, explains schedule changes, and calls attention to violations of rules. He eventually gives over the platform to the music teacher for group singing. This is regular weekly routine in this school, varied by occasional seasonal pep sessions, band music, athletic awards, and guest speakers. But always the principal presides.

Rural Union High School is a four-year secondary school with only sixty-five pupils, seven miles from the county seat. There are three full-time teachers, and the superintendent teaches three classes and acts as principal. He must also be responsible for four elementary teachers, coach all athletics, and advise the senior class. The many problems of a lunchroom, building repairs, equipment and supplies, operating five school buses, and planning the budget are among his general administrative duties. Miss Jones, the new inexperienced English and social studies teacher, is handed a state-required course of study at the first teachers' meeting in September and is told by the principal-superintendent to "follow it in every detail." Subsequent meetings discuss certificates, discipline, textbook accounting, the Christmas program, salaries, county tests, and the proposed new gymnasium. Miss Jones is visited twice for a few minutes during the year by the superintendent, but she is not assisted with her problems nor does the superintendent actually know what she is doing. In early May, the superintendent regretfully tells her that the board of education is not renewing her contract because of "persistent discipline problems."

Laissez Faire and Autocratic Leadership.—The two illustrations given above are descriptions of poor administrative practices in secondary schools. Dozens of similar examples could be given. Similarly, we could give many illustrations of more functional and democratic secondary school leadership. It is important for the beginning teacher to realize, however, that he may find himself in such a school as either one of those described above. He ought to be prepared to meet the situation, even though it is not one in which he can function most effectively.

The two schools described briefly illustrate the lack of sound principles of democratic educational leadership. The criterion of good administration is the degree to which the principal secures cooperative efforts in improving learning. In applying this criterion to the sample of administrative practices revealed by the two principals above, the appraisal seems fairly clear. The Townville High School principal, in the very brief picture given, apparently operated upon the elite concept of leadership. He seemed to make most of the decisions, and he personally saw that each was executed. Pupils apparently carried out orders. One wonders if there are not both frustration and aggression among faculty and pupils. As students of education, we might well ask what happens in this high school when the principal is absent. This example illustrates, in part, autocratic or dictatorial administration. From the sketchy picture given, we have little direct evidence of the principal's role in curriculum improvement. But from his handling of the assembly program, we might assume that he permits little shared leadership in instructional procedures.

The principal-superintendent of Rural Union High School represents, in some respects, the opposite extreme in administration, that of laissez faire. He is so busy with the mechanical and routine details of "running a school" that he has practically no time to help teachers cooperatively improve the educational program of the school. He gives them plenty of freedom, but little encouragement or assistance. He assumes that state-prescribed courses of study will serve all the pupils of his school; when problems of discipline result, he holds the teacher responsible. His administrative philosophy is not clear-cut, it is a mixture of both unlimited freedom and dictatorial practices, with each reflecting his overconcern for mechanical detail. This statement can well summarize one type of secondary school administration prevalent today: a conflicting welter of opposing ideals resulting from pressure and expediency.

Improvement of Instruction Subordinated to Mechanical Details.
The generalization made just above merits further consideration, for
it explains so many administrative practices in secondary schools today. If any one statement can be documented and demonstrated, it is
that many high school principals still spend an excessive amount of
time in administering various mechanical and routine details. These
principals are so busy with absence slips, basketball schedules, assembly programs, honor rolls, discipline violations, attendance records,
service club programs, reports, and the like, that they have little time
or energy left for working directly with pupils, parents, and teachers
to improve the curriculum and instruction. One reason is that the
administrative activities are immediate concerns that cannot be safely
neglected; the improvement of the curriculum is a long-range activity
often with no apparent pressures demanding that it be done.

There are other reasons for this prevailing condition. One must
recognize the fact that a large majority of communities fail to provide
anything approaching adequate clerical and secretarial assistance for
their schools. If a report is to be ready for the superintendent or state
department, the principal must in many cases tabulate the data and
type it personally. This is an example of penny economy operating
in education, but it is still a prevailing practice. In small high schools,
the superintendent usually functions as the principal. In such schools,
the principal is a designated full-time teacher who keeps certain records and may have a few other similar routine administrative duties.
Any consistent leadership in curriculum improvement is consequently
difficult if not impossible.

These valid conditions and pressures explain much administrative
neglect of curriculum improvement, but not all of it by any means.
There are many high schools, both large and small, where fairly adequate clerical assistance is available and the principal either does not
have a heavy teaching load or does no teaching. Why, then, the persistent neglect of the instructional program? The reasons, we believe, are these:

1. Many principals find greater security in mechanical details than
   in curriculum development.
2. They are psychologically unwilling or unable to delegate these
   routine duties to others.
3. They lack adequate training and experience in coordinating a
   curriculum improvement program for their schools.
4. They sincerely believe that a well-administered school is one that
   runs like clockwork.

5. They do not know how to assist teachers with instructional problems.
6. Such activities as attention to routine details are less time consuming.
7. They can "get by" without attention to instruction—not so with respect to other responsibilities.

The concept of educational leadership held by the high school principal will largely determine whether he submerges himself in administrative details or gives major time and energy to help coordinate a functional modern curriculum for the school. The factor of inadequate training and experience will be discussed in detail in a later chapter. It is sufficient to point out that in the past the education of high school administrators often emphasized the mechanistic aspects of the school. Courses in general and secondary school administration glorified the role of the efficient high school principal. Educational psychology, philosophy of education, curriculum courses, and workshops were relatively neglected. Furthermore, in many administration courses, the more mechanical and purely administrative details predominated over the more vital aspects of improving the curriculum. Hence, when principals began their work, they were predisposed toward relatively routine administration. Fortunately this picture is slowly changing, and many graduate schools of education now offer a more balanced program for the education of secondary administrators. In some states, however, requirements for state administrative certificates still emphasize courses in school administration.

Many Administrative Functions of Secondary School Principals. —The beginning teacher will often find his principal having many additional responsibilities in the operation of a modern high school. A major responsibility of his leadership is that of putting basic school policies into effect. In addition to implementing curriculum policies, he must see that policies affecting building and grounds, use of library and other facilities, athletic program, distribution of textbooks, faculty committees, publications and dramatics, and the like, are carried out effectively. The principal serves as the direct official representative of the superintendent in all except very small high schools. Although democracy and autonomy should reside in each high school faculty unit, beginning teachers must recognize that in the typical situation many decisions are made by the superintendent and passed down the line as policy for the principal and faculty. The principal may act as official school and faculty representative to the community in medium-sized and large high schools. He often represents the high school officially in P.T.A. activities, service clubs, youth-serving agencies, and system-wide administrative meetings.

Responsibilities of Additional High School Administrative Staff.—The typical high school of 100 to 250 enrollment will have a principal who teaches part time. In addition, he has many administrative duties and little assistance, although he may have one teacher who gives limited time to counseling, another to visual education, athletics, clubs, and the like.

In large city high schools ranging from 800 to 3,000 pupils, the administrative organization will be rather complex. An assistant or vice principal is the rule; sometimes more than one may be found. The assistant principal usually has responsibility for discipline, attendance, and daily schedules. He may also serve as the guidance coordinator. Some schools call their counselors deans of boys and girls, although these titles are slowly disappearing. Large schools frequently have permanent department heads who may perform some administrative functions. They coordinate instruction, represent their department at meetings, requisition supplies, and possibly supervise instruction. Directors of guidance, audio-visual aids, music, dramatics, athletics, health, and art may also have numerous administrative duties.

Most large high schools have a head clerk or secretary who may be given considerable responsibility for supplies, equipment, books, attendance, reports, budget, and other details. School physicians, chief nurses, dietitians, lunchroom managers, librarians, and chief engineers always exercise considerable authority in their fields. The principal's task is one of coordinating their efforts to place emphasis upon educational values rather than efficiency and order.

The Teacher's Administrative Responsibilities.—There are three broad areas in which the teacher may expect to carry on certain administrative duties and responsibilities. First, within his own home room or classroom he is expected to keep attendance records; to record grades, marks, test scores; and to write pupil reports to parents. He must coordinate school drives and campaigns among his pupils. He will have to order, account for, and distribute supplies, equipment, and textbooks.

Another responsibility of the classroom teacher is to serve on certain schoolwide administrative committees. These committees may be primarily service agencies, but they often perform administrative functions as well. Typical committees commonly found in medium-sized and large high schools include those which help administer the lunchroom, assemblies, athletics, musical organizations, library, ticket sales, and the like.

A third area of administrative responsibility in which teachers participate is that of representing their department or school at citywide, regional, or state meetings. Thus a teacher may be selected to explain the purposes of the school honor society to a city service club. He may represent his school at a community meeting to plan drives for the Red Cross or Community Chest. Finally, in fewer instances, he may be appointed to represent the high school principal at a P.T.A. committee meeting or at a city curriculum meeting.

Teacher Participation in Formulating Administrative Policies.— A recent study of teacher participation in the determination of administrative policies in a sample of thirty-two smaller Minnesota high schools reveals a number of interesting conditions. Approximately 81 per cent of the teachers in the study reported that they helped determine the content of individual courses of study in the curriculum. In only seven other functions out of fifty-eight listed did a majority of the teachers feel that they participated directly. This study reported teacher participation in policy formulation independent of administrators and when working jointly with them. Not over 41 per cent of the teachers indicated that they cooperated directly with administrators in determining policies in any one of the fifty-eight functions studied. Administrative areas in which most cooperative policy formulation was reported were in community relations, use of buildings and equipment, school control, reports, and records. Areas in which relatively little cooperative participation was found included faculty administration and school finance. Principals consistently reported more teacher participation in formulating administrative policies than teachers reported for the same schools.[4]

One nationwide study [5] revealed that in only the following four administrative activities did as many as 50 per cent of the teachers responding share democratically:

> Evaluating pupil progress
> Preparing daily programs
> Selecting textbooks
> Building and evaluating courses of study

---

[4] Raymond C. Carlson, *Teacher Participation in Formulating Administrative Policies in Minnesota Secondary Schools,* an unpublished research paper, Minneapolis: University of Minnesota, 1949, 119 pp.

[5] Eldridge T. McSwain, "Cooperation As Teachers And Administrators View It," *Cooperation: Principles and Practices* (Eleventh Yearbook), Washington, D.C.: Department of Supervisors and Directors of Instruction, National Education Association, 1939, pp. 153-76.

Teachers desired, in contrast, to participate more fully than they were permitted in all but one of the thirty-one administrative activities. For example, the findings of the study revealed that 69 per cent wished to take part in determining promotion policies and practices, but only 41 per cent had opportunities to participate. Only about one fifth took part in preparing salary schedules while two thirds wanted to participate. Less than half as many reporting teachers were able to plan and conduct teachers' meetings as wished to do so; more than five times as many teachers wanted to help prepare the budget as had been participating in this activity. This same study revealed that nearly 60 per cent of the superintendents responding did not believe teachers had the necessary competency to participate in the various types of given administrative activities, while only 55 per cent of them thought teachers had any desire to participate.

The Minnesota study revealed that, in the responding schools, faculty meetings were largely planned and conducted by the administrators. Only two of thirty-two schools used a committee to plan meetings for the year. Only about 20 per cent of the schools reported the election of a chairman to conduct faculty meetings. About one half of these high schools reported their faculty meetings being conducted as lecture sessions by the administrators. Only 20 per cent of the high schools had a superintendent's administrative council. About one third of the schools had standing committees; six schools reported the election of standing committee members by the staff. The ten schools which had most teacher participation in administrative policy making all described their faculty meetings as open forums with active staff discussion. Seven of the ten schools with most teacher participation held regularly scheduled faculty meetings. These schools also reported more P.T.A.'s and local units of the state teachers' association. Over 75 per cent of the reporting teachers and principals believed that more teacher participation in policy making would be desirable. They agreed that such practice improved morale and the general efficiency of the high school.[6]

Pupil Participation in Organization and Administration of Secondary Schools.—The extent and degree of pupil activity in various aspects of organization and administration varies markedly from school to school. Frequently, they have no voice in helping plan the curriculum nor in carrying out learning activities. In other cases they may be full participants in every phase of the learning process. In many schools, pupils have a responsibility in determining many school

---

[6] Carlson, *op. cit.*, pp. 108-16.

policies and practices through student councils. However, in too few have they been delegated real responsibility. (See Chapter 10.)

It is common practice in many high schools, regardless of size, for pupils to do responsible work in offices, libraries, lunchrooms, gymnasiums, and in custodial jobs. Hall traffic, safety, discipline, clubs, and publications are frequently pupil-sponsored and administered. These practices will be described in detail in the following section.

3. Practices in the Better Secondary Schools

Although democratic administration is an ideal difficult to achieve, many schools follow democratic practices in some areas of organization and administration. Some modern high schools are following democratic administrative practices in the total operation of their institutions. We shall present some of these outstanding practices found in better secondary schools today. The reader is also referred to the illustration from Oakland High School given in Chapter 5, showing how teachers participated in curriculum planning. In these illustrations, there is evidence of the many people taking responsibility for a job that they have helped to plan and consider as theirs. The principal delegates responsibility to teachers who serve as chairmen of committees, to department heads, and to whoever has special abilities and interests for performing the task at hand.

A Pattern for Cooperative Planning.—In the Drury High School, North Adams, Massachusetts, the principal uses the following plan [7] as a basis for democratic, faculty-administrative school planning:

1. Each teacher states one or more problems that he believes should be solved before Drury may become maximally effective.
2. A committee of teachers with the principal plans a program of problems to be worked upon and arranges to have every one of the faculty assigned to a problem of his choice.
3. The committees on different problems meet and elect chairmen.
4. The committee chairmen meet from time to time with the principal.
5. The principal meets from time to time with the committees, especially when his services are needed and requested.
6. Each committee defines its problem, reads the best literature on the subject, brings in parents, pupils, administrators, and other

---

[7] Adapted from *Cooperative Planning*, Principal's Bulletin (mimeographed), North Adams, Mass.: Drury High School, 1946, p. 7.

teachers, if help may thus be secured in solving the problem. A report showing progress is given to the entire faculty from time to time, for the purpose of keeping the faculty informed and to secure its help and cooperation. After a satisfactory solution is agreed upon, the proposal *in written form* is presented to the faculty for criticism and adoption.

7. Committees meet at 8:00-9:00 A.M. on Fridays.
8. The school helps to provide the necessary books and references needed.
9. Faculty meetings are arranged for the purpose of considering committee reports.

Cooperative planning meetings and departmental meetings are held on alternate Fridays until the spring when chairmen report and action is taken on plans for the following year. The principal states that most of the worth-while improvements for the school have come out of these discussions. Pupils are excused from reporting in the morning until 9:00 on the days of faculty meetings. The administration, teachers, and citizens have all supported this plan and found that it contributes to the improvement of the school.

Preschool Planning.—For the past few years, the Minneapolis public schools have held a week's planning and orientation program prior to the opening of school. All elementary and secondary school teachers report for work a full week in advance of the pupils' return and engage in an intensive program of planning and preparation for the year's work. All principals, in turn, begin working one week before the teachers.

The program for the week is planned cooperatively by teachers and administrators. It has included in the past a general meeting of the total teaching personnel at which the superintendent of schools and chairman of the Citizens Committee on Public Education were principal speakers. Such a meeting has been followed by citywide workshops in which elementary and high school teachers jointly explored critical and crucial educational problems and issues. Both local and outside specialists served as discussion leaders and consultants. Teachers, principals, and central office staff members met and discussed common problems in these workshop sessions. Following the workshops, individual high schools held meetings in which they formulated plans and policies. Departmental and committee meetings rounded out the week's activities. Such cooperative preschool planning has proved its value in improving the organization, administration, and curriculum of the city's schools.

Many high schools across the nation are holding similar preschool planning periods. Some, as in Minneapolis, extend for a week's duration. A majority operate for only one, two, or three days. These usually serve general orientation functions, especially for new staff members; inspirational purposes; explanation of school routine; and general and special planning. Frequently, outside specialists and consultants from higher educational institutions, state departments, and publishing and supply agencies participate. Occasionally, the total staff—both secondary and elementary—concentrate upon a single workshop problem, such as guidance or marking.

Fortunate, indeed, is the beginning high school teacher who has these opportunities for preschool orientation, planning, and cooperative thinking. Only a decade before World War II, the inexperienced teacher typically arrived at his new teaching environment the week end before school opened, desperately sought a "rooming house," probably attended a short Saturday morning teachers' meeting, and then reported for his first day's work on Monday along with the pupils! Programs as described above are further evidence of the progress of American secondary education. The Portland, Oregon, public schools have a well-organized program for welcoming, assisting, and orienting the new teacher. Special assistance is given in finding a place to live and in getting adjusted to school and community. A teachers' handbook gives pertinent information about the school and community. One person in the central office has been assigned to this work as her main responsibility.

Democratic Planning in a Small High School.—The faculty of the Floodwood Community School in northern Minnesota for many years played a vital part in planning the total activities and program of the school. Staff meetings were held weekly, usually after school, but sometimes partly on school time. The agenda were usually not planned in advance, but teachers and administrators informally presented problems pertaining to the schedule, extraclass activities, discipline, class work, schoolwide projects, and the like. Decisions were reached democratically and the principal, a teacher, or a committee was delegated to carry out the decision of the group.

Three of the four monthly staff meetings were usually devoted to curriculum planning under the leadership of an elected curriculum chairman. These meetings were often conducted as workshops in which class units were preplanned, test data analyzed, and parent reports prepared. The expenditure of large budgetary items for textbooks and supplies was usually a joint responsibility of the staff and the administration. Teachers worked directly with the superintendent and the board of education in building a salary schedule. Recently, when a new superintendent was to be selected, the teachers were asked by the board to appoint a committee to assist in interviewing candidates and in making final recommendation for the position.

Democratic Planning in a Large School System.—A few years ago, the teachers and administrators of Battle Creek, Michigan, began cooperative planning to improve their schools. The following steps [8] were taken to secure the cooperation of laymen and teachers for their important task:

1. Representatives of the administration and all teacher groups planned and worked together for the improvement of the schools.
2. First concern was given to special problems of teacher salaries, teacher morale, inadequate school budget, and the apparent indifference in the community attitude toward school welfare.
3. Complete enrollment of all teachers was secured in the local, state, and national education associations.
4. The teachers' association, the Parent-Teacher Association, and the board of education developed an educational advisory council, with wide elective lay-organizational membership. This council is purely advisory and operates democratically under lay leadership.
5. Wide parent participation in high schools has been secured through what is called the parent-teacher-student organization, affiliated with the P.T.A.
6. A council on instruction was organized as a means of getting teacher participation in curriculum development and in the improvement of teaching. Each building elects a teacher representative to the monthly meetings, and principals and supervisors are also represented. Teachers are provided with substitutes when they attend council meetings.
7. A joint teacher-administrative-board of education committee on teacher welfare has, with the assistance of lay groups, been able to adopt a fair salary schedule.
8. Evaluation and in-service education have been promoted through emphasizing self-appraisal and growth. No relationship exists between supervision and administrative employment practices.

---

[8] Virgil M. Rogers, "Schools Can Plan Cooperatively," *NEA Journal,* 38 (September, 1949), 436-37.

9. A policy of involving parents and laymen in a wide variety of school activities has brought better understanding of school needs, interest, enthusiasm, and excellent financial support.

A Faculty Chooses Its Committees.—At Alhambra City High School, California, the faculty elects its committee on committees at the opening faculty meeting each fall. Each teacher checks five names on the mimeographed faculty list; the five receiving the highest number of checks make up the committee, with the member who stands first among the five acting as chairman. This committee appoints all standing committees, such as the social committee, assembly committee, faculty meeting committee, and others. It also appoints various special committees as the need arises; examples are the nominating committee, scholarship committee, and bond election committee. There is student representation on many of these committees, with student representatives selected by the student commission, the executive body of the student government. The principal is ex officio member of all committees but has no vote. All committees have complete responsibility for their respective assignments. This plan has promoted the morale of pupils and faculty alike, building good rapport between them.

A Small High School Planning Council.—The Sunnyside, Washington, High School teacher's planning council is an organization composed of all regular faculty members of the high school. The purpose of this council is the promotion of good student-teacher relationships, democratic teacher-administrator relationships, and a better understanding among pupils, parents, teachers, and administrators.

A chairman and secretary are elected annually by the council; these two officers, two elective board members, and the principal as an ex officio member compose the executive planning board. This board meets prior to regular council meetings to discuss problems, issues, and suggestions emanating from pupils, parents, or school staff; it prepares the agenda for the planning council which is made available in advance to the faculty.

The planning council meets regularly twice each month and more frequently when necessary. It considers carefully the items on the agenda, and all faculty and administrative personnel are given opportunity to express themselves. Special committees are sometimes appointed to investigate problems and to report to the council. A consistent effort is made to use group process techniques in order that the council may make decisions representing the unanimous approval of all teachers and administrators.

The Principal as a Leader of People.—In forward-looking secondary schools, the beginning teacher can expect to find a principal who is, first of all, skilled in human relations. The principal in such a school is a person who knows how to administer a good secondary school, but he does not attempt to do it all himself. He knows his faculty members and gives them an opportunity to take responsibility where they are able to do so. He understands that morale will be highest and people will best carry out policies if they have a part in making them.

The vice principal, the guidance director, the athletic director, the student council, and the teachers are all given freedom to make their own decisions within the sphere of activity in which they operate and within the general policies developed by the group as a whole. In such a situation, the principal has a part in selecting his own faculty and he, in turn, has his teachers assist him in this responsibility. In large high schools, administrative councils of teachers to work with the principal as representatives of the teachers are becoming more common.

Consequently, the principal has time to work with teachers in improving the instructional program, his most important job. He works with committees, has conferences with his teachers, takes extension courses with them, and serves as consultant to summer workshops participated in by the teachers of his school.

Helpful Supervisory Assistance Available.—Although the beginning teacher will find little supervisory help in some schools, in others he will receive helpful, sympathetic assistance. (Specific assistance available to beginning teachers is discussed in Chapter 19.) The supervisory policies and the services available to all teachers in the better situations are these:

1. The teachers and the principal develop together policies for the instructional program; this process in itself gives the principal many opportunities for helpful supervision.
2. Supervision is a process of working *with* teachers where there is committee work on curriculum problems, in-service courses, summer workshops, and other forms of cooperative work.
3. In this kind of cooperative work, the principal finds many opportunities to visit teachers' classrooms, hold conferences with them, and serve as a consultant to ongoing projects.
4. In large school systems, the supervisors for the system are made available as consultants to such groups.
5. The principal makes use of the abilities represented in his staff to

help other teachers. Thus, a teacher with special education in reading will assist English teachers with the improvement of reading; a guidance director will work with teachers in improving guidance in the classroom and home room; a teacher with special training in child and adolescent development will serve as chairman or consultant to curriculum study concerned with this area.

6. Good human relations are the fundamental basis for supervision in such secondary schools, for it is realized that people must gain the confidence and respect of others before they can help others.

The Group Process in Leadership.—Good group procedures are evident in the above description of practices which involve cooperative work. Leadership, whether by the principal, vice principal, committee chairman, or department head, makes wise use of group dynamics in an increasing number of secondary schools. Good leaders have the group participate in defining its problems, as the policy of the Drury High School illustrates (see page 362). Principals plan with the faculty how they should tackle their problem and set up a situation in which there are groups small enough for study and action. Gone are the days when most teachers accepted with docility the type of faculty meeting where the leader spends half of the time in announcements. More principals are using staff meetings to work on curriculum problems. A few schools make use of the observer in group meetings to facilitate the work that is to be done. But, most important, the principal or superintendent makes it a point to see that he helps carry out the action decided upon by the group.

4. First Steps

Throughout this chapter we have indicated many ways in which the administrative leadership of secondary schools can be improved. We have emphasized that educational leadership must be democratic, but that it need not be inefficient. Teachers and pupils need to participate actively in many aspects of administration. The following practical suggestions point out steps which can be taken by high school principals and beginning teachers in order to further democratic leadership in their institutions.

1. The high school principal can actively promote better human relationships among his faculty and student body. He can be cheerful, friendly, and helpful at all times. Too many principals are feared by their staffs; the most effective leader is respected but never feared. He can be interested in the personal as well

as the professional problems of his staff. He can often help
teachers secure professional advancement, and find satisfaction
in their growth and progress. He can reveal the same friendly
interest in the problems, progress, and success of pupils in the
school; he can follow their work in community and college after
graduation. Such qualities and practices on the part of principals in high schools, large or small, will always improve morale,
effectiveness, and service.

2. Basic to improving secondary school leadership is the need for
   sharing policy-making functions among pupils, adults of the
   community, nonteacher personnel, and teachers. Many matters
   of school policy, such as discipline, various phases of school
   activities, assemblies, publications, athletics, and home rooms
   can be determined satisfactorily by the student council. Curriculum policy and planning can best be done through faculty meetings, workshops, and committees. Parents and other community
   adults can help determine policies regarding lunchrooms, homework, and sex education. They can also send representatives to
   school and citywide curriculum councils and committees. The
   clerical and custodial staff can assist in determining policies for
   rush periods, overtime, holidays, and sick leave. All such sharing in policy making will strengthen and improve the total school.

3. Much of the policy making suggested above can best be carried
   out in pre-school staff planning workshops. If the board of
   education cannot finance a full week of work or even a few days
   prior to the opening of school, then at least one or two days
   should be taken during the first week. Such a workshop serves
   as orientation for new teachers, provides socialization for all
   through picnics and parties, and gives ample time for sharing
   in policy making, planning, and room arranging.

4. All planning cannot be carried out prior to the opening of school;
   hence some plan of organized group meetings and work needs to
   be followed throughout the year. Regularly scheduled teachers'
   meetings, planned and directed in part by the faculty, are most
   helpful. Teachers should share both in planning agenda and in
   presiding at meetings. They should suggest committees and
   have some voice in determining committee membership. The
   time, length, and organization of all such meetings can best be
   determined by the total teaching and administrative staff.

5. As a result of policies made jointly by the teachers and principal,
   a continuing program of curriculum improvement can be carried out. In a large system, this usually means working through

citywide committees representing all schools and the central office. In a single high school, all teachers can work directly on different committees and in larger group meetings. Resource people and consultants can be secured, and extension courses can often be arranged with institutions for higher education. Whichever plan or combination is followed, *it is imperative that teachers and administrators plan and work together cooperatively in all endeavors.*

6. The principal can help improve the curriculum of the school by providing democratic supervision. No matter how busy he becomes with administrative details, his first responsibility is to help improve instruction and learning. By delegating and sharing as we have indicated, he can have more free time to visit teachers, to consult with them, and to observe learning situations. In city systems, he can secure additional specialized assistance in supervision when he needs it. He can provide at least minimum free time for teachers to visit other departments and buildings. Highly effective help can often be given beginning teachers by others more experienced. The principal can encourage all teachers to come to him freely to discuss curriculum problems.

7. Not only can policy making be shared, but also the administration of many of the mechanical details of operating the school. Teachers, parents, and pupils can share in the supervision of playground, gymnasium, activities, and lunchrooms. Pupils can serve as hosts to visitors, as receptionists, as observers of traffic within the building, and as office assistants. Schools can successfully utilize class projects to provide printing, notices, newspapers, bookkeeping, school equipment, and the like. All this sharing not only frees the principal but also improves the quality of leadership and the morale of the school.

8. Even though many schools cannot provide adequate office and clerical assistance, it also is true that many administrators do not seek diligently and persistently to secure more help. Too many principals and superintendents are content to accept the status quo in regard to office assistance. Surely, it is not good business practice to have teachers do clerical work which is more efficiently done by trained personnel. Even more uneconomical and inefficient is the common practice of having principals type their own letters. It is the definite responsibility of the high school principal or superintendent to point out to the board of education the penny-pinching economy involved.

9. The wideawake high school principal who is seeking to improve

his school can secure many kinds of professional services from other agencies. The curriculum library services, the audio-visual aids services, and supervisory services are often available in city systems or, in some rural areas, through the county superintendent's office. State and private colleges and universities have extension classes and services available to many schools. The state department of education always has helpful specialists in a variety of school functions who can be secured to work with teachers. County and state health departments, conservation departments, welfare departments, libraries, and historical associations also stand ready to serve. Local service clubs, churches, and other organizations are willing and eager to assist those schools seeking to improve themselves.

10. The beginning high school teacher should first accept the administrative status quo of a school in which he has chosen to teach. If he has serious questions or reservations regarding administrative policies, then he should not accept a position in the school. As the beginning teacher starts his work, he should cooperate with his principal and superintendent in every possible way. Being an unfriendly rebel or "radical" will only lead to further misunderstandings and frustration.

11. While first accepting the administrative status quo—assuming that it is less than democratic—the beginning teacher should not compromise his own educational point of view. Frequently young teachers become discouraged quickly, and accept the common statement that "it's a fine theory, but it will not work in practice." They may also be intimidated by the principal and admonished by veteran teachers to accept present practices indefinitely without question. Progress will come as beginning teachers hold to their democratic beliefs and experiment with them in practice. If the existing situation becomes so intolerable to the beginning teacher that he can no longer be true to his educational values, then he can resign. An extreme step, this should be taken only as the last possible alternative and after seeking the counsel of experienced colleagues and community friends.

12. As has been pointed out, the best insurance of a democratically administered secondary school is the practice of democracy in all aspects of the school. Hence, the most important step the beginning teacher can take is to work democratically and cooperatively with pupils in all his classes, in extraclass activities, in home rooms, and in the community.

13. The beginning teacher should participate in as many community activities as his interest, ability, and time warrant. Such participation will give him status with teachers, administrators, and community adults. It will give him valuable experience in working with others on projects of common concern. These experiences will demonstrate the value of cooperative effort to pupils, teachers, and administrators.

14. There will be many opportunities for the beginning teacher to work democratically with his fellow teachers in schoolwide activities. All high schools have at least a few committees, and new teachers are usually given opportunities to serve. As these committees fulfil their functions, they will demonstrate further the values of shared administrative practices. Most principals will give more and more responsibilities to committees and to the faculty as a whole as they demonstrate their competency.

15. After serving a few months in a high school, a beginning teacher may occasionally find opportunities to suggest tactfully to the principal or superintendent ways of sharing in the formulation of school policies. Such factors as precedent and the personality of the administrator will help determine the strategy of such action. Some opportunities may arise naturally in faculty and committee meetings. Again the beginning teacher may join with one or two experienced teachers in taking suggestions directly to the principal. Finally, if these techniques work, the new teacher may be confident enough to go individually to the administrator when he feels that he has a sound proposal.

SELECTED REFERENCES

ALEXANDER, WILLIAM M., and SAYLOR, J. GALEN. *Secondary Education: Basic Principles and Practices.* New York: Rinehart & Co., Inc., 1950, chap. 9.—An excellent overview of the purposes, agencies, and processes involved in administering the modern high school, together with illustrative practices.

ASSOCIATION FOR SUPERVISION AND CURRICULUM DEVELOPMENT. *Group Processes in Supervision.* Washington, D.C.: National Education Association, 1948, 130 pp.—Valuable for its outstanding discussions of the characteristics of a democratic school and of group processes, with a great number of accounts of group processes in action.

ASSOCIATION FOR SUPERVISION AND CURRICULUM DEVELOPMENT. *Leadership Through Supervision* (1946 Yearbook). Washington, D.C.: National Education Association, 163 pp.—This yearbook gives the status of supervision and presents a wealth of information from an extensive questionnaire study of the goals, practices, problems, and trends. Many valuable illustrations are included.

CASWELL, HOLLIS L. (ed.). *The American High School.* (Eighth Yearbook of the John Dewey Society.) New York: Harper & Bros., 1946, chap. 12.—Deals with the organization and administration of secondary schools. It is a lucid presentation of the democratic approach to supervision and administrative leadership, emphasizing guidance and curriculum improvement.

DOUGLASS, HARL R. (ed.). *Education for Life Adjustment.* New York: The Ronald Press Co., 1950, chap. 15.—A discussion of how faculties work together for in-service growth.

KOOPMAN, G. ROBERT, MIEL, ALICE, and MISNER, PAUL J. *Democracy in School Administration.* New York: Appleton-Century-Crofts, Inc., 1943, 320 pp.—The meaning of democratic school administration and its implications for individual teachers and for teacher groups are well presented.

MELCHOIR, WILLIAM T. *Instructional Supervision.* Boston: D. C. Heath & Co., 1950, 485 pp.—The many concrete illustrations of supervision in practice should be of interest to the beginning teacher. These illustrations show how the teacher can work cooperatively with other teachers, principals, parents, and pupils.

WILES, KIMBALL. *Supervision for Better Schools.* New York: Prentice-Hall, Inc., 1950, 330 pp.—The whole book can be read profitably by pre-service teachers. The stress placed on human relations, leadership, the group process, staff morale, and staff meetings should make the book a helpful one to teachers.

YAUCH, WILBUR A. *Improving Human Relations in School Administration.* New York: Harper & Bros., 1949, 299 pp.—Valuable for its presentation of the concept of democracy in school administration. Although written for elementary school principals, many principles and practices are applicable to the secondary school.

In the United States since about 1890, we have attempted to educate at public expense all the children of all the people. In order to carry out such an ambitious undertaking, local communities and states work together to maintain a public school system. In planning how to educate children and youth, basic policies are established which evolve from a philosophy or belief about the purposes of education. Communities through elective boards of education plan how to operate their schools. The structure or plan which results is the organization of the school. It includes the number and kinds of school units, their interrelationship and articulation, and the plans by which the schools will arrange their programs to educate children and youth. While the organization of the school is the plan or pattern, administration is the process of putting the plan into operation.

The organization of a secondary school is a crucial factor in determining how well it attains its objectives. Little consideration may be given to basic purposes when the organization of a high school is planned and developed. Unfortunately, school organization frequently is not carefully planned but may be determined more or less arbitrarily by school administrators or boards of education and modified neither by changing conditions nor by cooperative faculty thinking. A high school may well operate for years upon practices long outmoded but never critically appraised.

What should be the major criterion by which the organization and administration of a modern high school is evaluated? We believe there is one basic principle: *it must promote maximum pupil growth and development.* School organization exists only to help pupils learn and develop most effectively; it has no other purpose nor function.

Tradition and misconceptions of efficiency have long dictated a mechanical school organization out of harmony both with democracy and conditions promoting pupil growth. Thus, we often find in high schools today that effective pupil growth and learning are handicapped by traditional administrative practices. In this chapter we shall outline desirable principles and practices of organization and administration and point out how a smooth-running mechanical organization may determine the policy of a school, its schedule, length of school period and day, and even the quality of pupil learning.

1. THE PRINCIPLES

The organization of a secondary school should promote the maximum learning for all pupils.

The organization and administration of a high school may become ends in themselves rather than means to the development of sound pupil growth and learning. Principals and teachers often come to cherish mechanical efficiency and precise schedules *in themselves,* rather than considering how they promote or hinder the achievement of desirable pupil behavior. Since learning is the basic goal of schools, all aspects of the school, including its organization and administration, should be judged according to their contribution to the promotion of maximum learning for each pupil.

In planning or evaluating the organization of a modern high school, therefore, we need to consider how it can best promote desirable adolescent growth and development. Does it provide for utilizing pupil-teacher planning and determination of objectives? Does the organization permit active participation in meaningful situations? Does it give basic consideration to adolescent interests and needs? Does it provide the means for carrying principles into social action? Does the day's program make it possible to help youth attain sound emotional adjustment? Can pupils progress in unifying and integrating their learning experiences into broad principles and generalizations? These, then, are aspects of learning which the school organization must promote and enhance. If it does not, then it fails in serving its primary purpose.

The size of the school and the organization of the school day should make it possible for the principal and teachers to know and understand the pupils as individuals.

Basic to learning is the principle of individualization of instruction. In order to plan best to meet the individual interests, needs, and problems of youth, the teacher should have a situation in which he may become well acquainted with each pupil. As we have previously emphasized, learning is both social and individual. The modern high school, therefore, is experimenting with many techniques and plans of organization which permit teachers to know and understand the individual pupil in order to guide his learning most effectively.

Individualizing instruction and learning relates both to school size and class size. In the large high schools of one, two, and three thousand enrollment, it is difficult at best to plan carefully for each pupil. The youth may easily become just a name on the room roll of a given teacher. Plans and programs need to be developed whereby such large schools may be subdivided in order to help teachers know pupils individually and to assist pupils in identifying themselves with and participating more effectively in school activities.

In a typical high school that is organized departmentally, the teacher has five classes with an average of thirty pupils each. How, then, can he possibly know and understand each of the 150 different pupils? How can the teacher teach each as an individual when faced daily with so many different pupils? Is it possible to know the home background, community experiences, work experiences, habits, needs, problems, interests, goals, and plans of 150 growing, changing youth? Surely the organization of the day's work in the modern secondary school must make it possible for the teacher to know and understand each individual if maximum pupil growth and learning are to be achieved.

The modern high school should be organized so that a wide variety of learning experiences may be provided.

As we have shown in earlier chapters, functional learning requires a wide variety of direct and vicarious pupil experiences. Hence the modern high school should be organized to provide adequately for many kinds of learning situations. The typical forty-five- or fifty-five-minute period, each with a different teacher, makes difficult—if not impossible—the flexibility necessary to provide many kinds of vital learning experiences.

The school day should consist of periods sufficiently long to permit the use of field trips, excursions, community surveys and study, work experience, interviews, resource visitors, audio-visual materials, laboratory work, and panel discussions. Classes need to be scheduled so that two or more groups may occasionally work together on a common project. Then, too, the organization of classes needs to be sufficiently flexible to permit two or more teachers to work with a single group of pupils when learning situations require their joint effort.

The school organization should make possible the scheduling of classes which may relate the work of different subject matter departments.

As long as high school classes are scheduled for a single period according to subject matter, certain desirable learning experiences will be handicapped and curtailed. Some kinds of desirable learnings can well be achieved within this traditional framework; other learning experiences cannot be so developed.

It is possible to schedule several different classes for a given group of pupils to work under the guidance of two or more teachers in adjacent classrooms. These teachers can plan their work together so that the pupils can relate information learned in different classes. Sometimes it is possible to schedule two consecutive periods with one able teacher so that in studying such problems as the conservation of forests, the class could use social, historical, economic, scientific, industrial, and literary information in seeking possible solutions. When a teacher is competent to guide pupils in this kind of broad learning, maximum growth results. High school organization needs to facilitate such pupil experience.

The development of functional study habits and learning skills must be facilitated by the school program.

Modern secondary education is based upon the assumption that the pupil is increasingly able to direct his own learning. We must recognize, however, that pupils differ markedly in their mastery of study habits and skills, and that each high school teacher has the responsibility for furthering this process. This means, for example, that the mathematics teacher should likewise be a teacher of reading and spelling.

In the typical high school, study habits and skills are largely assumed, and the pupil is supposed to work independently in study halls and at home. There is much evidence that this system fails to secure maximum learning or the further development of important skills. Most authorities agree that poorly supervised study periods and unsupervised home work are largely wasteful, if not actually harmful.

Modern high school organization, however, permits the teacher to diagnose the learning problems of pupils and to give adequate time to help them directly in improving their study skills. When the teacher has a longer period to work with pupils, he can understand them more completely and assist them more directly in improving their work habits. These habits and skills are more functional, too, when learned directly in relation to class problems.

The organization of the high school should make it possible for all pupils to participate in the total program of the school.

The organization of the total school day should be carefully planned so that all pupils may be able to participate in all aspects of the program of the school—extraclass as well as class activities. As we pointed out in Chapter 10, there should be no sharp distinction between these two kinds of pupil experiences. The so-called "extra-curriculars" actually are part of the curriculum if they help pupils in achieving the goals of the school. Hence, no barriers should be erected which might prevent the equal participation of pupils in all vital aspects of the entire program of the secondary school.

When extraclass activities are held after school, transportation by school bus and part-time employment combine to prevent many pupils from engaging in these activities. The total program of the school day needs to be so planned that *all activities* are programmed within the regular school day.

2. SOME TYPICAL PRACTICES

The principles discussed above indicate that the administration and organization of a high school exist only as a means of insuring that desirable pupil growth will take place. Are secondary schools today meeting this dynamic criterion? Are they organized and administered in such a way that maximum pupil growth and development will occur? Is the mechanical organization of the high school a means to the end of more effective learning, or does it become an end in itself? For answers to these and other questions regarding high school organization today, an examination of some common practices in typical American secondary schools will be made.

Fragmented High School Class Periods.—The typical high school today is organized upon a subject matter, departmentalized basis. Class periods are relatively short, and pupils change classrooms and teachers several times during a day. There is often little continuity or correlation between the subjects studied throughout the day. The following examples illustrate some of these problems.

Blank City High School with an enrollment of about fifteen hundred pupils in Grades 10, 11, and 12, is located in a city of thirty thousand. A considerable number of pupils are transported by school bus, although the great majority live in the city proper. School opens at 8:45 A.M., with a five-minute period immediately following for roll-taking. The first class begins at 8:50; each period is fifty minutes in length, with three-minute intermissions for class changing. Two periods in the middle of the day are five minutes shorter. At 11:30 half the student body has a forty-five-minute lunch period; the other half at 12:15. Afternoon classes begin at one o'clock, with dismissal time at 3:40 P.M. Most pupils have two study hall periods. Practically all extraclass activities take place after school.

Townville Junior-Senior High School with an enrollment of 250 pupils is located in a small village with a population of twelve hundred. One third of the pupils are transported by bus; the remainder live in the village. School opens at 8:45 A.M. with a home room period of a half hour. Each teacher has thirty pupils for typical home room and guidance activities. Three fifty-five-minute periods follow, which include class changing time. Lunch for all pupils is from 12:00 to 1:00. Two one-hour periods make up the afternoon program. A few organized activities occur during the noon period, but most are held after school. Most pupils have one study hall period; a few have classes all five periods.

Rural Union High School, a four-year secondary school located in a rural area, has only sixty-five pupils. Practically all arrive on buses; many ride twelve miles to school. School does not open until 9:00 A.M., and there are four morning classes, each forty-five minutes in length. Since there is no lunchroom, pupils bring lunches, eat in their room quickly, and have thirty to forty minutes for play and extraclass activities. Afternoon classes begin at 1:00, extend for forty-five minutes, with school closing at 3:15 P.M. Most pupils have two study periods. No organized activities are held after school except basketball practice just prior to the county tournament.

Although the pattern varies somewhat in each of these three schools, basically it is similar. Class periods range from forty-five to sixty minutes, each terminated by the traditional bell-ringing or buzzer signal. Pupils move on schedule from one teacher to another, each of whom teaches his subject, with little if any correlation between the subjects. Pupils must establish their own relationships and integration if any are to be made. Teachers often plan within their departments but infrequently between departments.

A majority of schools do not have home rooms of a half hour or more in length. Extraclass activities are either offered hurriedly at noon or, more leisurely, after school for those pupils fortunate enough to be able to remain. *Does this typical kind of high school organization promote maximum pupil learning and development?*

High Schools Organized Around Subjects.—The average high school today is one organized into subject matter departments, i.e., English, social studies, science, mathematics, physical education, and others. Such an organization assumes that learning is best accomplished through studying those bodies of logically arranged disciplines as determined and classified by scholars. These subject matter disciplines are then reorganized professionally for use with secondary school youth. For example, the social science disciplines, such as history, geography, political science, sociology, and economics, become the social studies in the modern high school. Similarly, English and American literature, speech, and composition become the language arts curriculum.

Even though the teaching areas in secondary school are fairly broad, and the specialization not as narrow as in scholarly research, there must still be departmentalization if this plan of organization is followed in high school. Since the large majority of high schools still have a subject organization, they find departmental teaching necessary.

High Pupil-Teacher Ratios.—Departmental teaching means that a teacher usually is a type of specialist and teaches his subject to a large number of different pupils. For example, an English teacher often teaches five different classes of English. With an average class load of thirty, he meets a total of 150 different pupils per day—not counting those he may have in study hall, home room, or extraclass activities. Inevitably, the very nature of the organization itself assumes considerable if not greater emphasis upon subjects than upon pupils.

In high schools of five hundred or over, departmental teaching increases markedly the pupil load for each teacher. Teachers typically prefer to teach not just "English," but often seek to have only "English II and III." The larger the school and the more teachers in each department, the greater the specialization. Since it is unlikely that a given teacher will teach the same boy or girl in two different classes, the total number of different pupils that he teaches each day will be correspondingly greater. In addition, pupils may change teachers at the end of one semester.

In high schools with enrollments of two hundred or less, most teachers have two or more subjects. In such schools they may have the same pupils in two or more classes, thereby reducing their total pupil load considerably.

In the average high school, teachers are not likely to have fewer than a hundred different pupils per day; a few teachers may have the responsibility of two hundred. As has previously been emphasized, this situation makes extremely difficult the task of understanding adequately the individual pupil. With all the variation in abilities, problems, and interests, the task of knowing well so many rapidly changing youth seems impossible. An ever increasing number of high schools sense this problem and are experimenting with techniques for reducing the heavy pupil load.

A Relatively Short School Day.—The length of the high school day in the United States has traditionally been six hours, exclusive of the lunch period. Just as typical for many years was the plan of four morning and afternoon periods of forty-five minutes each. Until World War II, the average high school opened at about 9:00 A.M. and classes ended at approximately 4:00 P.M.

Within the past decade there has been a definite trend toward lengthening class periods and shortening the total school day. Fifty-five- to sixty-minute periods are now fairly common, as is the five-period day. Noon periods are much shorter than formerly. In certain sections of the nation, the end of the high school day is 2:30 P.M., in some schools—particularly in the East—even as early as 1:30 P.M.

Although the early closing time is supposed to give pupils an opportunity for working at part-time jobs in the afternoon, there is usually no relation of such work to the school as a part of the educational program. Moreover, many pupils do not have jobs and, unless the school provides recreational programs for this time, they either help at home, loaf, or enter into other community activities—good or bad. The theory that this time should be used for homework is well evidenced by the heavy assignments so labeled, but is not sound educational practice. The result is often a development of poor study habits or a type of class session which is of the lesson-hearing variety. The extraclass activity is usually relegated to an "after school" position. The secondary schools that carry on this practice will sooner or later answer to the public why they are not taking their responsibility for youth in a complete, well-rounded educational program. The taxpayer is very likely to question how his tax dollar is spent.

Large Study Halls.—The typical study hall with a large number of pupils to be supervised by one teacher still exists in a number of secondary schools, although many secondary school people are convinced that it is not effective as a device to promote study. The teacher in charge can be of little assistance to many pupils in the study hall, since they work on different subjects and usually the group consists of fifty or more. To the teacher who has seen much service in supervising study halls, they represent a "policing" situation where there is often little reference material at hand and more temptations to talk than incentives to study.

More and more schools are eliminating study hall periods and incorporating supervised study into the work period of the regular class. This change is a genuine improvement, removing a long-standing source of "headaches" for teachers as well as a source of poor habits and behavior for generations of adolescents.

Large Proportion of Relatively Small High Schools.—The 25,000 odd public high schools in America today vary in size from the small rural school of twenty to the complex large city institution of over five thousand. Even in the face of rapid consolidation and reorganization of rural districts throughout the nation, nearly half of the secondary schools still enroll one hundred or fewer pupils. About 15 per cent enroll more than five hundred, while nearly 8 per cent have more than one thousand pupils. City high schools, although they include only about 10 per cent of the total number of secondary schools, nevertheless enroll considerably more than half of the total pupils. Less than 30 per cent of all pupils, on the other hand, still attend small town and rural high schools of fewer than fifty enrollment.

Many problems result from these extremes of secondary school size, yet agreement as to what is optimum size is difficult to discover among authorities. It can readily be seen that a high school of less than one hundred enrollment can hardly have a rich and varied program, adequate equipment, and adequate staff. On the other hand, gigantic city institutions which attempt to coordinate the development of thousands of pupils within a single school face an impossible task. Many of these large high schools seem to operate efficiently, but few would claim for them the best environment conducive to democratic pupil growth.

Reorganization to Include Junior High School and Junior College.—After the introduction of the first junior high school in 1910, many types of reorganized school units were tried at various places throughout the nation. This reorganization resulted from long study and thinking about the functions of American elementary and secondary schools. In order to make the curriculum more interesting and meaningful, to provide for more guidance, to plan an environment more in line with the principles of adolescent psychology, and to reduce the pupil mortality between grades eight and nine, the junior high school came into being.

The first type of experimental organization was the six-two-four plan, including in the junior high only grades seven and eight. This plan was rapidly replaced by the six-three-three division in which grades seven, eight, and nine became the junior high school and ten, eleven, and twelve the senior high school. Six-six plans, which combined the junior and senior high school, became common, especially in small towns. Basic psychological and physical facts seemed to favor the six-three-three organization, with a relatively distinct junior high school as a transition unit. Hence—though only very approximately—the elementary school would contain the physically immature; the junior high school, the maturing; and the senior high school, the mature groups of pupils.

Since 1900, we have also had the interesting rise and growth of the junior college. Usually organized as a separate two-year institution, it has served both as the first two years of college and as terminal general and vocational education. More recently the junior college has been considered as a part of secondary education—the thirteenth and fourteenth years of general education. Hence came the growth of the idea of a new plan of organization in which the senior high or upper school would include grades eleven, twelve, thirteen, and fourteen. Most secondary education authorities favor this plan today. There are now thirty-seven junior colleges thus organized.

Departmentalization in Junior High Schools.—The modern junior high school has adequately met many of its declared objectives. It has offered more activities, provided more centralized guidance services, eliminated certain duplications in subjects, and has helped to increase the holding power of secondary education. But in many instances it has offset these gains by overemphasizing preparation for high school, interscholastic athletics, and departmental specialization of subject matter.

The seventh grade pupil, usually immature, has frequently been plunged into a high school pattern of departmental teaching before he can adjust to the sudden change from the elementary school. Even though most of his courses carry the caption of "general," they are often taught by high school teachers representing departmental specialization. More serious, he is thrown into a welter of ringing bells, changing rooms, classes, and teachers, often with no real home room. If the school is large, he may not find any one teacher who really knows him well. The security of feeling that he belongs to a group, as in the elementary school, is often shattered by the size and complexity of the organization with its shifting class periods.

As will be pointed out in the next section, it is possible to keep the desirable features of the junior high school and yet remedy its major weaknesses.

Extent of Reorganization.—It is difficult to secure figures accurate for any specific time, and the wide variation in types increases the difficulty. About 40 per cent of American high schools, with an enrollment of nearly 60 per cent of the secondary school population, have undergone reorganization to a more or less major degree. A majority of the small high schools of the nation still are not reorganized. The six-six plan is most popular in small town schools since it permits the maximum sharing of faculty, building, and equipment. In cities, the six-three-three type predominates, and the trend is still toward that plan. The six-four-four organization is slowly gaining favor.

3. Practices in the Better Secondary Schools

There are several high schools that are experimenting with new ways of organizing the school, the day's schedule, and the activities within the school in order to achieve a better learning situation for their pupils. Illustrations are drawn from schools in different parts of the country, both medium-sized and large high schools. The illustrations show how the larger high school can be organized internally to provide some of the advantages of a smaller school.

Programs Permitting Teachers to Understand Pupils More Adequately.—In the Floodwood, Minnesota, Community Junior and Senior High School the daily schedule is so arranged that pupils remain in one room with the same teacher for three consecutive periods in the seventh grade and for two periods in the eighth, ninth, and tenth grades. In the seventh grade, the pupils take English, social science, geography, and science with the same teacher, within the consecutive three-period block. In the eighth grade, pupils are with the same teacher for English and social science in consecutive periods; in the ninth and tenth grades, world history is followed by English with the same teacher. This plan has varied somewhat from year to year. At present, the separate subjects are named within this block of time. At one time, Grades 7 through 12 had a three-hour block of time called "general education."

In the Red Wing, Minnesota, High School, there is a core program for a two-hour block of time daily for all pupils in the junior and senior high school.

In the Folwell Junior High School, Minneapolis, Minnesota, the curriculum is organized on the core basis, called a "common learnings program." Each "common learnings" teacher has a single group of pupils for at least two hours in which instruction in English and social science is combined. Each teacher teaches one class group for two hours in the morning and another similar afternoon group. The fifth period for these teachers is set aside for pupil personnel work, for parent conferences, and for developing units and teaching materials with other teachers. Pupils have departmental teachers for arithmetic, science, typing, industrial arts, home economics, art, physical education, and music. The principal of this junior high school reports that by this organization— [1]

1. We have a core of teachers who have fewer pupils. The core teacher has the responsibility of knowing and understanding each child in his classroom.
2. We endeavor to interest more pupils through meeting their needs and interests. Units of work at each grade level have been added to the content. We do more than follow a textbook. Pupils are given more opportunities to participate. Excursions are possible because of the two-hour period.
3. Teachers are given time to hold parent conferences without interruption.
4. Teachers are provided an opportunity to work and share with other teachers in the building.

In the Jefferson Junior High School of Long Beach, California, the seventh, eighth, and ninth grades each has a daily program which includes a double period for a course called social living. This is a core program which has replaced the former social studies and English courses. The schedule is given on page 386.

In each of the programs described above, teachers work with a given group of pupils for more than a single class period. These programs occupy from one and one-half to three hours of time daily. These schools have been able to reduce their pupil-teacher ratio markedly, since one teacher works for more than one period with a class group. Such an organization of the school day illustrates several of the principles given at the beginning of this chapter: it enables teachers to understand individual pupils better, it makes possible a wide variety of learning experiences, and it permits the correlation or integration of different subjects.

[1] Malcolm B. Keck, *A Personalized Program to Improve Instruction and Human Relations* (Common Learnings in Folwell Junior High School) (mimeographed), Minneapolis: Folwell Junior High School, 1950.

NINTH GRADE COMPOSITE PROGRAM—Jefferson Junior High School, Long Beach, California

Period	REQUIRED COURSES*								ELECTIVES
	A	B	C	D	E	F	G	H	
1	Social Living	Social Living	Social Living	Social Living	Social Living		Social Living	Social Living	General Mathematics Mechanical Drawing Clothing 1b-1a Woodworking II Printing Typing I Art
2	Social Living	Social Living	Social Living	Social Living	Social Living				General Mathematics Business Practice 1st Year Science Reading Woodworking I Typing I Art Senior Orchestra
3	Social Living		Physical Education		Physical Education		Social Living	Physical Education	General Mathematics Foods 1b General Mechanics II Clothing 1b Boys' Glee Club Typing I B Orthography G Exploratory Language
4	Social Living	Physical Education				Physical Education	Social Living	Social Living	2d Year Science Spanish Business Practice Printing Home Arts
5							Physical Education		Agriculture
6	Physical Education		Physical Education	Social Living		Social Living			General Mathematics Business Practice Reading Orthography G B 8th Glee Club Printing Typing I
7				Social Living		Social Living			Girls' Glee Club Speech & Dramatics Business Practice 2d Year Science Woodworking II General Mechanics I

* A given group of pupils takes the required courses, social living and physical education, in the periods indicated under the letter columns. For example, if they were scheduled in Section A, they would have social living the third and fourth periods and physical education the sixth period. These pupils would then choose suitable elective subjects to complete their program from those elective courses offered in the first, second, and seventh periods.

The core program at West Junior High School, Kansas City, Missouri, called "common learnings," permits each of the common learnings teachers to work with one group of pupils for two and a half hours in the morning and another group for a similar time in the afternoon. Each of these teachers has an open period for conferences and planning with other teachers. Guidance, planning, field trips, and all-school projects have been facilitated by this organization. Each period is fifty-five minutes except the first, which is sixty-five minutes to allow for administrative aspects of the usual home room. It should be obvious that such a core program takes over the home room functions.

In this high school, there are six common learnings groups in each of Grades 7, 8, and 9. The seventh grade schedule [2] below is illustrative of the organization of all three grades:

SEVENTH GRADE PROGRAM
West Junior High School, Kansas City, Missouri

Periods	Group A	Group B	Group C	Group D	Group E	Group F
I	Art Music	Arithmetic	Physical Education Health	Art Music	Arithmetic	Physical Education Health
II	Common Learnings	Common Learnings	Common Learnings	Arithmetic	Art Music	Art Music
III	Common Learnings	Common Learnings	Common Learnings	Physical Education Health	Physical Education Health	Homemaking Industrial Arts
IV	Common Learnings Lunch	Common Learnings Lunch	Common Learnings Lunch	Homemaking Industrial Arts	Homemaking Industrial Arts	Arithmetic
V	Physical Education Health	Physical Education Health	Arithmetic	Lunch Common Learnings	Lunch Common Learnings	Lunch Common Learnings
VI	Arithmetic	Art Music	Art Music	Common Learnings	Common Learnings	Common Learnings
VII	Homemaking Industrial Arts	Homemaking Industrial Arts	Homemaking Industrial Arts	Common Learnings	Common Learnings	Common Learnings

[2] Roscoe V. Cramer, "The Common Learnings Program and Its Evaluation In West Junior High School," *Minnesota Journal of Education*, 30 (April, 1950), 26-27, and "Organization of the Common Learnings Program," *Minnesota Journal of Education*, 30 (March, 1950), 29-30.

Extraclass Activities as a Part of the Day's Schedule.—The Abraham Lincoln High School of San José, California, has developed a flexible daily schedule which brings the activities program into the regular school day. This plan permits maximum pupil participation and adequate faculty supervision. It also provides for assemblies, student government, clubs, and other meetings, as well as for shortening the school day without disturbing regular classes. The following schedule [3] indicates the organization of this program:

Daily Periods	Tenth Grade	Eleventh Grade	Twelfth Grade	
Conference Period	PRE-PERIOD—for individual guidance and instruction—optional or required			*REQUIRED* for General education
1	HEALTH AND PHYSICAL EDUCATION			
2	SOCIAL STUDIES	SOCIAL STUDIES	SOCIAL STUDIES	
3	ENGLISH	ENGLISH		*ELECTIVES* Interests— avocational and vocational— including a fifth subject or study period
4	LIFE SCIENCE			
5	CURRICULAR ELECTIVES			
6				
7	CO-CURRICULAR ELECTIVES (government, assemblies, clubs and other activities)			

Abraham Lincoln High School Daily Schedule.

The pre-period or conference period, from 8:00 to 8:30 A.M., enables the faculty and counselors to provide individual assistance to pupils and also gives them opportunity to carry on class committee work. This period is optional, except for pupils who are deficient in their work.

The seventh or activity period is of the same length as the other periods. It actually is a "floating period" and may be scheduled in between any other periods or at the beginning or end of a school day. Announcement of the daily scheduling is made through the faculty bulletin board and the principal's bulletin to the pupils. The

[3] Frederic T. Shipp, "A Flexible Daily Schedule for a Modern High School," *American School Board Journal,* 3 (October, 1945), 58.

following list [4] indicates how the "floating period" is used without interrupting or eliminating the regular subject periods:

1. Before first period to collect materials for the Red Cross.
2. Registration period for enrollment purposes or for the issuance of report cards.
3. Extension of second period for war bond organization and drive.
4. Assembly between the second and third periods.
5. Clubs between fifth and sixth periods.
6. Excusing the entire school an hour earlier to attend a cross-town baseball game.
7. On an average of twice each week there is no all-school activity for this special period. This floating period then becomes an "S" (for "study") period and a subject period is repeated, in rotation.

When the "floating period" becomes an "S" (study) period, a regular class subject period is either repeated or else comes later in the day. The "S period" is informal and permits supervised study and individual conferences. It also allows time for the weekly meeting of the student government group, for committees, and for class meetings and other groups while the remainder of the school continues its classwork. As a result, over a semester class periods gain additional time, averaging fifty-five rather than the scheduled fifty minutes.

Watertown Senior High School, Watertown, South Dakota, has a somewhat similar plan for home rooms, activities, and schoolwide meetings. The sixth period daily is scheduled exclusively as an activities period; all kinds of school activities (all supervised) are held during this period. In addition, a so-called "interim period" of thirty-five minutes daily is scheduled between two of the morning classes. Home rooms are regularly held twice a week during this period; otherwise it is reserved for pupil and faculty committees and for any kind of schoolwide meeting. Such an organization prevents interruption of classes, provides for home rooms, brings activities into the curriculum, and allows some relatively free time for the faculty to engage in curriculum improvement.

Home Room Teachers and Counselors Scheduled with Groups for Longer Periods.—Another procedure for achieving the teacher's understanding of pupils so necessary to good instruction and guidance is to schedule the home room teacher to stay with a group of pupils

---

[4] Shipp, *op. cit.*, p. 56.

for two to four years. Provision would need to be made for adequate time for the home room in the day's schedule. This plan is in operation in some schools which have found that it could be put into effect without too much difficulty, particularly where teachers are interested in guidance. In some schools, the home room teacher is assigned to teach the home room group for a period a day in addition to his work with them during the home room period. Scheduling this period next to the home room period has made possible some activities comparable to those in the core program.

More frequent is the policy of scheduling a specialized counselor to retain the same counseling group throughout the years they are in the secondary school. This is done especially in large high schools that have such specialized services.

Schools Within a School.—In attempting to gain some of the advantages of the small secondary schools, the William A. Bass High School of Atlanta, Georgia, has spent over twelve years in evolving a radical departure in secondary school organization. The basic purpose is the building of more "wholesome relationships between teacher and student, teacher and teacher, teacher and parent, student and parent, student and student." [5]

Previous to 1947, when the five-year community high school program absorbed the junior high school organization, the William A. Bass Junior High School was divided into nine little "schools," three in each grade, with an average enrollment of approximately one hundred and sixty pupils in each little school. The total school had an enrollment of about fifteen hundred pupils.

In adapting the idea to the five-year high school, William A. Bass High School (grades eight through twelve), each of the five grades was organized as a little school with an enrollment of approximately two hundred and twenty pupils in each unit, divided into six to eight heterogeneous sections. Each little school has its own separate faculties, teaching the same group of pupils. The staff includes the chairman of the little school, the co-chairman, and a part-time counselor. The pupils elect a president of their little school, and the general P.T.A. president appoints a parent chairman.

Each little school operates relatively independently as a unit within the total school community. Staff, parents, and pupils jointly plan a program within the general curriculum framework, arrange their own assemblies, activities, parent meetings, and the like. The little

---

[5] W. Joe Scott and Others, *The Little School,* Atlanta, Georgia: Atlanta Public Schools, 1947, p. 1.

school, therefore, functions more or less as a small high school with an enrollment of approximately two hundred and twenty; it does, however, have the advantage of the many specialists, specially equipped rooms, and resources available only to a larger school. Teachers of art, music, physical education, home economics, and industrial arts serve all the little schools.[6]

At least twice each week, when pupils are engaged in work with special teachers, the regular staff has a planning and conference meeting. These conferences may involve teachers, pupils, and parents. Monthly, the respective little school staffs and parents come together to discuss informally their plans and problems. Much of the school guidance program stems from these meetings, which may become clinical situations discussing problem cases. The parent chairmen of the little schools have a monthly luncheon at the school to exchange ideas, to plan, and to evaluate.

In order to unify the little schools within the framework of the total school community, the principal appoints a chairman and a co-chairman for each unit; these chairmen compose the principal's cabinet. The cabinet meets biweekly and determines policies, organizes schoolwide activities, and promotes school and community understandings. Parent relationships are similarly coordinated through the parent chairmen of the little schools serving as members of the executive committee of the P.T.A. The P.T.A. president serves as representative to the principal's cabinet for matters of community interest. The total school is unified further through an elective student council composed of the respective pupil presidents of each little school. The student council president often appears before the principal's cabinet to present matters and problems of common interest.

Consolidation of Small Rural High Schools.—Small high schools, especially those with an enrollment of less than a hundred, tend to offer relatively limited educational opportunities to their pupils. This condition may result from inadequately trained teachers, the inability to offer a rich program, a lack of such specialized services as guidance and health, fewer school activities, and frequently poor or inadequate equipment and supplies. Consequently, educational leaders have long recommended that small rural high schools be consolidated into larger institutions in order to offer more effective educational programs for youth.

Many states are rapidly enlarging the size of their educational

---

[6] *Ibid.*, pp. 1-2.

units through permissive legislation which results in the reorganization of local school districts. Such legislation has already made possible the elimination of hundreds of small high schools and the development of larger and more efficient secondary schools. Washington, Colorado, Illinois, and Minnesota, for example, are states in which this movement has been accelerated in recent years. As a result, modern high schools have been developed, adequate in size to permit the organization of sound educational programs. Mt. Baker-Union High School in Deming, Washington, for example, now has an enrollment of 450; this school transports pupils as far as twenty-three miles and now includes in its enrollment young people who formerly attended four small rural high schools.

Some states, too, have developed the county educational unit, with a single senior high school serving the entire county. Minnesota has two county high school units, Lake and Cook counties. Grand Marais High School in Cook County enrolls 154 pupils; Two Harbors High School in Lake County has 450 pupils.

Block Scheduling to Achieve Cooperative Planning.—Schools that do not provide opportunities for teachers to work with one group of pupils longer than one period are using a form of scheduling that permits cooperative planning among a group of teachers responsible for the same group of pupils. Shumway Junior High School, Vancouver, Washington, for example, has secured flexibility and cooperative planning through "block scheduling." Blocks of 150 pupils are grouped together under a social studies, language arts, and mathematics teacher, and are assigned adjoining rooms. The groups have a concurrent planning period. Although each subject retains its identity, the social studies units serve as centers of class activities. The teachers of each block or group of pupils plan their work together and secure special help from the art, music, and home economics teachers. Considerable emphasis is given to diagnostic work, to case study techniques, and to guidance. Pupils and parents are asked to come for occasional conferences. As a result of this scheduling for cooperative planning and work, pupils are making good progress in attaining the goals of the school.[7]

Organization of Special Services to Facilitate Pupil Growth.—

The High School Library. Every first class high school has its own central library directed by a well-trained librarian and cooperating with the public library. High school libraries are ordinarily

[7] William H. Dunn, "The Whole Child in the Whole School," *College of Education Record,* 16 (December, 1949), 27-30.

financed and controlled by local school boards, and they naturally fall under the administration of the school superintendent and principal.

There is a great scarcity of school librarians today; hence the beginning teacher may find that he does not have the opportunity of working with a trained person in this important activity. Large city high schools always employ experienced librarians to assist in guiding and stimulating the learning of their pupils. Smaller high schools frequently have part-time teacher-librarians who typically spend from one to three periods daily working in the library. Too often, no school time is assigned to any person for library work. For example, in a recent study sponsored by the secondary school principals' organization, made for the Governor's Fact Finding Commission in Connecticut, it was found that of schools under 250 in the state, 77 per cent had no school time assigned to librarians.[8] Beginning English and social studies teachers in very small schools may find that they are given the additional responsibility of serving as librarian in addition to teaching a full class load. Few accredited high schools today fail to have an organized library, although in many the facilities and services are wholly inadequate.

The library serves an important function in the instructional program of the modern high school. It provides materials for laboratory work in classrooms, references for individual and group research on units, stimulation for recreational reading, and materials for various schoolwide service programs and agencies. Schools organized upon forty-five minute periods provide opportunities for library reading and study throughout the day. One-hour periods provide fewer opportunities to work and read in the library; hence the central library must service classroom groups more carefully with books and learning materials of all kinds. In this plan of organization, all teachers must work closely with the librarian in order to plan the most effective use of materials.[9]

In addition to the activities described above, the librarian has the responsibilities of selecting and ordering books and other materials, organizing them for most effective use by pupils and teachers, making known the total informational resources of the community, and instructing pupils in their use.

---

[8] From a mimeographed bulletin, *Preliminary Report of Findings in a Survey of 106 Connecticut Secondary Schools,* 1950. (Compiled by Kimball Wiles of New York University.)

[9] G. H. Reavis, "Relations of Superintendents and Principals to the Library," *The Library in General Education* (Part II, Forty-Second Yearbook), National Society for the Study of Education, Chicago: University of Chicago Press, 1943, chap 9.

In high schools where trained assistance is limited, pupils take a large share of responsibility under the guidance of the librarian. Many schools with full or part-time librarians make good use of the library as a resource for valuable learning experiences through having pupils serve as assistants. Some have library clubs for this purpose.

The School Lunchroom. The school lunch program is a valuable part of the total educational program of many modern high schools. It helps develop good nutritional habits, socialization, cooperation, social graces, and responsibility. The beginning teacher will find that well-organized lunchrooms are a real asset to his work, no matter what his responsibilities may be.

The superintendent and principal have the basic responsibility for initiating a school lunch service. Many high schools today have a school-community lunch committee which serves the following functions: [10]

1. Planning to make the lunchroom attractive
2. Suggesting standards for manners
3. Publicizing the lunch program
4. Planning exhibits and posters of good lunches
5. Checking the kinds of lunches eaten in order to build a program to meet the needs discovered
6. Giving pupils experiences in planning menus, buying food, and preparing and serving food
7. Working with the school garden committee to plan foods to be produced for school lunches.

In small high schools, the home economics teacher frequently is appointed to manage the lunchroom, while larger high schools often have a trained dietitian as lunchroom manager. Such a manager may have faculty status, since she holds an important responsibility. She plans menus and sees that good food is secured, prepared, and served. She also plans work schedules, prepares budgets, and keeps accounts. She works closely with the school lunch committee, teachers, and pupils in achieving the goals of the program.

High school pupils often are employed to work in the lunchroom. Good school lunchroom programs never exploit the services of their pupils, but remunerate them adequately and attempt to make their experiences educational. A growing number of schools consider

---

[10] Adapted from *School Lunch Management,* Nutrition Education Series, Federal Security Agency, Office of Education, Pamphlet No. 3, Washington, D.C.: Government Printing Office, 1944, p. 2.

the lunch period as an important educational period, not just a place and time to eat. Pupils take responsibility for the lunchroom and serve in various capacities. Especially in some junior high schools is the lunchroom tied in with teaching good nutrition in the classroom.

Audio-Visual Services. The beginning teacher in a modern high school is able to utilize many audio-visual teaching aids in his instructional program. In some small high schools he will not find much organized material, while in other schools he will be able to use a great variety of teaching aids.

The superintendent or principal has the responsibility for setting up a planned program for the use of audio-visual aids in the high school. In small high schools, the administrator usually appoints as part-time audio-visual coordinator an interested and qualified teacher who is given some time freed from teaching and other responsibilities for this work. In large high schools, the coordinator may be a well-trained, full-time specialist in audio-visual education. In either case, additional interested and competent teachers serve in previewing and annotating films and in producing audio-visual aids. Many secondary schools have a teacher advisory committee to assist in determining policies and in planning the total program of audio-visual education.

Many high schools today have an audio-visual center of at least one room for making repairs and keeping equipment, supplies, and catalogs. Teachers and pupils are sometimes taught how to operate projectors and recorders in this center, which also serves as headquarters for audio-visual clubs. These clubs provide recreation, hobby, and service functions for interested high school pupils. With pupils operating projectors, the teacher is free to concentrate upon the actual learning process. In a recent study, 80 per cent of the responding schools used pupil operators for 16-mm. sound movie projectors.[11]

4. First Steps

What can teachers and administrators do to organize their high school to promote learning more effectively? How may the principles outlined at the beginning of this chapter be implemented? What part does the classroom teacher play in helping improve the organization

---

[11] L. C. Larson, "Suggested Answers to Some Pertinent Questions in the Audio-Visual Field," *Audio-Visual Materials of Instruction* (Part I, Forty-Eighth Yearbook), National Society for the Study of Education, Chicago: University of Chicago Press, 1949, chap. 11, p. 236.

of a high school? Some of the answers to these questions have been discussed throughout this chapter. In this section are suggested certain basic first steps to be taken in improving the organization of any high school—be it large or small.

1. The school day and class period can be gradually extended in order to bring the various school activities into the regular daily program. Lengthening the class periods will reduce the necessity for study halls and will provide time for real supervised study in smaller, more natural class groups. Lengthening the school day will provide an activity period and a home room period.

2. A first step that can usually be taken without too much difficulty is to provide for an activity period within the day's schedule. Teachers who are responsible for activities ought to work for such a plan if they find that some pupils are being denied equal opportunities to participate because school activities are held after school.

3. The daily program can be arranged so that all teachers who work with a given section, group, or grade can plan their work together. For example, in Grade 9 those who teach mathematics, English, general science, and social studies to a particular group of pupils could then meet regularly to discuss their common problems, plans, requirements, and evaluation. In this way the work of the pupils can be coordinated and related. Learning difficulties of individual pupils can be considered clinically and more carefully than is possible through individual effort.

4. It is possible to arrange the program so that pupils will have their home room period followed by a class taught by their home room sponsor. Home room periods are often too short and serve purely administrative purposes. By scheduling them prior to a class taught by the home room teacher, a more flexible arrangement of work and activities can be made.

5. In order that a teacher may have fewer pupils with whom to become acquainted, such related subjects as history and geography can be taught during consecutive periods by the same teacher. The teacher can request such a schedule for himself. After considerable planning and experimenting, these related subjects might be fused within a single or double period.

6. After careful experimentation with combining such subjects as geography and history, one or two teachers are often willing to try to combine two other and less closely related subjects. Frequently, English and social studies are combined, or at least closely

correlated within a double period. The curricular implications and characteristics of the core program have been discussed in Chapters 6 and 8.

7. In large city high schools, teachers, parents, pupils, and administrators can cooperatively plan to subdivide the school into smaller groups in some type of plan such as "schools within a school." Such a program requires concerted planning and careful experimentation. It involves the exclusive use of certain teachers with "little school" groups of pupils, while other more specialized teachers (such as art and music) work with pupils in several different "little schools." This plan requires maximum cooperation between parents and faculty, as well as careful coordination of the "little schools" into the larger school community. It combines the strength of a small, compact school with the greater resources and specialized services and facilities of a large secondary institution. Such a school plan of organization has much to commend it for our consideration in attempting to individualize the learning experiences for youth today.

SELECTED REFERENCES

ALEXANDER, WILLIAM M., and SAYLOR, J. GALEN. *Secondary Education: Basic Principles and Practices.* New York: Rinehart & Co., Inc., 1950, chap. 8.—Contains information on the organization of the secondary school, size of secondary schools, and types of secondary schools.

BENT, RUDYARD K., and KRONENBERG, HENRY H. *Principles of Secondary Education.* (2nd ed.) New York: McGraw-Hill Book Co., Inc., 1949, chaps. 1, 4, 5.—Contains a good deal of information on statistical data relating to size and types of secondary schools and extent of reorganization of secondary education.

DOUGLASS, HARL R. (ed.). *The High School Curriculum.* New York: The Ronald Press Co., 1947, chaps. 14, 18.—Both chapters contain some discussion of organizational aspects of the school as they relate to curriculum.

DOUGLASS, HARL R. *Organization and Administration of Secondary Schools.* New York: Ginn & Co., 1945, chaps. 1, 6.—These two chapters are specially pertinent: "Types of Secondary School Organization" and "Constructing the School Schedule."

GRUHN, WILLIAM T., and DOUGLASS, HARL R. *The Modern Junior High School.* New York: The Ronald Press Co., 1947, chaps. 2, 4, 15.—Deals with grade organization, the length of the school day and period, and the school schedule as applied to junior high schools; the functions and advantages and disadvantages of the junior high school organization; and the growth of the movement to reorganize secondary schools.

JACOBSEN, PAUL B., REAVIS, WILLIAM C., and LOGSDON, JAMES D. *Duties of School Principals.* (2nd ed.) New York: Prentice-Hall, Inc., 1950, chaps. 12, 14, 15.—This text on duties of school principals deals in some detail with their responsibilities for school organization.

LANGFITT, R. EMERSON. *The Daily Schedule and High-School Organization.* New York: The Macmillan Co., 1940, chaps. 1, 7, 10.—This is an older reference which goes into considerable detail as to the construction of the daily schedule.

PIERCE, PAUL R. *Developing a High-School Curriculum.* New York: American Book Co., 1942, 367 pp.—This book, which describes how a functional program of education was developed at Wells High School, Chicago, has no specific chapters devoted to the topic of the present chapter, but a reading of the entire book will reveal how the school was organized internally to provide a good learning situation.

PINCKNEY, PAUL W. "Organization for Improved Learning." *Educational Leadership,* 6 (March, 1949), 385-91.—This article is an excellent supplement to the section in this chapter on better practices. A high school principal discusses the need for teachers learning to know pupils and how it can be accomplished in a large high school.

THUT, I. N., and GERBERICH, J. RAYMOND. *Foundations of Method for Secondary Schools.* New York: McGraw-Hill Book Co., Inc., 1949, chaps. 4, 15.—In these chapters, the size and type of secondary schools, the day's schedule, class periods, and other administrative devices and aspects of the organization of the school are discussed from the point of view of how they affect the curriculum.

Chapter 17

RELATION OF THE SECONDARY SCHOOL
TO OTHER SCHOOL UNITS

The public secondary school does not exist as a separate institution in American society; it has since its inception been related to other educational institutions. The original American secondary school, the Latin grammar school, was established in most of the colonies, and its growth paralleled that of the first colleges. During the colonial period, the Latin grammar school served almost exclusively as a preparatory institution for colleges; hence, the purposes of the two institutions were similar though their support and control were unrelated.

Although the academy which arose following the Revolutionary War had for its main purpose preparation "for the great end and real business of living," as the Latin grammar school declined, the academy was forced to take over college entrance preparation. In time it became identified almost exclusively with that function. The high school in the beginning was the "people's college," but it, too, soon had to provide the training demanded by the colleges. Gradually the high schools came to look upon this as their major function. In the early part of the twentieth century, in spite of the small number of pupils involved, this emphasis unfortunately was maintained.

There have always been other kinds of schools in America. In the earliest colonial days, provision was made for elementary schools by the church, state, or private agencies. Most of these schools had little or no relation to the Latin grammar schools. During the middle of the nineteenth century, however, the free, public, graded elementary school became established as the single "common school," serving both as terminal education for the many and as preparation for the rapidly growing high school.

By 1900, therefore, we find that the American "ladder system" of free public education was established, one continuous state school system extending from the first grade through the state university. Yet, these different units forming our educational ladder were not carefully articulated to present a unified educational experience for the children and youth of our nation.

399

We shall in this chapter present an overview of the American elementary school, with emphasis upon the trends of its curriculum. We shall give a general statement of the goals of the elementary education and show their relationship to secondary education. The need for a cooperative approach by elementary and secondary teachers toward solving their common problems will be emphasized.

Not only must the secondary school build upon the program of the elementary school, but it must also plan for those pupils who seek higher educational experiences in college and university. We shall attempt to examine this function closely, to observe its influence upon the secondary school, and to describe programs which prepare adequately for higher education without jeopardizing the welfare of the large majority of youth who do not go on to college.

1. THE PRINCIPLES

There should be basic agreement on the common objectives of elementary and secondary education.

Elementary and high school teachers need to come together to discuss their common and distinctive purposes. When this is done, it is usually found that these two schools have many common objectives. All too often, elementary teachers do no understand what the high school teacher is seeking to attain and vice versa. Misunderstandings between these teachers commonly result from failure to know what kinds of pupil growth are desired.

Separate faculty meetings for elementary and secondary teachers are usual. Consequently, we often find two separate systems of objectives existing, with little opportunity for one faculty to understand the goals of the other. How, then, can we expect a program of continuous and related learning experiences when there is not an integration of purposes?

Child growth and development is a continuous process which should be recognized and promoted throughout the elementary and secondary schools.

Modern psychology holds that individual growth follows patterns which develop throughout life. Growth curves, though sometimes irregular, generally follow fairly definite patterns until adulthood. Early childhood is not distinct from middle childhood, which in turn merges into adolescence. Adolescence, though bringing some fairly sharp growth changes, still is related closely to the previous growth patterns. The fourth grade boy, after all, is the same individual who later becomes an adolescent.

Too frequently, our schools violate this principle of continuous growth. Elementary schools are planned for young and immature children who, we believe, must be guided, directed, controlled, and protected. We assume that all these childhood characteristics are left behind in the elementary school and plunge pupils too suddenly into the complex, departmentalized junior and senior high school. We then expect them to "grow up" rapidly, to accept mature responsibilities and to be able to direct their own study habits. Gradual maturation must be considered as important in various phases of growth.

Recognizing the principle of continuity of growth, the school should develop a common program of general education extending from Grade 1 through Grade 14.

The basic and common purpose of the elementary and secondary school is that of general education. The curriculum of these two units consequently should provide pupils with all the necessary skills, understandings, and attitudes requisite for living in and improving modern society. It must emphasize citizenship, good physical and mental health, homemaking, critical thinking, and aesthetics. It should provide for the richest possible development of the abilities of each individual pupil, and promote also the common interests and purposes which young people need in a democratic society.

The development of this common, continuous program of general education should be a cooperative enterprise. Elementary and secondary teachers, administrators, pupils, and community adults should work together through committees, councils, and consultation to build a functional curriculum that will enable children and youth to attain the goals of general education.

Such a functional curriculum of general education cannot be constructed in isolated segments and then added together to achieve integration. It must be planned as an entire, continuous program and developed as such in order to provide for maximum pupil growth. In other words, curriculum planning must be a responsibility of *all teachers*—elementary and secondary working together, continuously and cooperatively. The elementary social studies curriculum will not be separate from the secondary, but rather will be one inclusive, continuous, integrated program of social education designed for and functioning through the entire school—kindergarten through junior college.

The secondary school should give recognition to individual differences by accepting the pupils where they are in skills, attitudes, and understandings when they enter high school.

All good elementary school teachers today are keenly aware of the wide range of individual differences in each class of pupils whose learning they guide. They do not expect all first grade children to read at the same time. They know that some second grade pupils will have relatively good large-muscle coordination while others will not. Elementary teachers have learned from experience that it requires many different kinds of art media to satisfy the wide interests of fifth graders. Every good sixth grade teacher has learned that he usually faces a wide range of reading comprehension among his pupils, often extending from second through tenth grade ability.

Elementary teachers usually have in a single class several informal, flexible learning groups in the areas of reading and arithmetic. A child may be in the first reading group and in the third arithmetic group. Children normally progress from one group to another. Much of the day, however, they are working as an entire group or upon individual projects.

When working with small groups and in individual projects, elementary teachers should have learning materials adapted to the ability and skill of the child or group. It is not uncommon, for example, for a fourth grade boy to be reading a junior high school adventure story. On the other hand, a small group in the fifth grade might be reading books of a second grade reading level.

Secondary teachers should not only *know how* the elementary school builds its program around the individual differences of its pupils, but *they also need to continue this practice in high school.* Pupils, whether in Grade 2, 6, 10, or 14, need to be *accepted where they are* in skills and understandings, given learning materials suited to their level of achievement, and helped to make the maximum growth possible for themselves as individuals. No other kind of group, grade, or norm standard should be substituted for the individual standard in the program of general education.

Since modern elementary schools no longer employ nonpromotion practices and fewer elementary pupils fail and drop out of school, high school teachers need to understand that there will be a wider range of abilities and skills than formerly among their pupils.

For the past decade an ever increasing number of elementary schools have abandoned rigid programs of failure or nonpromotion. A significant body of research has shown that children differ markedly in ability when they enter school and that these differences continue throughout the total formal educational period. In fact, these differences become greater with each new learning experience, with increased maturity, and with superior teaching. Recognizing the existence of wide ranges of individual differences, elementary teachers have come to expect wide variations in pupil achievement; hence, they do not attempt to hold to a single arbitrary grade standard. Retention of pupils in the same grade for two or more years tends to increase rather than decrease these differences.[1]

There should be a continuation in secondary schools of the practice in elementary schools of pupils working under one teacher a considerable portion of the school day.

The elementary school of today is organized to facilitate a flexible, individualized curriculum, since a given teacher normally works with only one group of pupils. Elementary classes vary in size, but most good schools try to keep their groups under thirty. This number, though not ideal, does become significant when we compare it with the average secondary teacher load of 150 pupils. As a result, the elementary teacher is able to study and understand his pupils individually. The same need is apparent in high school. Especially is this true in junior high school.

Although the total pupil load of the elementary teacher is lighter than that of his secondary colleague, he must be more broadly educated and oriented. Since the modern elementary school is organized upon the basis of the "self-contained classroom"—a classroom with all the day's activities centered under one teacher—the teacher must be qualified to guide the learning of children in all major areas of living. This type of organization places an emphasis upon the individual rather than upon the subject and permits a more functional organization of the curriculum. It strengthens the pupils' security in that they have one teacher who is their counselor, guide, and friend. High school youth have need of a program which provides similar understanding of their problems, as indicated in the previous chapter.

---

[1] Walter W. Cook, *Grouping and Promotion in the Elementary School,* Minneapolis: University of Minnesota Press, 1941, 65 pp.

Pupils should proceed from the elementary school through the secondary school until their general education has been completed.

The principles of child development which underlie modern elementary education should similarly be basic to secondary education. Not only should these principles operate within the program of the secondary school, but they should, moreover, help to eliminate the gap between the two units of our public schools. The reorganized high school has increased its holding power significantly, but even today approximately 50 per cent of fifth grade pupils fail to complete the twelfth grade. All normal pupils should be encouraged to have the benefit of a high school education regardless of their ability to achieve an arbitrary standard in academic classes.

There are several related assumptions which may guide us in strengthening the holding power of the secondary school. First, we may assume that *all American youth need to complete a program of general education adapted to their abilities and needs.* Second, *all normal adolescent youth should work together in a separately organized school,* rather than retaining overage, slow-learning adolescents with younger, immature children of the elementary school. These assumptions lead naturally to a third, namely, that *the basic criterion for determining when a pupil is ready for high school is to determine which school (elementary or secondary) can help him best in guiding his learning and solving his personal and social problems.* These three assumptions point clearly to the need for providing a continuous program of general education for all young people, a program based upon individual abilities and needs extending from age five through twenty.

A sound program of general education in high school constitutes a desirable preparation for college.

For many years there has been apparent conflict between the college preparatory and the life preparatory functions of secondary education. Originally, as we have seen, the principal aim of the early American secondary school was preparation for college. Slowly, this function was modified to include considerable emphasis upon life functions. Today, the college preparatory function is still dominant, although relatively decreasing.

Two factors, however, have operated to modify the situation. First, there is a multiplying body of research which indicates clearly that the nature of the high school pattern of courses is not a significant factor in determining college success. Able pupils pursuing college preparatory curricula generally succeed in higher education, but so, too, do superior pupils who take vocational courses in high school. Research reveals that such factors as high school rank, recommendation of high school principal, general scholastic aptitude, study habits, interests, and such basic skills as reading are related fairly closely to college success. Such competencies as the last three on this list can be developed through a great variety of learning experiences and from different types of curricular organizations. Hence, an increasing number of institutions for higher education are accepting for admission students who meet their entrance requirements regardless of their pattern of courses taken in high school.

A second factor which is modifying the influence of the colleges upon secondary education is the increasing emphasis upon general education in higher institutions. Starting about 1930, many colleges and universities began experimenting to improve their programs of liberal and general education. These institutions examined their offerings in liberal arts, defined their objectives, reorganized courses, and began to develop systematic programs of evaluation. Today, few institutions remain which have not, at least in part, reoriented their liberal arts program toward the more functional and dynamic goals of the generally educated citizen. Consequently, the modern college no longer seeks high school graduates who have "specialized," but rather those who have made a successful beginning of a program of general education designed to help youth solve their personal and group problems in a society of free men.

2. SOME TYPICAL PRACTICES

The explanation of principles indicates how the elementary school, the secondary school, and the college should be articulated in order to provide a program of continuous learning for young people. Some of the outstanding characteristics of elementary education were described and compared with those of secondary education. Elementary schools in general have recognized principles of child growth and development, functional learning, individual differences, and socialization more adequately than secondary schools. Are these desirable practices of elementary schools related to the child's further growth in the secondary school and in college? Does each unit of our public school system relate closely to the next higher segment? Is learning a continuous or an isolated, unrelated process in our schools?

Not only is there the problem of relating the policies and program of the elementary school to those of the secondary school, but also there is the more difficult situation of coordinating the learning experiences of high school with those of higher educational institutions. The latter is the more difficult, for the colleges are almost always remote in distance, administration, and control from the local elementary and secondary school units. A long history of independence and prestige has given the American college considerable domination over the curriculum of the secondary school. Is this influence desirable? How has it affected our elementary and secondary schools? For an answer to these questions, we will examine some typical practices found today among elementary and secondary schools and colleges.

Historical Development of the Elementary School.—Early elementary schools in America were small and ungraded, taught by inadequately trained teachers in independent school districts. These schools usually had no administrative relationship to the secondary schools. During the middle of the nineteenth century, great strides were made in extending educational opportunities, in freeing schools from sectarian control, in providing adequate support, and in developing an organized administrative system. This period was followed by the rapid extension of free public secondary education. Elementary and secondary schools were slowly brought under a single administrative head in towns and cities, but in rural areas the small, independent elementary school was supreme and became glorified as the "little red schoolhouse."

The curriculum of the early elementary school was largely restricted to the "Three R's," with strong emphasis upon religious and moral training. During the nineteenth century, practically all the other regular elementary school subjects were added, while the twentieth century has seen the addition of home economics and industrial arts.

In early colonial schools, one teacher taught all the subjects or skills to the children; "grades," as we know them, did not exist. In the earliest organization, one teacher would teach two or three classes or combinations of classes. By 1880, in towns and cities, the favored practice was to have one teacher work with a single group of children in one grade.

After about 1920, the "platoon system" came into prominence in many of the larger city elementary schools. The school was divided into two platoons, each platoon containing half the pupils in each grade. Continuous use of the facilities was obtained by having one

platoon do regular class work while the other platoon used the special
rooms (provided for science, music, art, etc.); these two platoons
alternated throughout the day. The plan was designed to enrich the
curriculum and to provide more activities, as well as to make more
efficient use of the school plant. Since one group of teachers taught
the regular subjects, and others such special subjects as science, shop,
home economics, physical education, and supervised auditorium activities, the platoon encouraged departmental teaching. This influence extended to schools without platoons. Today, though in a
minority, some elementary schools employ different teachers for
subjects taught in the intermediate grades.

A Typical Elementary School Today.—A typical American
elementary school is usually found housed in a building separate from
the high school and has its own teachers and a teacher-principal.
In small towns and large cities, elementary schools are an integral
part of larger school districts which usually include some kind of a
secondary school. In the Middle West and much of the West and
South, the typical elementary school is an ungraded rural school
employing one or two teachers, with enrollments commonly under
thirty. In large cities, on the other hand, elementary schools frequently enroll four hundred to one thousand pupils, and employ a
full-time supervising principal.

In the primary grades, each teacher operates a self-contained classroom in which he provides all the learning experiences for the children
of a particular grade. In the intermediate grades (four, five, and
six), the teacher usually teaches all subjects with the exception of
music and physical education. Teachers frequently exchange these
more specialized responsibilities, i.e., one will teach physical education
for two or more grades while another will similarly handle music. In
cities, these subjects may often be taught by special teachers within a
single building, or sometimes by teachers working with several buildings.

An Elementary School Day.—The following program illustrates
how a typical elementary teacher organizes her program for the fifth
grade in a large city system. It is an example of a self-contained
classroom in which one teacher works with a given group of pupils all
day, even handling her own children's work in art, music, and physical education, with the periodical assistance of a visiting consultant in
each field. Often the schedule is considered as flexible, so that a
teacher can combine the time from different subject areas to teach integrated units.

8:45 — 9:15	Civic club
9:15 — 10:30	Social studies, science, health
10:30 — 10:45	Recess
10:45 — 11:45	Language arts
11:45 — 1:15	Noon lunch period
1:15 — 2:00	Arithmetic
2:00 — 2:20	Music
2:20 — 3:05	Art, physical education, library period (on alternate days)
3:05 — 3:15	Evaluation and planning period

Problems in Transition to High School.—Elementary school pupils often have considerable difficulty in adjusting to high school upon completion of the sixth or eighth grade. This is especially true if they enter a junior high school in the seventh grade after passing through several self-contained elementary classrooms. In such elementary schools, the pupils have had one teacher each year who had the major responsibility for directing their learning experiences. They spent almost the entire day working with this one teacher, in one room, with one group of children, studying related problems.

Upon leaving the elementary school and its self-contained classroom, the young adolescent pupil suddenly finds himself in an institution with a different organization of the school day, and in many cases in a much larger institution—the junior or senior high school. He will usually be placed in a home room, but finds little time to spend there. Roll is taken, announcements are made, and then the procession of new classes, new teachers, and changing periods begins. He is likely to feel that no one teacher knows him well. No one helps him study. He returns to his home room again only at the end of the school day.

Too often, there is inadequate guidance given the eighth grade pupil in his transition to high school in the eight-four type of system. He may arrive the first day in high school without any previous counsel in selecting the electives that most nearly suit his abilities and needs. In the case of a city system that has specialized types of high schools, such as vocational high schools and commercial high schools, the problem is augmented. The eighth or ninth grade pupil must, at an age when he has little basis for choice, choose between a certain specialized kind of a high school and an academic or general high school. The assumption is that he will have made some selection of a field of vocations by this time. However, research shows that permanent choices can rarely be made this early.

The transferral of inadequate records from the one school unit to the other makes the guidance job more difficult. Especially when pupils come from one of the small independent rural schools, the records transferred often contain nothing more than a listing of the pupil's marks.

Lack of Agreement and Cooperation Among Elementary and Secondary Teachers.—Within elementary and secondary schools, there are many desirable practices found in the organization, curriculum, guidance, and administrative programs, several of which have been described in earlier chapters. Unfortunately, however, these superior practices and programs are often limited *either* to the elementary *or* to the secondary school. Few school systems have developed a curriculum planned and organized to provide for continuous pupil growth from kindergarten through the twelfth grade.

The lack of planned, continuous experiences extending through both the elementary and the secondary school results from a number of factors. First, these two units have had an independent origin and early development. Only within the twentieth century have both schools become part of a single unified school district. High school teachers have generally had a longer period of training than elementary teachers, and have consequently considered themselves superior. This factor has been exaggerated in the eyes of laymen until elementary teachers generally have come to have less status and prestige than secondary teachers. Better salaries, resulting from the more extensive training of high school teachers, have added to the inferiority complex of elementary teachers. Better buildings and equipment, the prestige of "extracurricular" activities, the preponderance of women in elementary education, and the college preparatory function of the high school have all added weight to the assumed superiority of the secondary school.

As a result of these and other factors, the elementary school and the high school have frequently developed more or less independent programs. Many teachers, as well as the community, have often assumed that the job of the elementary school was primarily to prepare for high school. Similarly, the high school was expected to prepare for college. As long as both functions seemed to be met adequately, there was little inclination to raise further questions.

Meetings, committees, and activities commonly are held independently for elementary and for secondary teachers. Not understanding each other nor each other's purposes, they find it difficult to secure common participation toward unified objectives. When committees are organized on a school or citywide basis, it often requires considerable effort and leadership to break down misunderstandings between elementary and secondary teachers. These barriers must be removed if we are to make possible the kind of understanding and agreement that will result in working for consistent goals in the development of children and youth.

Influence of College Entrance Requirements.—Colleges and universities today are still powerful agencies in helping determine the curriculum of the high school. High school graduation requirements of foreign languages, mathematics, and science frequently reflect college entrance requirements rather than life needs. In small high schools the single curriculum organization of the program of studies is usually provided, and it frequently is one primarily designed for meeting college entrance requirements. (See Chapter 6.) This fact often holds true even if there is only a very small percentage of graduates continuing their education.

Not only is the college pattern superimposed upon the total high school curriculum, but its impact also descends upon the secondary school in other ways. High school textbooks are often written by college professors. Some professional organizations are largely controlled by these same professors and likewise exert a strong influence.

Influence of College Board Examinations.—In the eastern and New England states, the colleges make their influence felt directly upon the secondary school curriculum through entrance examinations developed by the College Entrance Examination Board. Practically all private higher institutions of the eastern area require, as a condition for admission, successful achievement on special examinations on subject matter. Many of these colleges prepare and administer individual entrance examinations; others have cooperatively developed such evaluation instruments. The best known of the latter are the College Entrance Examination Board's tests, which are given five times a year at more than five hundred centers throughout the world to approximately eighty thousand secondary school senior candidates for admission to the ninety-three member American colleges and universities. Colleges other than the member institutions use the College Board's examinations for admission purposes.

Prior to 1942, essay-type examinations were given by the Board, and definite requirements were given in each subject as guiding references for teachers and those who constructed the examinations. As a result these examinations exerted a very strong influence upon the curriculum and evaluation programs of many high schools throughout the nation, as pupils, parents, and teachers concentrated upon preparation for them.

Since 1942, however, all Board examinations except English composition are of the objective type, subject matter fields are no longer defined, and copies of old tests are not published. Tests are offered in every academic subject, but the whole battery now requires only six to seven hours' time. Current tests measure understandings, applications, and interpretations as well as factual knowledge. Candidates are compared with each other on their test performance; there is no passing or failing point, since they are not rated on any absolute standard. A study of scores on recent physics tests indicates that there seems now to be no advantage resulting to those pupils who made special preparation for the Board examination. Most colleges using these examinations also consider high school marks, recommendations, and interviews in determining the selective admission of candidates.[2]

Influence of the New York Regents' Examinations.—Since 1877, Regents' examinations in New York State have been used in that state as a standard for high school graduation and college admission. When the law was passed, the secondary schools of New York were largely college preparatory and the examinations logically served the dual function. Today, however, with approximately 20 per cent of the graduates continuing into higher education, these examinations in practice deny equal opportunity to pupils in the state who do not complete their high school program. Many pupils who drop out do so apparently because they are not interested and are unsuccessful in the academic curriculum which has resulted from the Regents' examinations and the Regents' diploma. These examinations are discussed here because they represent a pattern that has had an influence on practices in American education.

An increasing number of school systems in New York State have set up graduation requirements and local diplomas independent of Regents' examinations. The Summary Reports of the Regents' Inquiry into the Character and Cost of Education in New York State recommended that high school graduation be determined by the pupil's readiness to leave school, that the Regents' diploma be discontinued, and that the Regents' examinations be discontinued as graduation tests and be used for diagnostic purposes.[3] Within the past few years there have been continuing efforts to have the state department

---

[2] *The College Entrance Examination Board Handbook—1949, Terms of Admission to the Member Colleges,* Princeton, N.J.: College Entrance Examination Board, 1949, pp. 5-8.

[3] The Regents' Inquiry, *Education for American Life,* New York: McGraw-Hill Book Co., Inc., 1938, p. 48.

put these recommendations into effect and to define the function of the Regents' examinations as being exclusively for college entrance.[4]

Lack of Concerted and Courageous Action to Overthrow College Domination.—While recognizing the influence of the college on the secondary school as an important historical factor, we must also point out that the control once exercised by the college and university is declining, a development resulting from many factors. First, while an ever-increasing *number* of high school graduates enter higher education the *percentage* of graduates who pursue further formal education has declined. Many research studies, such as the Eight Year Study of the Progressive Education Association, have indicated that the pattern of courses taken in high school has little relationship to college success. Finally, the increasing prestige of the modern high school has led to a degree of professional independence from college and university.

In spite of these changes, however, the vast majority of communities in this country seem to "love their chains." A closely prescribed college preparatory curriculum gives a sense of security to high school faculty and administration. Such a program is traditional, respected, respectable, and dignified. The college success of its selected graduates brings prestige to the local school. College academic honors are prima facie evidence in most communities of the effectiveness of the high school program. Some administrators and teachers frankly declare that they would not like to see the subject requirements for college entrance eliminated because they want this support for retaining the present subject patterns. The domination of the college may be more imagined than real in a number of cases.

Secondary school administrators and teachers need to build programs to meet the needs of *all their pupils,* not merely offer prescriptions for the success of the relatively few college-bound youth. Only dynamic and fearless leadership in the secondary school will improve this situation by:

1. Determining how much freedom they have within their area from the requirements of higher educational institutions, and setting about to change the situation by concerted action in their own group.
2. Building a curriculum which will meet the needs of all youth—both college-bound and job-bound.

---

[4] Robert W. Frederick, C. Currien Smith, and Lyndon H. Strough, "A Call for Leadership," *New York State Education,* 33 (January, 1946), 317-21.

3. Conducting careful follow-up studies of *all graduates* to determine not only their college achievements but also their success in adjusting to vocational, civic, leisure, health, and family relationships and activities.

3. Practices in the Better Secondary Schools

An increasing number of modern high schools are planning their goals and programs jointly with elementary schools and are developing cooperative programs with colleges and universities. Some of these outstanding practices will be presented in this section.

Common Purposes for Elementary and Secondary Schools.—The St. Louis public schools have developed a common philosophy of education for their elementary and secondary programs. Their statement was developed through the cooperative efforts of elementary and secondary school teachers and principals, working in committees and through discussions of faculties in the separate buildings. It illustrates a dynamic point of view, and points the direction which the growth of pupils should follow. A brief example [5] is given below:

. . . education is the lifelong process by which the individual grows or develops as the result of all his experiences;
. . . education is a basic means whereby a given social order strives to perpetuate, improve, and transmit its cultural heritage or way of life;
. . . the obligation of American education, therefore, is the development of citizens who will function effectively and constructively in a democracy.

A Twelve-Year Curriculum Program.—For more than ten years, the Eugene, Oregon, public schools have been developing a functional curriculum. A curriculum coordinator initiated the program, and citywide committees of elementary and secondary teachers and administrators worked jointly for several years to develop statements of goals and outcomes in terms of pupil behaviors, to prepare resource units, and to develop evaluation instruments. Their work centered around a twelve-year social living or core program, extending from the first grade through the twelfth. It has been revised several times by committees of elementary and secondary teachers always working together to build a continuous learning program for children and youth—a program aimed toward definite goals.

---

[5] See *The St. Louis Public School Journal*, Courses of Study Series, Vol. 1, No. 6, September, 1946, St. Louis: St. Louis Public Schools, pp. 2-5, for complete list.

Each grade has a theme which serves as a guide for the year's work: [6]

Grade 1. How to live more effectively in the home and school
Grade 2. How to cooperate with community helpers
Grade 3. How our environment supplies our basic needs
Grade 4. How man has adjusted to his environment
Grade 5. How man has developed the Western Hemisphere
Grade 6. How Europeans developed and spread their culture
Grade 7. How the people of the Pacific Northwest contribute to the world today
Grade 8. How the American people have developed their culture
Grade 9. How Americans strive toward intelligent, productive citizenship
Grade 10. How mankind has developed a sense of the worth of the individual and his responsibilities within conflicting social patterns
Grade 11. How the people of the United States have struggled to achieve a democratic way of life
Grade 12. How youth may develop status, security, personal responsibility, and participation in society.

Liberalized College Entrance Requirements.—Independent colleges throughout the country have liberalized their requirements for admission as a result of research evidence on factors that influence or do not influence college success. The state universities of Minnesota, Michigan, Washington, Colorado, Kansas, Iowa, Oklahoma, and Illinois are examples of larger institutions that will now accept accredited high school graduates into certain colleges regardless of the pattern of secondary school courses.

Many institutions retaining typical high school course requirements in their catalog also provide for students of high rank in the graduating class and high rank on a college aptitude examination to be admitted without regard to the courses presented from high school. Most institutions give graduates the privilege of taking an examination for admission in lieu of the required courses. Some place more stock in the recommendations of the high school principal and teachers than they do in course patterns, or even course marks. As college counseling departments increase their staff and facilities, they are requesting more information on test records, activity records, special abilities, and other cumulative data from the high school records.

One recent investigation found that, among the colleges and universities which are members of the College Entrance Examination

---

[6] *Social Living Program—Grades One to Twelve,* Scope and Sequence Chart, Eugene, Oregon: Eugene Public Schools, 1949.

Board, an increasing number no longer prescribe patterns of courses, although conventional academic subjects are still favored. In September, 1949, less than 4 per cent required all applicants to take the Board achievement tests for entrance.[7]

The Michigan Secondary School-College Agreement.—Although the colleges still influence the secondary school curriculum unduly, there are increasing evidences of understanding between these institutions. The Eight-Year Study, completed in 1941, gave considerable impetus to the movement to free secondary schools from rigid college entrance requirements.

School people participating in The Michigan Study of the Secondary School Curriculum, which began in 1937, found that a serious obstacle to curriculum change was college entrance requirements. After careful discussion of this problem with the Michigan College Association, an agreement was made between the Association and the fifty-four cooperating high schools to admit selected graduates from these schools, regardless of their pattern of courses, upon the recommendation of the school faculty. This agreement was to run from 1940 to 1950. As a result of the successful operation of this agreement, it was revised in 1946 to include any accredited high school in the state, and it contained no terminal date. In order to continue in this program, however, high schools agreed to observe the following four conditions:

1. Gather significant personal data about each student and summarize it for submission to the college.
2. Provide a continuous study and evaluation of the curriculum.
3. Carry on a continuous follow-up study of former students.
4. Provide a program of vocational orientation and information relating to college courses.

Eighty-four high schools were admitted to the program in the first two years of its operation; these represented more than 20 per cent of the secondary school pupils in the state of Michigan.[8] In July, 1950, 121 high schools were participating in the program.

Complete Cumulative Records Transferred to High School.— The Rochester, Minnesota, guidance program begins with the pre-school child through the work of its Child Development Project. As

---

[7] Richard A. Mumma, "Further Modification in College-Entrance Requirements," *School Review,* 58 (January, 1950), 24-28.

[8] Leon S. Waskin, "The Michigan Secondary School-College Agreement," *Bulletin of the National Association of Secondary School Principals,* 33 (January, 1949), 49-64.

a result of the records furnished by this project, the school can give attention to the individual needs of each child entering school. Cumulative records are kept as each pupil moves upward through the elementary school. These records are supplemented by data from the Public Health Department and the Mayo Clinic. The social service departments of the County Welfare Office and the Mayo Clinic also work with the schools on individual problem cases. Test data for individual pupils are made available to individual teachers through a special testing bureau in the city school's junior college.[9]

After the pupil's completion of the elementary school, the most pertinent information is transferred from the elementary school record to a record which accompanies the pupil through junior high school and senior high school and is used by many teachers and counselors for guidance purposes. When the pupil completes the twelfth grade, the most significant data are again condensed and transferred to the permanent files. Should the pupil continue to college, the information is summarized and accompanies him.

Orientation of Elementary Pupils to High School.—Modern elementary schools have succeeded in helping more of their pupils to make a satisfactory transition to high school. Even though large numbers still fail to graduate, improvement has been marked. The junior high school has helped to bridge the gap between the elementary and the secondary school; it has, however, at the same time introduced this problem in the sixth rather than the eighth grade. When the elementary school is located apart from the junior or senior high school, a definite guidance program must be planned to insure a satisfactory adjustment to the secondary school. The following are some steps taken by good elementary schools to facilitate this process:

1. Cumulative records are kept throughout the elementary school.
2. Pertinent information is summarized and sent to the high school.
3. Home room periods are used to give information pertaining to high school work.
4. Teachers, school counselors, and the elementary principal interview the pupils individually regarding high school courses.
5. Senior or junior high school counselors come to the elementary schools for group and individual conferences with pupils.
6. Elementary pupils about to enter the junior or senior high school are taken to the secondary school building for group orientation

---

[9] Lila M. Argue, "Guidance Benefits All," *Minnesota Journal of Education,* 30 (April, 1950), 29.

meetings, a tour of the building, assembly programs, and participation in activities with high school pupils.

7. Pupils' parents are invited to attend interviews when various high
school programs are planned.

Orientation of High School Pupils to College.—Most colleges and
universities carry on somewhat similar programs for the orientation
of entering freshmen. These programs are variously called Freshman Week, Orientation Week, and the like. At the University of
Minnesota, all freshmen and new students come to the campus in
small groups in August and early September for an orientation conference. Each group is assigned to a counselor and a student sponsor
for the two-day meetings. Each student is given a battery of tests,
has an individual interview with a faculty adviser for program planning, and meets in a group conference with a representative of the
college in which he is enrolling. The Student Activity Bureau in-
terprets its varied program for students, and also provides some recreation and social events during the short conference. This orientation program is followed in late September by the large "Welcome
Week" for all freshmen and new students just prior to the beginning
of classes.

Cooperative Guidance Planned by High Schools and Colleges.
—Some colleges and universities hold joint conferences with high
schools to help teachers and counselors plan more effective guidance
for the college student. These conferences go beyond planning for
freshmen orientation and attack many of the fundamental problems
of college students. Such problems as employment, housing, activities, career planning, family life counseling, and recreation are considered along with academic problems of high school work and its
relationship to college success. A number of college students usually
meet first with their former high school teachers and counselors and
raise questions and problems. High school and college staffs meet
together for discussions, and finally the students and the high school
and college staffs meet to discuss the questions previously raised by
the students. Such meetings have proved valuable in improving high
school and college relations.

4. First Steps

The American secondary school exists as an integral part of a total
school system. It should never stand alone. Its purpose and program must be cooperatively determined and related to total educational needs by elementary and secondary teachers and community

adults. Only through cooperative effort can a functional program be constructed to meet the needs of all American children and youth to-day. Here are suggested certain first steps which any high school faculty can take to provide continuous learning for youth.

1. High school and elementary teachers can work closely and co-operatively together to determine their basic educational philos-ophy and purposes. Community adults and children can also be included. The goals of general education are common from pre-school until the completion of secondary education; there is only a difference of emphasis and interpretation as a child pro-gresses upward through the grades and into high school. Chil-dren, youth, and community adults must share in determining these goals if maximum understanding and cooperation are to result. A total educational program cannot be coordinated with-in a community unless first there is agreement upon the kinds of behavior changes which are desired among the children and youth.

2. Communities can organize a central planning council or coordi-nating curriculum committee representing elementary and sec-ondary teachers, administrators, community adults, children, and youth. All schools, buildings, and departments should be repre-sented. Its primary function should be coordination. Only broad general policies and programs should be determined by the planning council; the actual curriculum should be worked out within individual buildings.

3. Elementary and high school teachers, community adults, and pupils can work together to plan twelve-year curriculum pro-grams. The central planning council can block out the general language arts program, for example, by indicating what its scope should be. It can also determine themes for each grade level.

4. The elementary school and the secondary school can undertake the joint study of many common problems. The problems and needs of children and youth are basically similar and a continu-ous program will be fruitful. When teachers on all levels work together, they discover common interests and ways to relate and improve instruction. Problems having significance for both ele-mentary and high schools include pupil adjustment, reporting to parents, records, guidance, health and safety, and classroom control.

5. Individual teachers can make it a point to learn more about the elementary school and get acquainted with elementary school teachers.

6. Elementary schools, junior high schools, and senior high schools can work together to develop a sound program of guidance to assist pupils in their transition into secondary education. Careful planning can help the pupil adjust to the highly organized secondary school program. Achievement, personality, and interest tests will give valuable guidance information in planning individual high school programs for pupils. Parent-teacher-pupil conferences are helpful. Visitation days and open house programs will assist the adolescent in understanding the ninth or tenth grade program. High school counselors can come into each elementary room and explain their programs.

7. Teachers with special interests and abilities can be selected as home room teachers for seventh, eighth, ninth, or tenth grade pupils, and they may move upward with a given group through the high school.

8. Individual teachers can use every opportunity to help pupils obtain a better understanding of the secondary school, its courses, and organization.

9. Careful planning with parents and good public relations with the entire community can overcome the erroneous idea that certain combinations of courses give the best preparation for college entrance. P.T.A. programs can be planned on themes of functional general education. Local newspapers will help interpret this function if given the facts and the opportunity. Through these avenues, the results of studies of factors in college success can be publicized.

10. High schools do not find it difficult to obtain cooperation with the colleges in the area relative to the admission of their graduates. The high school administration should first ascertain the percentage of its graduates who go to college, where they go, their courses, and their college success. The next step is to learn exactly what entrance requirements are held by the colleges. High schools can assist colleges in recruitment programs, in professional and vocational guidance, and in checking periodically upon the achievement of their graduates as college students. If high school administrators will do a careful job of recommending graduates for selective college admission, representatives from the higher institutions will often grant them more freedom. The amount of freedom will naturally depend upon the nature of the college, its purposes, and its educational philosophy, but many institutions are liberal when cooperative relationships have been successfully established.

11. Teachers can guide pupils to take courses that will give them a good broad, general education instead of insisting on a limited college preparatory program. In their own classes, the best preparation for college—substantiated by research—is to assist pupils in the improvement of their reading skills, study skills, reading interests, and attitudes toward school work. Of course, one of the responsibilities of teachers is to give pupils the facts about college entrance requirements and to acquaint them with the nature and demands of college life. They must be extremely careful in their remarks and attitudes not to place greater prestige value on so-called college preparatory programs.

SELECTED REFERENCES

AIKIN, WILFORD M. *The Story of the Eight-Year Study.* New York: Harper & Bros., 1942, 157 pp.—This is the first volume of the report on the eight-year experimental study, with recommendations. It summarizes the experiences of the graduates of the experimental schools in their college work.

ASSOCIATION FOR SUPERVISION AND CURRICULUM DEVELOPMENT. *Organizing the Elementary School for Living and Learning* (1947 Yearbook). Washington, D.C.: National Education Association, 211 pp.—States the purposes of a modern elementary school including how children learn, and how it serves the community, nation, and world.

BOSSING, NELSON L. *Principles of Secondary Education.* New York: Prentice-Hall, Inc., 1949, chap. 11.—This deals, among other things, with the relationship of the secondary school to the elementary school and to adulthood.

COOK, WALTER W. *Grouping and Promotion in the Elementary School.* Minneapolis: University of Minnesota Press, 1941, 65 pp.—This excellent monograph discusses and summarizes research dealing with individual differences, grouping, and promotion practices in the elementary school.

LEE, J. MURRAY, and LEE, DORIS MAY. *The Child and His Curriculum.* New York: Appleton-Century-Crofts, Inc., 1950, 710 pp.—This standard book dealing with the elementary school child and the elementary curriculum treats all aspects of learning and the different areas of the curriculum; well documented with research studies.

PRESIDENT'S COMMISSION ON HIGHER EDUCATION. "Establishing the Goals." Vol. I of *Higher Education for American Democracy.* Washington, D.C.: Government Printing Office, 1947, 103 pp.—This first volume of the Commission's report outlines a democratic point of view for higher education, emphasizing the importance of general education.

SEXSON, JOHN A., and HARBESON, JOHN W. *The New American College.* New York: Harper & Bros., 1946, 312 pp.—The basic principles and purposes of the junior college are set forth in this volume, with descriptions of its program. The curriculum of the Pasadena, California, Junior College is described in detail.

SPAULDING, FRANCIS T. *High School and Life.* The Regents' Inquiry. New York: McGraw-Hill Book Co., Inc., 1939, chaps. 10, 15.—These two chapters in this report of the Regents' study describe certain outcomes of secondary education and examine critically the Regents' examinations. Contains recommendations regarding the elimination of these examinations and the Regents' diplomas.

PART V
THE SECONDARY SCHOOL TEACHER

THE SECONDARY SCHOOL TEACHER

The authors of this book believe that a growing, dynamic type of pre-service and in-service education for secondary school teachers is fundamental to progress in attaining the kind of secondary education that adequately serves all youth. It is pointed out in these three chapters that the education of the teacher is a continuous process from the time he enters the teacher education institution until he completes his years of teaching. The institution's services for the beginning teacher, the type of assistance he can receive from his immediate supervisors, and his own responsibility for continuing his professional growth are discussed. In the last chapter of this section, the student will find assistance with the many questions he may have concerning certification, contracts, what will be expected of him in a teaching position, and other responsibilities.

Chapter 18

PRE-SERVICE EDUCATION OF THE SECONDARY SCHOOL TEACHER

The type of education that the secondary school teacher receives helps to determine what the secondary school is like now or will be like in the future. Pre-service and in-service education must go hand in hand if the long overdue changes in secondary education are to be made. Public schools, teacher education institutions, and state departments of education are involved in this important enterprise of teacher education.

A good deal of study and experimentation in the field of teacher education has been going on in recent years. Until that time, the patterns for preparation of the high school teacher had changed but little in two decades or more. Outdated teacher education does not adequately serve the modern secondary school. We need to be concerned seriously about questions such as these: What kind of preparatory program is needed for a teacher of core classes? What has happened, or failed to happen, in universities where the teacher education program is a disjointed one, with bickering, mistrust, and misunderstanding between education and subject departments engaged in a joint project? What effect does this situation have on the development of potentially good teachers?

The future teacher should study the problem in connection with his own institution. Probably one of the best means for him to understand what good teaching involves is to analyze his own experiences in different classes that are part of his preparation as a teacher. To serve as a basis for such critical evaluation, as well as to consider the whole pattern of teacher education in relation to the American secondary school, certain principles are presented in this chapter indicating what should be the experiences in undergraduate teacher education.

It should be made clear that if these principles are to be applied effectively certain conditions should exist:

1. Promising, well-adjusted young people in high school must become interested in the teaching profession as a career.

2. There needs to be a selective process for admission to teacher education, as well as a process of continuous selection during the pre-service period, a selection that considers qualifications broader than academic ability.
3. The continuation of teacher education in service, as described in the next chapter, should be a corollary to pre-service experiences.

1. THE PRINCIPLES

The general education of the future teacher should develop broad cultural interests, provide a good foundation for understanding the scientific development and social processes in a democratic society, develop techniques for improving that society, and foster a continuing interest in its advancement.

It has been stressed in many sections of this book that the teacher in the secondary school should understand the meaning of a democratic society and the many current social problems that we face in to-day's world. The first years of the teacher's college education should serve as a period of rounding out and expanding the general education begun in the secondary school. Deeper, more mature interests in the world's affairs and in society should result from this period of study. Cultural and special interests should be developed and expanded. The foundations for better understanding of human development can be laid through the study of biology, anthropology, and psychology.

It would seem, however, that some better means will have to be found to select the important understandings and attitudes that should be the aim of a general education in these years and to develop a working arrangement among college or university instructors whereby they can plan together to achieve these aims. The elective system, whereby a college student chooses one course from science, one from social studies, and one or more from other specified areas hardly seems to provide an adequate solution. This plan lacks the type of coordination that will help the student integrate knowledge from the different fields. Survey or broad fields courses which include important aspects from larger fields of study, or continuous planning together by instructors particularly concerned with general education, hold far greater promise.

The early nonprofessional education should be planned for the purposes of general and cultural education, not as a preparation for future courses in specific fields. It should have as its basic focal point the study and improvement of democratic understandings, techniques, and attitudes, and a greatly expanded culture horizon.

The pre-service education of the teacher should be rich in opportunity to study and work with children and adolescents from the time that the student first makes his decision to enter the profession.

The heart of any teaching situation is the pupil. It logically follows that the prospective teacher should use every possible occasion to become acquainted with children and adolescents, their nature, their problems, their interests, and their needs. Teacher education institutions that have laboratory schools are especially fortunate in this respect. Students can begin observation and study of pupils in the first or second year of college through psychology courses and through child and adolescent development courses offered in other departments, such as home economics. The campus school can become a real functioning laboratory for all education courses, for case studies of pupils, for observation of teaching and keeping anecdotal records, and for working with pupils in extraclass activities.

There are, however, relatively unexplored resources in many colleges and universities that have no laboratory schools. Cooperative arrangements can be made with nursery schools on campus and with nearby elementary and secondary schools. Certainly, in a program of education of the secondary school teacher, experiences need not be confined to working with adolescents. The high school teacher can profit greatly by understanding the child in his various stages of growth.

The innumerable boys' and girls' activities found in any community furnish another source. Scouting, young people's groups in churches, YMCA or YWCA work, and other youth organizations are usually on the lookout for leaders and would welcome assistance from college students. The possibilities of serving as a camp counselor in the summer should not be overlooked. Perhaps no other experience gives as close insight into young people's problems and ideals as living with them for a month or more.

Arrangements of the kind suggested here cannot be left to chance. They must become a part of a planned curriculum for teacher education, with the responsibility to arrange for them delegated to someone on the staff. A program consisting of only course-taking would not suffice unless these activities become a part of those courses. An important part of all education courses should be experiences and activities that center around the study of the child and the adolescent.

*In the professional preparation of the teacher, courses should
be fused into an integrated program, a continuous sequence of
significant experiences and problem solving, drawing from various aspects of education.*

Are teacher education programs following a pattern of covering
much subject matter while, at the same time, advocating more attention to pupil needs and interests? It is extremely doubtful if the relationships between methods and learning or between curriculum and
the adolescent nature can be well understood if taught in separate
courses, hoping that the applications will be made. Entirely too much
faith has been placed on acquiring "background" that is supposed to
prepare a person for another course. We know that the facts about
learning do not substantiate such an assumption.

Developing the content of education courses around problems of
interest to students, motivated in part by their contacts with children
and with schools, is the sensible answer to making experiences in
professional undergraduate courses meaningful. Interrelationship is
needed in education rather than division of subject matter. The pattern of separate courses in educational psychology, methods, curriculum, and principles, fails to meet the test of the criteria of a good learning situation.

At the same time, the need extends to seeing and understanding
relationships between the content of courses in subject matter fields
and the courses in education that deal with methods and curriculum.
Both are a part of the professional equipment of the high school
teacher.

*The program of teacher education should help students to de-
velop a system of carefully analyzed values to guide their actions.*

Immediately, upon reading this principle, someone might say,
"Add a course in philosophy of education to the undergraduate program." Nothing could be farther from the correct interpretation of
this principle. Although a course in this subject would undoubtedly
be of value to many undergraduate students, the additive method of
curriculum development does not furnish the solution.

This principle refers to helping education students—through all
courses—to develop a point of view which will guide them in making
wise choices in teaching. A teacher without some system of values,
carefully thought out, is like a plane without flying instruments. New
ideas may come along but what values will determine whether the
teacher should use them? Are these new methods helpful in pro-

moting learning? Would they give children new confidence or a sense of frustration? Will they square with our ideals of a democratic society?

In other words, throughout all courses the student should be developing a point of view, analyzed in terms of democracy, the modern world, the adolescent and his nature, and facts about how people learn. Although specific facts about methods and curriculum may often be meaningless to the inexperienced teacher, a set of values can be developed in undergraduate education courses. The values will be there in any case—perhaps hazy and unanalyzed to be sure—but they will govern the kind of teaching the student will do. If those who are engaged in teacher education do not concern themselves about values, changes in secondary education will continue at a snail's pace.

It indicates a lack of courage to say that we cannot train teachers for the more modern procedures because schools are not using these procedures. Again, this statement represents a point of view in itself, and a misunderstanding of the problem. An understanding of adolescents is good in any teaching situation; skill in pupil-teacher planning would be useful in both the more traditional and the more modern schools. Most of all, the secondary schools need teachers who are convinced that something needs to be done and have a vision of what that something is. Turning out mechanical robots with teaching skills alone will never do that job.

The student's experiences in all his college courses should furnish him an example of how learning can be promoted most effectively in a democratic atmosphere.

If the principles in Chapter 1 are accepted as applying to the secondary school, they should be put into practice in college classes of future secondary school teachers. There is nothing in the nature of democratic principles that would indicate that they should not be applied to classes of older youth and adults. In fact, democratic skills are acquired only through continuous experiences that become increasingly appropriate to mature responsibility and judgment. Good learning situations are similar in high school and college; in neither case do desirable changes in behavior result from an authoritarian "telling" process in which the teacher knows all the answers and dominates the entire learning situation, where little regard for human relationships or individual adjustment problems is evident.

It is essential that the future teacher should have worth-while experiences in his own college classes. He should have numerous opportunities to set goals for himself and the group, to plan cooperatively the experiences of the class, to work in committee groups in order to investigate problems, and to use varied sources and types of materials. Educational classes should hold no monopoly on good teaching procedures, but they ought to be expected to take the lead in good instructional practices. The instructors who have charge of undergraduate education courses should, first of all, be inspiring teachers who can demonstrate effectively the principles and practices that they teach.

The sequence of courses in professional education should provide for a continued contact of instructor and student as a means of effective counseling and guidance of learning activities.

Much of the undergraduate program of professional courses, familiar to campuses of universities and colleges preparing secondary school teachers, has been based on the assumption that the best learning situation can be provided by dividing courses among staff members expert in their fields. Thus, the psychological aspects have been taught by one person, the sociological aspects by another, general methods by a third staff member, and special methods by still another person. Parceling out courses to experts has tended to result in "learning the subject matter" rather than in focusing on competencies of the students who will be the future teachers. Many staff members of colleges and universities, even though they teach in such a situation, are convinced that a reorganization of the program is needed.

Teacher education needs to recognize that, for efficient learning that results in changed behavior, the teacher must know his pupils well. Guidance of a personalized type rather than mechanical schedule-making and course-selecting is possible only if students can work with an instructor for a long enough period. Real assistance in developing abilities and latent talents can be given if some continuous contact with students is provided.

The college teacher of education courses should work with the student in classes over a longer period than one semester, certainly over a full two semesters. For example, an instructor might be assigned a group of thirty students throughout a year's teaching in education courses and in practice teaching the following year. Follow-up in the schools, as discussed in Chapter 19, will naturally be added contact. Continuity in counseling is essential. The principle dovetails with the need for a more integrated program centered around significant problems. The latter can be carried out with the best results in classes where the instructor knows students' abilities, interests, personalities, and idiosyncrasies. The assumption here is that in professional courses much greater use will be made of other staff members so that the student will also have broader contacts than before.

All courses intended to prepare the student for teaching and certification, professional courses and courses in subject fields to be taught, should form a closely related program of professional education developed around the needs of teachers and adolescents.

If courses in the subject matter fields, required as preparation for teaching, are to be taught by subject matter departments, there needs to be constant planning together by education and other departments to achieve a common understanding of the purposes of the teacher education program. The kind of situation in which the subject departments scoff at education courses, or where there is division and mutual suspicion, is mere mockery and pretense at good teacher education.

Courses that develop the student's understanding of the subject area are far removed from the needs of the prospective teacher unless they have a direct bearing on the subject matter that is suited to the secondary school. Instructors of such courses should understand the purposes and nature of the secondary school through keeping in touch with public schools.

All three phases of teacher education—general education, professional education, and the teaching fields—should form an integral part of a whole. Each is a necessary part of education for effective professional participation. Those who teach in these three areas should work together as a team. Unless present university organization can reform itself to encourage this type of teamwork, probably a drastic revision of the whole scheme of education of the secondary school teacher will be called for.

A great deal of direct laboratory experience in schools and in the community is fundamental as preparation for teaching in the modern secondary school.

The secondary school that wants to prepare youth for active participation in a challenging world has no place for lesson-hearers or order-keepers. Both of these types of teachers would be easy to secure without any training for teaching. Instead, the good teacher has to be able to guide pupil clubs or other activities, work with young people and adults in the community, take charge of P.T.A. programs, make intelligent and planned studies of the community and of pupils, lead faculty committees, and teach classes in such a way as to help pupils achieve social skills and develop changed behaviors in several ways. He needs pre-service experiences in as many of these activities as possible.

The opportunities for direct experiences in the pre-service program should be many and varied and should be provided through working arrangements between teacher education institutions and schools and community organizations. These experiences should be included:

1. Observing pupils and studying adolescent behavior.
2. Observing good teaching continuously over a period of time long enough to see the completion of plans developed by teacher and pupils.
3. Student teaching under teachers who know what is effective education and who understand children.
4. Assisting with student activities in schools.
5. Serving as director or counselor of youth groups in the community.
6. Studying a community and its organizations.
7. Assisting in teaching groups of students, both on campus and in the public schools.
8. Assisting in speech, reading, and psychological clinics.
9. Visiting schools to discuss the program with teachers and principals and to see the school in operation.
10. Serving as an apprentice or intern teacher in public schools.

More direct experience means student teaching in both campus laboratory schools and public schools of the state, the latter during extended periods of time when the student lives in the community. It means that, when a fifth year is added to the curriculum, it will be more than course-taking. The apprentice or internship programs with seminars to discuss experiences, hold considerable promise.

2. Some Typical Practices

In this book, we have attempted to appraise the American secondary school by applying principles as criteria against which practices may be judged. We have seen what some good secondary schools are doing in adjusting their programs to become real youth-serving agencies. The question will always arise as to what kind of teacher education is needed for a revised and reoriented secondary education such as described. Does the present kind of teacher preparation fit people for the exacting job of providing for youth the kinds of experiences that will help them grow and develop in desirable ways? Does it help to formulate the kinds of values that are consistent with a democratic society? Does it give a better and deeper understanding of that complex organism, the adolescent?

In this section is presented an overview of what teacher education is in some institutions of higher learning that prepare teachers for the secondary schools. It is not an encouraging picture. The conditions described here are those that need to be improved. They may apply to universities, liberal arts colleges, or teachers colleges. It is recognized that there are individual differences among these institutions. Some have the kind of program that has seen few changes in many years; others have gone a long way toward implementing the principles outlined in this chapter. The promising view is given in the next section, where programs of colleges with vision, courage, and imagination are discussed. It is the intention to present conditions as they exist, but no educator sincerely interested in improving secondary education can describe these conditions without comment.

Since it is recognized that the teacher is the major factor in determining pupils' experiences, it must follow that the education of the teacher to take his place in the schools of tomorrow is of vital concern. The modifications of secondary education proposed in this book will not come about unless teachers change in point of view and procedures; this is a cooperative task for both pre-service and in-service education.

A Minimum of Attention Given to Professional Education.—It has been stressed in this chapter that courses in general education, professional education, and the teaching fields are complementary, that it is not an either-or proposition. Yet, some institutions seem to consider professional courses as a necessary nuisance instead of as an important part of this trio. Evidence of that point of view can be found in the fact that sometimes people not trained in professional education, or without teaching experience in the public schools, teach those courses. These institutions offer only the minimum of education courses required by the state. Their staff members are rarely found providing leadership in the improvement of secondary education in the state. In fact, the preparation of teachers is regarded as an unwanted stepchild of the liberal arts function.

A Disjointed Type of Teacher Education.—In large colleges or universities, the whole institution has not always accepted its proper responsibility for teacher education. Different departments have built their courses without considering the needs of teacher education, and the college of education has not received the necessary cooperation to develop a good program. In these institutions, various subject departments in the liberal arts college and schools of business, home economics, and agriculture have a hand in the process of educating the teacher. Usually, he takes his first two years in one of these schools or colleges; during his last two or three years, they offer the courses in the subject matter fields which make up the major part of the student's program.

In some institutions, the arts college, which is a multipurpose college offering courses for students of medicine, law, dentistry, journalism, and education, is not genuinely interested in teacher education. The result may be that each of the colleges helping to educate the teacher goes its own way. Instances of group work among colleges of education and other colleges, in which staff members meet together to make decisions cooperatively, are few in number.

General Education Based on the Elective System.—Although the trend is toward broad fields and survey courses to provide the general education in the first two years of college, there are many colleges that follow the plan of providing within selected areas a certain number of electives from which a student can make a choice. He may, for example, be required to take two social science courses from specified courses in economics, government, anthropology, sociology, or history. Or perhaps ten credits in social sciences, fifteen in foreign languages, ten in science, and ten in English are required of all students, the choice of courses being open to them. In the case of many students, the choice is based on such criteria as well-liked instructors, "pipe" courses, courses not scheduled for Saturday, or courses not already filled. Often the resulting program does not represent a broad general education. The usual specialized chemistry or zoology course, or a history course that deals with only a small segment of history, for example, is not very suitable for general education purposes. Just as bad is the more comprehensive course superficially covered, emphasizing facts and recitation because the instructor feels he must cover the material and consequently has time for little else.

Preparation for Advanced Work Stressed.—In the liberal arts courses, there is a strong tendency to prepare for upper division or graduate courses. Many of the lower division courses, in the usual four-year liberal arts department or college program, are prerequisites to advanced courses. Consequently, the instructors make it their primary aim to provide basic foundations for further work rather than the understandings and skills needed by the student who will become a teacher. In some institutions, a comprehensive examination is given in the major field in the senior year. The result is that the student aims toward taking courses that will help him pass the examination rather than the ones he will need most for teaching the subject.

Research Ability Given Priority over Teaching Ability.—Research and professional writing in most universities have been more important criteria for advancement in rank than good teaching. The instructor who remains satisfied with teaching undergraduate students has been looked upon as a curiosity. Fundamentally, in universities and liberal arts colleges operating under this policy, the function of teacher education has taken a back seat. Not until good teaching in universities becomes as important as good research will teacher education be given the attention it deserves. Such a plan would call for selection of the best teachers for pre-service courses, not necessarily individuals with doctor's degrees, and a staff primarily responsible for teacher education that could plan and work together for the best interests of the students.

Graduate Teaching Considered Most Desirable.—Universities have a tradition, often strengthened by personnel policies, that the most desirable positions are those that involve teaching and counseling graduate students only. Consequently, undergraduate courses in colleges of education in universities have tended to be assigned to graduate students working for a doctor's degree, or as a secondary responsibility for those staff members whose major interest is in the graduate area. More serious is the related practice of assigning a hundred or more students to undergraduate lecture sections, while graduate classes are confined to twenty or thirty students. Some universities have given up entirely the function of pre-service education of teachers and confine their work to the graduate program. Only in recent years has the field of teacher education been developing as a desirable field in which to specialize.

Division of Education Courses into Specialties.—The criticism is sometimes made that content and problems discussed overlap considerably from one course to another. This criticism may be valid if the program of courses is an uncoordinated one, following the traditional college pattern of subdivision of courses into different phases of the subject. The sequence of professional courses provided frequently includes introduction to education, principles of secondary education, educational psychology, methods, special methods, and practice teaching. The pattern has grown up over a period of years and in many cases little has been done to question it. Too often instructors in each of the courses have planned their own work as specialists in that area with little or no cooperative planning with the other staff members. It has generally been assumed that the specialist in educational psychology could more effectively teach that course than one who has a broad view of education, knows the needs of teachers, and knows well the students whom he is teaching. Classes are shifted from one instructor to another at the end of each quarter or semester at a time when the instructor is just becoming well acquainted with the students, their problems, needs, and interests. The guidance function and the instructional function are seldom combined.

For teacher preparation, science, social studies, English, mathematics, agriculture, and all the rest of the high school subjects are typically divided into separate special methods courses; little experimentation has been attempted with other patterns. Grouping within a class to take care of these differentiated needs and interests is still a relatively unexplored procedure at the college level.

Specialization in the Subject Fields.—The pattern of courses in the subject fields presents a somewhat similar picture. In many cases a student can major in only such specialized fields as botany, zoology, chemistry, history, or government. For the purposes of the secondary school, such a major is similar to one in English literature. Usually the student is required to complete a minor in a second teaching field which will make a logical combination of the teaching subjects found in the secondary schools. This plan helps to develop specialists in a subject, but does not provide for the broader background needed in recent developments in the secondary school, such as the core curriculum, or for teaching in the junior high school. There is, however, a desirable trend toward a major in a broad field, such as the social studies or science. In some institutions this is known as a "distributed major." Unfortunately, the emphasis in the education of secondary school teachers has been toward making subject matter specialists rather than specialists in learning, adolescent development, and the knowledge and selection of instructional materials and content that are suitable for different levels of maturity.

Limited Period of Student Teaching.—The typical plan of student teaching in colleges and universities preparing secondary school teachers provides one period of teaching, usually during the senior year. Many institutions place their students in schools in the immediate community or in their own laboratory school. In such cases the period of time extends over a quarter or more, but frequently involves only one period of teaching a day for the academic subjects. There is little opportunity for studying the total school and community, for the student is at school for only the single period, or possibly two, and has responsibilities for other campus classes during the period of student teaching. Observation is usually made available as a separate course in itself and is only loosely coordinated with the other professional courses.

Lecture Method Widely Used.—In college classes taken by the future teacher, the method used is still predominantly the lecture. Large classes, tradition, and the lack of professional training on the part of many instructors have all contributed to this condition. This is perhaps the weakest phase of the education of the teacher for carrying out modern principles of secondary education. The inexperienced teacher is likely to use the methods he has experienced in his own high school and college classes, especially when he lacks confidence in himself.

When this method is used almost exclusively, there is no opportunity for cooperative planning of goals and experiences. Grouping within the class is a rare procedure, and visual aids may be used infrequently. The student, through his experience in this type of class, is likely to learn to be an "expert" as a teacher, one who gives out information and answers all the questions. The use of the subject-centered curriculum in his classes on campus does not make him proficient in the use of the experience approach.

The Textbook As a Basis for the Curriculum.—Most college courses taken as a part of preparation for teaching are to a large extent based on the contents of the textbook selected for the course. The single text is more common than multiple texts or use of reference books alone. Less frequent are direct experiences through observation, visits to schools, the use of individuals as resources, the use of campus resources, the use of audio-visual aids, work with young people, and the like. These laboratory experiences are coming to the fore in the reorganized teacher education program described in the next section.

As a result, evaluation is done largely in terms of objective or essay examinations, given at mid-term and at the end of the semester. Self-evaluation, cooperative evaluation, observation, anecdotal records, and evaluation of growth in attitudes are used mainly in situations where there is cooperative student-teacher planning.

3. Forward-Looking Practices in Teacher Education

In part, the improvement of the secondary school of the future will depend upon the point of view, the interest in children, the desire for change, and the ability to use modern procedures that the new teacher going into these schools will have. Principals increasingly are looking for the kind of teacher who has broader competencies than teaching one or two subject fields; they seek one who has had pre-service experiences in cooperative planning, studying pupils, and working with young people in many ways.

Teacher education institutions that practice what they preach are constantly striving to find better ways of preparing secondary school teachers. They go beyond producing teachers who can teach a major and a minor subject. They go beyond the stage of arguing whether the subject matter or professional education is most important. In the accounts of how these colleges have developed their programs, we read about the cooperative work of the education staff and staff members in other departments. They see their jobs as a joint project for the preparation of teachers.

In the practices described here, the student of education will see an application of the principles discussed at the beginning of this chapter. Furthermore, he will see put into use the principles of a good learning situation, for good teaching and learning are much the same at all school levels.

Providing a Broad General Education.—In institutions that have studied the problem of improving the means for providing a good general education for students, some cutting across of departmental lines to provide broad fields or survey courses has usually resulted.

In the Troy State Teachers College, Troy, Alabama, revision of the curriculum resulted in a plan that included study of the biosocial development of the individual (biology, physical education, psychology, and sociology) and a fused course on arts in individual development in the freshman year; a course on man and his natural environment, one on socioeconomic problems of the region and nation, and another on arts in contemporary society in the sophomore year. These are called core courses and are in some cases scheduled for more than one period a day. Teams of faculty members worked together in planning the courses.[1]

---

[1] Earl Armstrong, Ernest V. Hollis, and Helen E. Davis, *The College and Teacher Education,* Washington, D.C.: American Council on Education, 1944. pp. 66-78.

Another example, from New Jersey State Teachers College, Upper Montclair, New Jersey, indicates how general education is provided in a series of courses common to all students.[2] These courses include the various areas considered important phases of general education. The required work in each of four major areas is indicated:

	Semester Hours	
Social Studies		
Civilization and Citizenship	6	
Contemporary Economic Life	2	
Contemporary Political Life	2	
Contemporary Social Life	2	
		12
Literature, Language, Art and Music		
World Literature	6	
Composition	3	
Fundamentals of Speech	3	
Foundations of Language	2	
Art Appreciation	1	
Music Appreciation	1	
		16
Science		
Survey of Physical Science or Survey of Biology	4	
Survey of Earth Science	2	
Hygiene and Health	2	
		8
Mathematics		
Social and Commercial Uses of Mathematics	2	
Educational Statistics	2	
		4
		40

It is evident in these programs that the general education of the future teacher is not left to the hit-or-miss system of electives, but provision is made for the common learnings considered significant for all students.

Integrating of Experiences in Professional Courses.—Recent approaches in teacher education indicate a promising trend away from separate courses in education, taught by different instructors, toward developing integrated courses that fuse much of the content in the old courses and provide for a problems approach to the study of education. These courses usually extend over a longer period of time.

The need for fusion of courses within the field of education is be-

---

[2] John G. Flowers and others, *School and Community Laboratory Experiences in Teacher Education,* Oneonta, N.Y.: Charles Hunt, Secretary, American Association of Teachers Colleges, State Teachers College, 1948, pp. 46-47.

ing recognized. The Commission on Teacher Education, a national body appointed by the American Council on Education to study teacher education, has committed itself in this direction:

We are ready to suggest abolishing as separate and autonomous courses such subjects as general psychology, principles of secondary or elementary education, organization and administration, or classroom management.[3]

The content of these offerings is included in the integrated courses and organized around problems. Much useless duplication is eliminated and valueless content discarded. In other words, there is an emphasis on solving problems rather than on covering subject matter.

Promising attempts are being made to relate information from the subject areas and the professional courses. Future teachers are helped to see how the content studied in English courses, for example, can be used with high school students. As these concepts are developed in various courses that are required for professional purposes, the teacher education program actually becomes institution-wide in scope and function.

New Jersey State Teachers College, Jersey City, New Jersey, has a junior practicum course that serves to integrate professional courses and observation and student teaching experiences.[4]

The College of St. Catherine, St. Paul, Minnesota, has moved in the direction of a planned sequence of courses in social understanding in the junior year and an integration of special methods and practice teaching in the senior year. Guided observation and study of children, the community, and the school situation are integrating factors throughout the professional courses. In the senior year of student teaching and special methods, the instructor brings in other members of the department of education and supervising teachers from the public schools to work with students in the course.[5]

The situation at the Ohio State University presents an example of teamwork within the institution, rather a group of individual stars each proceeding in his own direction, a rather common picture of university staffs a decade or so ago. Here staff members from education and the subject matter fields work together on committees to consider the problems of teacher education in a group attack.[6]

At the University of Connecticut, the juniors in the School of Education take an integrated course, secondary education: learning and

3 Armstrong, Hollis, and Davis, *op. cit.,* pp. 306-7.
4 Flowers and others, *op. cit.,* pp. 83-87.
5 Armstrong, Hollis, and Davis, *op. cit.,* pp. 129-37.
6 *Ibid.,* pp. 276-86.

the adolescent. It combines the areas of learning, understanding the adolescent, and evaluation of growth of adolescents, with the study of the secondary school, its curriculum and organization to provide for significant learning experiences. Problems are developed around the study and observation of children and adolescents in surrounding elementary and secondary schools, and around the study of the curriculum, guidance, extraclass activities, and organization of secondary schools visited. Plans for the senior year are to fuse general and special methods together with related phases of educational psychology. The center of interest of this course, taught over two semesters, is the study and observation of children and adolescents, their growth, development, adjustment problems, and school experiences.

Extending Student-Instructor Contacts.—The scheduling of students with the same instructor over a period of time longer than a semester or a quarter for classes or for counseling is a practice that is complementary to provision for integration of experiences. Only as the instructor has the opportunity to work with students for a longer period of time can real integration be accomplished. Instead of the typical sequence of educational psychology taught apart from methods, the concepts of learning are related to method by the same instructor. Continuous counseling is provided through the assignment of a student to one instructor as his counselor for two or more years. Smaller classes, where the instructor knows his pupils well, have been found essential to effective teacher education.

The plan provides for (1) a fusing of the guidance and instructional functions in one person, (2) better individualization of instruction, and (3) a possibility of planning a continuous sequence of experiences over a longer period. Cooperative planning by instructor and students brings about many contacts with other staff members, who serve as resource persons to the group. Continuous planning on the part of the staff frequently becomes a part of this plan. At the University of Connecticut, in the example given above, a staff member works with a group of about thirty students for a year. He also serves as their counselor for a longer period.

The Willimantic State Teachers College, Willimantic, Connecticut, has developed a plan whereby an instructor, who is called a coordinator, works with a group of about twenty-five students during both the junior and senior years. The coordinator has charge of this group for all their work except physical education and music. He is responsible for supervising their student teaching. The group meets with the coordinator to plan their programs in order to see what resource people and community and school resources will be used. This is not a one-man contact proposition, for a good many resources are used; at least six other instructors work with a group during the year, for a period of from a week to eight or more weeks. The instructors who serve as resource persons have this work as their teaching assignment and have no regularly scheduled classes. This is an example of a well-integrated program and the use of a great deal of student-instructor planning.

Using the Experience Approach in Pre-Service Courses.—Perhaps one of the most important and far-reaching changes exemplified in the forward-looking programs of teacher education is the changed procedures used by staff members in their own classes. The day of the college professor who taught one type of theory and practiced another in his classes is fast approaching an end. Teacher education institutions are realizing that, first of all, they need good teachers as staff members responsible for professional undergraduate education. They have found it necessary to extend the usual three periods a week of class time to three two-hour "laboratory" sections, or some other plan that gives time for the many types of activities.

Such institutions are aiming in these courses to give students the kinds of experiences that they expect them to use with their own pupils. To some extent, the practices described in the following sections are also spreading into the subject content courses. Specific examples can be found throughout the literature listed in the bibliography of this chapter. For example, the complete discussion of the program in Troy State Teachers College, cited above, has many illustrations of good teaching procedures.

Cooperative Planning by Students and Instructor.—There is a genuine atmosphere of cooperation in the better college classrooms. Instead of the instructor's deciding what students are to cover and giving daily assignments, there is a cooperative planning of goals to be accomplished in the course. Decisions on types of activities, visits to schools, and observation are made by the group as a whole. Many students are experiencing for the first time the opportunity to select their own reading and their own projects instead of being told what to do. No longer does the dreary lecture set the stage for dozing and nonparticipation in those courses. Excerpts from a statement of one instructor, quoted in one of the volumes of the study of the Commission on Teacher Education,[7] illustrates what is happening:

---

[7] Armstrong, Hollis, and Davis, *op. cit.,* p. 178.

To continue drawing upon the instructor's memorandum, the "questioning attitude" of undergraduates led to "the first venture in teacher-student planning" for the conduct of the class. In succeeding quarters with other students the originally "unwieldly group procedure" got "streamlined" but the instructor ended by doubting if he would "ever go back to a teacher-planned and directed course."

Studying the Needs of Students.—There is an increased attention being paid to the student's background, special abilities, potentialities, activities, and living conditions. A course planned for any one group, in which all students have the same assignments, is scarcely an appropriate setting for provisions for individual needs. Personal interviews, inventory tests, check lists, sociograms, and anecdotal records are but a few of the means used to gather data about the student. The combination of guidance and instructional functions in one person permits a better knowledge of the student. A centralized counseling service, which functions for referrals, testing, case conferences, and special problems, supplements and assists the individual instructor-counselors.

Building Courses on Students' Needs.—As courses are planned cooperatively with students, units are built around problems with which the student is concerned. The observation of and work with children, experiences with youth groups, student teaching, and other direct experiences included in the better teacher education programs all stimulate questions and furnish motivating centers around which to build the course. Problems, not subject matter, are the bases for the unit in these courses.

Grouping Within the Class.—Instructors have discovered that students will learn how to group within classes more readily if they experience that kind of situation in their college classes, rather than merely being told about how it is done. Investigating problems, developing means of evaluation, and preparing for observation offer many opportunities for committee and small-group work. Students plan together with the instructor the problems that need to be explored, search out the information, work in groups in the class in order to plan and to share findings, and report to the total class.

Using Many Types of Teaching Aids.—The better programs of teacher education are child-centered and people-centered, rather than book-centered. College instructors in these programs realize that, in order to teach others how to use many sources of information, they must use such procedures in their own courses. They use many such audio-visual aids in their classes as "A Broader Concept of Method," a film which illustrates teacher-pupil planning in an experience unit.[8] Their students operate the projectors, after learning how to use them by working in the audio-visual aids center on campus as part of their class experiences. Individuals, schools, curriculum laboratories, bureaus of educational research, and community organizations are also used as sources of information. The single textbook is being replaced in many courses by more than one book, and a good deal more use is being made of reference books.

Evaluating Growth in Terms of Behavior.—The trend is away from emphasis on marks and toward a stress on the measurement and recording of growth of many types that cannot be included in a single mark symbol. As students plan their goals with the instructor, they also periodically evaluate their progress toward those goals. The instructors are genuinely concerned with growth of students in understanding children, in developing values, and in improving skills of working with children. These are important changes in behavior not measurable by written examinations. Students keep their own records, rate themselves and other class members, and evaluate continuously their experiences in the course. Observation of attitudes, of ways of working in groups, of ways of working with children and the like, is an important technique in the instructor's evaluation of progress, because change of behavior rather than learning facts in order to repeat them on a test is his main objective. Attitude inventories and questions presenting a problem situation are more frequently used as written tests.

Providing Direct Laboratory Experiences.—"Professional laboratory experiences" is a new term used in teacher education literature to refer to various contacts with children, adults, community organizations, and schools, planned for the purpose of better understanding children and communities as related to the teaching situation. The study of the community, study of children and adolescents, student teaching, and internship all are such experiences.

The following is a rather comprehensive list of the kinds of direct experiences forward-looking teacher education programs are providing for their students. They are included in the professional courses or planned in those courses for vacation periods. They serve to make those courses more meaningful and alive to students. Moreover, they help develop skills of working with communities and with

---

[8] Issued by McGraw-Hill Book Co., Inc., New York.

adolescents. Observation tends to be an integral part of other courses rather than a course by itself.

Visiting schools
Observing good teaching procedures over a continuous period
Working with children and adolescents in schools
Assisting in student activities
Teaching Sunday school
Doing recreational work in summer camps
Directing Scouts, church groups, and other youth groups
Directing playground
Assisting in remedial and guidance clinics
Assisting in audio-visual aids centers, testing bureaus, and curriculum
    laboratories
Working with social and service clubs
Working with welfare organizations
Assisting in libraries
Assisting in recreational work
Doing 4-H Club work
Working with community music groups
Working in child care centers
Working in YMCA or YWCA
Participating in forum discussions
Participating in student activities on campus
Student teaching

Many of the examples given in this chapter illustrate the use of laboratory experiences. Another type of such experience is "The September Field Experience Plan" of the Ohio State University. Students in the freshman through the senior year are given the opportunity before the opening of university classes to spend full time for two or three weeks in a high school, as a general exploratory service experience. The students function both as assistant staff members and as observers. They give clinical and administrative assistance in the office, to the teacher, and in the library; assist the teacher in the classroom in many ways; assist with extraclass activities; observe the school as a whole and its community activities.

Studying the Community.—We can look forward with considerable optimism to how future teachers will understand and utilize the community and function as community members. These are likely to be teachers who will have received their education in institutions which include direct contact with the community as a part of professional or related courses. Experiences in these colleges are generally of these types:

1. Participation in parents' meetings, forums, and civic meetings.
2. Excursions into the community.

3. Work with youth groups in the community: church, YMCA, YWCA, Scouts, Grange, etc.
4. Work with welfare and service organizations.
5. Survey of a community or phases of community life.
6. An extended period away from campus studying a community.

Students receive actual experience in working in a community as a part of the curriculum of the education courses. In the University of Wisconsin course on the community, excursions, surveys, and participation in civic organizations are an important part of the work in learning more about the community and its relations to the school.[9] At Miner Teachers College, Washington, D.C., community experiences are an integral part of courses in introduction to education and educational psychology.[10]

· The New York University curriculum for students planning to teach provides for some experience in community agencies. During their freshman year, students are placed in such social welfare agencies as the Red Cross, neighborhood houses, orphans' homes, and community centers to spend time with social workers for two afternoons or evenings a week. At Ohio State University, students must have some paid group experience and some service experiences.

At the University of Minnesota, in its integrated program in the junior year, students spend two to three hours of community youth participation per week in addition to attending three one-hour lecture sessions and two two-hour laboratory discussion periods. In the laboratory periods, students help plan with their instructor these experiences with community agencies. The youth work is coordinated through the Volunteer Service Bureau, where representatives meet regularly with the steering committee that carries on continuous planning for the course.

Intensive community study is carried on at Michigan State College, East Lansing, where students choose either six hours on campus or eighteen hours off campus in community study. In the latter plan, a group of ten to twenty students lives off campus for three months. The group gets an over-all view of all areas of community living. They participate in the Community Chest and Red Cross drives, P.T.A. events, and other worth-while experiences. The Willimantic State Teachers College, Willimantic, Connecticut, provides for field trips of a week's length to study a community and its

---

9 Flowers and others, *op. cit.*, pp. 109-12.
10 *Ibid.*, pp. 116-19.

social problems, such as a trip to a Pennsylvania coal mining district.

Studying Children and Adolescents.—Perhaps one of the most important experiences for undergraduate students in education, if we are going to move away from subject-matter-mindedness, is frequent guided contacts with children of different ages, maturity levels, and socioeconomic backgrounds. In the teacher education programs that live up to the principles of good education, a large proportion of time is spent on the study of child and adolescent growth and development, partially through reading research and books, but largely through actual work with children. Case studies are frequently made in courses whose center of interest is the adolescent and his nature. Living educational psychology replaces the dry, unlifelike textbook courses where a child is seen in statistical form rather than in a dynamic situation.

These courses often begin in the freshman and sophomore years and are definitely planned to have numerous laboratory experiences, such as work with children in nursery schools, elementary schools, child guidance clinics, and playgrounds. It is correctly believed that the secondary school teacher will have a better understanding of adolescents and their growth if he is familiar with the different stages of children's growth.

In the junior and senior years, a considerable portion of the education courses is devoted to the adolescent and to experiences in the curriculum suitable for his development and interests. At that time, the student has a chance to work with young people in school activities, in summer camps, in youth groups, and in other ways. He may make further case studies and keep anecdotal records or other records of growth of pupils that he observes.

An interesting procedure has been found useful at Ball State Teachers College, Muncie, Indiana, in helping prospective teachers cut across subject lines to see themselves as teachers of children. In the course in principles of teaching, students select certain junior and senior high school pupils whom they follow throughout the school day in order to see them in a variety of situations. They also see their pupils outside of school at community functions, at restaurants, and the like.[11] The course, the child: his nature and needs, provides many direct experiences with children at the University of Wisconsin. Students select some activity which provides for con-

---

[11] *Ibid.*, pp. 74-79.

tinuous contact with and study of the child throughout the semester, such as a school club, Sunday school class, or a Scout troop.[12]

Student Teaching and Internship.—Student teaching is generally regarded as the most practical phase of the prospective teacher's professional preparation. Although it is a part of all teacher education programs, some colleges have progressed farther in making student teaching a vital experience.

Teacher education institutions that have secondary schools on campus, known as laboratory schools, use them to good advantage for observation, work with pupils, and student teaching. Opportunities are available in these schools for supervision by competent teachers who are a part of the college staff. It is an advantage to receive teaching experience in a school that has a curriculum adjusted to youth needs, as a number of laboratory schools have.

However, experience in a laboratory school is supplemented by practice teaching in the public schools, where the college student actually spends from six to twelve weeks living in the community and taking part in all the activities that make up the life of a teacher. This provides a complete and rounded-out experience, rather than a half-day or a few periods a day. The University of Connecticut; State Teachers College, Upper Montclair, New Jersey; and Florida State College for Women, for example, as well as other institutions, have provisions for such extended periods of off-campus teaching.

Supervising teachers in the schools and college staff members jointly supervise the student teacher. Experiences that a student receives, in addition to teaching in the classroom, are guiding extra-class activities, participating in faculty meetings, assisting in the school library, conferring with parents, participating in parents' meetings and other community activities, making a study of the community, finding out about the administration of the school, working with counselors, supervising playgrounds, helping to plan assemblies, following pupils through various classes, and assisting with other duties of the school.

As student teaching is made an integral part of the professional education of the teacher, many opportunities are used for planning together the experiences before students begin to teach and using the student teaching as a basis for further discussion of procedures.

Few colleges have developed extended plans of internship teaching, in the sense that the medical profession uses the term, that is,

---

[12] *Ibid.*, pp. 110-12.

guided teaching as a member of the staff of a school. At Northwestern University, a fifth year of internship is planned which, combined with two summer sessions of work, will lead to a master's degree. The plans include a year of internship in a school, for which some pay is received, supplemented by a seminar course at the university on Saturdays to plan experiences, discuss problems, and exchange ideas.

The new teacher education program in the state of Washington provides that the beginning teacher is to have an initial year of teaching experience after which he shall immediately begin his fifth year of college work; this he may complete (after his year of experience) either in summer school or in a full academic year. The school district and the pre-service institution help him to evaluate his first year of teaching and plan for his fifth year of college work. Four-year graduates receive a provisional general certificate which is valid for one year and renewable annually for four years. Their undergraduate preparation emphasizes either elementary or secondary education, but all will have professional laboratory experiences in both levels. The assumption is that teacher education is the responsibility of the profession as a whole, and emphasis in the program is upon increased cooperation between public schools and teacher education institutions in the education of the teacher.

4. First Steps

Recommendations presented here relate both to what teacher education institutions concerned can do as first steps toward an improved situation and to what the beginning teacher himself can take as his first steps. In this case, we are concerned with the student's experiences before he goes out to teach on a full-time job. There are a number of things that he can do within the framework of his present college courses to make them more vital and useful.

For teacher education institutions:

1. Teacher education institutions should examine the competencies needed by good teachers in order to determine the best type of program for their students. This kind of group study can begin with education staff members and gradually bring in people from other departments.

2. The appointment of a coordinator of teacher education from the education staff, who has at least part of his time assigned to coordinating and developing the program, would be a good step to

take in order to get people together from different areas. Mutual understanding is secured by people getting together, not by throwing slurs at each other from desks across the campus.

3. Those concerned with preparing teachers for the secondary schools should get together often with public school teachers and administrators to discuss the kind of secondary school teachers needed in the schools and to work out ways in which direct experiences can be provided to meet these goals.

4. Visits to secondary schools by subject department staff members concerned with the education of teachers should be required as a starting point for better understanding of what the secondary school is trying to do. A closer relationship with secondary schools and their problems should be striven for by those institutions whose education staff members have kept themselves relatively isolated from the schools.

5. College instructors who are genuinely interested in improving teacher education might well start in their own classrooms by discussing the matter with students.

6. College staffs should examine all unused possibilities in the institution and surrounding community for opportunities for study of and work with youth and the community and for direct laboratory experiences that can revamp sterile book learning, lecture, and paper courses into better learning media.

For students in education:

7. Students in education courses can make those classes more valuable for themselves through visits to schools and discussions about education with principals, teachers, and college staff members, at every opportunity.

8. Prospective teachers should strive to build for themselves a set of values or principles that will help them to guide their thinking in teaching situations.

9. Prospective teachers should use every opportunity to participate in campus activities, such as journalism, speech, forums, dramatics, music organizations, and others that will help them to develop skills for directing class or extraclass activities.

10. Students in college who expect to go into teaching can work toward becoming students of society through participation in social studies courses, forums, discussions, and independent study.

11. There are many opportunities for work with youth groups, summer camps, observation of adolescents, and other contacts with

children and youth that can be taken advantage of by the individual student who wants to become a good teacher.

SELECTED REFERENCES

ALBERTY, HAROLD, and OTHERS. *Preparing Core Teachers for the Secondary Schools* (Mimeographed). Columbus, Ohio: College of Education, Ohio State University, 1949, 46 pp.—This is a monograph devoted to the type of pre-service education needed by core teachers. One chapter reviews the status of teacher education for core teachers in a number of institutions.

ARMSTRONG, W. EARL, HOLLIS, ERNEST V., and DAVIS, HELEN E. *The College and Teacher Education.* Washington, D.C.: American Council on Education, 1944, 311 pp.—Contains illustrations of teacher education programs—general education, education in the subject fields, and professional education—from many teacher education institutions.

ASSOCIATION FOR STUDENT TEACHING. *Professional Laboratory Experiences: An Expanding Concept of Teacher Education* (1948 Yearbook). Lock Haven, Pa.: State Teachers College, 1949, 138 pp.—Describes pre-service education in a number of institutions, including specific examples that relate to many of the points discussed in the last section of this chapter.

CASWELL, HOLLIS L. (ed.). *The American High School* (Eighth Yearbook of the John Dewey Society). New York: Harper & Bros., 1946, chap. 10.—Discusses desirable emphases in pre-service education for the modern secondary school.

COMMISSION ON TEACHER EDUCATION. *Teachers for Our Times.* Washington, D.C.: American Council on Education, 1944, 178 pp.—Outlines the type of teachers needed by our schools, with implications for teacher education.

COOK, LLOYD ALLEN, and COOK, ELAINE FORSYTH. *A Sociological Approach to Education.* New York: McGraw-Hill Book Co., Inc., 1950, chaps. 19, 20.—Gives a vivid picture of campus community life as it affects the future teacher. Discusses the social skills the teacher needs to develop as a leader.

FLOWERS, JOHN G., and OTHERS. *School and Community Laboratory Experiences in Teacher Education.* Oneonta, N.Y.: Charles Hunt, Secretary, American Association of Teachers Colleges, State Teachers College, 1948, 340 pp.—The entire book is a report full of illustrations of the kinds of laboratory experiences being provided by teacher education institutions all over the country.

MacCONNELL, CHARLES M., MELBY, ERNEST O., and ARNDT, CHRISTIAN O. *New Schools for a New Culture.* New York: Harper & Bros., 1943, chaps. 11, 12.— These chapters deal with the kind of a teacher and teacher education needed for modern, democratic schools.

Ch. 19]   PRE-SERVICE EDUCATION OF THE TEACHER   449

Chapter 19

THE BEGINNING TEACHER'S IN-SERVICE EDUCATION

Most educators know the difficulties encountered by beginning
teachers. The difficulty with the "problem" class, with adjustment
to a new community, with making new friends, with "keeping ahead"
of the pupils in subject matter, with planning interesting activities,
with locating a variety of instructional materials—these are only a
few of the problems encountered by the teacher in his first year of
service. It is the purpose of this chapter to discuss some of these
problems and to suggest how the beginning teacher can meet them.

1. The Principles

*The beginning teacher should make plans for the opening
activities of school before the completion of his pre-service education.*

Usually, the beginning teacher reports for work in his first position a day or two before school officially opens. He has probably
made little specific preparation for beginning the year satisfactorily.
As a result, he may be so overwhelmed during the first few weeks
with various duties and responsibilities that it is difficult for him to
do effective teaching. For this situation the teacher is only partly
responsible. Without experience he is not able to make adequate
preparation for the many responsibilities which attend the opening of
the school year. It is important that he have much assistance in
planning to meet those responsibilities. Since this may be done best
with the help and guidance of the education faculty at his college or
university, it should be included as a significant part of his pre-
service education.

The planning for the opening of the school year, presented as a
part of pre-service education, should be definite and specific, and
should include such matters as the following:

1. How to find a suitable place to live in a new community.
2. How to become oriented to the policies, rules, and regulations of
   the school system.

3. How to become familiar with the curriculum and courses of study in the school.

4. How to get acquainted with the pupils—their individual characteristics, personality and character qualities, abilities, interests, previous achievement, and out-of-school backgrounds.

5. How to plan the work for the term or the year, particularly if there is not an adequate course of study or a series of regular planning meetings by the teachers.

6. How to plan teaching activities for the first week or two of school.

7. How to get acquainted with the instructional aids and resources in the community.

8. How to get acquainted with reference materials and teaching aids in the school system.

9. How to discharge administrative responsibilities effectively.

Because of their importance to the success of the beginning teacher, activities such as these need to be carried on either before school opens or early in the year. For prospective teachers who are placed in their first position before the close of their pre-service education, the planning may be done in terms of the school where they are to teach. They can visit the school, study the community, obtain programs of studies and courses of study, study school policies and regulations, and locate a place to live. For students who obtain positions during the summer, such planning must be in more general terms. Even so, these students can be fully informed concerning the activities for beginning their first year's work before they complete their pre-service education.

The beginning teacher should make plans for in-service growth before the completion of his pre-service education.

It is not sufficient merely to help the teacher begin his work satisfactorily. He should also be assisted in making plans for in-service growth during his years in the profession. Often, the beginning teacher is so tired of attending school that, upon graduation from college, he has no desire to make plans for advanced study. Consequently, several years may pass before he seriously plans activities leading to in-service growth. This is particularly unfortunate because he will probably need the most help during his first years of teaching. The assistance to the beginning teacher in planning for in-service improvement before the completion of his teacher education program should emphasize the following:

1. He should be helped to see the importance of activities for growth and improvement in service.
2. He should become familiar with the various sources of in-service help—advanced study at colleges and universities, professional reading, participation in the activities of professional organizations, assistance from supervisors and consultants, travel, and experiences in other vocational areas during summer vacations.
3. He should plan for membership in selected organizations in his teaching fields and in the profession as a whole, both at the state and the national levels.
4. He should prepare plans for budgeting his time to provide for in-service improvement.
5. He should become inspired to contribute to the profession through experimentation, study, research, and writing.

The beginning teacher should have the assistance of his preservice institution through follow-up activities.

The responsibility of the teacher education institution for its students does not end on commencement day when the graduate walks across the platform to receive his diploma. In fact, the responsibility of that institution extends beyond its own students; it is ultimately responsible to the children in our elementary and secondary schools, to the parents of those children, and to the state and the nation as a whole. In other words, a teacher education institution is ultimately responsible for the success of its graduates in the schools where they serve as beginning teachers. This responsibility can be discharged satisfactorily only through well-planned follow-up activities.

Follow-up activities may be of various types, including correspondence with beginning teachers who have serious problems, mimeographed or printed suggestions that are sent to all graduates, periodic conferences on the college campus for beginning teachers, regularly planned extension and summer courses designed for beginning teachers, and visitation of teachers by college supervisors. All these activities have some merit.

Follow-up activities should be planned cooperatively by the teacher education institution and the school authorities where the graduates are employed. The teacher education institution is interested in helping the beginning teacher implement the philosophy, theory, and practices which he has studied. The teacher, however, is under the immediate supervision of a local principal and superintendent; he is expected to adapt himself to the philosophy of the school where he is employed. His success, which will be measured by his effectiveness in the school situation where he finds himself, will be most effective if there is complete cooperation and understanding between the teacher education institution and the local school authorities concerning the follow-up activities.

How long the follow-up activities should be carried on is debatable. Surely, they should continue until the beginning teacher has developed confidence in his professional abilities and has gained reasonable success in his work. All teachers should have rather close follow-up for the first year or two, while for some teachers a longer period may be desirable. The pre-service institution should, however, keep in touch with all its graduates indefinitely, noting their successes, encouraging and assisting them with their problems, and aiding them in their professional advancement.

The beginning teacher should have assistance in becoming oriented to the community.

The success of the beginning teacher will be measured to a large extent by the adjustment which he makes to the community where he begins his professional career. The home in which he lives, the church he attends, the community activities in which he participates, the recreation in which he engages, the friendships he forms—these have a significant bearing on his personal happiness and, in turn, on his professional success. It is exceedingly important, therefore, to help the beginning teacher find happiness in the community where he teaches.

Various persons should have a part in helping the teacher become adjusted to the community: the board of education, the superintendent of schools, the principal, the other teachers, the members of the P.T.A., the pastors of the several churches, and leaders in community activities and organizations. If all these persons were to assist the beginning teacher, it would go far toward making pleasant his life away from home.

The teacher himself also has some responsibility in this matter. Beginning teachers frequently expect the people in the community to make all the advances, while they wait to be urged to participate in the life of the community. Sometimes they are so attached to their "home town" that they do not find it easy to develop a new community loyalty. Some years ago one teacher informed the writer that she could not contribute to the Community Chest because she was already contributing liberally in her "home town." This is an immature attitude on the part of a beginning teacher. He should make every effort to meet people in the new community, to attend church, to join some civic organizations, and to participate in community activities. Community participation will help him greatly in becoming fully adjusted to the community where he is doing his professional work.

The beginning teacher should have a teaching assignment which he is able to discharge effectively.

It seems only reasonable to give the beginning teacher an assignment which recognizes his lack of experience. Certainly, he cannot succeed as well if the demands that are made upon him compare with those of the teacher who has developed background and skill through years of experience. The beginning teacher should be assigned a lighter class load than the experienced teacher. He should have time to study the community, accumulate teaching materials, develop interesting and worth-while activities, plan the year's work, and prepare teaching plans. In large schools, it is customary to give teachers one or two free periods, while in small schools they often have no free time during the school day. It is a desirable practice to give the beginning teacher one more free period daily for planning and study than is provided for other teachers. The beginning teacher should also be assigned the less difficult classes. Pupils with the more obvious social and emotional adjustment problems should be placed with teachers who have sufficient skill and background to work effectively with them.

In extraclass activities, the same consideration should be shown in making assignments to the beginning teacher. In most pre-service teacher education programs, there is inadequate preparation for supervising these activities. It seems best, therefore, to have the beginning teacher serve as an assistant for a year or two to other faculty members in these activities. He could be an assistant club sponsor, serve as a committee member for social functions, and in other ways assume responsibilities in cooperation with experienced teachers. But he should assume a major responsibility for such activities only after he has had sufficient experience with them to assure his success as a faculty sponsor.

The beginning teacher should participate in professional improvement activities in the school even the first year, but such participation should not involve a major responsibility. It should serve as a learning experience for him, recognizing that his greatest contribution to the development of an effective instructional program in the school will best be made after he has had some teaching experience.

The beginning teacher should have adequate supervision from the superintendent, the principal, and other supervisors.

Adequate supervision—more than any other one thing—is essential to the success and professional growth of the beginning teacher. It should be based on a feeling of mutual confidence and understanding between the teacher and the supervisor. The teacher should realize that the supervisor's major responsibility is to assist him to succeed and improve, that the supervisor comes to him in a friendly, helpful spirit, and that he should feel free to call on the supervisor to assist him with any professional problems.

The assistance that the teacher can expect from the supervisor should be concerned with any problems that confront the beginning teacher, such as the following:

1. How to organize a year's work in a given subject area.
2. How to prepare unit and daily plans.
3. How to become acquainted with the characteristics, abilities, and interests of the pupils.
4. How to meet the needs, interests, and abilities of individual pupils.
5. How to locate instructional materials, references, and aids.
6. How to prevent or meet group discipline problems.
7. How to take care of administrative records, reports, and other matters that concern the teacher.
8. How to study the community as a basis for instructional activities.
9. How to improve himself professionally.

The supervisor should not confine his assistance to the beginning teacher to classroom visitation alone. He should have scheduled conferences with the beginning teachers as a group, he should prepare mimeographed materials for them, and he should have frequent individual conferences with them.

In most schools, the principal is the supervisor with whom teachers work most closely. They should ordinarily take their problems to him. The superintendent should be called upon only when the principal and the teacher believe that he has a particular contribution to make to the beginning teacher's work. In some schools a department head, the assistant principal, or general supervisor share in the responsibility for assisting the beginning teacher.

The beginning teacher should have the assistance of his fellow teachers with various professional problems.

It is only natural that the beginning teacher is reluctant to take all his questions and problems to the principal. He realizes that the principal is a very busy person, especially at the beginning of a school year. Furthermore, he may be hesitant to discuss some matters with the principal lest he give the impression that he is not competent in his work. The college supervisor, through follow-up activities, can be exceedingly helpful until the teacher and principal have established a feeling of mutual confidence and an effective working relationship. Other members of the faculty can also be of assistance to the beginning teacher in making an adjustment to the community, becoming oriented to the school, getting acquainted with pupils, understanding policies with regard to courses of study, and learning school policies, rules, and regulations.

It is even more important, however, that experienced teachers realize the influence they have on beginning teachers in developing enthusiasm for their work and in gaining a wholesome attitude toward their professional responsibilities. In a recent follow-up visit to one of his former college students, the writer offered the suggestion that she plan her work in more detail. The teacher replied that she lived with several fellow teachers, and that they did very little planning. Furthermore, they discouraged her from planning, stating that no one would ever know the difference. At the end of the year, she left the profession because she was disgusted with the nonprofessional attitudes of experienced teachers in her school. Present members of the profession have far more influence in shaping the professional attitudes of beginning teachers than they realize. They should make every effort to assist the beginning teacher with his professional responsibilities, to help him enjoy his life in the community, and to grow in professional thinking, enthusiasm, and effectiveness.

The beginning teacher should have assistance in becoming oriented to the profession.

Many members of the teaching profession are quite concerned by the fact that it takes several years for most beginning teachers to become enthusiastic members of the profession. They may be conscientious and enthusiastic about their work, they may engage in activities for professional improvement, and yet they may not identify themselves with the profession in their state or in the nation. It is important that teachers—like lawyers, doctors, and dentists— have a feeling of belongingness toward their professional group, that they keep in touch with state and national developments in education, that they develop contacts with leaders in education, and that they become participating members of professional organizations.

The professional organizations should take the initiative to encourage and assist beginning teachers to become oriented to the profession and to become identified with state and national groups. They not only should invite teachers to join, but they should encourage them to attend meetings, to write for their publications, serve on committees and study groups, and in other ways to become active in the work of the organizations. Likewise, the beginning teacher should be receptive to suggestions to become professionally active. He should realize that he will receive greater satisfaction from teaching if he has definitely identified himself with other members of the profession. He can do much to develop professional contacts and gain professional recognition through participation in the activities of local, state, and national organizations.

The beginning teacher should be placed in a school where he can best develop his talents and ideas.

While it is not always possible to carry out this principle, much more attention should be given to it than has been true in the past. In too many instances, teachers who have formed beliefs in harmony with the facts of the psychology of adolescence and of learning are placed in a school where they are told to "forget about the theories of education."

Placement officers in colleges and universities need to know the schools well and know what kind of a person would be happy in each. In large city systems, it is important that teachers be placed in a school where the staff might be congenial. If some school does not welcome young people with modern ideas about education, older experienced teachers preferably should be moved into that situation when vacancies occur. Placement in a school where principal and teachers are sympathetic to the beginning teacher's problems is a most important factor in his success.

2. Some Typical Practices

The assistance which teacher education institutions, elementary and secondary schools, and professional organizations provide for beginning teachers is indeed limited. There are, of course, many activities for in-service education, but they are usually designed to meet the needs of all teachers in the profession rather than the beginning teacher. Since the problems of the beginning teacher are unique, they are usually overlooked in the broader programs of in-service education. This discussion of typical practices in in-service education for beginning teachers, therefore, may be rather discouraging. If it focuses attention upon the need for improving these activities, it will serve a useful purpose.

In-Service Activities by Teacher Education Institutions.—The typical college or university which educates teachers for the secondary schools does very little to assist those teachers to succeed during their first years in the profession. The institution gives them their pre-service education, it grants them a degree, and it helps them obtain a position. Apparently, at that point the responsibility comes to an end; the teacher then becomes little more than a name on the alumni list of his alma mater.

There are, of course, certain informal ways through which an institution keeps informed about the success of its graduates. Members of the faculty in the department, college, or school of education may meet the employing superintendents and principals at professional conferences and seize upon that opportunity to ask them about the success of the beginning teachers. Then, too, many institutions suggest that superintendents and principals inform them if their beginning teachers encounter difficulties. Although this is a rather negative approach to in-service education, it does give the institution an opportunity to assist those teachers who clearly are having difficulty.

In some institutions, the placement office makes an organized effort to keep informed concerning the success of its teachers, particularly as a basis for recommending teachers for better positions. Various devices are used for this purpose. A common one is the sending after a year or two of a simple check list or questionnaire concerning the success of a teacher to the employing superintendent or principal. Such information is not used, however, to assist the beginning teacher to succeed in his present position.

These activities assist the institution to keep informed about the success of its graduates, but they do not make provision for the in-service education of the beginning teacher. Follow-up activities, such as visitation by a college supervisor, conferences for beginning teachers, and mimeographed aids for beginning teachers are carried on by so few institutions that they cannot be considered typical practices. Teacher education institutions should study this aspect of their responsibility to their graduates and to the schools of the state in an effort to provide more adequately for in-service education for beginning teachers.

In-Service Activities by Secondary Schools.—The activities provided for the in-service education of beginning teachers by the secondary schools are almost as limited as those provided by the teacher education institutions. There are some things, however, which are done. A handbook for teachers which outlines the policies and regulations of the school is provided for teachers in some schools. The handbook is intended for all members of the professional staff, but it is particularly helpful to the beginning teachers. In some schools, the teachers' handbook is sent to all new teachers several weeks before the opening of school so that they may be thoroughly oriented in the policies and regulations of the school before they arrive.

The teachers' handbook ordinarily includes such information about the school as its philosophy and aims of education, a description of the curricula and course offerings, a summary of the extra-class activities, the provision for supervisory help, the guidance program, the rules and regulations for pupils, the administrative rules and regulations for the professional staff, and such special services as the library, cafeteria, and health department. Some school systems have a handbook for the entire school system as well as handbooks for the individual schools. Beginning teachers should make it a point to ask the principal or the superintendent of schools about such a handbook.

In some schools meetings are held for all new teachers to orient them in the philosophy and the program of the school. Although these meetings are for all new teachers, they are especially valuable to the beginning teachers. In the typical school, these meetings are limited in number, usually being confined to one or two sessions. It would be helpful to beginning teachers if these group conferences were greatly expanded, both in number and in the topics covered.

The social life of the new teacher, and of course the beginning teacher, is given attention in a number of schools. Parties, picnics, and similar activities are provided to help the new teacher get acquainted with other teachers. These activities are particularly helpful if they include teachers from other schools in the system. The beginning teacher should welcome such activities as a means of forming acquaintanceships and friendships which will contribute to the happiness he may find in the community.

Few schools do anything to lighten the load of the beginning teacher. In fact, it seems to be the typical practice to give preferred assignments to the teachers on a seniority basis. The teacher who has been in the school the longest is likely to have the college preparatory groups, the best classroom, and the fewest different preparations. The new teacher takes what is left. This policy often means that the beginning teacher has the "problem" classes, the least desirable classroom, and the most teaching preparations. It is only in extraclass activities that he may receive some consideration, since frequently he is given a rather light extraclass load for the first year or two. Much thought needs to be given in our secondary schools to the kind of teaching load that beginning teachers should have.

In-Service Activities by Professional Organizations.—A number of the professional organizations encourage students, through student memberships or affiliated groups, to identify themselves with the professional groups during their pre-service education programs. The student membership dues are usually low, although they entitle the students to the publications and most of the privileges of regular members. The Future Teachers of America, sponsored by the National Education Association, is an example of a student professional organization. Some state educational associations also have such student groups.

After the completion of their pre-service programs, beginning teachers are invited, often urged, by various professional groups to become members. There is little done, however, to make them participating members. The officers, committee members, and participants at conferences and conventions are usually drawn from the membership of some years' standing. Few organizations make an organized effort to have beginning teachers become immediately active. Unless there is such a policy, beginning teachers are likely to be passed by for some years in favor of those who are better known because of long membership in the organization.

3. Some Outstanding Practices

Follow-Up Activities by the Pre-Service Institution.—A few teacher education institutions are providing for well-planned follow-up activities. Some have full-time supervisors to assist beginning teachers during their first year or two, while others have the regular staff carry on follow-up activities. At the University of Connecticut, the supervisors in the student teaching program are also responsible for follow-up supervision.[1] The advantage of this plan is that the faculty member who played an important part in the teacher's pre-service professional education—and consequently knows the teacher—is responsible for helping him become oriented to his in-service work. The supervisors plan to visit each beginning teacher three times during the first year, and perhaps once during each of the next two years. The number of visits may be increased for beginning teachers who need more help. The Connecticut program is not limited to the teachers who are having serious difficulty. Successful as well as unsuccessful teachers are given help in the belief that those who are doing satisfactory work may become outstanding teachers much sooner under proper supervision and encouragement.

The University of Connecticut also has follow-up conferences for beginning teachers. They are invited to return to the campus for a Saturday morning session several times during the year to discuss informally some of the problems they have encountered and how to meet them. At these meetings, there is no program of speeches on professional topics; the beginning teachers themselves present problems to the group for discussion. Faculty members are present to assist when that seems advisable.

A few teacher education institutions provide adequate staff for carrying on follow-up activities, since they realize that follow-up work contributes greatly to the success and satisfaction of the beginning teacher in his work. Likewise it is helpful to the institution, as it provides a continuous check on the effectiveness of its program of teacher education.

Adjustment in the Teaching Load.—It has been stressed that the load of the beginning teacher should certainly be lighter than that of the experienced teacher. Such a plan was tried experimentally at the Ridgefield, Connecticut, High School several years ago. Beginning teachers were given a lighter load; they served as assistants to experienced teachers in certain activities; and they were given planned assistance with their problems by the other teachers and the principal. The outcomes of this plan were more effective teaching, fewer serious discipline problems, and much greater satisfaction in his work for the beginning teacher.

Adequate Supervision for Beginning Teachers.—Some local school systems provide special supervisory activities for beginning

---

[1] William T. Gruhn, "When Teachers Leave the Campus," *Educational Leadership*, 5 (December, 1947), 141-44.

teachers. In small systems where there are only a few beginning teachers each year, this is done on an informal basis. In large systems there may be enough beginning teachers to justify a well-planned program of supervisory activities. These activities include:

1. A series of meetings to orient the beginning teacher in the policies, practices, and regulations of the school.
2. Planned conferences with supervisors and specialists, such as the physician and nurse, the guidance director or counselor, the librarian, and the director of audio-visual aids.
3. Planned social activities designed particularly to help the beginning teacher, as well as other new teachers, get acquainted with the faculty members and people in the community.
4. Frequent visitation by the principal or supervisor to classes taught by beginning teachers, followed by conferences.

4. FIRST STEPS

There are some things which can be done immediately to help the beginning teacher succeed and make reasonable professional growth. Some of these can be done by the teacher himself, while others concern the teacher education institutions or the local schools.

These are first steps in in-service education which may be carried on by the beginning teacher himself:

1. Prepare a plan for in-service education, preferably before leaving the pre-service institution and with the help of the faculty there.
2. Be enthusiastic about becoming the most effective teacher possible.
3. Take his problems immediately to his supervisor or principal instead of waiting until they become serious.
4. Go to the community where he is to teach several weeks before school opens to find a place to live, to obtain copies of courses of study and basic study materials, and to become acquainted with the facilities available for teachers in his department.
5. Come to the community to remain several days before school begins and devote this time to planning and study; organize the equipment, textbooks, and other study materials that he may use early in the year; and become acquainted with the materials in his field available in the school library, in the public library, and in the audio-visual aids center. If possible, he should become acquainted with the backgrounds of pupils he will have through a study of their previous records.

6. Prepare tentative but detailed plans for the first two or three weeks of school for all the classes he is to teach.

7. Affiliate immediately with several selected professional organizations, such as the National Education Association, the state association, the local association, and an organization in his subject field or field of special interest.

8. Attend the conferences and meetings of the various professional groups to which he belongs and begin to participate as soon as possible in their activities.

9. Consult frequently with his supervisor or principal concerning his work, taking the initiative to request such conferences if the supervisor or principal fails to do so.

10. Plan his time during the first year or two to provide for professional reading in current periodicals and recent books.

11. Take the initiative to affiliate with a local church, recreation groups, service clubs, lodges, or other community groups that interest him.

12. Become well acquainted with the community during his first year or two, studying the economic and social life of the people, the educational and recreational facilities, and the human and material resources that will help him in his work.

The teacher education institution may take these steps to help beginning teachers succeed and grow professionally:

1. Provide some activities late in the pre-service program which will help the beginning teacher with his work during the first year.

2. Provide for supervision of the beginning teacher by its faculty members in cooperation with the local supervisor or principal for the first year or two.

3. Provide follow-up conferences for beginning teachers, either on the campus or in convenient centers near the schools where the teachers are employed.

4. Have a long-term program of follow-up for all graduates, keeping in touch with their successes and assisting them in their professional advancement.

5. Attempt to place its graduates in schools in which they will be best adjusted to the type of faculty, the type of community, and the philosophy of the school.

The school system employing the beginning teacher may carry on activities such as these as first steps to improve its in-service education program:

1. Study the possibility of giving the beginning teacher a reduced load for at least one year, preferably one class less per day than for other teachers.
2. Provide a series of orientation conferences for all new teachers, including the beginning teachers.
3. Provide mimeographed or printed materials for all new teachers, summarizing the philosophy, aims, program, practices, and regulations of the school system.
4. Provide for considerable visitation of the classes of the beginning teachers, followed by individual conferences concerning their work. The supervisor or principal should provide this supervision.
5. Provide frequent conferences for beginning teachers with such specialists as the physician, nurse, librarian, guidance director, and director of audio-visual aids.
6. Provide social activities to help new teachers become acquainted with the other members of the professional staff and with people in the community.
7. Set up a plan whereby an experienced teacher makes it his special responsibility to assist a beginning teacher.
8. If there is more than one secondary school in the system, place the teacher in the type of situation in which he will have the best chance for success.

The professional organizations can also operate in certain ways to assist the beginning teacher, among them the following:

1. Have present members contact the beginning teachers to invite them to meetings and conferences, to help them get acquainted with the members, and in other ways encourage a feeling of interest by the organization in the teacher as a person as well as in the membership fee.
2. Have a definite policy concerning the appointment or election of young teachers to some positions of responsibility in the organization.
3. Make it a point to have some young teachers participate on all programs, contribute to the publications, and in other ways become contributing members of the organization.

SELECTED REFERENCES

BAXTER, BERNICE. *Teacher-Pupil Relationships*. New York: The Macmillan Co., 1946, chaps. 3, 5.—Presents some of the factors involved in successful personal adjustment to children. In Chapter 3, a contrast of successful and unsuccessful teachers is presented; in Chapter 5, the effective teacher is described.

DOUGLASS, HARL R., and MILLS, HUBERT H. *Teaching in High School.* New York: The Ronald Press Co., 1948, chap. 26.—Gives suggestions for the in-service improvement of beginning teachers.

LAMB, MARION M. *Your First Year of Teaching.* Cincinnati: South-Western Publishing Co., 1939, 35 pp.—An attractive monograph which presents informally some of the problems encountered by the beginning teacher.

PRALL, CHARLES E., and CUSHMAN, C. LESLIE. *Teacher Education in Service.* Washington, D.C.: American Council on Education, 1944, chaps. 2-6.—Discusses various types of in-service teacher education activities, particularly those planned and carried on with teacher participation. This volume is one of a series on teacher education sponsored by the Commission on Teacher Education of The American Council on Education.

REAVIS, WILLIAM C., and COOPER, DAN H. *Evaluation of Teacher Merit in City School Systems.* Supplementary Educational Monograph No. 59, January, 1945. Chicago: University of Chicago Press, 138 pp.—Describes many different ways of evaluating a teacher's effectiveness. Should help the beginning teacher to understand devices for teacher evaluation.

REAVIS, WILLIAM C., and JUDD, CHARLES H. *The Teacher and Educational Administration.* Boston: Houghton Mifflin Co., 1942, chap. 20.—A discussion of the improvement of teachers in service.

SCHORLING, RALEIGH. *Student Teaching.* New York: McGraw-Hill Book Co., Inc., 1949, chap. 14.—A discussion of things the beginning teacher may do to get started right in his first position, to make professional growth, and to add prestige to the profession.

"These Are Our Concerns." *Educational Leadership,* 5 (December, 1947), 145-54. —Summarizes the problems of beginning teachers in widely scattered parts of the country through material received in reply to a request for such information. Helpful to beginning teachers, to faculties at teacher education institutions, and to principals and supervisors who assist beginning teachers in service.

TROYER, MAURICE E., and PACE, C. ROBERT. *Evaluation in Teacher Education.* Washington, D.C.: American Council on Education, 1944, chap. 8.—Suggests ways of evaluating teacher growth in service. Another volume in the series sponsored by the Commission on Teacher Education of the American Council on Education.

WILES, KIMBALL. *Supervision for Better Schools.* New York: Prentice-Hall, Inc., 1950, chap. 12.—Gives practical suggestions for helping teachers evaluate their effectiveness as a basis for improvement. Although the suggestions apply to all teachers, they are especially helpful to the beginning teacher.

Chapter 20

RESPONSIBILITIES AND DUTIES OF THE TEACHER

The secondary school teacher of today has many responsibilities and duties other than classroom teaching. Although some of these responsibilities are relatively new, most of them have been assumed by the teacher in one form or another since the earliest secondary schools. The more important of these include responsibilities related to classroom teaching; responsibility for such extraclass activities as the home room, guidance, clubs, and assemblies; certain administrative responsibilities; responsibility for professional improvement and growth; and community responsibilities.

1. RESPONSIBILITIES RELATED TO TEACHING ACTIVITIES

Keeping Well Informed.—Every teacher, regardless of his experience, has the responsibility for keeping himself well informed. Only in that way can he have the background to be an intelligent, effective professional person. First, he should keep himself informed concerning cultural, social, economic, political, and scientific developments in general; this is important no matter what his area of subject specialization may be. It means a program of planned reading in various areas of interest. Furthermore, the teacher's reading concerning current questions should be so chosen that it covers various points of view, giving him that breadth of background and understanding which marks the well-read, cultured person.

Second, the teacher should continue to improve himself in the subject areas that he is to teach. This may be difficult on a teacher's limited salary because it is likely to involve, in addition to reading, such broadening experiences as travel, study abroad, work experience, graduate study at summer school and in extension classes, and attendance at workshops and conferences. If this study is to be most effective, it cannot be planned in terms of narrow subject areas. The teacher of a foreign language may, for instance, profit most by studying history, literature, economic and social life, and geography as related to the peoples whose languages he teaches. Work experience may be especially helpful to the teacher of English or social studies who has had little contact with life outside the secondary school or college classroom. A planned program of study and experiences will, over a period of years, add much to the background of information and ideas upon which the teacher may draw.

A third area in which the teacher should keep himself informed is in developments in professional education and such closely related fields as psychology of adolescence, psychology of learning, sociology, and anthropology. There is a wealth of information available on developments in the curriculum, teaching methods and procedures, and educational thinking which will be helpful to him in the improvement of his work as a teacher. Much research in psychology and sociology is especially pertinent to the teacher. He should avail himself of the opportunity to keep up with developments in these various areas.

Locating and Using Resource Materials.—Reference has just been made to the importance of having the teacher acquire broad backgrounds of ideas, understandings, and information. It is equally important that he accumulate materials that may be helpful to the pupils. The day of textbook teaching is indeed a thing of the past for the teacher who tries to work most effectively with his pupils. Today the textbook is supplemented by a variety of reference materials: films, film strips, slides, recordings, radio programs, library materials, bulletins and pamphlets, newspapers, magazines, and many other types of materials.

The teacher's work has increased greatly with the introduction of these new materials. Not only must he organize and arrange them so that they may be used effectively in a learning situation—he must first locate these materials. The latter task is often the larger one. The teacher today should keep in touch with the libraries of audio and visual materials; he should study publishers' catalogs for library materials; he should examine newspapers and magazines for current reference materials; and he should place his name on the mailing list of historical societies, industrial and business agencies, and civic and governmental agencies for informational materials which they may prepare.

The teachers in a secondary school will save much time for themselves by pooling their efforts in the location of reference materials. Professional publications in some subject areas are very helpful in listing study materials as they appear. Then, too, pupils can be helpful in locating certain types of materials. In fact, this is one way in which teachers may have pupils participate in planning and carrying on learning activities. In accumulating pamphlets, bulletins, charts, and similar materials, it is suggested that teachers obtain a sufficient number of copies for class use. Many agencies which distribute free and inexpensive materials are perfectly willing to make available a sufficient number of copies to meet the needs of secondary school groups.

Once the teacher has accumulated a file of reference materials, he is confronted with the problem of arranging them for ready reference. Although every classroom should have adequate cupboard space and filing cabinets for pamphlet materials, many schools have little or no space of this kind. An energetic teacher might be able to persuade the board of education, through his principal and superintendent, of the need for such space. If not, he may have to improvise filing space of his own. Some teachers find it helpful to arrange these materials according to the units in which they are to be used, while others arrange them by subject or title.

Locating and Using Community Resources.—The effective teacher today makes much use of the material and human resources in his community in planning and carrying on instructional activities. If he is going to use the community effectively as a laboratory, he must explore the possibilities which it offers for instructional aids and materials, such as the historical places that may be visited; the professional, business, civic, and labor leaders who may participate in the program of the school; and the business, industrial, and civic agencies that may be used for field trips. These resources must be located, studied for their contribution to the instructional program, and contacted to solicit their cooperation in the program of the school. Every teacher must work constantly at this task.

Planning for Instruction.—Teachers frequently do not see the importance of planning for the instructional activities which are carried on in the classroom. This is particularly true of beginning teachers. The daily routine of meeting classes, supervising extra-class activities, assisting pupils after school, reading the tests and papers prepared by pupils, and keeping records, consumes so much time that planning for instruction is frequently neglected. Yet, thorough planning is more important to the success of the teacher's work than any of the other duties he performs. The planning which a teacher does should therefore take precedence over his routine duties and responsibilities.

The amount of planning required in an experience-centered curriculum is far greater than that in a subject-centered curriculum. In the subject-centered curriculum, the teacher prepares a unit or lesson plan in terms of subject matter which, once it is completed, is transmitted to the pupils with little or no modification. There are no uncertainties in such a plan; the teacher can determine definitely and specifically in advance the work to be covered, the study materials needed, the assignments to be given, and the activities to be carried on.

In an experience unit, however, the pupils participate in planning the unit, the activities, and the study materials. In preparing for such a unit, the teacher becomes a resource person. As such he provides motivation for the class, brings in many suggested activities, and has a variety of study materials ready. The teacher should try to be ready for any turn that the unit may take. It is essential, therefore, that the teacher working in an experience-centered curriculum so organize his day that he will have much time to prepare for the learning activities of his classes.

The details of planning are the concern of a book on teaching methods rather than one such as this on the broader aspects of secondary education. Some suggestions concerning the teacher's responsibility for planning are appropriate, however, in this discussion. In an effective secondary school curriculum, especially when the experience-centered approach is employed, the following suggestions may be helpful:

1. There should be much cooperative planning between teachers in related areas of study as a step toward more effective integration in the instructional program of the school.
2. There should be much cooperative teacher-pupil planning in the daily activities, in the units of study, and in the total program for the year.
3. There should be participation in planning certain aspects of the school program by parents and other citizens. Such cooperative planning is especially appropriate in certain units in social studies, homemaking, industrial arts, and business education.
4. The teacher should do much planning far ahead, particularly if the experience-centered approach is employed. The teacher must be prepared to motivate, encourage, and assist pupils with all learning activities as the need arises. The day-by-day planning, so common a few years ago, is not appropriate for this purpose.

Working Effectively with Pupils.—The teacher's major responsibility is of course that of working with pupils. For the present, we shall concern ourselves particularly with his responsibility for working with pupils in the classroom type of learning situation.

In the secondary school, there was a time when the teacher assigned
lessons which the pupil was expected to complete with little or no assistance. Under the assign-study-recite method, as it has been called,
the teacher had these responsibilities: (1) he gave the assignment,
(2) he assisted the pupils only if they encountered difficulty, (3) he
heard the pupils recite and received their written work, and (4) he
evaluated the pupils' recitation and written work. The experience-
centered approach to teaching has greatly changed these contacts between teacher and pupil. Today, the teacher works closely with pupils
in formulating objectives, in planning learning activities, and in locating source materials; he supervises the pupils as they engage in the
learning activities, helping them whether they encounter difficulties or
not; and he helps the pupils evaluate their progress step by step as the
learning activity develops. With this approach, the entire learning
activity is a cooperative venture between teacher and pupil. It necessitates much more teacher-pupil contact than the assign-study-recite
approach. It may require teacher-pupil conferences during the class
period, after school hours, and occasionally on days when school is not
in session. The effective classroom today demands that the teacher
have the willingness and the skill to work with pupils in this cooperative manner.

Evaluating Pupil Growth.—The teacher is responsible for helping
the pupil make progress toward well-formulated and accepted educational goals. This means that there must be continual evaluation of
the pupil growth that is taking place. The teacher should have a well-
planned evaluation program which includes observation, check lists,
informal tests, formal teacher-prepared tests, standardized achievement tests, diagnostic tests, and any other measuring devices that help
answer the question: What progress are the pupils making toward
recognized objectives? The various methods of evaluation which the
teacher may employ were discussed at some length in Chapter 12.

There should also be much cooperative teacher-pupil evaluation.
In some instances pupils may participate in deciding how the evaluation should be made and in preparing the measuring instruments. In
any case, they should work with the teacher to interpret the results.
The pupil's participation in evaluation is essential if he is to analyze
his strengths and his weaknesses as a basis for improvement.

Supervising Extraclass Activities.—In addition to classroom
teaching responsibilities, most teachers have responsibilities for other
types of learning activities, such as guidance, the home room, clubs,
assemblies, and social functions. These activities make certain contri-

butions to the educational growth of the child which are not realized through typical class activities. For instance, they offer opportunities for developing leadership qualities, personality and poise, the ability to work with others, and good citizenship attitudes and skills. If they are to be effective, the various extraclass activities demand the same imagination, skill, and planning as any other aspect of the instructional program. The extraclass activities in the secondary school for which the teacher assumes responsibility are discussed at greater length in several other chapters.

2. Responsibility for Administration of the School

Supervising Pupils.—One responsibility in which all teachers share is in the supervision of pupils everywhere in the school. In most states, school authorities are responsible for the supervision of pupils from the time they leave home in the morning until they return home after the close of the school day. The principal alone cannot discharge this responsibility. Every member of the school faculty must share in it.

Some of the places where teachers share in supervision are in the corridors, the cafeteria, on the school grounds, in the school buses, at athletic functions, at school parties, and at other school functions. Usually, the members of the faculty are given definite assignments for such responsibilities in order that adequate supervision of pupils may be assured. It is important, however, that every teacher recognize and assume his share of the responsibility for supervising pupils in all places and at all times. This statement does not mean that the teacher must always do this supervision himself. The best type of supervision is that which helps pupils gradually to assume greater control and responsibility for their own conduct as they develop maturity and skill in democratic self discipline. Some of these possibilities were presented in the illustrations in Chapters 8 and 10.

Keeping Records.—Every well-administered school has an efficient system of records and reports covering various aspects of the administrative, supervisory, and instructional program. The most important of these are the ones that concern the backgrounds, participation, and educational progress of pupils. Although the permanent pupil records usually are kept in the principal's office, the teachers share in the keeping of pupil records and the preparation of pupil reports. The records for which teachers ordinarily assume considerable responsibility include :

1. *The school register*—this is the official record of pupil attendance at school. In many states the register is required by state law, and a uniform type of register is required of all schools in the state. The register is of considerable importance in states where state aid to local school districts is based on average daily attendance, average daily membership, or some other measure of pupil attendance.

2. *The permanent cumulative record*—this record, kept in the main office, includes attendance, achievement, and other information concerning individual pupils. It is cumulative in the sense that the entire school record of the child is kept on one record form or a group of forms arranged as a packet. It usually follows the pupil from one school to another within the system. In some school systems, there is a cumulative record for the pupil's work from kindergarten through the high school, while in other schools there are separate records for the elementary and the secondary schools.

3. *The anecdotal record*—this is a more recent development which is not as widely used in secondary schools as the school register and the cumulative record. This record consists of "anecdotes" concerning the individual pupil in every phase of the life of the school. It is in the form of a separate file for each pupil in which may be placed any item of interest concerning the child and his participation in the life of the school. The teachers are responsible for accumulating the "anecdotes" concerning individual pupils.

4. *The guidance record*—this is a record of the counseling service that is given each pupil. In some schools it is maintained by the home room teacher, while in others it is kept in the office of the school counselor. In most schools, however, the home room and classroom teachers participate in keeping such records and have ready access to them.

5. *The textbook record*—in most schools textbooks are issued to pupils by classroom teachers. Each teacher, then, is expected to maintain a record of books so issued, the condition of the books when issued, and the return of the books. In some schools a record form with appropriate instructions is given teachers for this purpose, but in others the teacher is permitted to keep the record of textbooks in any form he prefers. The teacher is urged to keep an accurate record of books issued, the age of each book, and the condition of each. In a few school systems, textbooks are issued to pupils from a central storeroom by a clerk. In these

schools the teacher has little or no responsibility for textbook records.

6. *Equipment records*—some teachers are responsible for school equipment other than textbooks. That is true of coaches, librarians, and teachers of science, art, physical education, homemaking, industrial arts, and instrumental music. These teachers need to maintain a careful record of all equipment, depreciation, breakage, and loss.

The records dealing with information necessary to the understanding and guidance of the pupil were discussed in greater detail in Chapter 13.

Preparing Reports.—The teacher has considerable responsibility for the periodic preparation of certain reports. These vary with the teachers' subject fields. For instance, most teachers need to prepare an annual inventory of reference materials and equipment issued to them. For most teachers, the inventory consists of little more than the furniture in the room, encyclopedias, dictionaries, and similar items. For teachers of such subjects as homemaking, physical education, and industrial arts, the annual inventory is a lengthy detailed report of equipment issued to the teacher. Maintaining a careful record of such equipment greatly simplifies the teacher's work for the annual inventory. The importance of the inventory becomes more apparent when it is recognized that all school equipment is public property and needs to be accounted for periodically to the school authorities in the audits of school records and accounts. Teachers also need to prepare periodic reports of pupil attendance. Usually these are made as part of the school register referred to above.

The most significant responsibility of the teacher for reports, however, is the periodic report to the pupil's parents of his progress in school. Formerly these reports were prepared on forms called "pupil report cards." In recent years, they are being called more frequently "reports of pupil progress." The pupil progress reports have caused more concern to educators in recent years than any other single aspect of school administration. This is particularly true in schools that have been interested in introducing some aspects of the experience-centered approach to curriculum development and classroom planning and teaching. Again and again teachers have found their efforts to implement the experience-centered approach seriously handicapped by the marking system and the pupil progress report system. There is at present a decided trend in the junior high school toward a new type of progress report which gives consideration to aspects of child growth and development other than subject matter. The senior high school has made little progress toward developing a type of pupil progress report which is more in harmony with our present philosophy of education. The trends in pupil progress reports are discussed at some length in Chapter 12.

Teachers should study carefully the policy of the school concerning marks and progress reports. The report to the parents of their child's progress in school will be more meaningful if the teachers who prepare the various parts of it are consistent in their implementation of that policy. A thorough analysis and a careful record of each pupil's total progress and achievement are essential as a basis for the preparation of the pupil progress reports.

Participating in Administration of the School.—Until recent years teachers did not expect to have a part in formulating administrative and supervisory policies or in making administrative decisions. These were the functions of the administrators—the superintendent, assistant superintendents, principals, and supervisors. But in the last two decades a great change has taken place in the manner in which schools are administered and school programs developed. Today we hear much about democratic administration and supervision. In schools that are administered according to democratic principles, there is much participation by all members of the professional staff in formulating school policies, in developing the instructional program, and in the performance of certain administrative functions. The superintendent and principal hold positions of leadership in these schools, but it is leadership from a democratic rather than an authoritarian approach.

It might be well to suggest how the teacher may function most effectively in a democratic school organization. The following suggestions may be helpful:

1. The teacher should be willing to give of his time and effort to help formulate school policies and assist in their administration. The democratic approach takes much teacher time as compared with the authoritarian approach to supervision and administration.

2. The teacher should be willing to share in the responsibility for the actions of the group of which he is a part. In an authoritarian school the superintendent or principal makes the decisions and assumes the responsibility for them. Where policies and decisions are democratically arrived at, all persons sharing in these activities should also share in the responsibility for the outcomes.

3. The teacher should be willing to abide by any decisions which are reached by the group, even though he may not be in complete agreement with them.

4. The teacher should develop a democratic attitude in his relations with all his colleagues. He should avoid any tendency to dominate the group, to coerce individuals within the group, or to impose his point of view in any manner other than through democratic discussion of the issues involved.

Further discussion of the teacher's participation in the administration in the school was presented in Chapter 15.

Protecting Pupils Against Accidents.—During the time that pupils are under the supervision of the school, the principal and faculty are responsible for their safety. That is true not only in school buses, in the gymnasium, and on the athletic field, but in the shop, the homemaking laboratory, the science class, and all other classes as well. The broken chair in the English classroom, the lack of safety devices for power machines in the shop, the inadequate supervision of pupils on the playground, the failure to explain safety measures to pupils in the foods laboratory—these are a few examples of negligence on the part of teachers which may lead to the injury of pupils. Every teacher in school has a responsibility for providing safeguards against injury to pupils while they are under his supervision.

In recent years, teachers have become increasingly concerned about accidents to pupils because it is recognized that they are legally as well as morally responsible for protecting pupils from injury while they are participating in any kind of school activity. There are numerous cases of lawsuits brought by parents against teachers for damages resulting from accidents in which pupils were involved. Since a teacher may be held liable in a suit for damages if there is evidence that a child was injured as a result of negligence on the teacher's part, it becomes important for the teacher to be fully informed concerning the best safety practices in school activities. The following suggestions may be helpful:

1. He should be thoroughly informed about the policy of the school concerning accidents, including safety measures in various aspects of the school program, the supervision of pupils in all types of activities, how to reach quickly the school nurse or physician, and the procedure for reporting accidents.

2. He should be thoroughly informed concerning the appropriate safety measures in all types of activities which are under his super-

vision. If the activity is one with which he has had no previous experience, he should consult the principal about safety measures.

3. He should provide adequate supervision for pupils engaged in any activity. If necessary, he should request the assistance of other teachers or parents. Field trips, club parties and picnics, and after-school rehearsals are examples of activities for which the teacher may need help in the supervision of pupils.

4. He should immediately report to the principal or other appropriate person any broken furniture, equipment, lighting fixtures, or other defective facilities which may cause injury to pupils.

5. He should be sufficiently skilled in first aid to protect an injured child until competent medical attention can be given.

Protecting the Health of Pupils.—The school has much responsibility for safeguarding the health of pupils. Although the school nurse, physician, and principal are particularly concerned with this problem, it is the teacher who comes most closely in contact with the pupils. He sees them in the home room when they first come to school at the beginning of the day and in his classes throughout the day. It is the teacher who can most easily detect the flushed face or the mild rash which frequently is the first sign of a communicable disease. It is the teacher who may have to take care of the child with an epileptic seizure, the one who has fainted, or the one with some sudden illness, until the nurse or physician arrives. In fact, in the thousands of small rural high schools, it may be some time before medical help can be reached. Then, too, the teacher can do much to protect the health of his pupils by proper regulation of light, temperature, and ventilation, by giving them guidance on health matters, and by supervising them in the lunch period.

It is exceedingly important, therefore, that the teacher be informed on matters pertaining to the health of the child, such as the symptoms of the common communicable diseases, the attention that should be given an epileptic, and the treatment for a person who has fainted. Furthermore, he should formulate a simple but effective policy for maintaining the proper light, heat, and ventilation in the room. In matters that require specialized assistance, he should be sure to consult the principal, nurse, or physician, preferably before a serious situation arises.

3. Legal and Ethical Responsibilities

Obtaining a Certificate to Teach.—For many years it has been the practice in most states to permit only persons with a certificate issued by the state to teach in the secondary schools. In some states, certificates are required in both public and private schools, while in others only public school teachers must be holders of a certificate. In effect, the certificate serves as a license to teach, similar to the license granted in such other professions as medicine, law, dentistry, osteopathy, and nursing. The certificate is issued by the state board of education, or a similar agency, on the basis of authority granted to it by the state legislature.

The provisions for a certificate vary so much from state to state that it is difficult to summarize them. For secondary school positions, particularly above the eighth grade, a baccalaureate degree is usually required for certification in most subject areas. Furthermore, a prescribed amount of course work in professional education is also required. The professional course requirements usually total at least eighteen semester hours and in most states include supervised observation and practice teaching in a secondary school. In such fields as music, physical education, homemaking, business education, art, and vocational agriculture, the requirements for certification are often more detailed and specific than in English, history, mathematics, science, and other similar areas. Besides a specified amount of college credit in professional education and subject matter areas, most states have other requirements for a certificate to teach, such as evidence of United States citizenship, character testimonials, and evidence of satisfactory health.

There is at present a strong trend toward five years of preparation for secondary school teaching. The Commission on Teacher Education and Professional Standards of the National Education Association has urged for several years that five years of college preparation be required of both elementary and secondary school teachers. Several states, including Arizona, California, New York, Washington, and the District of Columbia, at present require five years of college education for secondary school teachers. Other states have indicated an interest in demanding five years of college education as a prerequisite for a certificate to teach, at least for secondary school teachers.

The teacher is responsible for obtaining the certificate and for having it properly renewed periodically. Furthermore, it is unlawful in most states to reimburse a teacher for services unless he holds the proper certificate at the beginning of the period of employment. The teacher should have a certificate to give the superintendent of schools or the principal when school opens. In order that the teacher may be properly certified in the state in which he plans to teach, it is suggested that he do the following:

1. Write to the commissioner of education or state superintendent of public instruction to ascertain requirements for a certificate in the subject field in which he plans to teach. This should be done early enough in the student's college work to enable him to plan his program to meet these requirements.
2. Apply to the commissioner of education or the state superintendent of public instruction for a certificate immediately after completion of the college program. It may take several weeks to gather the necessary information before the certificate may be issued.
3. Study the requirements for the renewal of a certificate so that they may be satisfied at required intervals.

There is reciprocity in certification between only a few states, as in New England, and then only under certain conditions. In other words, a certificate in one state is not necessarily honored in another. The differences in requirements between states are often greatest in such fields as homemaking, business education, vocational agriculture, physical education, and music. A few states have special requirements for certificates that compel a teacher to do some college work within the state, such as a course in state school law or state history.

There are usually additional requirements for certification for such positions as supervisor, assistant principal, principal, counselor or director of guidance, librarian, and superintendent. Usually a teaching certificate and teaching experience are basic requirements for a certificate for a supervisory or administrative position. Teachers interested in preparing for such positions should consult the appropriate official in the state department of education concerning such requirements so that they may make the necessary preparation for it.

Fulfilling the Obligations of a Contract.—The agreement between the employing board of education and the teacher usually takes the form of a written contract. The contract sets forth certain conditions of employment, such as (1) the annual salary, (2) when the salary is to be paid, (3) the period during which service is to be required of the teacher, and (4) the conditions under which the contract may be terminated. The contract ordinarily does not state the grades or subjects to be taught, although administrative and supervisory positions are usually specified.

The most common practice is to limit the contract for teachers to one year, but for administrative and supervisory positions it may be granted for a longer period of time. In some states teachers have "tenure." That is, after a teacher has served in a school system for a certain number of years, designated by state law, he has permanent tenure, which means that he may be discharged only for serious short-comings, such as immorality, inefficiency, or insubordination. In states granting permanent tenure, teachers who are discharged may demand a hearing before some designated authority. The continuing contract is another practice for assuring some degree of permanency to the teacher's position. In states with a continuing contract plan, the teacher is automatically re-employed from year to year unless properly notified, before a date specified by law, that he is not to be retained for the coming year. Under both the permanent tenure and the continuing contract plans, the teacher has some assurance of a position from year to year, although the salary may be changed.

Frequently, teachers do not understand the obligations which they assume when they have signed a contract. A contract is an agreement between two parties, and it imposes obligations on both. For the term of the contract, the board of education cannot refuse a position to a teacher, reduce the salary, or make other changes once a contract has been duly signed by both the teacher and a representative of the board. In return, the teacher cannot resign to accept a position elsewhere—or for any other reason—during the period of the contract.

Unfortunately, there are numerous instances when teachers have failed to live up to their agreements. Once under contract, a teacher may leave a position only after an understanding has been reached with the board of education. Some contracts have a clause which gives the conditions under which a teacher may resign during the duration of the contract. For instance, the contract frequently provides that a teacher may resign after thirty or sixty days' notice in writing. Some contracts permit resignations up to a certain date, such as July 1 or August 1. Teachers should fulfil all the conditions of any contract as faithfully as is expected of the board of education. If unusual conditions warrant it, the teacher may be justified in requesting a release from a contract. That release, however, should be arrived at only through a frank discussion with the superintendent of schools as a representative of the board of education and with their complete approval. Any other action on the part of the teacher is both illegal and unethical.

Complying with Professional Ethics.—There are certain standards of conduct which are generally recognized as appropriate for members of the teaching profession. Those which deserve particular emphasis are as follows:

1. The teacher should maintain professional confidences. In other words, information concerning pupils, other teachers, and the administration of the school should not be discussed with anyone except those members of the professional staff whom these matters concern. Certainly, they should not be discussed with persons not on the school faculty.

2. The teacher should refrain from critical comments concerning other members of the professional staff.

3. The teacher should discuss matters that concern school policy only with his fellow teachers and his immediate administrative and supervisory superiors. He should not discuss such matters with members of the board of education except with the previous approval of the superintendent.

4. The teacher should adhere faithfully to the conditions of his contract of employment until it is dissolved by mutual agreement.

5. The teacher should not tutor his own pupils for pay nor should he refer them to members of his immediate family for tutoring.

6. The teacher should apply for a position only to the superintendent of schools or other official designated by the board of education. Political influence or other pressure should not be used to obtain a position.

7. The teacher should not apply for a specific position currently held by another teacher, unless he is informed that a vacancy in this position is impending.

8. The teacher should not accept any gift or compensation for endorsing a textbook or other school materials which are under consideration for selection in the school system where he is employed.

9. The teacher should refrain from using his classroom to promote partisan politics, sectarian religious views, or propaganda of any kind.

10. The teacher should maintain confidences placed in him by his pupils, unless it is for the best interests of the child and the public that confidential information be revealed.

4. Responsibility for Contributions to the Profession

Professional Growth.—Most teachers realize that, upon graduation from college, they have only begun their professional growth. They have some preparation in their teaching fields and usually a minimum of preparation in professional education. Before they are prepared to make a significant contribution to the development of a more effective program in their schools, as well as to the profession as a whole, they need to complete a great deal of study in their teaching fields and in various aspects of professional education. Teachers should, therefore, have a planned program of in-service education as a step toward professional growth.

One avenue of professional growth followed extensively by teachers today is advanced study through extension courses, late afternoon and Saturday classes, and summer sessions at colleges and universities. Salary schedules which provide higher compensation for teachers with the master's degree and the doctor's degree have encouraged such advanced study. The beginning teacher should not delay long such a program of advanced study. Moreover, the experienced teacher who has earned advanced degrees may profit by taking selected courses at colleges and universities.

This does not mean that professional growth should be considered primarily in terms of advanced study at teacher education institutions. This is indeed a narrow concept of what in-service education includes. There are numerous other avenues for in-service education which are fully as valuable as study at a college or university, among them travel, professional reading, experimentation on instructional problems, projects carried on by faculty committees, workshops conducted by the local school, attendance at professional conferences, participation in the activities of professional organizations, and visitation of other schools. All these activities should form, over a period of years, a part of the teacher's program of in-service education and professional growth.

Participating in Professional Organizations.—It is rather generally recognized that teachers, to remain professionally informed, should belong to various professional organizations. The advantages to the individual teacher of such membership are numerous, particularly the following:

1. It brings the teacher into contact with teachers from other schools and with leaders in the profession.
2. It helps to keep teachers informed about significant developments in the profession through the publications and professional meetings sponsored by the organization.
3. It enables teachers to keep abreast of the thinking of the profession as a whole on matters that concern the profession.
4. It gives the individual teacher an opportunity to participate in activities to improve education and to build a more effective profession.

It is, of course, for each teacher to decide what professional organizations he should join. He should, however, consider the following types of organizations: The National Education Association; the education association in his state; the national and state organizations in his subject; an organization that cuts across subject fields; and an organization in a special interest area, such as guidance or audio-visual aids. A few organizations that help teachers get a perspective broader than their own subject fields are these: National Association of Secondary School Principals; Department of Classroom Teachers of the National Education Association; Association for Supervision and Curriculum Development; American Education Fellowship; and the National Vocational Guidance Association.

Teachers can profitably spend some time investigating what these and other professional organizations offer in the way of state, regional, and national conferences; publications such as periodicals, bulletins, and yearbooks; and opportunities to participate in active projects of the organization. Criteria, such as these, might be developed for the evaluation of professional organizations:

1. Does the organization take active leadership in promoting modern educational principles?
2. Do its conferences include small work-discussion groups?
3. Does it deal with teachers' problems?
4. Do teachers have any opportunity to serve in positions of leadership in the organization?
5. Will its periodicals, yearbooks, and pamphlets be of value to the teacher?

Most professional organizations have a few active members and a large number of others who pay their dues but participate little in its activities. Obviously, the effectiveness of any organization is no greater than the enthusiasm and interest of its members. Furthermore, the teacher will derive much in professional growth for himself if he enters enthusiastically into the activities of a professional organization—attending its meetings, serving on its committees, contributing to its publications, and serving as officers. The teacher who is active in professional organizations will enjoy and profit from that participation.

Contributing to the Improvement of the School.—The most immediate professional responsibility of the teacher is, of course, to the school in which he is employed. That responsibility is not limited to meeting classes, teaching pupils, and supervising extraclass activities.

It goes far beyond that. *Every teacher must realize that the educational program is no more effective than he is willing to make it.* In other words, it is the teachers and administrators as a group who make the program of a school; they determine how forward-looking it is to be, how much it is in harmony with their philosophy of education, and what improvements can be made from time to time in its program.

The individual teacher can contribute a great deal to the improvement of that program. He may do much experimentation in his classes, serve on curriculum committees in his school, and carry on activities in his advanced professional study which are directed toward developing a more effective educational program for the boys and girls in his community. The teacher's first responsibility naturally will be in those subject areas which he teaches. But in a school which emphasizes the experience-centered curriculum it will also go far beyond his subject areas. In an experience-centered program, the teacher must keep in touch with other members of the faculty, drawing upon their talents and contributing to their work. The teacher should therefore assume some responsibility for developing a more effective program in all subject areas and in extraclass activities as well.

5. RESPONSIBILITY FOR COMMUNITY PARTICIPATION AND SERVICE

Participating in Community Activities.—In recent years there has been much emphasis on making the school the center of the life of the community. This is true not only of the school building, but of certain aspects of the school program as well. For instance, in many communities adult education classes and recreational activities for the entire community are sponsored by the school in the evening, on Saturdays, and during summer vacations. Furthermore, there is a tendency to integrate the secondary school program more closely with the life of the community. The social studies program is based to a large extent on the social, economic, and civic life of the community. The programs in industrial arts, homemaking, business education, and other vocational subjects, likewise are based on the economic and industrial life of the community. This close relationship between the school program and the life of the community demands understanding of the community and its problems by the teacher.

One of the best ways for a teacher to develop an understanding of the community and to keep closely in touch with it is for him to take part in various civic, religious, recreational, and social activities. It is only through actual participation in the activities of the community that a teacher truly becomes a part of it. Some of the organizations and activities that are particularly appropriate for teachers are the churches, the service clubs, the women's organizations, the veterans' organizations, the YMCA and YWCA, community recreational groups, and organizations that have as their specific purpose the improvement of human relations and conditions for the youth in the community. The teacher will enjoy and profit from participation in these activities and through them may be able to make a considerable contribution to the life of the community.

Participating in Political Activities.—It is generally agreed among educators and some laymen that teachers have an obligation to participate in the political life of the local community, the state, and the nation, much like any other citizen. As such, they should vote, identify themselves with a political party, study political issues, and in other ways discharge the political obligations of a citizen. Teachers are urged to recognize and assume their political responsibilities as citizens.

It is not so generally agreed that teachers should assume positions of leadership in political parties, engage actively in political campaigns, and hold public office. In fact, in many communities such activities by teachers are frowned upon by laymen, boards of education, and superintendents. It is to be hoped that the attitude toward political activities by teachers will become more liberal so that teachers may engage in these activities much like other citizens. Teachers should study the thinking of their community on such matters and conform judiciously until such time as they can bring about a more forward-looking point of view.

Summary

The responsibilities and duties of teachers cover a wide variety of activities. In the school, they include responsibility for teaching activities in the classroom, for extraclass activities, and for the administration of the school. In the profession, they include responsibility to professional organizations, for the development of a more effective school program, and for professional growth by the teacher. In legal and ethical matters, they include responsibility for certification, for discharging the obligations of contracts, and for complying with recognized professional ethics. In the community, they include responsibility for leadership in civic activities, for keeping in touch with the social, economic, and civic life of the community, and for the discharge of political obligations. The teacher is urged to study carefully these various responsibilities and to discharge them fully and conscientiously.

Selected References

ASSOCIATION FOR SUPERVISION AND CURRICULUM DEVELOPMENT. *Toward Better Teaching* (1949 Yearbook). Washington, D.C.: National Education Association, 282 pp.—Presents a forward-looking point of view concerning instructional practices, with many examples of how that point of view is being implemented in the schools. Should be helpful to the teacher who is interested in improving his effectiveness in the classroom.

CHAMBERLAIN, LEO M., and KINDRED, LESLIE W. *The Teacher and School Organization.* New York: Prentice-Hall, Inc., 1949, chaps. 10-20.—Presents a very complete discussion of various types of teacher responsibilities, such as working with supervisors, improving the school's program, preparing reports and keeping records, using the school plant, participating in school administration, and improving community life.

COOK, LLOYD ALLEN, and COOK, ELAINE FORSYTH. *A Sociological Approach to Education.* New York: McGraw-Hill Book Co., Inc., 1950, Parts II, V.—Some good information on the teacher's life in the community and on community attitudes and pressures. The section on "The Community Frame of Life" should give future teachers a better insight into the community in which they may work.

GOULD, GEORGE, and YOAKAM, GERALD. *The Teacher and His Work.* New York: The Ronald Press Co., 1947, chap. 4.—Deals with ethics and the teacher's contact with various professional organizations.

NATIONAL EDUCATION ASSOCIATION. *1948 Report of the Professional Ethics Committee.* Washington, D.C.: The Association, 1948, 64 pp.—This report gives the Code of Ethics of the National Education Association and each of the state codes. A single copy may be obtained free on request.

OTTO, HENRY J. *Principles of Elementary Education.* New York: Rinehart & Co., Inc., 1949, chap. 15.—Presents a discussion of the teacher as a person, citizen, and professional worker. Although written primarily for the elementary school teacher, it should be helpful to secondary school teachers.

REAVIS, WILLIAM C., and JUDD, CHARLES H. *The Teacher and Educational Administration.* Boston: Houghton Mifflin Co., 1942, chaps. 5-8, 12, 13, 19.—Presents a discussion of the teacher's relationship with the administration of the school. Chapters 5 to 8 cover administrative responsibilities; chapter 12, the teacher's relation to the principal; chapter 13, the teacher and professional organizations; and chapter 19, professional ethics.

WILES, KIMBALL. *Supervision for Better Schools.* New York: Prentice-Hall, Inc., 1950, chaps. 2-4.—Gives suggestions concerning leadership in the improvement of the instructional program. Although written primarily for the supervisor, it will help the teacher understand better his part in democratic action to improve the instructional program.

WOELLNER, ROBERT C., and WOOD, M. AURILLA. *Requirements for Certification of Teachers, Counselors, and Administrators for Elementary Schools, Secondary Schools, Junior Colleges.* (14th ed., 1949-50, mimeographed.) Chicago: The University of Chicago Press, 1949.—Provides a summary of certification requirements in the various states and the District of Columbia. New editions are prepared to keep the publication up to date with changes in requirements. Helpful to the student who must meet certification requirements in any state or the District of Columbia.

PART VI

A LOOK AHEAD FOR
SECONDARY EDUCATION

A LOOK AHEAD FOR SECONDARY EDUCATION

No one can prophesy what will happen to the secondary school in the next twenty-five to thirty-five years—during the future teacher's professional life. However, there are certain pressing needs of secondary education that should challenge the teacher, problems which he will have a part in solving. Many issues have been raised throughout this book which were intended to assist the future teacher in becoming an intelligent thinker about education for youth, one who weighs evidence and acts on his principles. This chapter is a summary for the book, focusing specifically upon what needs to be done by secondary school people if they are interested in making the American secondary school a community-youth service institution.

Chapter 21

CHALLENGING NEEDS OF SECONDARY EDUCATION IN THE UNITED STATES

The authors of this book have continuously pointed out that the student of education should formulate his own beliefs and his own principles, basing such conclusions upon careful study, thought, and exchange of ideas. These are the values by which a teacher makes his decisions. No pre-service education program can hope to answer all the questions that will arise in the teaching situation. Problems arising daily can only be solved intelligently if the experiences of the teacher have resulted in a well-thought-out set of values to guide his action.

The essential long-range needs of secondary education indicated in the following pages should require thinking of a similar character. They are questions with which the future teacher will have to deal if he has a sincere desire to participate in the improvement of secondary schools during his lifetime. Each need is stressed briefly; most of them summarize what has been said previously and give an indication of what further work needs to be done. None of them has any easy or simple answers.

These needs are "essential" in the sense that they present challenging problems concerning which educators must do some serious thinking and take action—individually and cooperatively—if the secondary school is to keep up with the times as an institution that truly serves all youth of the nation. We are confident that educators, the public, and youth working together as a team can meet these needs. They are the need for :

1. Kindling the desire for carefully evaluated change and, consequently, accelerating the tempo of change.
2. Clarifying the relationship between educational theory and practice.
3. Putting into action the results of research in education, psychology, biology, anthropology, and sociology.
4. Gearing the secondary school to a philosophy that considers change of behavior as the primary function of its program.

5. Changing over from a book-centered to a life-centered and community-centered school.

6. Finding some means to supplant outmoded practices that are dead weights on progress, i.e., credits, marks, traditional college preparation, the traditional school day.

7. Breaking down departmental barriers to a well-integrated program of instruction.

8. Creating a situation in which it is possible for the teacher to meet fewer pupils in a day in order that he may get to know them well.

9. Reducing the total teaching load of the teacher in order that he may be able to give the individual help and attention to adolescents needed in a modern school.

10. Securing dynamic and democratic leadership.

11. Getting democracy to function in pupil-pupil, teacher-pupil, and teacher-administrator relations.

12. Developing ways of working with adults in the community in a joint enterprise for improving experiences and services for youth.

13. Breaking down barriers between academic and vocational education; between teachers of so-called academic and nonacademic fields; between elementary and secondary teachers; between supervisors and teachers.

14. Attaining for all secondary school teachers freedom from fear: that they shall be free to discuss all sides of a question, free to give mature pupils an opportunity to read materials on different points of view, and free to work for the extension of democracy to all peoples and groups within our society.

15. Extending the services of the secondary school in many ways to out-of-school youth and youth beyond the twelfth grade.

16. Providing facilities, services, and instruction for the increased enrollments in secondary schools.

17. Achieving an optimum size of the secondary school unit for the best possible growth of adolescents.

18. Providing for a type of teacher education that educates by putting into practice, in all its phases, the kind of philosophy it advocates.

19. Interesting competent youth to go into secondary school teaching as a life career.

1. *Kindling the desire for carefully evaluated change and, consequently, accelerating the tempo of change.* New findings in research, new developments in society, and new experiences will necessitate change. The principles presented in this book, which represent the

authors' beliefs, are based upon their experience and upon present knowledge of children, learning, and society. There is no claim, however—and note this point carefully—that these principles, or the practices that illustrate them, are the final answers. The very basis of scientific thinking and democratic principles is opposed to such a stratification. Values ought to be subject to modification, and one important value to hold is to have a desire for well-ordered change and a conscious interest in improvement of educational practices. As more is discovered about how good education can be provided, educators should be willing to slough off outmoded beliefs. Only thus can the education of youth narrow the gap between its practices and advancements in society.

2. *Clarifying the relationship between educational theory and practice.* Many a beginning teacher may find that some administrator or fellow teacher will say, "You will be all right as soon as you forget about those theories you have learned; out here we run up against practical situations." The implication is that theory and practice are something entirely separate. Actually, there is always a theory behind any practice. The only difference is that, in the case of individuals who make such statements, the theory has never been carefully thought out. Another important consideration is that theory must be ahead of practice if progress is to result. The development of electric lights, the airplane, television, or atomic energy would never have happened unless that had been true. Some would say, "All the better for us!" But they do not place the blame where it should be placed— on the failure of social invention to keep up with scientific invention. We need to understand that progress in secondary education will come to a standstill unless we are willing to try out theories, and that some people who scoff at theory would like nothing better than to see that condition occur. Certainly, such a statement by school people should also challenge teacher education institutions to include more laboratory experiences in pre-service education.

3. *Putting into action the results of research in education, psychology, biology, anthropology, and sociology.* One of the serious problems that secondary education faces is how to put research in education, psychology, biology, anthropology, and sociology into action. Case after case in this book has illustrated that dilemma. It is hoped that the student's own investigation has helped him to sense this problem. For example, we are constantly finding out more about learning; yet the out-dated S-R bond theory still dominates secondary education. What does this mean? Have teachers failed to keep up with

research findings? Have research people operated in isolation from schools? Have the results of research been disseminated inadequately? Or do we lack the know-how of putting theory into practice? There seems to be a need for teamwork on the part of practitioners and research workers in the fields of psychology, sociology, biology, anthropology, and education. Some of the most significant research in recent years has been of this type, or has stemmed from the areas of social psychology and sociology; for example, research in group dynamics and in social behavior and the class position of youth.

4. *Gearing the secondary school to a philosophy that considers change of behavior as the primary function of its program.* It has been stressed in this book that it is doubtful if many fundamental changes in the secondary school curriculum will come about until there is a change in the direction of the experience approach to curriculum development and away from the subject-centered curriculum. This is a tremendous job for leaders in the field since there is still a strong belief on the part of many that learning the subject matter is the most important aim, one which will somehow result in adequately learning how to live in modern society. This belief is a far cry from one that considers the changing of the child's behavior as the primary aim of instruction, one in which subject matter is used to attain desirable growth in skills, attitudes, appreciations, and understandings. Considering the curriculum in terms of the kinds of experiences that pupils have with subject matter, with people, in speaking, reading, writing, investigating, living with each other, making decisions, taking responsibilities, and the like, is a necessary step.

5. *Changing over from a book-centered to a life-centered and community-centered school.* Many secondary school people are keenly aware of the fact that the secondary school does not meet the needs of the many youth whose interests are not scholarly and whose abilities are not of the verbal type. Many are also becoming more concerned about the lack of use of the rich resources a school and community offer for all pupils. Only a few youth will become research scholars, but all will deal with people and live in a community. Much of their success will depend upon their skills in human relations—success in occupations, success in making emotional and social adjustments, and success in being a person whom people like and respect. The increased percentage of youth going on into high school, as a result of increased family incomes and less opportunity for those under eighteen to get worth-while jobs, will mean a larger proportion of pupils who are not verbal-minded. The Life Adjustment Education pro-

gram of the Commission on Life Adjustment Education, appointed
by the United States Office of Education, has as its objective a better
life-centered secondary education for all youth.

6. *Finding some means to supplant outmoded practices that are
dead weights on progress, i.e., credits, marks, traditional college preparation, the traditional school day.* The use of the Carnegie unit has
ceased to serve the best interests of secondary education. It now
blocks new developments, such as putting into effect the core curriculum and giving status to music, physical education, work experience,
camping, and other activities that are an important part of the education of youth. The competitive mark protects the weak teacher, sup-
ports the recitation-drill-factual examination type of teaching, and
stands in the way of good, friendly relations between teacher and pupil, pupil and pupil, and teacher and parent. There is enough evidence
to show that single marks are not desirable incentives to use, do not
give the necessary information about pupil growth, and are not consistent with the principle of individual development to the highest possible degree. The traditional idea as to what constitutes effective college preparation has no longer any solid foundation on which to stand.
The concept of the traditional school day as beginning at 8:30 A.M.
and ending at 3:00 P.M. impedes progress in school camping, in the
community school idea, in cooperative teacher planning, in the use of
the community for work and service experiences, and in further development of pupil activities. When we can move away from these
devices—that are conveniences, to be sure—greater strides in improvement will be possible.

7. *Breaking down departmental barriers to a well-integrated program of instruction.* As long as rigid departmental divisions are
maintained, the orientation of curriculum improvement in the secondary school is likely to be in the direction of adding courses to or sub-
tracting them from the curriculum. Moreover, the chances are not
good for the development of any integrated types of courses based on
broad problems which draw upon many subject areas for their solution. When teachers see the total growth of the pupil as a joint enterprise, they begin to question the bell-ringing and shifting of the pupil
from subject to subject every hour without much relationship among
the four or five shifts.

8. *Creating a situation in which it is possible for a teacher to meet
fewer pupils a day in order that he may get to know them well.* This
is one of the most promising fronts on which to work toward a better
secondary education for youth. Teachers everywhere are concerned

about the large numbers with which they need to become acquainted. The many records for which the teacher is responsible, the responsibility for making administrative reports to the office, the time taken to see many parents, and the demands on their strength in attempting to understand the many personalities, all tend to make them receptive to doing something about the situation. The increased interest in guidance, the growing number of secondary school teachers who understand adolescent psychology, and the stress in modern education on home contacts and parent conferences are all powerful factors stimulating a desire for this change. It is essential that some plan be developed whereby high school teachers can get to know their pupils' abilities, interests, and problems—to know them as individuals. The core curriculum, or some variation of it, will probably be the type of solution that will be used by a growing number of secondary schools.

9. *Reducing the total teaching load of the teacher.* As just pointed out, the teacher cannot possibly understand pupils as individuals, keep adequate records, or make adequate reports and home contacts if he has more than a hundred different personalities to deal with. Broadened responsibilities of the teacher for guidance, for pupil-teacher planning, for community relations, for curriculum improvement, and for other tasks which the school must carry on, all are a drain on the administrators' and teachers' energies. They take far more time and effort than did the former "school-keeping."

Reduction of the class size to less than twenty-five pupils will not solve the problem. Most teachers would still work with 125 different pupils a day. While class size needs to be reduced to that number in crowded school situations, the real solution must go further. It is an essential need of secondary education that will require a willingness to break away from some traditional practices in order to explore ways by which the school can be organized to meet new demands and responsibilities. The need is closely related to the one above, but it stresses the need for more time for recreation, for community participation, and for the continuous study of education and society required of the good teacher today.

10. *Securing dynamic and democratic leadership.* The job of the principal should be to help the neophyte teacher put his ideas into practice successfully. The leader of a secondary school should be familiar with research and with modern theories of education. He should be a leader of instruction who can assist teachers—traditional teachers and modern teachers alike. He should, by all means, make

use of the leadership that he finds in his staff, delegate responsibility to teachers and committees, and develop policy with his staff. The real leaders among principals are found in such schools whose practices are described in the "better schools" sections of the various chapters in this book; however, such leadership is sadly lacking in too many instances in American secondary schools. Leadership of the democratic type is needed to bring about any of the suggested changes for making the secondary school an institution that serves youth needs in a modern democratic society. Such leadership is a mixture of courage, friendliness, intelligent information, respect for personality, belief in the democratic process, know-how, and ingenuity and creativeness.

11. *Getting democracy to function in pupil-pupil, teacher-pupil, and teacher-administrator relations.* Authoritarian ideals do not fit a school for a democratic society. As cooperation in making policy and carrying out responsibilities is necessary to a school in which the morale is good and the staff professionally alert, so the cooperative relations between teacher and pupils in classroom and in extraclass activity is essential to the desired kinds of growth in social skills on the part of the pupils. The task is not an easy one. There are those who ridicule cooperative planning with pupils because "you're just trying to fool them." There are others—many others—who do not understand how to do cooperative planning. There is another group who, because they want to sabotage the whole idea, talk loudly about "letting pupils do what they want to do," identifying good group planning with the laissez faire type of situation, which differs from democratic cooperation just as much as it differs from authoritarian domination.

12. *Developing ways of working with adults in the community in the joint enterprise of improving experiences and services for youth.* We are woefully lacking in the know-how of planning with lay people for the improvement of the school program, perhaps because in the past the school often tended to be set apart from community life. Now, when the majority of educators are convinced that they must work more closely with community groups, they are searching for the ways through which such cooperation can best be achieved. Boards of education may be jealous of their "prerogatives"; school people may be afraid that there will only be a series of complaints about the school; laymen criticize the techniques of teaching, which are part of the professional knowledge and skill of the teacher. Where should the parent and the community member fit in?

Most educators agree that there should be considerable planning by laymen and school men to help determine the goals of the school. Parents have done yeoman service as resource people for elementary school teachers, but have functioned less often as a resource for instruction at the secondary level. In order to make changes that are accepted by the public, community adults should certainly take part in the planning of those changes—not just as listeners, but as participants who have ideas to contribute. Effecting a change in the curriculum of secondary schools today is too closely tied in with the total community for school people to do the task alone. Many persons in the community need to understand the new developments and practices in education so that they may support sound programs and reduce opposition that arises from lack of information and hearsay. The questions of adequate support for secondary education, of better salaries and working conditions for teachers, and of a wholesome community attitude toward teachers obviously need to be studied with laymen.

13. *Breaking down barriers between general and vocational education, between elementary and secondary teachers, between teachers of so-called academic and nonacademic fields, between supervisors and teachers.* The barriers that have grown up between teachers of federally aided vocational subjects and other teachers, between elementary and secondary teachers, between supervisors and teachers, or between various specific groups, *all* of whom are concerned with some phase of the total education of the child, are obstacles that must be removed if progress is to be made. Most of them are the result of tradition and precedent and are difficult to eliminate because of vested interests. The factor that can effect the breakdown is a consideration of the development of the child as a joint enterprise. The group process in working for a common goal has proved itself a powerful medium for shattering misunderstandings, fears, and suspicions among peoples who differ.

14. *Attaining for all secondary school teachers freedom from fear: that they shall be free to discuss all sides of a question, free to give mature pupils an opportunity to read materials on different points of view, and free to work for the extension of democracy to all peoples and groups within our society.* Many secondary school teachers are disturbed by the growing tendency in recent years of pressure groups to ban books or periodicals from the school and to make it uncomfortable for teachers to discuss in their classes both sides of controversial issues. These teachers realize that democracy can best be sustained

and improved in an atmosphere where people get the facts. The propaganda and thought control techniques of fascist and communist ideologies are inimical to the interests of democracy. School people ought to be on the alert to detect such insidious methods; there is certainly no place for them in the American secondary school. When people become afraid to say what they think about political or educational questions, democratic institutions suffer.

Teachers who desire to extend the practices discussed in this book, or other practices they believe to be desirable educational trends, should inquire into the question of what forces are working against progress toward improvement of secondary education, or against the public schools in general. *Open and frank discussion, based on facts, will result in progress in secondary education.*

15. *Extending the services of the secondary school in many ways to out-of-school youth and youth beyond the twelfth grade.* There is no valid argument why free public education on a higher level than the twelfth grade should be made available to those who plan to go into professional work or wish to further their cultural interests and not to those who will go directly into community occupations of a skilled, semiskilled, semiprofessional, or unskilled type. The next few decades will undoubtedly see the problem coming to the fore. The occupational life span is being shortened. Civic intelligence to solve modern complex social problems demands more study by the citizen than ever before. Community institutes or colleges that serve larger community areas than the small secondary schools, or an extension of secondary education through the thirteenth and fourteenth years, are becoming more and more realistic needs in American life. Moreover, there is no justification for a secondary school's dropping its services to youth when they drop out of full-time school. Guidance services, placement services, shop facilities, recreation facilities, and evening classes are all a part of the services of the secondary school that should serve all youth.

16. *Providing facilities, services, and instruction for the increased enrollments in secondary schools.* Provision for the various facilities and services recommended here for youth will be a task in itself, for carrying out the principles outlined will mean an *extension* of these facilities and an addition of services. However, population figures indicate that the increased birthrate of the mid and late forties will affect the secondary school in the late fifties, probably doubling the secondary school population in many areas in the early sixties. And yet many existing school buildings are outmoded and bulging at the

seams. Thus the resulting problem—providing better facilities for a much larger school population—becomes a real challenge. Increased school-community cooperation, increased consciousness on the part of the public of the value of secondary education, and new ways of financing education, such as federal aid, are called for. As secondary school people, we should realize that we have an obligation to make the program of education so worth while that the public will consider an improved secondary education for all youth as indispensable.

17. *Achieving an optimum size of the secondary school unit for the best possible growth of adolescents.* Decisions determining the size of secondary schools built within the next ten years will govern the size of schools that youth will attend for many years to come. Neither the extremely large nor the small high school will provide the most desirable learning situation. In the enthusiasm to do away with the small, expensive, and meagerly equipped high school units, the disadvantages of the high school too large to be a community center and in which pupils are known by but a few of the staff have been lost sight of.[1] The excesses of departmentalization, the difficulties of cooperative study by the staff, and the impersonal relations between staff and pupils are real dangers in a large high school.

18. *Providing for a type of teacher education that educates by putting into practice, in all of its phases, the kind of philosophy that it advocates.* The discussion in the last section of the book showed that this kind of teacher education is being developed in a number of institutions and by many individual instructors in other institutions. The problem is one of extending it far and wide so that future teachers will have an opportunity to work in situations and practice good educational procedures as a most important aspect of learning how to teach. Most inimical to good teaching is the idea that techniques can be learned only from a book or from a lecture. Future teachers need to experience the kind of teaching that is recommended in education courses and books.

19. *Interesting competent youth to go into secondary school teaching as a life career.* This final—and extremely important—problem is one for which all teachers, administrators, the public, future teachers, and college professors must assume responsibility. First of all,

---

[1] See the author's criteria for determining the size of a secondary school in I. N. Thut and J. Raymond Gerberich, *Foundations of Method for Secondary Schools,* New York: McGraw-Hill Book Co., Inc., 1949, p. 66. Also, A. I. Oliver, "How Large Should the Small High School Be?" *School and Society,* 69 (February 19, 1949), 127-28.

salaries and working conditions must be made attractive to the most competent people. But there is still the job of finding and encouraging those young people to go into the profession. The secondary school of the future that serves the American public well will have to be staffed by alert, intelligent, well-adjusted people with broad cultural and civic interests and, above all, a liking for, an understanding of, and a faith in young people.

SELECTED REFERENCES

ASSOCIATION FOR SUPERVISION AND CURRICULUM DEVELOPMENT. *Toward Better Teaching* (1949 Yearbook). Washington, D.C.: National Education Association, chaps. 1, 9.—These chapters present a new orientation for the evaluation of good teaching. The rest of the book discusses and illustrates each of the characteristics of "better teaching."

CASWELL, HOLLIS L. (ed.). *The American High School* (Eighth Yearbook of the John Dewey Society). New York: Harper & Bros., 1946, chap. 1.—Cites eight issues that must be faced in the redirection of secondary education, which are good questions for study.

DOUGLASS, HARL R. (ed.). *Education for Life Adjustment.* New York: The Ronald Press Co., 1950, chaps. 1, 2.—Discusses the meaning and origin of the "life adjustment education" movement and what changes it seeks to make in the education of youth.

DOUGLASS, HARL R. *Secondary Education for Youth in Modern America.* Washington, D.C.: American Council on Education, 1937, chaps. 6, 7.—Contains suggestions for the secondary schools, made about fifteen years ago during the depression, many of which are still a long way from attainment.

EDUCATIONAL POLICIES COMMISSION. *Education for ALL American Youth.* Washington, D.C.: National Education Association, 1944, 421 pp.—This report is one of the most comprehensive guidelines of what a secondary school that serves youth should be like.

GRUHN, WILLIAM T., and DOUGLASS, HARL R. *The Modern Junior High School.* New York: The Ronald Press Co., 1947, chaps. 17, 18.—These chapters, on "Criteria for Evaluating Junior High School Practices" and "The Junior High School of Tomorrow," both contain recommendations for improvement of the junior high school program.

PIERCE, PAUL R. *Developing a High-School Curriculum.* New York: American Book Co., 1942, chap. 10.—Desirable kinds of administration, curriculum, community relations, teachers, and school plant for the future high school are envisioned by one high school principal.

SPEARS, HAROLD. *The High School for Today.* New York: American Book Co., 1950, chap. 21.—Another schoolman gives his views of what "the people's high school" should be like.

STILES, DAN. *High Schools for Tomorrow.* New York: Harper & Bros., 1946, 212 pp.—A book written by a layman, formerly a teacher, who is dissatisfied with many practices in the American secondary school. He suggests needed reforms and cites examples of practices from good schools.

THAYER, V. T. *American Education Under Fire.* New York: Harper & Bros., 1944, 193 pp.—Deals with crucial issues that confront the citizens and the professional educator. Issues not discussed here, such as religion and the public schools, are included.

INDEX

LIST OF SCHOOLS WHOSE PRACTICES ARE DESCRIBED

Secondary Schools

Aberdeen Public Schools, South Dakota, 233, 235
Abraham Lincoln High School, San Jose, California, 388-89
Acalanes High School, Lafayette, California, 258-59
Albuquerque High School, New Mexico, 255-56
Alhambra City High School, California, 366
Allen-White School, Hardeman County, Tennessee, 253-54
Amarillo Public Schools, Texas, 129
Anoka High School, Minnesota, 256
Appleton High School, Wisconsin, 277
Ascension Parish, Donaldsonville, Louisiana, 173
Avenal High School, California, 132
Battle Creek Public Schools, Michigan, 105, 365-66
Baxter Seminary, Baxter, Tennessee, 208
Benjamin Franklin High School, New York City, 254
Brockton Public Schools, Massachusetts, 336-37
Bruton Heights School, Williamsburg, Virginia, 250
Bulkeley High School, Hartford, Connecticut, 165
Burdick Junior High School, Stamford, Connecticut, 278
California, Public Schools of, 258
Central High School, Aberdeen, South Dakota, 228, 315
Central High School, Pueblo, Colorado, 229
Central High School, St. Joseph, Missouri, 236
Cleveland High School, Portland, Oregon, 173
Cloonan Junior High School, Stamford, Connecticut, 167
Colin Kelly Junior High School, Eugene, Oregon, 314, 334, 339
Denby High School, Detroit, Michigan, 137
Drury High School, North Adams, Massachusetts, 362-63
East High School, Denver, Colorado, 334-35
East Rockford High School, Rockford, Illinois, 163, 164, 314, 318
Elkridge High School, Baltimore, Maryland, 257
Elma High School, Washington, 203
Eugene Public Schools, Oregon, 413-14
Evansville Public Schools, Indiana, 307
Fairview High School, Cullman, Alabama, 171-72
Faribault Public Schools, Minnesota, 259, 284
Floodwood High School (Floodwood Community School), Minnesota, 127, 254, 364-65, 384
Folwell Junior High School, Minneapolis, 384-85
Frost Community School, Navarro County, Texas, 203, 258
Gallatin County High School, Bozeman, Montana, 316
Glencoe Public Schools, Illinois, 256
Hanson High School, Hopkins County, Kentucky, 173, 249-50
Hartford Public Schools, Connecticut, 255
Highland Park High School, Illinois, 132-34, 163, 172, 200-1
Holtville High School, Alabama, 250
Indianapolis Public Schools, Indiana, 252
Jefferson Junior High School, Long Beach, California, 385-86
Jesup W. Scott High School, Toledo, Ohio, 236
Kalamazoo Public Schools, Michigan, 104, 281-83, 338
Keene High School, New Hampshire, 308-9
Kirkville Senior High School, Missouri, 255
Manual Arts High School, Denver, Colorado, 164
Middlebury High School, Middlebury, Vermont, 235
Milwaukee Public Schools, Wisconsin, 175-76, 178
Minneapolis Public Schools, Minnesota, 250-51, 363-64
Minot Junior High School, North Dakota, 230
Mt. Baker-Union High School, Deming, Washington, 392
New London High School, Connecticut, 204
New Trier Township High School, Winnetka, Illinois, 130

507

Teacher Education Institutions